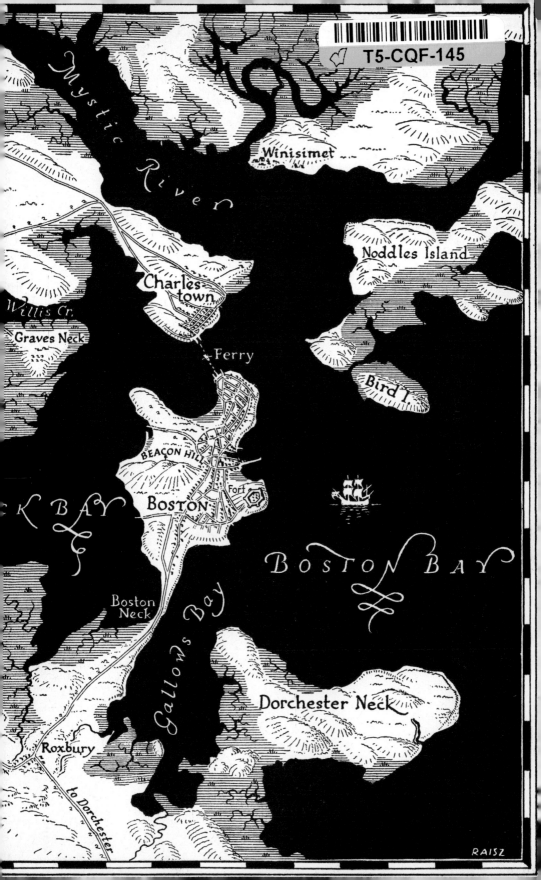

THE TERCENTENNIAL HISTORY OF
HARVARD COLLEGE AND UNIVERSITY
1636–1936

LONDON: HUMPHREY MILFORD

OXFORD UNIVERSITY PRESS

HARVARD COLLEGE IN THE SEVENTEENTH CENTURY

BY

SAMUEL ELIOT MORISON
CLASS OF 1908

PART II

Cambridge, Massachusetts

HARVARD UNIVERSITY PRESS
1936

COPYRIGHT, 1936

BY THE PRESIDENT AND FELLOWS OF HARVARD COLLEGE

PRINTED AT THE HARVARD UNIVERSITY PRESS

CAMBRIDGE, MASS., U.S.A.

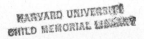

CONTENTS

PART II

LIST OF ILLUSTRATIONS
AND MAPS

PART II

The Map of Boston, Cambridge, and their environs in the Seventeenth Century, used for end-papers, is by Dr. Erwin Raisz.

LIST OF ARMS AND SEALS

PART II

The arms of William and Mary, surrounded by inscription in two borders: — (1) GVLIELMVS · III · ET · MARIA · II · D · G · M · BR · FR · ET · HI · REX · ET · REG   (2) SIG : REG : PROVINCIÆ · DE · MASSA- CHVSETS BAY · IN · NOVA · ANGLIA · IN · AMERICA.

From the Harvard Charter of 1697.

ABBREVIATIONS IN FOOTNOTES

A. A. S. .... American Antiquarian Society, Worcester. *Proc. A. A. S.* are the *Proceedings* of this Society, 1812–.

B. P. L. .... Boston Public Library.

C. S. M. .... *Publications of the Colonial Society of Massachusetts*, 1895–. Vols. xv, xvi, xxxi contain Harvard College Records.

Coll. .... See M. H. S.

D. A. B. .... *Dictionary of American Biography*, New York, 1928–.

D. N. B. .... *Dictionary of National Biography*, London.

H. C. L. .... Harvard College Library.

F. H. C. .... S. E. Morison, *The Founding of Harvard College* (1935, the previous volume in this series).

H. U. Arch. .... Harvard University Archives.

Magnalia .... Cotton Mather, *Magnalia Christi Americana*, 1702.

Mass. Archives .. Massachusetts Archives, State House, Boston.

Mass. Bay Recs... *Records of the Governor and Company of the Massachusetts Bay in New England*, 5 vols. in 6, 1853–54.

M. H. S. .... Massachusetts Historical Society. *Coll. M. H. S.* are the printed *Collections* of this Society, 1792–. *Proc. M. H. S.* are the *Proceedings*, 1859–. Numerical prefixes indicate numbers of series.

N. E. D. .... *The New English Dictionary*, Oxford, 1888–1928.

N. E. H. G. R. ..... *New England Historical and Genealogical Register*, Boston, 1847–.

N. E. Q. .... *The New England Quarterly*, 1928–.

Paige .... Lucius R. Paige, *History of Cambridge* (Boston, 1877), with *Supplement and Index* (1930).

Proc. .... see A. A. S.; M. H. S.

Quincy .... Josiah Quincy, *History of Harvard University*, 2 vols., Cambridge, 1840.

Sibley .... J. L. Sibley, *Biographical Sketches of Graduates of Harvard University*, 4 vols., Cambridge, 1873–1932.

HARVARD COLLEGE IN THE SEVENTEENTH CENTURY

PART II

XVIII

FINANCIAL HISTORY OF CHAUNCY'S ADMINISTRATION [1]

1654–1672

One gains the impression that college finances were better managed in Chauncy's administration than before. The new President made no attempt to keep college accounts himself; Thomas Danforth, named Treasurer in the Charter of 1650, but as yet Treasurer in name only, now assumed the active exercise of his office, obtained an accounting from the retired President, searched the records to find what property the College was entitled to, and began the keeping of regular accounts.[2] Danforth used 'charge and discharge' accounting, a method that is found as far back as Sumerian tablets, and is still used in the judicial department of the Commonwealth of Massachusetts. Current assets, including accrued rents, annuities, debts, real estate that the Corporation hoped to dispose of, and the Mowlson-Bridges scholarship fund which they were trying to pry loose from the General Court, were listed as 'the Colledge Stock.' Fixed annual income was known as 'the Colledge Estate.'[3] A five-year or nine-year account of disbursements plus final stock is headed 'Harvard Colledge is Debtour'; the account for the same period of receipts and initial stock is headed 'Harvard Colledge is Creditour.' These two have to balance; and a variable item called 'advance of the Stocke' on the credit side appears to do the trick.[4]

1. See notes at head of Chapter XVI, and *F. H. C.*, p. 292 n. In addition to the sources there mentioned, many items for Chauncy's administration may be gleaned from the ms. Journal and Ledger of Treasurer Richards (1669–82) in the H. U. Archives.
2. *C. S. M.*, xv. 180–81, 186–87, 212–17, 53–54. For Danforth's career, see above, p. 22 n.
3. *C. S. M.*, xv. 216, and cf. 53. The Stock amounted to £863 4s 9d in 1668; the Estate, to only £50 10s.
4. *Id.* 212–15; Professor William A. Hosmer has kindly analyzed these accounts.

Thomas Danforth was one of those busy men of affairs who are burdened with unremunerated responsibilities, which they discharge cheerfully and effectively — the first of a long line of such men who have served Harvard College. The office of Treasurer was no sinecure. 'I know it is a busy time of the year,' writes his brother Sam to Thomas Danforth on March 31, 1670, 'and you have more need of a beast at hand for service (in regard of your Care of the Colledge) then ten other men.' So Tom may keep the family horse.[1] His need for transportation was due to the frequent collecting of rents on college property and interest on loans. Most of the investments that he made were involuntary ones. For instance, the trustees under the will of Governor Edward Hopkins sent to the College from Hartford £100 'in provisions,' about the year 1665. They were consigned to Deputy-Governor Willoughby, merchant of Charlestown, who already had charge of £75 in money belonging to Harvard. As the College Steward was trying to get out of the provision business, Treasurer Danforth left the sale of the Hartford consignment to Willoughby, who credited the College with £100, less £7 6s freight, and probably shipped the meat and corn to the West Indies. By June 1669, the £75 and the Hopkins bequest, with accumulated interest, were reckoned by the College Treasurer at £80 10s and £119 10s, respectively, on which Willoughby agreed to pay interest at 8 per cent, but failed to do so. This worshipful magistrate died in 1671; and in 1684 his executors still owed the College £200 principal and £63 accrued interest.[2] Such delays were inherent in the cash-barter system of currency prevalent in New England. Money and other commodities became mingled with a merchant's stock of goods, and were often shipped to distant ports, so that he could not produce them on demand;[3] nor could he pay for them until his creditors paid him.

By necessity Chauncy and Danforth used much the same financial expedients as Dunster to keep the College alive. After the General Court had assumed responsibility for the President's

1. *Proc. M. H. S.*, XIII. 306. I cannot find what salary, if any, Danforth received from the College. He left it some valuable land in Framingham, the rents of which were used to endow a study in Stoughton College. See *C. S. M.*, XVI. index.

2. *Id.* 216, 53, 245, 251; cf. 385.

3. The New England Company had the same difficulty in the handling of its funds in New England, and for the same reason. See G. P. Winship, *The New England Company and John Eliot* (1920), pp. lii–lvii.

salary, two distinct drives for funds were started, and a third, planned in Chauncy's administration, bore fruit later.

PRESIDENTIAL SALARY GRANT

The matter of replacing voluntary town contributions by a tax levy had been attended to a few days before President Dunster's resignation. On October 18, 1654, the General Court of Massachusetts ordered

that, besides the proffit of the ferry formerly graunted to the colledg, which shall be continewed, that there shall be yearly levied, by addition to the countrie rate, one hundred pounds, to be paid by the Treasurer of the countrie to the colledg treasurer, for the behoofe and maintenance of the president and fellowes, to be distributed betweene the president and fellowes according to the determination of the ouerseers of the colledg, and this to continew during the pleasure of the countrie. . . . [1]

Those who had signed the subscription papers in the drive of 1652–54 for voluntary contributions [2] were allowed to deduct the amount paid from their future tax.

This was an important step toward putting the college finances on a sound basis, and assuring the President a regular salary. The fellows never shared in this grant. On November 2, 1654, the Overseers voted the entire sum of 'One hundred pound per annum to be payd out of the Country Treasury' as a salary to Charles Chauncy, if he should accept the Presidency; [3] and that sum continued to be paid to him annually, by the Colony Treasurer, during his incumbency. [4] Moreover, this grant inaugurated a policy which long continued. Throughout the colonial and even the revolutionary period, the President

1. *Mass. Bay Recs.*, IV. part i. 205.
2. See above, pp. 27–30.
3. *C. S. M.*, xv. 206; and note (*id.* 194) that the salaries of teaching fellows were paid in 1666 out of the College Treasury.
4. Eliot, *Sketch*, p. 153, says that it was paid only for seven years; but town records, and other sources, prove that it continued annually. In Chauncy's petition of 1663 for increased salary (Mass. Archives, LVIII. 45) it is implied that the £100 had been paid regularly; and in Elnathan Chauncy's petition of 1673 (*id.* 88) he says that his honored father, during his entire presidency, 'never receiued for allowance any other payment but such as the Country rate brought in.' Moreover, the votes of October 8 and 11, 1672, respecting President Hoar's salary, prove that Chauncy's £100 a year continued until Hoar's £150 began; and he also had a grant of £20 'as a gratuity' in 1666 (*Mass. Bay Recs.*, IV. part ii. 314).

of Harvard College received his salary from the General Court of Massachusetts Bay.[1]

The General Court raised this sum, during Chauncy's administration, in the manner initiated by Concord.[2] The £100 was considered an additional annual tax, which was levied on the towns of the Bay Colony according to the basic rate.[3] The Colony Treasurer issued a warrant to the constable of each town, ordering him to collect, in addition to the 'country rate,' so much 'college proportion.' This was assessed on individuals in the same manner as any other rate or tax, and in like manner was collected by the constables and delivered to the Colony Treasurer. Thus, the constable of Dorchester 'payd vnto the treasurer for the Country rate in the yeare: 1657, £52 6s 4d . . . to the treasurer for our parte to the Colledge, £5 5s.' [4]

Although this was a great improvement over the corn collections of Dunster's day, it can hardly have increased the popularity of Harvard or of her President; and after Chauncy's death the General Court wisely made the President's salary a regular item in the annual appropriation bill, instead of raising it by a special rate.

President Chauncy regarded his annual stipend of £100 wholly insufficient for his proper support, and on May 9, 1655, the Corporation presented to the General Court a gloomy

1. Excepting under the Dominion of New England. But the annual grant was renewed by the General Court in 1692. The latest salary grant of the General Court was in 1786 (Eliot, p. 157).

2. See Chapter II.

3. In 1646 the tax system in Massachusetts Bay was changed. From that date a 'rate' meant a fixed assessment on property — a penny in the pound, with 20d (or 30d, 1646–53) on polls (able-bodied males, 16 years and upward). If it was calculated that this rate would bring in more money than was needed, the General Court levied a fraction of a rate; if not enough, a 'rate and a quarter' or more; and during King Philip's War, seventeen rates were levied in one year (information furnished by Professor Harold H. Burbank).

4. *Dorchester Town Records (4th Report of Boston Record Commissioners)*, p. 95. In 1669, the country rate brought £37 2s 11d and 'Colledg proportion' was £3 1s 7d; *ibid.* 163. Other examples follow. Dedham: 1662, country rate £25 16s 8d and 'Colidge proportion' £2 11s 8d; 1666, 'Countrey charges' £50 0s 10d 'and the Colledg account £2 10s' (*Early Records of Town of Dedham*, iv. 37, 48, 89, 120, 138, 159, 203). Rowley: 1670, £16 0s 2d country rate and £2 18s 8d college proportion (*Rowley Town Records*, p. 219). Salem: 1657, 'rate for the Coledg' £5 6s; 1663, £6 12s; 1668, £8; 1671, £6 (*Essex Inst. Hist. Coll.*, ix. 205, 211; xl. 280; Felt, *Annals of Salem*, i. 432). These variations, Professor Burbank informs me, were due to the fact that the tax system in the Bay Colony was breaking down; the total yield declined about one-quarter from 1646 to 1675, while the community was growing richer. In Steward Chesholme's accounts for 1656–60 (*C. S. M.*, xxxi. 220–21, 232, 236, 238) there are several references

'briefe Information' of their financial situation.[1] The 'Real Revenue' of the College was about £12 from rents and annuities,[2] £15 from the Mowlson-Bridges fund, earmarked for scholarships, and the Charlestown ferry rent, at this time an uncertain quantity. College corn and town contributions had come to an end; £40 was still owing to Henry Dunster. The Old College as usual was desperately in need of repairs, although £127 had been spent on it within two years. Unless the roof is reshingled that summer, the scholars 'will be forced to depart. So that either help must be had herein, or else (we fear) no less than a Dissolution of the Colledge will follow.' And there were other pressing needs: replacement of utensils in kitchen and buttery, 'Accomodacions for the Scholars tables,' better commons (or the same commons for less charge), in order to reduce the cost of a college education.

The Deputies replied to these observations by proposing to levy a special rate, in order to pay over to the College for general purposes the Mowlson-Bridges scholarship fund which had been deposited in the colony treasury in 1643.[3] This misappropriation of a trust fund was very properly vetoed by the Assistants. Probably the Old College roof was patched up somehow; certainly the scholars were not 'forced to depart.' But the General Court felt it had done its duty in providing for the President's salary.

APPEALS TO ENGLAND

This was the more disappointing, since the other United Colonies of New England had done little or nothing for the College after the corn contributions expired in 1653. Application to the Society for the Propagation of the Gospel had indeed produced the Indian College; but that was no help to Harvard College revenues. Where to turn next? To England, of course; and if to England, why not start at the top?

Accordingly, the following petition to the Lord Protector

---

in both debits and credits to 'raites,' 'the Cuntry raite,' etc., and payments by 'constibells,' which I am unable to explain.

1. Appendix A, doc. 6.

2. This, I take it, meant the Newgate annuity of £5, the Cogan marsh rent of £4, a £2 instalment of John Wilson's gift, and the Shawshin farm rent, which by this time may have been raised from 10s to £1.

3. F. H. C., pp. 310–11.

was drafted and signed by President Chauncy and the clerical Overseers, and hopefully dispatched: [1]

The humble Petition of sundry of the Elders of the Churches of Christ in New England Humbly sheweth,

That whereas the Lord hath raised up your Highnesse for such a time as this, and hath graciously inclined the heart of your Highnesse to testify, many wayes, exceeding favour to his poore exiles in this Patmos, which hath beene to us as the dewe upon the mowen grasse; and allso hath set up your Highnesse to bee a nursing father to his churches, and Hezekiah-like, both to doe for and to speake comfortably to the Levites, that teach the good knowledge of the Lord; and moreover to be a guardian, and second founder (as it were) to the Universities and Schooles of Learning.

Forasmuch as wee have not a little cause to feare, least that vision should faile amongst us, by reason of the continuall wasting of the old stock of the Seers and Ministers of Christ in these partes; and because God's people here have no hopes of other supplyes, besides what is raysed out of one Colledge at Cambridge amongst us; and allso that one is but in a poore and mean condition, both in regard to buildings and maintenance, and likewise that the upholding therof in such a lowe condition, is very chargeable to the countrey, and too great a burthen for persons of inferior ranke (though serving the Lord with one shoulder therein;) and lastly, because the education of the Indian youth in Piety and Learning, in our Indian Colledge, erected and annexed to our English Colledge, doth depend much upon the welfare, comfortable support, and instruction of the English:

Your Petitioners therefore humbly request, that your Highnesse will be pleased to enlarge your pious and princely heart and hand, to the affording of more settled and comfortable subsisting and maintenance to our English Colledge in Cambridge, and the Members thereof, according as wisdome shall direct, Heroicall magnificence move and incline, and the love of Christ, his religion and the propagation thereof, constraine your Highnesse, that such abundant grace might through the thankesgiving of many, redound to the glory of God.

---

1. John Nickolls, *Original Letters and Papers of State, Addressed to Oliver Cromwell; Concerning the Affairs of Great Britain* (1743), p. 151. Nickolls assigns the date 1654. But as John Mayo, one of the signers, did not leave Eastham until the spring of 1655, and was only ordained over the Second Church in Boston on November 9 of that year, it is probable that the petition was sent late in 1655 or early in 1656. As Mr. Philip T. Nickerson, the authority on John Mayo, observes, the latter's ordination would have been a good opportunity to collect the signatures.

Unless it raised a smile at Whitehall, this petition had no effect. The combined rôles of nursing father, Hezekiah, and second founder to Harvard College in Patmos, appealed not to Oliver Cromwell.

Four years elapsed. A few individual benefactions had come in, but the Old College was falling apart as usual, and the need for fresh funds was more pressing than ever. President and Fellows now appealed to the Standing Council of Magistrates of Massachusetts Bay, whose personnel was identical with the non-clerical membership in the Harvard Board of Overseers.[1] The Council decided to make a new drive for funds in England, 'for the Inlargement of University Learning in New England.'[2] On their recommendation the General Court appointed on May 11, 1659 a board of trustees in England, with authority to solicit and receive gifts for Harvard College, and with them 'to purchase Lands, Rents, Reversions, or Annuities to and for the use aforesaid.' These trustees were well chosen. Their president was Nathaniel Bacon (1593–1660), historian and M.P. for Ipswich in the Rump.[3] The others, prominent New Englanders who had returned to the old country, were Herbert Pelham, the first Harvard Treasurer; Richard Saltonstall the younger; Henry Ashurst, alderman and woollen-draper of London, and Treasurer of the Society for the Propagation of the Gospel in New England; William Hooke, Master of the Savoy; John Knowles, lecturer at Bristol Cathedral; and Thomas Allen, sometime John Harvard's executor, now minister of a Congregational church at Norwich.[4] These gentlemen accepted the charge, and organized. Late in 1659

1. Namely, Governor Endecott, Deputy-Governor Bellingham, Simon Bradstreet, Samuel Symonds, Thomas Wiggin, Daniel Gookin, Daniel Denison, Simon Willard, and Humphrey Atherton. All but the Governor and Wiggin were fathers of Harvard alumni.

2. All that is known of this attempt is printed by Albert Matthews in *Proc. M. H. S.*, XLI. 301–08, where the text of the broadside here reproduced will be found.

3. *D. N. B.* Grandson (not son, as the *Index and Epitome*, 1903, of the *D. N. B.* states) of Sir Nicholas Bacon the Lord Keeper, and son of Edward, half-brother to Francis Bacon. He had been associated with Brampton (or John) Gurdon in attempting to insert a proviso in favor of Harvard in the act incorporating the Society for the Propagation of the Gospel in New England.

4. See *D. N. B.* for Ashurst (who was the father of Sir Henry Ashurst, the colonial agent); *F. H. C.*, Appendix B, for the rest. Pelham, Saltonstall, and Hooke were fathers of Harvard alumni.

or early in 1660 they published a broadside (here reproduced in facsimile) lauding the people of New England for their forwardness in promoting piety and learning, praising the quality of Harvard graduates, pointing out that the College 'hath not had, or ever shall, or can have the allowance of one farthing' from the Indian Corporation, and, in a burst of enthusiasm, predicting that Harvard College might have twenty-fold her then complement of scholars if there were a sufficient 'foundation for *University Learning.*' This foundation 'their deerly beloved Brethren, and worthy Christian Friends in *England*' were entreated to provide.[1]

Among the alleged upstarts of the republican régime who were mercilessly lampooned by the royalists was Judge Roger Hill, M.P. and Baron of the Exchequer:[2]

> Little *Hill* since set in the House,
>   Is to a Mountain grown:
> Nor that which brought forth the Mouse,
>   But thousands the year of his own,
> The purchase that I mean,
>   Where else but at *Taunton Dean?*
> Five thousand pound *per annum*,
>   A sum not known to his Granam.[3]

Judge Hill promised one thousand pounds to the Harvard fund, according to a letter from Saltonstall, Ashurst, and Hooke to the General Court.[4] This magnificent donation, they say, 'will be duly payde' and 'is to be kept for a Stock, or layd out in Lands, and the Rent therof imployed towards the education of youths in University learning with respect to preaching. And these youths must bee both well inclined; and of pregnant Capacities: as also the children of poore and godly parents (if it may bee).' Furthermore, they expect this gift to have 'a seminall virtue' which will breed donations from 'persons of Quality (whom we are now prepared to attend).'

1. *Proc. M. H. S.*, xli (3rd ser. i). 303–04.
2. See *D. N. B.* Hill's interest in Harvard may well have been aroused by his second wife Abigail (Gurdon), sister of the M.P. who tried to attach a Harvard 'rider' to the bill incorporating the Indian society in 1649, and sister-in-law of Richard Saltonstall.
3. *Rump Songs* (reprint of 1662 ed.), ii. 34; cf. p. 17.
4. *Proc. M. H. S.*, xli. 305–07. Mr. Matthews (*id.* 302) dates it between January 17 and March 24, 1659/60.

An Humble PROPOSAL, *for the* Inlargement *of* UNIVERSITY LEARNING *in* New England, *By the* TRUSTEES *hereafter named, to whom the Management of this Affair is committed.*

THE Good People of this Nation, as they are, and have been Honourable for their professed Love, to the hated wayes and truths of Christ in those perillous and evil times, which some years since we saw, so are they also no less worthy of acknowledgment, for their indeared affection to his Faithful Servants, who were then exposed to cruel sufferings by that evil Generation, of whom, as now it is, so, we hope it will be ever true concerning them, which the Prophet speaks in another case: *Thou art cast out like a Branch that is abominable, like the raiment of them that are slain, thrust through with a Sword, and as a Carcass trodden under foot.*

The special subjects of that wrath and rage which then appeared, in those wicked and unreasonable men, were the good old Non-Conformists, to which Tribe, the People of New England, both by joyning to bear witness against all Traditions of men in the Worship of God; and by pertaking with them in the afflictions of the Gospel are most neerly related, of them, it may be said, they feared not the wrath of man, when it was like the roaring of a Lyon, but they indured as seeing him who is invisible, esteeming the reproach of Christ greater riches then the revenues of *England*: Hence it was, that they so willingly suffered the spoiling of their goods, the leaving of their dearest friends, the loss of their native Country, to the peril of their lives, both by Land and Sea; and though the Lord hath led them to a Wilderness, where they have been as a People separated from their brethren and exposed to dwell alone in solitary places, yet they can and doe declare to the praise of his love and goodness, that he hath not been a barren Wilderness to them, nor a Land of Darkness; but hath testified his signal owning of them, by providing for them in those ends of the earth, where he hath set them down in quiet habitations, with rest round about, under the fulness of the blessing of the Gospel of Christ, accompanied with a Godly Orthodox and Learned Ministry, the propagation whereof (as the outward and visible means of such a blessing) is their present and great endeavour.

And because, as sometimes *David* said upon the like occasion, They will not serve the Lord with that which cost them nothing; they have according to their ability, if not above, and beyond it, (considering their late great losses, and other yearly burdens in reference to publick affairs) laid some foundation for a *Seminary of Learning*, the ordinary means whereby the Lord is pleased to make way for the free passage of his everlasting Gospel, which they look at and rejoyce in, as the standing portion and entailed inheritance of them and theirs for ever.

We cannot but be very sensible in their behalf, how much the Lord hath smiled upon their small beginnings, by succeeding the studious endeavours of those, who have been trained up in their *Cambridge*, of whom some are eminently useful among themselves at this present, and of the many, who have been called forth into other parts, both of *America* and *Europe*, have given large, and full proof of their faithfulness and fitness for the work of the service of the House of God, which we take as a token for good, superadded to all other obligations under Gods kind dealings with his People of *New-England*.

We must now crave leave, as in their names, humbly to recommend and propose that foundation for *University Learning* (which hath been laid by them) to be both every way inlarged, as also to be built upon, by the goodness and favour of their ever honoured, their deerly beloved Brethren, and worthy Christian Friends in *England*, who work the work of the Lord as they also do: And according to our present instructions, we shall only address our selves to such Persons of Worth and Reputation among the People of God, who are (in spiritual respects) neer of kin to the special objects of their deserved bounty. And we do beseech and intreat them humbly, unto whom we shall repair upon this occasion, that they will do the Kinsmans part in raising up, if we may so say, the name of Christ on his inheritance.

And for their necessary information touching this Work in hand, wherein the erecting and supporting of illustrious Schools and Colledges, adequately answerable to the increase of their Youth and Children in *New England*, is particularly intended; We must, and do declare, That all those sums of money, or other Donatives which have been given for the furtherance of *Preaching to the Indians*, are applied and appropriated to that Service only: So that this business of advancing *University Learning by illustrious Schools and Colledges*, hath not had, or ever shall, or can have the allowance of one farthing from that liberal Contribution.

One thing more must be offered to special consideration, namely, That all the provision which they have towards this great Undertaking, is not sufficient, according to a very low and moderate Computation, for the twentieth part of those who are born in that Country, and capable of such Improvement: So greatly hath the Lord been pleased to bless his People in those parts with increase of Children.

In pursuance of what we have proposed, we judg it expedient to give some account of that Authority by which we act in this Case, for which end we shall recite and extract some particulars, the Original whereof is in our custody, and at all times ready to be produced upon any just occasion.

'We the Governor, and General Court of the *Massachusets* in New England out of the knowledg and confident assu-
'rance we have of the Wisdom, Faithfulness and Sincerity of your selves, *hereafter named*, together with your natural
'care and readiness to promote so worthy a design; have requested, constituted and appointed, and by these presents
'do request, constitute and authorize you *Nathaniel Bacon* Esq; *Herbert Pelham*, *Richard Saltonstal* and *Henry Ashurst*
'Esquires; *Mr. William Hook* Master of the *Savoy*, Mr. *John Knowlles* of *Bristol*, Mr. *Thomas Allen* of *Norwich*,
'Ministers of the Gospel, you and every of you as *Trustees*, for the rayling and managing of a Revenue in *England*, to-
'wards the education of the youth and children of *New England in University Learning*; Giving and hereby granting
'to you, or any three or more of you, with such gifts as you shall receive, to purchase Lands, Rents, Reversions, or
'Annuities to and for the use aforesaid; and in case of death or removal of any of you the said Trustees, power is here-
'by given to the rest to elect and constitute one or more in his or their stead; as also to choose and appoint such Officers
'under you, as you or any three or more of you shall think necessary: And further to do and act in the Premises as in
'your wisdome and discretion you shall judg meet: And in testimony hereof, We have hereunto affixed the Seal
'of our Collony this eleventh day of May, *One thousand six hundred fifty and nine.*

Here was good news indeed! A thousand pounds already promised and more to come; a hundred pounds a year available for scholarships. But if President Chauncy ordered sack for all hands in hall the day that letter arrived, and commanded a fine stag's head sent to the honorable Baron of the Exchequer,[1] he later had cause to regret premature rejoicing. Judge Hill's promise was never carried out; one can easily guess why. The trustees' letter was written after Richard Cromwell had resigned the Protectorate, at a time when General Monk was in control of London, and when the return of Charles II was only a matter of months or weeks. With confiscation of property as the least of evils impending over active supporters of the 'usurpation,' it was no time to give away £1000 to a college overseas; and no trust formed for any such object would be safe.[2] The trustees simply disbanded.

Yet something less than Judge Hill's donation may have come of this attempt to create a Harvard fund. Treasurer Danforth's records inform us that in 1659/60 Richard Saltonstall sent from England, 'for the use of the Colledge,' £220 in money and £100 in goods.[3] A statement of Governor Hutchinson's to the effect that Sir Richard Saltonstall, who died in 1658, left money by will to Harvard College [4] has led to the assumption that this sum sent over by his son Richard represented the legacy. But Sir Richard died intestate;[5] there could have been no such legacy. The younger Saltonstall, who was his father's administrator, and who had already given £104 to the College, may have been making a second gift, and possibly in accordance with his father's wishes; but it seems much more likely that the £320 had been collected by him as one of the trustees in this 'drive' that was started too late.[6]

1. 'To a stags head sent to England to a Benefactor 10s' (College Treasurer's 'Abbreviate' for 1654–63, C. S. M., xv. 212).
2. See G. P. Winship, The New England Company and John Eliot, for the threatened confiscation of the landed capital owned by the Indian Corporation, averted by using an influence which the trustees of the Harvard fund did not possess.
3. C. S. M., xv. 198. In Danforth's accounts, he enters £453 3s 3d received from 'Mr Richard Saltonstall' between 1654 and 1663 (id. 214). This probably represents the £104 that Saltonstall had earlier subscribed toward the repair of the Old College, plus the £220 sent from England, and the price for which the goods were sold.
4. Hist. of Mass. Bay (2nd ed.), i. 16 n.
5. Somerset House, London, 'Administration Act Book, 1661,' fol. 99 b.
6. It is possible that the £100 received by the College in 1673 from Henry Ashurst

At all events, the money was put to good use; for the Overseers on July 16, 1660 appropriated £10 for the President, and the rest for teaching fellows' salaries, 'untill there be other provision made in their behalf.' [1]

Jonathan Mitchell's 'Modell'

Even under the Cromwellian régime, that subtle conservative force in Oxford and Cambridge which stifles every reformer whom it cannot absorb defeated the puritans' desire to make over the English universities. It seemed hopeless to expect governing bodies to give college fellowships to the right persons. Even at Emmanuel, the fellows had defeated their founder's intentions by changing the tenure of fellowships from twelve years to life; hence college resources became inadequate 'for holding out inducements to poor but promising students.' [2] In order to remedy this state of affairs Matthew Poole published in 1658 'A Model for the Maintaining of Students of Choice abilities at the University.' His scheme was to collect a fund to be administered by a board of trustees, who would nominate a certain number of Scholars and teaching fellows at Oxford and Cambridge, and maintain them during good behavior. Thus college nepotism would be defeated and the proper sort of young men prepared for the learned professions. Sundry benevolent puritans promptly subscribed to Poole's 'Model'; a board of trustees, including several persons with Harvard connections, was appointed; [3] and subscriptions were taken. But, as with the Harvard 'Proposal,' the time was too near the Restoration.

A copy of Poole's 'Model,' coming into the hands of Jonathan Mitchell, minister of Cambridge and Senior Fellow of the Harvard Corporation, inspired him to launch a similar vessel in New England. Harvard College seemed to be declining. Tutors were always resigning: in seven years, 1657–64, there were

---

'as a benevolence of sundry in England' was also an outcome of the same movement (*C. S. M.*, xx. 201).

1. Nicholas Sever's copy from College Book II (destroyed in 1764), H. U. Archives, H. C. Papers, i. 136. Also £10 was granted to the President.

2. Mullinger, *History of University of Cambridge*, iii. 585; William Sancroft's letter in Shuckburgh, *Emmanuel College*, p. 109.

3. Alexander Nowell must have been a kinsman of the brilliant Harvard tutor of that name; 'Mr. Higginson' was probably Francis, son of the first minister of Salem, and uncle of Harvard alumni; Mr. Pennoyer presumably was the founder of the Pennoyer scholarships.

eight new appointments to the three resident fellowships. Students were leaving early, too: of sixteen members of the Class of 1662, only six took their B.A.; and at Commencement that year, when nine graduates of 1659 were eligible for the M.A., not a single candidate appeared to take his second degree.[1] This meant, as Jonathan Mitchell pointed out, that 'Divers schollers after their first degree, are through necessity forced to remove or discontinue, or occasioned to enter into the ministry raw and unfurnished,' and that the standard for New England pulpits was being lowered. Not merely the poverty of the College — he mentions £250 as the total income available for 'president, fellows, scholars and Edifice'[2] — and the unhealthfulness and discomfort of the 'Colledge-Diet and Accommodations,' but the small material inducement to embrace learning as a career, was a hindrance. It was not so much that poor boys could not afford to go to college, as that ambitious parents did not care to send their sons, that troubled Mitchell.

These remarks — the gist of which has been echoed down the ages from one lover of learning to another — were embodied in 'A Modell For the Maintaining of Students and Fellows of Choice Abilities at the Colledge in Cambridge,' a manuscript which Mitchell presented to the General Court of Massachusetts Bay, probably in 1663.[3] After a long preamble on the importance of learning for churches and commonwealth, the 'languishing' state of the College, and the duty of the rich to support education, he proposes a scheme very similar to Poole's: that seven-year subscriptions be solicited for a fund which will be managed by a board of trustees. This will include all members of the Board of Overseers, together with seven laymen chosen by the seven towns then represented by their clergy on that Board. The trustees will provide exhibitions for which they themselves will examine and appoint the candidates; they will add to the stipends of fellowships in the hope that this may 'Incourage deserving Fellows,' not 'Idle Drones,' 'to a

1. *C. S. M.*, xxvIII. 14, 23. Samuel Willard's M.A., mentioned in the Quinquennial, was taken many years later. My figures are the total number of each class, not the number of graduates.

2. A generous estimate. President's salary, £100; rents and annuities (cf. *C. S. M.*, xv. 216–17), £50 10*s*; study rents, £30; Mowlson fund, £15; these are all that I can account for. The balance must have been tuition and Commencement fees.

3. Mass. Archives, ccxl. 142–51; printed in *C. S. M.*, xxxi. 303–22, where the date is discussed.

meet Continuance in the Colledge.' In order further to encourage learning, the trustees will establish four Harvard readerships, on the Learned Tongues, History, Law, and Divinity, which shall be filled by 'persons Chosen out of the exhibitioners or others.' Certain exhibitioners will be encouraged to enter the Church, especially 'in sundry out-places in the Borders of this Country,' others to be town schoolmasters and 'Teachers of the Mathematicks.'[1] And he hopes that out of the septennial contributions money may be found to enlarge the College Library, and even to replace the Old College by a new edifice.

'Though it is but Little that each single person can doe,' concludes Mitchell,

yet many drops united may make a small stream. . . . It is Hoped that in a little time God may raise up more Harvards whose Dying Bequeathments of their estates to this work (and Haply to be improved according to this modell) may give life to it. And thus the Contributions of many particular persons may be spared, In the mean time let us creep as we can and be doing something that Learning among us may not fall or Languish, but may stand and flourish to the Good of us and our posterity after us.[2]

Even that little was not done. 'Through the Discouragements of *Poverty* and *Selfishness*, the *Proposals* came to *nothing*,' wrote Cotton Mather.[3] Another disappointment! And it was not the last.

Treasurer Danforth now remembered the 'Commissioners for the College' of ten years before, the financial investigating committee which so infuriated President Dunster, yet made the General Court take a certain responsibility for the College. On October 20, 1663, he petitioned the General Court, of which he was a member, that whereas 'sundry inconveniences' had appeared in college finances, 'and endeavors for the removall thereof proving ineffectual,' his last refuge was that Honored Court. He craved leave 'Humbly to propound'

---

1. Meaning, probably, instruction in surveying and navigation. *C. S. M.*, xxxi. 317–19.
2. *C. S. M.*, xxxi. 322.
3. *Ecclesiastes* (1697), p. 95, and *Magnalia*, book iv. 181, where Mitchell's scheme is briefly described.

1. That a Committee may by this Court be nomminated and impowred, to Auditt my accounts of reseits and disburssments for the Colledge use

2. That a committee of meet persons may be intrusted and impowred, to improve the Colledge estate, by purchase of Lands, or other reall estate, according to the intent of the Donors, for the Colledges supply.

3. That some meet person for the trust reposed in my selfe may be nomminated and impowred by this Court, and my selfe orderly Discharged [1]

The Magistrates, having perused Danforth's address, 'together with Sundry other petitions referring to the Colledge,' [2] appointed a committee, including Danforth and Mitchell, 'to repajre to the colledge, and enquire concerning the true state thereof in all respects,' and to advise the Treasurer and report to the next General Court. Their report, unfortunately, has not been preserved; for the General Court, in voting thereon, referred to it only by sections. Numbers 1 and 2, they 'doe allow and grant'; and the Colony Treasurer is ordered to lay out the land claims that Nathaniel Ward had assigned to the College in 1646. As for the other recommendations, they were referred to the next General Court.[3]

THE PISCATAQUA BENEVOLENCE

North of Boston, the 'loud groanes of the sinking colledg' fell on sympathetic ears. The banks of the Piscataqua were teeming with activity. First-growth oak and pine were being rapidly converted into masts, spars, and ship timber for the English navy and merchant marine, pipe staves for the wine of Europe and barrel staves for West India rum, and boards and shingles for house building. Great mast-ships were carrying the heavier burthens to England, while a fleet of lesser craft took off the smaller stuff, returning with tropical produce, English merchandise, and pieces of eight. Dover and Exeter seemed in a fair way to eclipse the English towns from which they were named; little Strawberry-Bank blossomed into the town of Portsmouth, where the basis was being rapidly laid for a provincial aristocracy. A community so rapidly making

1. Mass. Archives, LVIII. 47–48.
2. Probably Mitchell's 'Modell' was one of the petitions.
3. *Mass. Bay Recs.*, IV. part ii. 113; cf. 92.

money is not often concerned with charity, beyond immediate sight and hearing; Boston certainly was not. Hence the College was doubly gratified when made cognizant of the following document:

To the much honoured the Generall Court of the Massachusets colony, assembled at Boston, 20 May, 69.

The humble addresse of the inhabitants of the toune of Portsmouth Humbly sheweth, —

That seeing by your meanes (vnder God) wee enjoy much peace and quietnes, and very worthy deeds are donn to vs by the favorable aspect of the gouernment of this colony vpon vs, we accept it alwajes and in all places with all thankfullnes; and though wee haue articled with yourselues for exemption from publique charges, yett wee neuer articled with God and our oune consciences for exemption from grattitude, which to demonstrate, while wee were studying, the loud groanes of the sinking colledg, in its present low estate, came to our eares, the releiving of which wee account a good worke for the house of our God, and needfull for the perpetuating of knouledge, both religious and ciuil, among us, and our posterity after us, and therefore gratefull to yourselues, whose care and studdy is to seeke the welfare of our Israell. The premisses considered, wee haue made a collection in our toune of sixty pounds per annum, (and hope to make it more,) which sajd summe is to be pajd annually for these seuen yeares ensuing, to be improoued, at the discretion of the honoured ouerseers of the colledge, for the behoofe of the same, and the advancment of good litterature there, hoping withall that the example of ourselves (which haue been accounted no people) will provoke the rest of the country to jealousy, (wee meane an holy emulation to appeare in so good a worke,) and that this honoured Court will, in their wisdomes, see meete vigerously to act for the diverting the sad omen to poore New England, if a colledge, begun and comfortably vpheld while wee were litle, should sinc, now wee are groune greate, especially after so large and proffitable an harvest that this country and other places haue reaped from the same.

Your acceptanc of our good meaning herein will further obleige vs to endeavour the approving ourselues to be

Your thankfull and humble servants,

JOHN CUTT,

RICHARD CUTT,

JOSHUA MOODY.

In the name and behalfe of the rest of the subscribers in the toune of Portsmouth.[1]

---

1. *Mass. Bay Recs.*, IV. part ii. 433. Jeremy Belknap, in his *History of New Hampshire* (1784), I. 117, described this as a subscription toward the Old Harvard Hall, a

Secretary Rawson's copy of this address, in the Bay Colony Records, concludes:

This addresse from the inhabitants of the toune of Portsmouth was presented by Mr Richard Cutt and Mr Joshua Moody, 20 May, 1669, and gratefully accepted of; and the Gouernour, in the name of the whole Court mett together, returnd them the thanks of this Court for their pious and liberall gift to the colledg therein.

Richard Cutt, who underwrote one-third of the annual contribution of £60, was the wealthiest of Portsmouth's newly-rich. Glorious tales of the magnificent style that he affected (silver candlesticks, tapestried rooms, private chapel and chaplain, steward and butler, and a drawbridge that let down by the front door) lived on in local tradition, to be garnered by Nathaniel Hawthorne.[1] We may safely credit Joshua Moody (A.B. 1653), the minister of Portsmouth, with steering in the direction of alma mater this uncommon urge of gratitude felt by his fellow Piscataquans toward the government from which they were soon to be severed by royal command.

Two weeks after the Piscataqua benevolence was promised, there was rejoicing in Cambridge, for the Overseers ordered that out of the first £60 the three teaching fellows should receive £16, £11, and £7 respectively, as an addition to their salaries, 'the Remainder to be for the Encouragement of Schollars as the Overseers shall see meet to order.'[2]

John Richards, who had succeeded Danforth as College Treasurer, now turned timber merchant. Every little while, over a period of years, the sloop *Strawberry*, Stephen Graffort master, or her unnamed rivals on this freight route, commanded by skippers Pendleton and Scarlett, would sail up Boston harbor with a cargo of pine boards and red-oak staves 'in part of Piscatoque benevolence.' Fortunately, Treasurer Richards owned a wharf where the shipping could tie up and customers

---

mistake which has been repeated by most of the local historians, by Quincy (1. 508), and by Sibley (1. 367). As Mr. Matthews has shown (*C. S. M.*, xv. lxxxv n.), the 'drive' for Harvard Hall began only in 1671; and as we shall see, the Piscataqua fund was used for other objects. The contributions of £32 from Dover and £10 from Exeter, mentioned in Nathaniel Adams, *Annals of Portsmouth*, p. 50, and G. Wadleigh, *Notable Events in Dover*, pp. 66, 75, as made in 1666 and 1669, were really made in 1672 for Harvard Hall, as the records (*C. S. M.*, xv. 223) prove.

1. *American Notebooks* (Randall Stewart ed.), p. 95.
2. *C. S. M.*, xv. 219. Other notes on the distribution, *id.* 58, 64.

examine the lumber. The College used 500 foot of board for fencing; Captain Davis took a few thousand to repair the Castle; the 'schoolhouse of Boston' and even 'Mother Richards' helped; but most of the boards and all the pipe staves were sold to local merchants, including John Hull the mintmaster, and Humphrey Davie, father of Sir John (A.B. 1681), our second Harvard baronet. Captain Brookhoern, doubtless a Dutch skipper who was helping the Bostonians in their congenial sport of evading the Navigation Acts, took 9000 foot of board at 37*s* per 1000, the top price; pipe staves fetched 60*s* per 1000; John Endecott, son of the late Governor, purchased 4000 barrel staves at 29*s*.[1] In the 'Great Storme' of August 1673, two vessels, driving against Treasurer Richards' wharf, smashed or scattered some 3000 foot of board, and many pipe staves proved unmerchantable; but something of the sort always happened with gifts delivered in kind. By 1673, when some of the original subscribers had lost enthusiasm or fallen victims to prosperity, the town of Portsmouth assumed their obligation for the remaining three years.[2]

SUBSCRIPTION FOR NEW COLLEGE BUILDING

Although the generosity of Portsmouth neither provoked 'the rest of the country to jealousy,' nor the General Court 'vigerously to act,' it may well have set an example two years later, when the Old College at Harvard was making its annual threat to tumble down over the scholars' ears.[3] This costly edifice had come to such a state that the Governing Boards resolved to sink no more money in reparations. 'Upon a serious and late debate,' in August 1671, they resolved to appeal for the wherewithal to raise a new college of stone or brick.[4] The Standing Council of Magistrates on September 12 officially sanctioned and encouraged a drive for subscriptions in every town of the Bay jurisdiction,[5] placing the responsibility for

---

1. Richards' ms. Journal and Ledger, H. U. Archives, ff. 4–7.
2. Adams, *op. cit.*, p. 56.
3. Quincy, I. 30, errs in stating that measures were 'immediately adopted for raising subscriptions in the Colony,' and that an agent was sent to England. The College had no agent in England between the expiration of the Weld-Peter mission and the appointment of Henry Newman in 1709; but cf. below, p. 392 n.
4. Letter of President Chauncy and other members of the Governing Boards, Aug. 21, 1671, *C. S. M.*, XI. 339.
5. *C. S. M.*, XV. 220.

raising money in the hands of local committees. If the Council endeavored to interest the other United Colonies in this good cause, only New Plymouth responded, and even there the people did not.[1]

From Massachusetts Bay, including the Piscataqua region, the response to this appeal was generous.[2] By the end of 1672 some £2280 had been promised, over half from the three towns of Boston, Charlestown, and Cambridge, £100 from that excellent merchant Sir Thomas Temple, and £50 from Benjamin Gibbs, a notorious attorney. Salem for the first time pulled her weight in a Harvard drive, with £130 2s 3d subscribed, including £40 from Mr. William Browne, ancestor of several Harvard graduates.[3] A subscription list was even handed about among resident bachelors at the College.[4] Every part of the jurisdiction was represented: the Connecticut Valley from Springfield up to Northampton subscribed heavily; even the fishing settlement of Hull promised £3 18s, and Scarborough in Maine, £2 9s 6d. All these places, it must be remembered, were being rated

---

1. In the *Plym. Col. Recs.*, xi. 232–33, under date of July 4, 1672: 'Wee being Informed that it is vpon the harts of our Naighbours of the Massachusetts Collonie to support and Incurrage that Nursary of Learning att harverd Colledge in Cambridge in New England from whence haue through the blessing of God Issued many worthy and vsefull persons for Publique seruice in Church and Comonwealth; being alsoe Informed that diuers Godly and well affected in England are redy to Assist therin by way of contributing considerable sumes prouided the Countrey heer are forward to promote the same; and that the seuerall Townes in the Massachusetts haue bine very free in theire offerings thervnto; wee alsoe being by letters from them Invited and Insighted to Joyne with them in soe good a worke; and that wee may haue an Interest with others In the blessing that the Lord may please from thence to convey vnto the Countrey; this Court doth therfore earnestly comend it to the Minnesters and Elders in each Towne, that they takeing such with them as they shall thinke meet; would particularly and earnestly moue and stirr vp all such in theire seuerall townes as are able to contribute vnto this worthy worke be it in mony or other good pay; and that they make a returne of what they shall effect heerin vnto the Court that shall sit in october next whoe will then appoint meet persons to receiue the contributions and faithfully to dispose of the same for the ends proposed.'
The list of Plymouth magistrates and elders, including two early Harvard alumni, Josiah Winslow and William Bradford, in the College Records (*C. S. M.*, xv. 20) probably has reference to this drive. Eastham is said to have voted £6 (Pratt, *Hist. of Eastham*, p. 36), and Bridgewater 'about £12 to be paid in Indian corn' (Nahum Mitchell, *Hist. of Bridgewater*, p. 52); but as there is no record of these sums being received by the College, they were probably never actually collected.

2. *C. S. M.*, xv. 222–23. Forty-four towns contributed.

3. A detailed list, in the Essex Institute, Salem, 'Subscriptions of Gentlemen and Inhabitants of the Town of Salem to the Colledge in Cambridge,' brings the total up to £158 5s.

4. See the accounts in Chapter XX and Appendix D.

annually for their share in the President's salary. But the most astonishing contribution was five pounds sterling from Sir George Downing.

Collecting the money subscribed is another story.

GIFTS AND LEGACIES

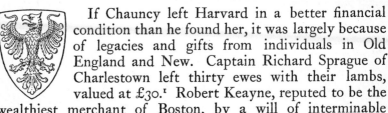

If Chauncy left Harvard in a better financial condition than he found her, it was largely because of legacies and gifts from individuals in Old England and New. Captain Richard Sprague of Charlestown left thirty ewes with their lambs, valued at £30.[1] Robert Keayne, reputed to be the wealthiest merchant of Boston, by a will of interminable length,[2] promised a conditional legacy of money which was probably never received,[3] together with half of his house 'scittuate in Boston near to the old meeting house,' which the College obtained. This property was the southeast corner of Washington and State Streets.[4] After some money had been laid out on it, the house rented at £10 to £15 per annum. Although, like all the early college real estate, it was free of rates and taxes, this property was sold in 1696 for the small sum of £160, which was let out at interest.[5] We have no record of what was done with the revenue until the early eighteenth century, when the eight or nine pounds that it brought in were used, in accordance with Keayne's will,

that the Godlyest and most hopefullest of the Poorer Sort of Scholars may have an Addition to that which their Parents allow them of 20s or 40s a year apiece. . . . Some may have the help of it for 2 or 3 years, and then others may have the help and Comfort of it 2 or 3 years after, and So in Order as long as the benefit of this Gift may continue.[6]

---

1. Eliot, *Sketch*, p. 161; *C. S. M.*, xv. 52, 215, and xvi, index. Danforth took over the sheep himself, and paid the College back in neat cattle. Treasurer Richards notes having received September 6, 1669, 'frome Mr. Tho. Danforth 4 Cowes, 3 Oxen and one steer prized at 35*l* which is in leiw of Sheep. Lt. Sprague's Gift. [sent the 3] oxen back againe to Mr Danforth. poor. not fitt for butcher and sold [*defaced*] 4 cowes and Steer att 21*l* to be paid in money.' Ms. Treasurer's book, 1669–80, H. U. Archives.

2. *Tenth Report of Boston Record Commissioners* (1886), pp. 1–54.

3. Danforth's Abbreviate of Accounts, *C. S. M.*, xv. 215, mentions only the 'Legacy . . . out of the reversion of his wives Thirds, not yet received, £147.' This, I think, means the house, valued at £147 10s (cf. p. 198). The College certainly received the whole house, the second half perhaps in lieu of the other bequest in money.

4. N. I. Bowditch, *Land Titles of Boston* (M. H. S.), iii. 345.

5. *C. S. M.* xv. 264.   6. From copy of will in *C. S. M.*, xvi. 835.

Continue it still does, for the Keayne fund, on the College Treasurer's books, now yields $234.74 per annum.[1] But the real estate that it represents was valued in 1932 at $741,100 for the land alone.[2]

Fortunately for Harvard finances, the Webb estate, only a few doors away from Keayne's, has never been sold. This was a house and lot on the present Washington Street, Boston,[3] which Henry Webb, merchant, left in 1660 'unto Harvard Colledge to be improved . . . forever either for the maintanance of some poor schollars or otherwise for the best good of the College,' together with £50 'in special good pay,' which he requested the Corporation to lay out in 'some pasture ground or small house that may yeeld yearly Rent to be Improved as aforesaid.'[4]

The £50 was spent on current expenses;[5] but the land is still yielding revenue. During the rest of Chauncy's administration it rented for £13 per annum,[6] which provided three under-graduate exhibitions, and one for a resident B.A.; in 1709 it was let out on a ninety-nine years' lease for £12 per annum ground rent. When repossessed by the College in 1789, for the lessee's failure to pay rent, the Webb property was re-leased for the same sum annually. Soon after, business began to en-croach on that neighborhood, the College Corporation made some improvements, and in 1811 the revenue was $1750. An office building, erected in 1860 and partly rebuilt since, yielded the College $18,700 rental in 1932.[7]

No other legacy that fell in during Chauncy's administration

1. *Id.* 415, and index; *Treasurer's Report, 1931–32,* p. 236. The income now goes to the College Benefit Fund. Keayne proposed as an alternative that the income might be disposed 'for an Addition or an Enlargment to the Commons of the Poorer Sort of Scholars, which I have often heard is too Short and bare for them.' It may have been used for this purpose in the seventeenth century.

2. Boston Real Estate Exchange, *Assessed Values* (1932), p. 444 (1 State Street).

3. Now numbered 254 and 256, and going through to Devonshire Street. It was not Webb's own mansion, of which he made the College legatee in case his daughter and grandchild died without issue, but a house which he had purchased from Henry Phillips.

4. Will in Suffolk County Probate Records, I. 388–89; cf. *C. S. M.,* xvi. 837.

5. *C. S. M.,* xv. 214. The £33 6s spent to repair the house probably came out of this £50.

6. *Id.* 215, 49; and see index to xvi.

7. *Id.* 270; *Treasurer's Statement* for 1833–34, p. 11; for 1859–60, p. 2; for 1931–32, p. 204; H. U. Archives, 'Lands: Miscellaneous,' ii. 6–8, 12, 14; ms. Treasurer's Journals, volume beginning 1856, p. 317, volume for 1871–77, p. 442. The estate has been carried on the Treasurer's books at a value of $164,604.79 since 1876.

bore such abundant fruit. John Glover, the Boston merchant who glutted Cambridge with shoes to pay his son's college expenses, left by will dated April 11, 1653, 'to Harvard College at Cambridge, for and toward the Maintainance of a Fellow there, five pounds a year forever,'[1] as a perpetual charge on his house, housing, yard, and tan-pits, situated in Dock Square, Boston.[2] This revenue did not begin until 1672, after the death of Mrs. Glover, when it was used toward the stipends of the teaching fellows.[3] The Glover annuity was regularly paid by the successive owners of the property on which it was a charge, until 1871, when the then owner, Samuel Torrey, commuted the obligation by paying to the College the sum of $350, which at 5 per cent yields the equivalent of £5 in the old 'lawful money of New England.' After accumulating interest for many years, this Glover fund amounts to $7,821.86, and yields an annual income of $410.65 towards salaries in Harvard College.[4]

Slightly different is the story of the annuity provided under the will dated 1671 of James Penn, ruling Elder of the First Church in Boston. Elder Penn left £10 per annum to the elders and deacons of the Church, 'out of the Rents of his Farm at Pulling Point' (now Winthrop), 'for the maintenance of such poor scholar or scholars at the Colledge as they shall see good.'[5] Elder Penn's farm, which covered 267 acres, and included most of the present Beachmont section of Winthrop, descended to his nephew Colonel Penn Townsend, Councillor and Speaker of the House, and to Townsend's descendant, Colonel John Sale, by whose heirs it was broken up in 1838. The control of this annuity has always remained in the hands of the First Church. Two of the stipendiaries in the nineteenth century were Emerson and Thoreau, who were accustomed to walk from Cambridge to the Sale Farm by way of Revere Beach, and collect the £10 ($33.33) from the owner themselves.[6]

---

1. C. S. M., xv. 286.

2. Now (1933) numbered 8 and 9; the property may readily be identified, as the buildings on both sides are modern.

3. C. S. M., xvi., see index under 'Glover, John.' From 1700 to 1704 it was used as an exhibition for William Rawson (A.B. 1703), a grandson of Glover. C. S. M., xv. 365-66, 369-70, 373.

4. H. U. Archives, Treasurer's Journal, 1871-77, pp. 49, 442, et passim; Ledger, 1868-84, pp. 176, 106 and ff.; Statement of the Treasurer, 1931-32, p. 219.

5. A. B. Ellis, Hist. of First Church, p. 132; C. S. M., xv. 287.

6. F. B. Sanborn, Recollections of Seventy Years, II. 458; Mellen Chamberlain, History of Chelsea, I. 254-61; letter of Mr. Channing Howard of Beachmont. In 1866

THE ROGERS FARM IN WALTHAM

John Ward of Ipswich, dying about 1656, made the College his residuary legatee. All that it obtained, after legacies and debts were paid, was somebody's note for £22, which proved worthless, and 'horses to value of £70,' of which a colt worth £7 10s died before the herd was sold.[1] Ezekiel Rogers, another of our university-trained pioneers, left to his wife in 1661 a life interest in his real estate at Rowley. At her death it went to Rowley Church for the maintenance of a second minister, Harvard College to have the reversion if the position remained vacant more than four years. The College invoked this clause at the end of the century, and began to receive rents from the Rogers estate in 1701. With the permission of the General Court, the scattered parcels in Rowley, almost thirty in number, were sold in 1737 for somewhat over £600, and the money applied toward purchasing a compact farm of about 160 acres in Waltham, which with its buildings rented for £140 3s 3d per annum.[2] This 'Rogers farm' was sold to Nahum Hardy in 1835 for $5000, which became the Ezekiel Rogers fund, the income of which is now used by the Graduate School of Education.[3] The exchange was better advised than the sale, for the site of the 'Rogers farm' in Waltham has lately been 'developed' for bungalow lots; the College Road that runs through it recalls the former ownership.

Not only bad judgment, but positive neglect, was shown by the College in respect of the Champney bequest of 1669. Elder Richard Champney left to the College 40 acres at the

---

the First Church obtained a legislative resolve (*Acts and Resolves* for 1866, cap. 45) empowering them to release the annuity; and accordingly did so to the Sales for the sum of $600 (Suffolk Registry of Deeds, Lib. DCCCLXXXVII. 76). This sum now yields $15 annually, which is paid by the Trustees of the First Church to the Harvard Theological School.

1. *C. S. M.*, xv. 53, 200, 213-14, 216. For Ward, see *F. H. C.*, p. 403.

2. *C. S. M.*, xv. 271, 292-97; xvi. 612, 642-43, 672, 812, 844, and see index. Original deed in H. U. Archives. The farm, which was purchased from Anthony Caverly for £2000 in paper currency, lay to the S. and E. of Hardys (formerly Means) Pond, on which it abutted, and on both sides of Lake Street and Lexington Street. A pew and horse-shed at Waltham meetinghouse went with it.

3. S. A. Eliot, ms. Catalogue of Donations (H. U. Archives), p. 40; Treasurer's ms. Journal for 1827-36, pp. 101, 162, 215, 259; Middlesex Deeds, CCCLXXXIV. 99; *Treasurer's Statement for 1931-32*, p. 251. The principal is now $4623.94, and forms part of the Charles W. Eliot fund for the School of Education. Similar in history was the 24-acre pasture of John Hayward on Fresh Pond in Watertown, bequeathed in 1672. It rented for £1 10s in 1696, $50 in 1797, $75 in 1813. In 1829 it was sold for $3254.20. *C. S. M.*, xv. 268, xvi. 413, and index under 'Hayward's Pasture'; H. U. Archives, 'Lands,' I. 14, II. 66; ms. Treasurer's Journal, 1827-36, p. 82.

Lower Falls of the Charles at Newton, as an expression of his 'willingness to further the Education of youth in all godly Literature.' Next to it was a lot of twenty or more acres granted to the College in one of the Cambridge divisions, in 1665. Although within the town of Cambridge, and surveyed as early as 1674, the College appears to have done nothing with this land until the early eighteenth century, when the falls which it adjoined were first utilized for an iron works. Nathaniel Hubbard, who apparently had squatted upon the Champney grant, was induced in 1713 to sign a ninety-nine years' lease, as from 1705, at 20s per annum ground rent. Both parcels, measuring 64½ acres, were sold in 1795 for the small sum of $450. The two lots together cover a considerable portion of the village of Newton Lower Falls, and the angle between Beacon and Watertown Streets; they are now covered with factories, shops, and dwellings.[1]

In addition to these larger bequests the College received many small gifts and legacies in the 1660's from New Englanders, both humble and great, such as £2 10s from Faithful Rouse, saddler of Charlestown; £4 from Bridget, widow of Faintnot Wines of Charlestown; and £16 from Deputy-Governor Willoughby.[2]

Nor was the College forgotten by her English friends. John Doddridge, Esq., of Bremeridge, Devon, Bencher of the Middle Temple and sometime Recorder of Bristol, bequeathed in 1659 'unto the College in New England towards the maintenance of scholars there the yearly sum of ten pounds forever, issuing and going forth out of my Rectory of Fremington in the County of Devon.'[3] Like several other English bequests, Doddridge's proved difficult to secure. John Knowles wrote to Governor Leverett in 1674[4] that he, who 'was the first (I thinke) that first moved Mr. Doddridge to

1. *C. S. M.*, xv. 267; H. U. Archives, 'Lands, Misc.,' i. 24–27, with plans; Francis Jackson, *History of the Early Settlement of Newton* (1854), pp. 103, 113; Middlesex Deeds, cxxiii. 185.

2. *C. S. M.*, xv. 199, 200, 214–15, and index to xvi.

3. *Id.* xv. 289–90; H. F. Waters, *Gen. Gleanings*, i. 660–61; C. H. Hopwood, *Middle Temple Records*, ii. 754–55, 855; iii. 1127, 1134. Doddridge left a like annuity to the trustees under Poole's Model, and to the Corporation of Bristol two silver-gilt tankards that are depicted in *The Connoisseur*, xxiii (1909). 157.

4. April 16, 1674. Hutchinson, *Collection of Papers* (1769), p. 448.

give,' was about to receive for the College 'neare an hundred pounds,' from which he was ready to 'accept of tenn pounds' commission, if urged. The college records show payments on account of the Doddridge annuity until 1687.[1] Shortly thereafter, it seems, the owners of the Fremington rectory simply declined to pay the annuity. In the eighteenth century, even as late as 1785, the Corporation spent considerable money attempting to recover their rights, without success.[2]

THE PENNOYER FARM

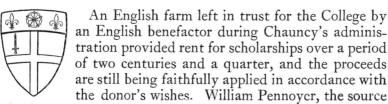 An English farm left in trust for the College by an English benefactor during Chauncy's administration provided rent for scholarships over a period of two centuries and a quarter, and the proceeds are still being faithfully applied in accordance with the donor's wishes. William Pennoyer, the source of this unique bequest, was one of that group of London merchants interested in the colonization of New England. With Maurice Thomson, sometime Governor of the East India Company, he early acquired fishing interests at Cape Ann. During the Civil War the two partners showed their political sympathies unmistakably, and often profitably. They subscribed over £6000 for the reduction of Ireland, and received a share of confiscated Irish lands. They purchased saltpetre from the East India Company and at one time were delivering a thousand barrels of gunpowder a month to the State. Their 'private man of war' *Paramoor* received letters of marque and reprisal; the *Alum* frigate took £7000 of their bullion to the Indies. On another vessel they shipped 'naggs' from England and 'steeres' from Virginia to Barbados, where they owned sugar works; their advice was asked by the Council of State as to 'reducing Virginia to the interest of the Commonwealth'; and they were joint adventurers in a project of the East India Company for establishing a colony in the island of

---

1. *C. S. M.*, xv. 80, 256; xvi. 411; Treasurer Richard's ms. Journal, fol. 12, October 8, 1687; Eliot, *Sketch*, p. 162. From the entry in the account of the College Stock for 1693 (*C. S. M.*, xvi. 411), it seems probable that Increase Mather obtained the last Doddridge payments during his mission to England in 1688–92.

2. *C. S. M.*, xvi. 452, 654, and index; *N. E. H. G. R.*, xlvi. 235; H. U. Archives, vol. 'Wills, Gifts, and Grants,' f. 60.

Assada (Nossi-Bé).[1] Pennoyer was a member of the Society for the Propagation of the Gospel in New England, to which, in 1670, he promised to give £600 for a building fund in return for an annuity of £20 'to be paid to or for the vse of the Colledge in New England forever.'[2] Before this agreement could be executed, Mr. Pennoyer died, when it appeared that he had already made provision for both Company and College by will:

And for and concerning my other Messuages Lands Tenements and hereditaments in the said County of Norff lett to Robert Moore att the yearly rent of Forty and Fower pounds per annum my will is that out of the rents and proffitts thereof Ten pounds per annum shalbe paid for ever to the Corporacion for propogacion of the Gospell in New England and that with the residue thereof Two fellows and two Schollars for ever shalbe educated maintained and brought upp in the colledge called Cambridge Colledge in new England of which I desire one of them soe often as occasion shall present may be of the lyne or posterity of the said Robert Pennoyer [3] if they be capable of it and the other of the said Colony now or late called Newhaven Collony if conveniently may be And I declare my minde to bee that Eight yeares or thereabouts is a convenient tyme for education of

---

1. Report by Walter K. Watkins on the Pennoyer family, in Pennoyer file at Harvard Treasurer's office. Pennoyer's name is frequently found in the different Calendars of State Papers (esp. *Colonial, 1574–1660*, pp. 329, 332–33 and *Ireland, Adventures for Land, 1642–59*); the 5th, 6th, and 7th *Reports of the Royal Historical Mss. Commission*; the *Court Minutes of the East India Company* (E. B. Sainsbury, ed.). For his Barbados interests, see L. F. Stock, *Proceedings and Debates of British Parliaments respecting North America*, I. 196–97; and for a petition to have Lord Baltimore's right voided, *Maryland Archives*, III (Council, 1636–37). 181. He was also a benefactor of his parish, of Christ's Hospital, and of the Clothworkers' Company of London, and left sundry small educational foundations, such as £10 apiece to 'two widows, each as shall be grave, sober, and pious,' to teach 40 poor children in Whitechapel. Summary in *Report of the Commissioners for Inquiring Concerning Charities* (Parliamentary Papers, 1840, vol. XIX. part i), pp. 141–43.

2. G. P. Winship, *The New England Company of 1649* (Prince Society, 1920), pp. 133–34, 137.

3. Robert Pennoyer came out in the *Hopewell* to Boston in 1635 at the age of 21. He appears in the *Mass. Bay Recs.*, I. 284, as having fled from the Colony rather than answer to the Court for an attempted rape or seduction. He next appeared at Gravesend, L. I., and then at Stamford in New Haven Colony, where in 1648 he was 'complained against for drinking wine and becoming noisy and turbulent, and abusing the watchman' (E. B. Huntington, *Hist. of Stamford*, p. 59). After that diversion he married and became a much respected citizen. There are also bequests in the will to a married sister Elinor Redding in Boston (cf. *C. S. M.*, XXX. 957), and to William Hooke, Master of the Savoy (see *F. H. C.*, Appendix B), and his sons John and Walter (Harvard, 1655 and 1656).

each Schollar respectively and about that standing others to be taken in their places which nevertheless as to tyme I leave to the Master and governors of the said Colledge. . . .[1]

The 'messuage' in Norfolk was a farm [2] of 92 acres in the parish of Pulham St. Mary the Virgin, near the borders of Suffolk, and about fifteen miles south of Norwich; a farm of heavy soil, suitable for growing wheat. This, with other lands in the neighborhood intended for pious uses, was left to a board of twelve trustees, headed by Sir John James and including Henry Ashurst. In 1708, in consequence of a decree of the Court of Chancery, the surviving trustees transferred the property to a new board, composed of twelve Governors of Christ's Hospital (the famous Bluecoat School), which was also a beneficiary under Pennoyer's will; [3] and Christ's Hospital continued to manage the Harvard College farm for another two hundred years.

The first payment of rent, £34 after deducting the £10 due to the Society with the long name, was received by the College in 1679 and divided between the two teaching fellows and two 'Schollars of the colonie of Nox or New haven.' [4] A few years later remittances fell off so sharply [5] that President Mather, when on mission to England, looked up Samuel Crisp, one of the original trustees under Pennoyer's will. He presented Mather with a Mercator's Atlas, a portrait of our benefactor, Mr. Pennoyer, and certain arrears of rent — exactly how much the President, with that indifference to money matters typical of

1. Will of William Pennoyer, Esq., citizen and clothworker of London, 25 May 1670. Prerogative Court of Canterbury, Duke, 25. Partly printed in H. F. Waters, *Gen. Gleanings*, I. 504–05 and *N. E. H. G. R.*, XLV. 158–59, and summarized in *Report of Commissioners* cited above.

2. Known as Pulham farm in Pennoyer's time, and Asten's farm in the nineteenth century and today; it is particularly described in the correspondence of 1897 in the Pennoyer file, Harvard Treasurer's Archives.

3. *Report of the Commissioners for Inquiring Concerning Charities* (1840), pp. 142–43.

4. *C. S. M.*, xv. 66. The word 'Nox' was the error of an English copyist, or of Treasurer Danforth, who copied the will into College Book III (*C. S. M.*, xv. 289), for 'now' — 'the Colony now or late called Newhaven Collony'; but the Harvard authorities took it to be a synonym for the Eaton-Davenport jurisdiction, and until 1737, when President Wadsworth obtained a new and correct copy of the will, seldom failed to mention the mythical Colony of Nox when referring to the Pennoyer bequest. See *Magazine of American History*, XVII. 243–44, 443; *Proc. Am. Antiq. Soc.*, n. s. IV. 266–70.

5. *C. S. M.* xv. 75–76, 262; xvi. 827–28.

the great, was unable to recall. 'To my best remembrance,' he wrote Mr. Crisp, 'I had of you 42*li* at one time, 11 [?] *li* at another time, and it runs in my mind that I had something more at another time, but I have perfectly forgotten how much it was.' [1] The actual amount, as Mr. Crisp reminded him, was £80 9s 9d, a sum which the Reverend President perfectly forgot to repay. As this Crisp-Mather route of remittance was not very profitable to the College, the Corporation appointed Richard Mico of London to collect the rent. His first instalment was '3 casque of pewter,' which sold in Boston for £74,[2] of which £20 was disbursed to each of the teaching fellows, John Leverett and William Brattle; £10 each to Jabez Wakeman and Nathaniel Collins, sophomores 'belonging to the Colony of Nox'; and £7 to Noadiah Russell (A.B. 1681), 'formerly a Newhaven Scholar,' which he had been promised when in college but had never received.[3] Richard Mico and his son Joseph continued to collect and remit the rent through the year 1769; their only reward, apparently, being the thanks of the Corporation and a box of bayberry candles.[4] After a short hiatus the agency was placed in the hands of Joseph's grandson Thomas Gibson, and remained in his family for almost another century.[5] Mr. Gibson faithfully collected the rent during the Revolutionary War, and sent it over in a lump sum shortly after the surrender of Cornwallis.[6]

Down to 1737 the Pulham rents were used to eke out the tutors' salaries, and to help support an occasional scholar from the former New Haven Colony who escaped going to Yale.[7] For over half a century thereafter, the income was allowed to

1. College Book V (Treasurer Brattle's Accounts), H. U. Archives, pp. 1, 2. Pennoyer's portrait was burned in Harvard Hall, 1764.

2. College Book V, p. 34.

3. C. S. M., xv. 348.

4. *Id.* xvi. 689; H. U. Archives, Harv. Coll. Papers, i. 186–88, 190–92, 194–99, 206, 207; ii. 7, 8, 15, 16, 23–29, 35, 36, 43. The annual rent from 1740 to 1769 varied from £26 17s 8d to £16 8s, or even less some years on account of disbursements and improvements.

5. Thomas F. Gibson notifies the Treasurer of Harvard College, Feb. 9, 1872, that he is about to resign the agency; he reports that the earliest power of attorney he could find was issued to his direct ancestor in 1740. Hence I infer that Joseph Mico was grandfather to the Thomas Gibson who acknowledges his first power of attorney from the Harvard Corporation on July 12, 1774, when he remitted the rents for 1770–73. Harv. Coll. Papers, ii. 71.

6. Treasurer Storer's Ledger A, H. U. Archives, p. 21.

7. C. S. M., xvi, index.

accumulate,[1] until in 1792 it amounted to £720, half of which was funded at 4 per cent, and the rest 'carried to the account of Salaries and Grants.'[2] The regular payment of stipends to scholars was then resumed. In 1802 appeared the first descendant of Robert Pennoyer to claim the preference; he was granted $100 a year while in college;[3] and in the present century at least one of the Pennoyer name and several of the blood have gone through college or graduate schools on William Pennoyer's foundation.

Although the revenue from the bequest was increased after 1792 by funding the income, the rent from the Pulham farm remained stationary, and in the agricultural depression toward the end of the nineteenth century it decreased. For many years the farm yielded but $117.63 annually, less than the original rent in 1671. Consequently, in 1897 the Corporation instituted proceedings to sell it. The Governors of Christ's Hospital were glad to be rid of a troublesome responsibility. But consent had to be obtained of Her Majesty's Charity Commissioners; the copyhold section of the farm had to be enfranchised, at a cost of £112 9s 11d paid to the lords of the manor; and a purchaser had to be found, which was not easy, as the farm was still subject to the annual charge of £10 payable to the New England Company. Finally, in 1903, Asten's Farm, parish of Pulham St. Mary the Virgin, County of Norfolk, was sold for $4029.52. This sum was added to the Pennoyer fund, which now stands in the College Treasurer's books at $13,686.25, and provides two annual scholarships of $450 each, the one incumbent to be of the 'lyne or posterity' of Robert Pennoyer, 'and the other of the said Colony now or late called Newhaven Collony if conveniently may be.'[4]

1. I can find no reference to disbursements between 1737 and 1792 in the Corporation Records.

2. H. U. Archives, College Book VIII, p. 337.

3. *Id.* 492. This was Jared Weed (A.B. 1807). Among the Pennoyer scholars of the nineteenth century were the historians Jared Sparks and John G. Palfrey; the theologian George Rapall Noyes; and William H. Appleton, later President of Swarthmore College.

4. Pennoyer file, Harvard Treasurer's Archives; Treasurer's ledger cards (Lehmann Hall), nos. 78, 270; *Statement of the Treasurer for 1931–32*, p. 233.

The College Stock

Treasurer Danforth entered all gifts not tied to specified objects, together with unexpended balances of other free income, in an account called College Stock, which had been begun by Dunster.[1] The College Stock amounted to £459 17s 11d when Danforth took over the treasury in 1654. He added £138 19s to it by 1663; and by February 1, 1668, this column in the Treasurer's accounts reached £863 4s 9d,[2] including a number of bad debts and rents in arrears, the first £100 of the Hopkins legacy, the Keayne house in Boston, the Mowlson-Bridges scholarship fund, still in the hands of the Colony Treasurer, and a number of loans. Whatever untied revenue the Corporation could spare from current expenses was let out by the Treasurer at 8 per cent interest. Thus, in 1669 Deputy-Governor Willoughby was paying interest on that part of the Hopkins legacy which he still retained; John Russell of Hadley owed £68 15s 7d, 'to be payd in Porke or wheat at currant price with the Merchant'; and there were several small bonds and obligations from £1 12s to £22 in value, some of them doubtless representing debts or rents due to the College, or money due on legacies from executors.[3]

Unfortunately Treasurer Richards left no such neat 'Abbreviate of the College Accounts' as Treasurer Danforth's; and stewards' records are wanting after 1660. But from the Danforth abbreviate, and other sources, we may make a rough calculation of the revenues of the College at the end of Chauncy's administration. The Colony's tax levy of £100 provided the President's salary, and the Piscataqua benevolence (£60), together with the Glover annuity (£5), and Charlestown ferry rent (about £30), and the tuition fees, took care of the teaching staff, leaving study rents (about £30) and 'detriments,' both much reduced because of the small number of students, to pay officers' salaries, servants' wages, and general upkeep. For scholarships and exhibitions there were available, besides the £25 that was already being received in 1654, £23 in rents from the Keayne and Webb properties, and perhaps five or ten pounds more in annuities. This was by no means a brilliant

1. See above, p. 361.
2. *C. S. M.*, xv. 213–16; see pp. 53–54 for inventory of the Stock in 1669.
3. *Ibid.* and *Proc. M. H. S.*, vi. 339.

showing. The other New England colonies had withdrawn their support from Harvard; the great magisterial families of New England, with the honorable exception of Hopkins, Rogers, and Saltonstall, showed as yet no signs of charity; the English trustees were no more; and the Mitchell 'Modell' had fallen flat. A new drive for subscriptions to replace the Old College by a brick building had been favorably begun; but the game of coaxing voluntary contributions from the community at large was almost played out. One really hopeful sign for the future was the generosity of merchants in Boston, Portsmouth, and Salem, continuing the English tradition of mercantile *Maecenates*, and portending Harvard's main source of revenue in the future.

XIX

LEONARD HOAR, PRESIDENT [1]
1672–1675

 A great deal of nonsense has been written about the 'isolation' of 'provincial' New England after the restoration of the English monarchy in 1660. From the Court of Charles II, and the Restoration dramatists (although she educated one of them), Harvard was indeed isolated; but with contemporary movements in science, scholarship, and theology, the College was in constant touch. As we have seen in previous chapters, hardly a year elapsed in Chauncy's administration without the passing of some gift or legacy or correspondence between the two Englands; and the dissenting clergymen and laymen who kept Harvard in mind were among the most eminent in the kingdom: men such as Dr. John Owen (the puritan Dean of Christ Church), Sir John Maynard, Henry Ashurst, and Dr. Thomas Goodwin.

If men of this stamp were disposed to forget the 'School of the Prophets' overseas, they were never allowed to do so by the several Harvard graduates and expatriated New Englanders who occupied English pulpits. Harvard's trials and prospects were often discussed at their dinner tables; and the recorded correspondence suggests that the Harvard presidency was a matter of real concern to them. As early as 1662, when it seemed likely that Chauncy might resign, Thomas Gilbert of Oxford had been approached on the subject.[2]

Prominent in this 'Harvard Club of London,' as we might

---

1. Almost all the available material on Leonard Hoar and his short but stormy administration will be found in Albert Matthews' paper on the Charter of 1672 (*C. S. M.*, XXI. 363–402); Sibley's sketch (*Harvard Graduates*, I. 228–52); Thomas Hutchinson, *Collection of Papers* (1769); accounts of the family by Senator George F. Hoar (descendant of Leonard's brother John) in *N. E. H. G. R.*, XLV. 285–89, and LIII. 92–101, 186–98, 289–300; and biographical sketches in the *D. N. B.* and *D. A. B.*

2. See above, p. 336.

call the group in modern terms, was John Knowles, pastor of a Congregational church in London, sometime fellow of St. Catharine's, Cambridge, former minister of Watertown and Overseer of Harvard College.[1] In the spring of 1671, Mr. Knowles wrote a letter to Governor Bellingham 'and other persons of note' in the Bay Colony, offering to call the needs of Harvard College to the attention of 'persons of speciall Interest, zeal, largnesse of heart, and singular affection to this weighty concernment of the glory of God.'[2] A change in the presidency must have been at least hinted, since the Board of Overseers, who took it on themselves to reply, adverted to that subject in no uncertain terms. They acknowledged (as was only decent, since the President signed the letter) the 'rich blessing' that Chauncy had been to their society, but observed that before a great while 'he must sleep with his fathers, and receive his reward.' It occasioned them 'afflictive thoughts' under this impending calamity 'to have none in view that might, as Eliazar be invested with the dignity of succession to dying Aaron'; and they begged their correspondents 'to advise and assist toward our supply.' The state of the College, moreover, was 'languishing'; that of the buildings, 'ruinous and allmost irreparable'; the students, sadly few in number; and 'it is wel known to your selves what advantage to Learning accrue's by the multitude of persons cohabiting for Scholasticall communion, whereby to acuate the minds one of another.' After the Class of 1671 graduated, not more than twenty-five students were left in college, a number pitifully inadequate for 'acuating' one another's minds, or for any of those social aspects of education that the founders valued.

This letter was addressed to Dr. John Owen[3] and to Dr. Thomas Goodwin, the two most distinguished dissenters of the

1. See *F. H. C.*, index; A. G. Matthews, *Calamy Revised* (1934).

2. The letter has not been found; these phrases are from the reply, August 21, 1671. *C. S. M.*, xi. 338–40.

3. A rumor to the effect that Owen was offered the Harvard Presidency was vigorously denied by Abiel Holmes in his *American Annals* (1805 ed.), I. 385 n., but has been repeated in the 1820 edition of Anthony Wood's *Athenae Oxon.*, IV. 98 n.; in William Orme, *Memoirs of John Owen* (1820), pp. 347–48; in the memoir to the Philadelphia (1860) edition of Owen's *Works*, I. p. xc n.; and in C. E. Whiting, *Studies in English Puritanism* (S. P. C. K., 1931), p. 78, with a reference to Eachard's *History of England* that I am unable to locate. The fact upon which this rumor was based is that Owen was warmly pressed by Governor Endecott and others in 1663 to succeed John Norton in the Boston Church (*Mass. Bay Recs.*, IV. pt. ii. 98), and that in 1665 he actually made preparations to sail for New England.

Independent camp; to John Collins (A.B. 1649), one of the leading Congregational ministers of London, and Dr. Leonard Hoar (A.B. 1650), a member of his church; to William Mead and William Greenhill of Stepney, the latter an early benefactor of the College; to William Hooke, formerly minister of New Haven; to Samuel Lee, an Oxonian of scientific tastes who later emigrated to New England; and to eleven other ministers.[1]

After discussing this letter at sundry private meetings and social gatherings, some thirteen of the reverend recipients, including Owen, Knowles, and Collins — but not Dr. Hoar — replied on February 5, 1671/72 to their 'Right Worshipfull, Reverend and Beloved' correspondents in the Bay.[2] They regret that, circumstances among dissenters being what they are, New England must expect little more than their prayers for her 'school of the prophets, from whence have issued such instruments as God hath need for service to himself, even in both Englands.' They propose, nevertheless, 'to indeavour to collect such summes of money' as may be a 'comfortable help' toward the 'repair of the edifice' and 'the maintenance of Fellows and Tutors.'[3] Respecting the presidency, they have sounded out a number of possible candidates, but found none 'whose hearts God hath touched to goe over to you, in order to a supply of that expected losse which you mention.' But they observe 'a speaking providence' in the fact that their 'beloved friend Dr. Hoar' intends 'a voyage towards you by this shipping'; and they 'doe judge that God hath so farr furnished him' with grace and 'gifts of learning,' that 'he may in some measure supply that want and help to make up this breach.'

Two years later, after Hoar had stirred up a tempest in the College, his former pastor John Collins tried to explain away

1. For the full list, see *C. S. M.*, XI. 341.
2. T. Hutchinson, *Collection of Papers* (1769), pp. 429–31.
3. Acting promptly on this suggestion, Governor Bellingham 'with the advice of the rest of the overseers of Harvard Colledge in New-England' issued on April 22, 1672 letters patent under the Colony Seal appointing 'our trusty and welbeloved friends Richard Saltenstoll Esq., Nicholas Gregson Merchant Taylor and citizen of London, the Reverend John Knowles minister of Gods word, Robert Newman vintener and Citizen of London, Anthony Wilson Gentleman' a board of 'Trustees for the Overseers of Harvard College in New England aforesaid to ask, demand, receive for the use of the said Colledge all such gifts legacies annuities already given or bequeathed thereunto or that shall or may be given.' H. U. Archives, 1.5.120. It does not appear that the gentlemen so addressed accepted this trust, or that any moneys were collected under it.

DR. JOHN OWEN

this letter, even to get it back. 'You will not find that wee did recommend him to bee your president,' he wrote to Governor Leverett,

nor did wee excite him to come or urge him upon such hopes; it was his own eagre desire after it and his thinking that hee might bee serviceable there; all wee sayd was, that since hee was prepared to come wee thought him one that might be helpfull in your colledge worke and left it with you to judge how.[1]

On February 19, 1671/72, while Dr. Hoar and his recommendations were on the high seas, the long expected demise of Chauncy took place. And not long after Chauncy had been laid away in the old Burying Field at Cambridge, Richard Saltonstall presented to the Overseers a memoir in favor of tendering the Presidency to John Knowles. The objection to his age — about sixty-six at that time — is waved aside, since Mr. Knowles is twenty years younger than Caleb, when Caleb told Joshua, 'I am as strong this day as I was in the day that Moses sent me' (Joshua xiv. 11).[2] Another passage in the memorial suggests that Knowles' chief rival was Urian Oakes (A.B. 1649), minister of Cambridge; for Saltonstall argues that no person 'hath sufficiency enough' to be at once pastor of a church and 'President to such a growing Colledge,' while 'to rend a Pastor or Teacher fitt for Collegiate worke from any Church, where they are,' would make for trouble. Indeed, there was always that trouble about filling the Harvard Presidency during her first century. In accordance with English tradition, a clergyman or a college fellow was wanted. But the fellows were too young, and every clergyman of presidential timber was a successful and beloved minister of some New England church which would not release him. So, unless you caught one on the fly, like Chauncy, or imported one from England, no clergyman was available.

Mr. Saltonstall's candidate was offered the Presidency, if not actually elected President. For on March 25, 1672, William Adams (A.B. 1671), a junior bachelor of Harvard College, copied out 'for the Governor and Mr. Saltonstall' a letter drafted by Thomas Cobbett of Ipswich, 'to be sent to Mr. Knowles for him to be Pres. of our Harvard Coll.'[3] No record of

1. April 10, 1674; Hutchinson, *op. cit.*, p. 445.
2. March 7, 1671/72, C. S. M., VIII. 196–98; also in N. E. H. G. R., XLIII. 354–56.
3. C. S. M., VIII. 194. Cobbett was still an Overseer.

Knowles' answer is preserved, but he must have declined. And this was probably fortunate: Harvard in 1672 was no place for a second Caleb.

On July 8, Dr. Leonard Hoar arrived in Boston.[1] The same ship brought the letter of the thirteen from which we have quoted. And that Providence might not speak alone, John Collins, evidently leader in this 'Hoar-for-President' club, had given the voyager a letter of introduction to Deputy-Governor Leverett, declaring the Doctor's 'ardent desire to serve God in what worke hee will allot to him in your parts, . . . which in the judgment of wiser men than myselfe is thought to bee in your colledge employment.'[2]

LEONARD HOAR

Leonard was a son of Charles Hoare, brewer, alderman, and sheriff of Gloucester in Old England, and of Joanna his wife.[3] Charles, dying in 1638, when Leonard was about eight years old, provided by will for his education at Oxford 'when hee is fitt for itt.' But Joanna was so discouraged by being deprived of the ministrations of the Reverend John Workman, to whom she and her husband were much attached, that after her pastor had been silenced and imprisoned by Archbishop Laud, this intrepid woman struck out for America with her family of five children. They settled at Braintree in the Massachusetts Bay.[4] Leonard was the son chosen to attend Harvard College, where he took his second degree in 1653. Returning to England, he was incorporated M.A. at the University of Cambridge, and presented by Sir Henry Mildmay to the rectory of Wanstead in Essex, whence he wrote the long letter to his freshman nephew at Harvard from which we have quoted in discussing the Harvard curriculum.[5]

1. *Diary of John Hull*, in *Archaeologia Americana*, III. 233. The mintmaster's wife was Hoar's niece; her mother, Mrs. Edmund Quincy, was Hoar's sister. Hull took care of Hoar's business interests during his residence in New England; a page in his account book at the A. A. S. shows expenditures of £838 14s 2d, and receipts of £790 19s 6d.

2. T. Hutchinson, *op. cit.*, p. 435; C. S. M., XI. 337.

3. N. E. H. G. R., LIII. 100–01. Joanna's name was Hinksman or Henchman.

4. *Id.* 186–88. Sibley's connection of Leonard with the founder of Hoare's Bank is incorrect; and it was the President's grandfather (not his father, as I stated in the D. A. B.) who was a saddler.

5. See Appendix C, and Chapter VII.

In 1660 Hoar was ejected from his rectory for refusing to conform. Of his movements during the next ten years we know little. By compiling a short *Index Biblicus* (printed in 1668),[1] he kept a hand in theology; but he also broadened out, cultivating the friendship of men of science such as the great Robert Boyle, and Dr. Robert Morison, senior physician to Charles II and first Professor of Botany at the University of Oxford. Hoar studied Botany (by correspondence, perhaps) with Alexander Balaam, an Englishman resident at Tangier,[2] and acquired sufficient knowledge of Medicine to obtain the recommendation of several members of the College of Physicians at London for an M.D. Through Dr. Morison, doubtless, he procured a royal command to the University of Cambridge to create him 'Doctor of Physick,'[3] which accordingly they did on January 20, 1670/71.[4] About the same time Dr. Hoar married Bridget, daughter of John Lisle the regicide; it was her mother, Alicia, who a few years later was sentenced by Judge Jeffreys to be burned alive for sheltering two of the Duke of Monmouth's fugitives, and who was actually beheaded in the market-place of Winchester.[5] Bridget accompanied her husband to New England.

The Presidential Election

The ostensible reason for Dr. Hoar's voyage was an invitation to preach at the Third (Old South) Church in Boston, with a view to being settled as colleague minister to Thomas Thacher. The Hoars put up at the near-by house of their kinsman, John Hull the goldsmith, and Leonard at once began preaching. But

1. For full title, see Sibley, i. 249. There was a second edition in 1669, and an enlarged edition, called *Index Biblicus Multijugus*, in 1672.

2. Letter to Boyle, Appendix C.

3. 'January 7th 1670[/71] A Letter was written to Cambridge to make Leonard Hoar Doctor in Physick having the Certificate of severall Doctors of the Colledge of Physicians London of his abilitys and fitnesse by standing in the University and My Lord Chamberlains concurrence. But with a clause that he should either then performe his exercises or give caution for performance at his returne from his Travells which he intended to make for his emprovement in that faculty.' Public Record Office, State Papers Domestic, Entry Book (S.P. 44/27), fol. 23.

4. Cambridge University Registry, Ms. Subscription Book, where Hoar, like the early Cambridge puritans, before taking the degree, signed his name to the 'Three Articles' of religion, entirely contrary to his professed religious principles.

5. See Macaulay's classic account, in his *History of England*, i. chapter v. It was upon petition of Bridget and her sister that Alicia Lisle's attainder was reversed under William and Mary.

on July 13, 1672, within a week of their arrival, Alexander Nowell, the senior teaching fellow who took charge of Harvard
after Chauncy's death, himself died. The College could not afford to remain headless any longer; and before the end of July,
Leonard Hoar was chosen President by the Board of Overseers.[1]

Although he seems to have accepted the presidency with alacrity, Dr. Hoar, for some unknown reason, declined to be installed in time to moderate Commencement on August 13. Perhaps he felt obliged to continue a few months with the Old
South;[2] more probably he deemed it wise, in view of his predecessor's financial troubles, to be assured of an adequate salary,
which could not be done before the General Court met in October. Urian Oakes consented to preside; and his witty salutatory oration on that occasion has been preserved.[3] Paraphrasing Cicero's famous speech for Quintus Roscius, he begins:

> If any of you (most splendid auditors) wonder why, when so many
> of the best orators, sharp dialecticians, famous philosophers, serious
> theologians, many incumbered with decorations for excellence in all
> manner of studies, remain sitting, I, their inferior in every respect,
> should rise to my feet in order to act in some sort as President; do not
> think it due to arrogance and ostentation on my part. It is an un-
> fortunate necessity, since all these renowned and learned men whom
> you see present, decided that somebody ought to undertake the office
> and duties of a President and that Commencement exercises should
> be held.[4] To postpone them to next year, they decided, would be in-
> jurious to the scholars.

After many more excuses, and self-deprecatory formulae, he
delivers short obituaries on President Chauncy and Alexander

1. *C. S. M.*, xxi. 365–67.

2. Although Dr. Hoar was not formally engaged to the Old South Church, it was
the proper thing to obtain from them a release; but this they were probably not loath
to grant, since, if Thomas Danforth may be believed, Hoar had not proved a popular
preacher. *Proc. M. H. S.*, xiii. 235.

3. Oratio 1. Cantabrigiæ Nov-Anglorum in Comitiis Academicis Habita, Idib.
Sextilib. Anno 1672 (à Reverendo admodum, atque Doctissimo Uriano Oakes C.
Harvardini Praeside). Ms. in John Leverett's hand in 'Leverett's Book of Latin
Orations, 1688,' H. U. Archives. Oakes's orations are so very prolix that I have made
(with the help of Professors Kittredge and Pease) abstracts rather than translations
of them, and have not indicated omissions even in direct quotations. This oration is
thickly strewn with quotations from and paraphrases of Cicero, Terence, Plautus,
Quintilian, Juvenal, Horace, Virgil, Suetonius, Pliny, Ovid, and the New Testament —
but not one from the Old Testament.

4. There was no graduating class of Bachelors in 1672; hence there was some reason
to omit Commencement, apart from the want of a President.

Nowell, with suitable remarks on the fleeting and unstable nature of human life. A witty passage follows, in which Oakes compares himself to C. Caninius Rebilus — a consul for seven hours, because his predecessor died the last day of the year, and he was chosen only for the remaining part of the day.

Cicero jocosely says, of a certain Caninius, who began and ceased to be consul on one and the same day, that he was a man of marvelous vigilance, since he slept not during his entire consulate.[1] This seems to fit my case, for I shall be so vigilant a President, that I shan't sleep during the entire time of my impersonation; for I avoid noonday naps, nor (as I hope) shall I sleep during these exercises. There is, however, this difference between Caninius and me. He was consul in the afternoon; hence Cicero remarks that nobody breakfasted *Caninio consule*. But a liberal collation will be served to you, *me Praeside*.

Two more pages follow, sprinkled with Greek and Hebrew, on his insufficiency; and then a very friendly address to President Hoar, who was in the audience.

Most honorable man, most friendly to me in many ways, whom I will call not only my friend but my kinsman;[2] thee, I say, Leonard Hoar, I will not leave unsaluted. Others I shall permit the gratulatory orator officially to salute; but thou must be particularly saluted by me. The scholars look upon thee as the rising sun (whom they adore not, to be sure, according to the Persian rite and custom), but desire, reverence, venerate, and pursue with love and honor. The very sight of thee refresheth me. A lively hope possesseth my mind that God, out of pity for the nursery of our afflicted and fatherless University, hath brought thee back to us safe and sound; hath led thee, walled and fortified by his protection, through ocean, through enemies,[3] through a thousand perils. One thing only distresses me — that thou, a President (I had almost said *divinely*) nominated and elected, and all but installed in the place of the deceased President, shouldst be spectator and auditor today. If thou wouldst only change place and bench with me, and mount this rostrum of preachers and moderators!

I need not praise these erudite men, who today by good grace of the Overseers are to be declared Masters of Liberal Arts. 'Good wine' (as the old but no less praiseworthy proverb saith), 'needeth

---

1. Cicero, 'Epistulae ad Familiares,' VII. xxx.

2. *Necessarius*, which also means 'indispensable'; again, Oakes calls Hoar his *familiaris*, which may mean relation, friend, or perhaps college mate. Oakes graduated in '49 and Hoar in '50, but they are not known to have been blood relations.

3. The Dutch war, which rendered Hoar's ship liable to capture.

no bush.' I am sure that they will display their eloquence and knowledge magnificently in this well-read circle of auditors, if only the Father of lights, Author of Arts and Sciences, Dispenser of all good things, will not disdain to favor the proceedings today. And so I spare you the tedium of a longer oration.

On October 8, 1672, the Court voted £150 per annum for the Harvard presidency, payable quarterly in money out of the treasury, 'provided Doctor Hoare be the man for a supply of that place, nowe vacant, and that he accept thereof.' At the same time, 'In answer to a proposall made by Dr Hoare,' the Court appropriated 'not exceeding' £300 worth of the money and materials then being collected for the new brick college, 'for the better repaire necessary to be donne to his lodging, by addition of a kitchen, etc, and making of fences for orchards and gardens, meet for such a place and society.'[1]

THE CHARTER OF 1672

On October 21, 1672, the General Court passed a new College Charter. We have to fall back on inference to explain the reason for it. Mr. Albert Matthews, who has studied this question from every angle, believes that President Hoar had two ends in view: to reaffirm those powers of the Corporation upon which the Overseers had repeatedly encroached, and to restore the fellowship to its full strength.[2] For, since the death of Nowell, the Corporation had been reduced to Treasurer Richards, tutors Browne and Richardson, and Samuel Danforth, the minister of Roxbury.

The Charter of 1672 mentions that of 1650, and is declared to be 'for the perpetuation and further advancement of so good a worke.' The Corporation is renamed 'The President, Fellowes and Treasurer of Harvard Colledge.'[3] 'Leonard Hoare Doctor in Phisick' is declared to 'be the present President of said Harvard Colledge,' the two existing fellows are confirmed in office, and

1. *Mass. Bay Recs.*, IV. pt. ii. 535, 537. Surely Dunster and Chauncy had a kitchen in the President's Lodging? They are not debited with food and drink in the Steward's book, nor are Chauncy's sons, when he was President and they were students.

2. *C. S. M.*, XXI. 393-94.

3. There is no engrossed copy of the Charter of 1672. The one recorded in the *Mass. Bay Recs.*, IV. pt. ii. 535-37, presumed to be the official one, is printed in parallel columns with the rough draft and with the Charter of 1650, in *C. S. M.*, XXI. 395-402. The title is on p. 398.

the Corporation is filled up by appointing as fellows senior to the two tutors 'Mr. Vrian Oakes Pastor of the Church of Cambridge' and 'Mr. Thomas Shepard Teacher of the Church of Charlstowne.' The language follows fairly closely that of the earlier charter. The substance of the Court's whipping order of 1656 [1] was incorporated in a clause giving the Corporation the full power of 'Sconcing [2] fineing or otherwise correcting all inferiour Officers or members to the said Society belonging.' And, again following English precedent, the fellows were given power, taking the town constable with them, 'to enter into any houses lycensed for Publick entertainement where they shall be informed, or may be Suspicious of any Enormities to be plotting or acting by any members of their Societie.' Expelled students shall not 'abide above ten dayes in the Township of Cambridge' unless it be their home.

Although the Corporation never used their new title in the Charter of 1672, and the former Charter of 1650 was expressly reaffirmed when Leverett was elected President in 1707, there is evidence that the Charter of 1672 was also believed to be in force, as a sort of supplement or explanation of the earlier document, as late as 1723. [3] Thereafter it fell into desuetude. With the growth of legal knowledge in New England, the college authorities probably realized that they must base their power on one charter or the other, not both.

PLANS AND VISIONS

Finally, after the Old South had been placated and the President's Lodging renovated and repaired, Dr. and Mrs. Hoar moved out to Cambridge. On December 10, 1672, [4] in the college hall where he had often recited and disputed as an

1. See above, p. 328.

2. 'Sconce,' meaning to fine, was a word used in the English universities — 'It is Ordered: That the Gentlemen Commoners of the severall Colledges and Halls in this University . . . in case of necglect . . . shall be punished with such sconce or imposed exercises as to the officers . . . shall seeme meete . . .' Montagu Burrows, *Register of the Visitors*, p. 366; cf. *N. E. D.* Being unfamiliar to the Secretary of the General Court, 'Sconcing' became 'Scourging' in one of his certified copies of this Charter, thus unwittingly adding another count to the sadistic charges against New England puritans.

3. Mr. Matthews, in *C. S. M.*, xxi. 375–88 disproves Sibley (i. 235) and Quincy (i. 33), who stated that this charter was never put in force.

4. *C. S. M.*, xv. 219; xxi. 366.

undergraduate, Leonard Hoar was formally inaugurated President of Harvard College. It was a quiet inauguration, since Governor Bellingham had died but three days before; Deputy-Governor Leverett presided.[1]

The omen was not unfavorable; for Governor Bellingham belonged to the founding generation that had almost passed away, while Governor Leverett, like the new President, was English born but New England bred, with worldly experience in the Old Country which he was eager to place at the service of the New.

It was a dramatic moment. After thirty-four years' existence, Harvard College was to be presided over by one of her own sons. Yet much in the situation was depressing. A mere handful of students were there to welcome their new President, compared with the throng which in his undergraduate days had filled the Old College with noise and laughter. All the 'edifices' but the refurbished Lodge were shabby and prematurely decrepit, the Indian College deserted. In Cambridge there were a few more houses, and more widely scattered than in Hoar's youth; the village had taken on an air of permanence and placidity; but it had very clear notions of how a Harvard president should behave, and was not disposed to look kindly on any departure from tradition.

It is not likely that Leonard Hoar was depressed by his surroundings, or over-sentimental from old associations. Forty-two years old, with a young wife, he had the world before him. Harvard College for him was an instrument to be quickened into vital service for God and man. He would have his alma mater no longer confine herself to suckling nurslings with spiritual milk, and conserving the culture of the past; he would rededicate her to the true advancement of learning, synthesize the great discoveries of the century, boldly experiment with the physical phenomena of this new world so rich in possibilities of human betterment — in a word, play the same dynamic rôle in colonial life as had Oxford and Paris in medieval Europe. The thoughts and dreams that were passing through his mind he communicated three days after his inauguration to Robert Boyle: 'A large well-sheltered garden and orchard for students addicted to planting' — a combination of his friend Dr. Morison's botanic garden at Oxford and a modern agricultural

1. Sibley, I. 235; 4 *Coll. M. H. S.*, I. 18.

experiment station; 'an ergasterium for mechanick fancies' —
a workshop to carry on the practical experiments of men like
Robert Hooke; 'and a laboratory chemical for those philosophers, that by their senses would culture their understandings.'
These, he continued, 'are in our design, for the students to
spend their times of recreation in them; for readings or notions
only are but husky provender.' And will his right honorable
friend be pleased 'to deign us any other advice or device, by
which we may become not only nominal, but real scholars'?[1]

No Harvard President before Eliot had a broader purpose.
As the late Theodore W. Richards remarked, in calling this
passage to my attention, President Hoar's design would have
given Harvard the earliest university chemical laboratory in
the English empire, if not in the world.[2] Yet all these splendid
visions came to naught; and within three years President Hoar
was forced to retire.

CONTROVERSY AND RESIGNATION

Exactly why this happened has never come to light. It was
one of those affairs that everyone discussed and fought over at
the time, without leaving anything definite behind. The out-
standing fact is that Hoar's administration was wrecked by the
young teaching fellows and students, entirely against the will
of the elderly Overseers, Magistrates, and ministers. This suggests that neither religion, nor the President's plans for a new
and better Harvard, had anything to do with the case.

Cotton Mather, who entered college a few months before the
President resigned, goes as far as any contemporary in stating
what was wrong. He writes of Dr. Hoar in the *Magnalia*:

Were he considered either as a *Scholar*, or as a *Christian*, he was
truly a *Worthy Man;* and he was generally reputed such, until happen-

---

1. See the whole letter, in Appendix C.
2. Cf. Irvine Masson, *Three Centuries of Chemistry* (1925), p. 53. John Allin (A.B.
1643) wrote in 1667, 'this week I met with an offer to go to Oxford with a friend for
one year, to work in the University chemical elaboratory' (Sibley, 1. 96); but this
'elaboratory' was a private affair, run by one Peter Sthael at the charge of Boyle.
R. T. Gunther, *Early Science in Oxford* (1920), 1. 22, 24. Arthur C. Cole, in *The
Irrepressible Conflict* (1934), p. 210, says 'the first chemistry laboratory in America
was set up in 1857' at the University of Michigan. But there was a chemical laboratory
in the Lawrence Scientific School from its opening in the second half of the academic
year 1847–48. *The Harvard Book* (1875), 1. 280–81.

ing, I can scarce tell *how*, to fall under the Displeasure of *some* that made a Figure in the Neighbourhood, the *Young Men* in the Colledge, took Advantage therefrom, to ruine his Reputation, as far as they were able. . . . The *young Plants* turned *Cud-weeds*, and with great Violations of the *Fifth Commandment:* set themselves to *Travestie* whatever he *did* and *said*, and aggravate every thing in his Behaviour disagreeable to them, with a Design to make him *Odious;* and in a *Day of Temptation*, which was now upon them, several very *Good Men* did unhappily countenance the *Ungoverned Youths*, in their Ungovernableness.[1]

Of the neighborhood figures and very good men who countenanced this student rebellion, suspicion has long pointed a finger at Urian Oakes, minister of Cambridge and Hoar's greeter and successor. Oakes was a year senior to Hoar at Harvard College, and had been a teaching fellow just before Dunster's resignation. Like Hoar, he had sought his fortune in England, and enjoyed an ecclesiastical benefice under the Protectorate; after the Restoration he had taught school for several years, and in 1671 accepted a call to the Cambridge Church, in succession to Jonathan Mitchell. A clever and brilliant man, ambitious but somewhat valetudinarian, 'Mr. Oakes hath had a distemper hang upon him that hath much weakned him,' wrote Governor Leverett to John Collins in August 1674.[2] 'The greatest occasion, I thinke, in some exercise in his mind, though he thinks it is the remayne of his sickness long agoe in England.' That Oakes had been the leading local candidate against Knowles and Hoar, we have already inferred; that Cambridge, where his father was a leading citizen, should have expected the election of such a brilliant Latinist, poet, and pulpit orator, would be only natural. But Oakes welcomed Hoar in so friendly a fashion, and after his resignation strove so strenuously to avoid the presidency, that unless he was a most consummate hypocrite, it is hard to believe that he was disappointed at the election of Hoar, or acted as ringleader of the opposition. Yet a number of

---

1. *Magnalia*, book IV. 129. Cf. John Hull's Diary, *Archaeologia Americana*, III. 236: 'Some troubles this summer arose in the College, so that Dr. Leonard Hoar, their new president, who was last year highly courted to accept the place, was now by some wished out of it again. I cannot say there was any apparent cause for it, more than that God seems to threaten to make division in all orders our punishment, as we too readily do make them our sin.'

2. T. Hutchinson, *Collection* (1769), p. 464. The fact that Hoar did not present letters of dismissal from John Collins's church in London seems to have been used as a count in his indictment; at least so I infer from a sentence in Leverett's letter.

contemporary hints do suggest that he was one of those responsible.[1]

Thomas Graves (A.B. 1656) of Charlestown, who had lately been a teaching fellow, seems to have been a disappointed presidential candidate who stirred up disaffection;[2] and Joseph Browne, one of the tutors, was a warm friend of Oakes and Graves. Thomas Shepard (A.B. 1653), named fellow in the new charter after Oakes, had been a tutor in the early part of Chauncy's administration. He showed his sympathy with the opposition by resigning with Oakes. The party alignment was clean-cut: Corporation and students against Overseers. The latter, who had elected Hoar, supported him consistently; but the fellows, whose powers he had endeavored to affirm by the new charter, and the students, whose curriculum he proposed to modernize and broaden, succeeded in driving him out.

In my opinion, the real trouble was some fault in Hoar's character or conduct. Governor Leverett refers to 'the check given him in his beginning' as President, 'which may make him more cautious for time to come';[3] but what that check was, we are not told. Surely there must have been something unfortunate in Hoar's manner, repellent in his personality, harsh in his disci-

1. Oakes told Samuel Sewall the junior fellow, on June 5, 1674 (*Diary*, I. 3), that 'he desired I would refrain from coming to his house, and that he did it *se defendendo*, least he should be mistrusted to discourage and dissettle me.' Oakes in his election sermon, in May 1673, told the General Court that they had 'done very well for the *Reverend President*' but should remember the Fellows also, since they are 'next to the *President*, the *Props* and *Pillars of that Society*, and have a careful and *Laborious Life* of it' (Sibley, I. 177). Later, when Samuel Danforth (A.B. 1671) was proposed for a fellowship, it was brought up against him that he had signed a petition for the removal of President Hoar. Oakes on that occasion said that 'except the Overseers would declare an absolute amnesty as to what had been done against' Dr. Hoar, he would refuse to accept the presidency, even *pro tempore*. Diary of Increase Mather, in *Proc. M. H. S.*, III. 318. And see his surprisingly warm defence of the seceding students in his Commencement Oration of 1675 (next Chapter).

2. Graves was so charged in one of the letters of Collins to Leverett. T. Hutchinson, *Collection* (1769), p. 471. Edward Randolph in 1676 (*ibid.* 502) wrote that Graves 'was put by his fellowship, by the late Dr. Hoar, because he would not renounce the church of England.' Graves may have been left out of the Charter of 1672 by Hoar's desire, but he had broken connection with the College before Chauncy's death, and he declined a fellowship offered in May 1673. *C. S. M.*, xv. 56, 226.

3. Hutchinson, *op. cit.*, p. 464. Governor Leverett also wrote that Hoar was 'not so cautious in his comeing off from former engagement as he ought before he enters upon new,' meaning the Boston ministry; but, after all, Hoar was only preaching to the Old South on trial. Sibley (I. 236) gives great weight to this; but J. Hammond Trumbull thought that Hoar's relation with the Old South as a 'half-way convenant' church caused the trouble (*N. E. H. G. R.*, LIII. 290–91).

pline, or unreasonable in his policy, to alienate the students. And Oakes, who lived within the present College Yard,[1] may well have come to an early conclusion that Hoar was impossible and allowed this opinion to be known. It is disappointing, but not surprising, that we cannot solve the mystery after two centuries and a half, since John Hull, who lived near by, could find 'no apparent Cause,' and John Collins, to whom both parties gave their views in full, wrote: 'by comparing report with report, letter with letter, I am almost confounded in makeing a judgment of this matter.'[2] From the same letter it appears that Governor Leverett, while blaming both sides, accused Hoar of untruthfulness — a charge that in New England (and possibly other regions) is apt to cover personal objections not easily definable or readily explained.[3]

Twice the controversy was appealed to the General Court. At an Overseers' meeting in 'Boston Towne house' on October 2, 1673, at which were present their worships John Leverett, Simon Bradstreet, Daniel Gookin, Edward Tyng, and Thomas Clarke, Esquires, and the Reverend Masters Eliot, Oxenbridge, Thacher, Danforth, and James Allen, the President's opponents entered their complaints. 'The Question being put whether upon all that had been said and alledged against Dr. Hoare President of said Colledge, there be cause found for his removall from the Presidentship. It was voted in the negative, *nemine contradicente.*'

Whatever had there been set down in writing was then shown to the General Court, which on October 18 voted:[4]

---

1. The 'Old Parsonage,' on the site of the eastern section of Wigglesworth Hall, had been built for him in 1670.

2. Collins to Leverett, March 19, 1675: Hutchinson, *op. cit*, pp. 471–72. John Knowles, writing to Leverett on April 16, 1674 (*ibid.* 447), expresses his grief at the 'great breach' made in the College. 'Wee wonder at the occasion of it, that they doe not either strengthen the hands of Mr. Hore that so the worke may go on, or else some other able man may be put into the place. For the wound will widen by delays, and if the colledge dye, the churches (some judge) will not live long after it. Mr. Penoyer's meanes given to it, about forty pounds per ann. I feare will goe another way when it falls, if there be noe colledge; and divers other intended gifts. Wee have some money offered to be payd for the colledge, etc. divers youths desire to come over to study there, but I doe give noe encouragement to them soe long as things are in such a broken condition in the colledge. . . .'

3. *Id.* 472. A former President of Harvard College once remarked in my hearing, 'I have observed that when people wish the Corporation to dismiss some member of the faculty, and all other arguments fail, they invariably accuse him of being a liar.'

4. Mass. Archives, LVIII. 89.

This Court hauing heard the Complaints of the Fellowes. and students of Haruard Colledge formerly exhibbited to the Honoured and Reuerend ouerseers. against the præsident Doctour Hoare whereof wee are (vpon seuerall Considerations) very sensible vpon the whole matter cannot but declare our Concurrance with the act of the said ouerseers vizt that we see not (Notwithstanding the said Complaints) ground for the present to remoue the sayd President: And although there may haue been some Greivances wee are very hope[ful] that the prudence and Council of the ouerseers to the said Præsident and the making a full supply of Fellowes may heale and Compose all distempers which is our earnest desire And we cannot but further declare that it will be very acceptable to this Court that the Students that haue withdrawne, doe returne to their former stations: —The magistrates haue past this their brethren the deputyes hereto Consenting.

A month earlier, Oakes, Shepard, Browne, and Richardson had resigned their fellowships. Three young graduates were promptly elected; but only one, Daniel Gookin (A.B. 1669), accepted.[1] For a few months there was peace, but the distemper broke out again in February 1674.[2] A few months later, Hoar presided with prayer at a painful scene in the Old College Library. Thomas Sergeant, a senior sophister, for 'speaking blasphemous words concerning the H. G.' was suspended from his degree and required to kneel down and be 'publickly whipped before all the Scholars' by Goodman Healy the local prison-keeper.[3] It is not likely that this did much to restore student morale. Indeed, it was not long after this that Cotton Mather, eleven-year-old freshman, was threatened with such terrible reprisals for telling tales to his father that he went home.[4]

On August 7 came a jolly interlude, the raising of the frame of 'New College,' Old Harvard Hall. Heavy drinking at New England house-raisings was the custom; and as this was the largest building yet put up in New England, the 'undertakers,' Deacon Cooper and William Manning, doubtless provided good cheer in proportion. By a special dispensation of Providence,

1. *C. S. M.*, xv. 57, 220–21. Samuel Sewall and Peter Thacher (A.B. 1671) were elected respectively on November 5, 1673 and June 15, 1674, and accepted.
2. *Archaeologia Americana*, iii. 238.
3. Sewall, *Diary*, i. 4. Healy was afterwards removed from his office for gross misconduct, and confined in his own prison after being well whipped. Paige, p. 580. Harvard presidents and fellows had probably done their own flogging hitherto, and the calling in of a professional may well have seemed the last straw to the students.
4. *Proc. M. H. S.*, iii. 317.

no lives were lost, although one of the workmen suffered a broken leg and thigh.[1]

Commencement, four days later, was a sad affair in contrast: only one member of the Class of 1674 graduated, and but four of the 'large yet civil' Class of 1671 took their second degree.[2] But Hoar presided with such dignity and urbanity that, so Governor Leverett wrote two weeks later, his 'opposers loose ground.'[3]

This was a bad miscalculation. So few students returned to college after Commencement that the General Court, in their October session, felt obliged to take the matter once more in hand. 'Understanding that, notwithstanding all former endeavours, the colledge yet remains in a languishing and decaying condition,' they order the President, present and former fellows, Overseers, graduates, and students to appear before them, that 'this Court may, if possible, take further effectuall course for the revivall of that great worke, and its future flourishing. . . .'[4] The hearing took place before the full Court on October 13. Except for Sam Sewall's 'sum' of his own speech, to the effect 'that the causes of the lownes of the Colledge were external as well as internal,'[5] none of the evidence has been preserved. After it was all in, the 'deputies voted to dismiss the President from his place,' but the Magistrates forced a compromise.[6] President Hoar 'vpon his oune voluntary motion, in consideration of the paucity of scholars,' took a salary cut of 33 per cent, and 'all the officers of sallery'— the Steward, butler, and cook — were dismissed. The President was directed to hold office until the 'next Election Court' in the spring, with the understanding that if by that time the Overseers were unable to remove 'all obstructions,' and the College remained 'in the same languishing condition,' he would 'be dismissed without further hearing.'[7]

So the Old College was closed for the winter, plate and other valuables were taken into the President's Lodging, and one by one the remaining students stole away, until by November 15

1. Sewall, *Diary*, I. 5.
2. Sibley, II. 412–13, 442.
3. Hutchinson, *op. cit.*, p. 464.
4. *Mass. Bay Recs.*, v. 20.
5. *Diary*, I. 5–6.
6. Diary of Increase Mather, *Proc. M. H. S.*, III. 317.
7. *Ibid.*; *Mass. Bay Recs.*, v. 20–21.

there were only three left in Cambridge.[1] Tutor Thacher was even encouraged 'to live in Boston provided he be tutor unto the scholars of the Colledg there residing, who shall desire it of him.'[2] At Commencement the next summer, President Oakes declared, in classical Latin,

I shall never forget that time, when the most beloved scholars, torn and wrenched from the bosom and embrace of their mother, went as it were into exile. *Mater academia*, naked, grieving, depressed, dragging out her life in filth and squalor, as in changed and torn garments, bewailed her childless misery in dust and ashes.

> Non alitèr quàm si nati pia Mater adempti,
> Portat ad extremos, corpus inane rogos.[3]

Bitter to me is the memory of those times, sad was the house of Harvard, silent was Cambridge, stilled were the studies of all good Arts; everything, everything I say, by the departure of these most flourishing young men, was deserted, savage, silent, full of mourning and lamentation.[4]

A gloomy winter it must have been for President Hoar and his wife. The short days passed slowly without college routine or cheery clatter of students coming and going. The small household was isolated and shunned. As they looked out of the windows, there was naught to see but the closed and deserted Yard, the tottering buildings from which (said Oakes) even the rats had fled, the gaunt frame of the unfinished Harvard Hall, and the inhospitable houses of hostile villagers. Even the printing press in the Indian College had no business that winter. There appears to have been nothing for the President to do ex-

1. *Proc. M. H. S.*, III. 317. The day after this entry in Increase Mather's diary, Thomas Danforth wrote to John Cotton (A.B. 1657) of Plymouth another of those exasperating letters that fail to elucidate the trouble. 'As for the Doctors grievance, you do not I suppose wonder at it. I doubt not but he hath been told of his evill in that matter from more hands then yours yet he does justifie his own innocency, and I perceive that Mr Corlet, both elder and younger were so taken with hopes of a fellowship, that they strenuously sought to excuse the Doctor and lay the blame else where; but by this time I suppose are out of hope of what they expected, the Colledge standing in more need of Students then of rulers. it would be too long to give you an account of particulars, but I think the Doctor, and all his friends do by this time see they have missed it greatly; but what the issue will be I canot divine.' November 16, 1674. Nineteenth-century copy in H. U. Archives, Harv. Coll. Papers, 1. 26 (printed in Paige, p. 368).
2. *C. S. M.*, xv. 60.
3. A paraphrase of Ovid, *Heroides*, Epist. xiv. lines 115–16.
4. Oratio secunda, 1675, p. 14, in 'Leverett's Book of Latin Orations.'

cept to check the books in the Library, list the utensils in the kitchen, and hold an individual Commencement for Thomas Sergeant, the blaspheming senior sophister, on the ground that he was 'going to sea the next week.' [1] Harvard College had reached her nadir. She could sink no lower and remain alive.

On March 15, 1674/75, Dr. Hoar tendered his resignation to the Board of Overseers, and it was promptly accepted.[2] 'The Colledge is still desolate,' wrote Increase Mather ten days later.[3]

So Leonard Hoar left the old President's Lodge, which he had entered with such high hopes less than three years before, and retired to Boston. But forty-five years old, he was completely broken by the '*hard* and *ill* Usage, which he met withal.' His grief, says Cotton Mather, 'threw him into a Consumption.' [4] On the night of November 27–28, 1675, Increase Mather was called out of bed 'to pray with dr. Hoar who [was] near vnto death. Hee desired me to take his Nephew John Hoar vnder my Tuition, and to write his Father, that hee would be Reconciled to his son.' [5] Before the next day was over, Leonard Hoar was dead, and on December 6 his body was laid in his mother's tomb at Braintree.

Malus celeri saucius Africo, mused Cotton Mather.[6] And John Hull recorded what, for want of better evidence, we may accept as the verdict of history: 'Would those that accused him had but countenanced and encouraged him in his work, he would have proved the best president that ever yet the college had.' [7]

1. *C. S. M.*, xv. 60–61.
2. *Id.* 231.
3. Ms. Diary, A. A. S., March 25, 1675.
4. *Magnalia*, book iv. 129.
5. Ms. Diary, A. A. S.
6. Horace, *Odes*, i. 14. The inscription on Hoar's tombstone, carved after his widow's death in 1723, may be read in Sibley, i. 247, where the later career of Hoar's widow, who married Hezekiah Usher, is related. Both this inscription and Josiah Flynt's preface to a posthumous edition of Hoar's *Sting of Death and Death Unstung* (Boston, 1680), indicate that family resentment over the President's treatment died hard; but the President's daughter Bridget and her husband Thomas Cotton of London gave the College £500 in 1724–26, £100 of it 'to be forever improved for an Augmentation in addition to the Salary of the President.' Sibley, i. 248; H. U. Arch. 1.15.490.
7. *Archaeologia Americana*, iii. 238.

The Triennial Catalogues [1]

Yet, futile as Hoar's presidency had been in comparison with what he hoped to accomplish, he left a permanent mark on the College, and on American university history, in a small matter which he probably tossed off without much thought. This was the simple but original device of issuing a catalogue of Harvard graduates.

So far as can be ascertained, no college or university in the world had yet undertaken to publish the names of her alumni.[2] Our little broadsheet, $10\frac{1}{2}$ by $17\frac{1}{2}$ inches, printed by the press in the Indian College in 1674, has the honor of heading a long line of university catalogues. The name of each Bachelor who took his second degree is followed by the abbreviation *Mr.* Anyone elected a Fellow of the Corporation is designated *socius*; and any degree he may have taken at another university, such as Oxford, Cambridge, Dublin, Aberdeen, or Leyden,[3] is duly recorded. By thus choosing the class, and the Bachelor's rather than the Master's degree, as the basis for distinction among graduates, President Hoar admitted the superiority of the first to the second degree in Arts, and created an important precedent. He recognized and emphasized the class unit, which has meant so much in the social life of American universities; and be provided a new motive for winning a degree by omitting the names of the student strikers of 1655–56, and of everyone who left college without taking a degree. This fashion, too, has been followed by all the successors to the Catalogue of 1674.

In arranging the names within each class, President Hoar followed the order of seniority as established at Commence-

1. On this subject, see J. L. Sibley's article, 'Catalogues of Harvard University,' in *Proc. M. H. S.*, VIII. 9–75, with reprints of the catalogues of 1674, 1682, and 1700; W. C. Lane, 'Early Harvard Broadsides,' *Proc. A. A. S.*, n. s. XXIV (1924). 264–304; *C. S. M.*, XV. clxi–clxiii; XVII. 232–34. The only known copy of the 1674 Catalogue is in the Public Record Office, London. *Cal. State Papers, Col., Am. and W. I., 1669–74*, p. 576.

2. The earliest University of Oxford catalogue is, *A Catalogue of all Masters of Arts, and Doctors of Musick: Who have regularly Proceeded, or been Created, in the University of Oxford, between the 10th of Octob. 1659, and the 14th of July 1688* (London, 1689; copy in B. P. L.). The earliest University of Cambridge catalogue, *Cantabrigienses Graduati, sive Catalogus ab anno 1659, usque ad annum 1787*, appeared in the latter year. Both these are arranged alphabetically, not by years. Scottish and Continental catalogues of alumni began only in the nineteenth century.

3. Henry Saltonstall, 1642; a mistake for Padua.

ment.[1] He probably took the names from a file of printed thesis sheets; but he did a certain amount of editing. The name of William Mildmay, which is not found on the Commencement theses of 1647, is inserted at the end of that class in the Catalogue;[2] and the latinized surnames in many instances are anglicized.[3] But most of the Christian names and many of the surnames are in the Latin form: Johannes Russellus, Josephus Dudlæus, Crescentius Matherus, and Robertus Painæus, for instance. A graduate's name had to be recalcitrant indeed — a Samuel Stow, Daniel Epes, or Ammi Ruhamah Corlet — to escape being twisted into some fancied resemblance to those of the ancient Romans.

President Hoar had begun a periodical publication, of which the last number appeared in 1930. The next Catalogue after that of 1674 of which we have any knowledge came out in 1682;[4] thereafter, with few exceptions,[5] the *Catalogus Eorum qui in* COLLEGIO HARVARDINO, *quod est* CANTABRIGIAE *Nov-Anglorum, ab Anno 1642 ad Annum* [6] (of its going to press), appeared at three-year intervals up to and including the year 1875. A five-year interval was then adopted; and in 1890 the Catalogue first appeared in English, as 'The Quinquennial Catalogue of the Officers and Graduates of Harvard University.'

1. Cf. the Catalogue with the six surviving thesis sheets of 1643–70, in Appendix B. The reprint of the 1642 theses in *New Englands First Fruits* (*F. H. C.*, p. 438) shows a slightly different order from that of the Catalogue, but may have also differed from the original thesis sheet.

2. Indeed, this is one of the intriguing things about the Triennial and Quinquennial Catalogues. You cannot be sure that a man put down under a given year actually graduated that year. He may have taken his degree at a later Commencement, and by courtesy been entered in the Catalogue among his old classmates. It may even mean, in some of the Catalogues, that he was a Yale man or a non-collegian subsequently admitted *ad eundem gradum* or *honoris causa*, who presumably *would* have graduated that year if he *had* gone to Harvard! Thus Franklin, on receiving an A.M. in 1753, was placed under the Class of 1724, when he was 18 years old; and Washington, who received an LL.D. in 1776, under that of 1750, when he was the same age; but in the 1782 Triennial Washington is in the Class of 1749!

3. Cf. Alcock, Brock, Stirk, and White in the Catalogue with their names in the theses of 1646, Appendix B.

4. There may well have been others in between. Proof that there was a Catalogue in 1685, for instance, was discovered quite recently; and others may yet turn up.

5. After 1689 a break of two years, and after 1754 a break of four years. It is not certain that there were catalogues in 1691, 1694, 1703, 1706, and 1709; and not likely that there was one in 1688. But we have copies of the catalogues of 1682, 1698, and 1700.

6. This was the title from 1698, the first Triennial without a dedication, to 1779, inclusive.

GOVERNOR JOHN LEVERETT

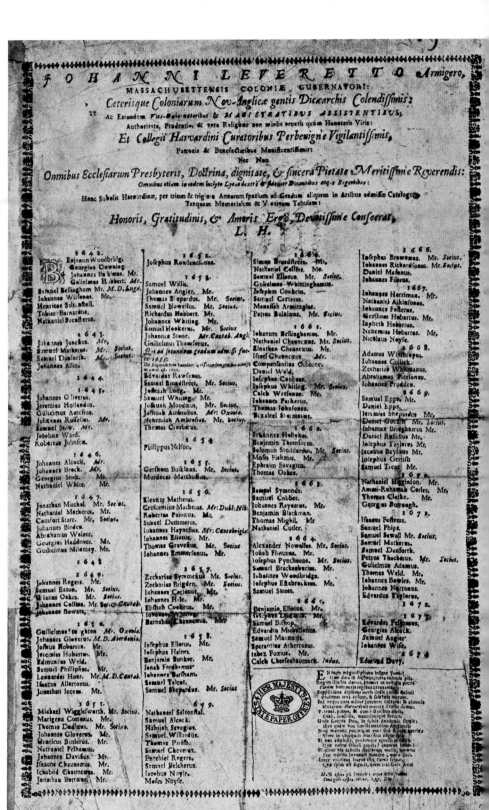

THE FIRST HARVARD CATALOGUE

Until the Revolution, one sheet of paper printed broadside, or two sheets pasted together, sufficed to hold all the names; in 1776 the Triennial Catalogue first came out in pamphlet form. In the meantime, Yale and the other colonial colleges had issued catalogues in the same style, and with similar devices. President Hoar's little broadsheet of 1674 set a fashion that American universities have, in the main, followed to this day.

A century ago, the Harvard or the Yale Triennial Catalogues, or both, were on the desk of every gentleman and scholar in New England. If your name was in it, that's who you were. If your name was not in it, who were you?[1] Every three years a new catalogue was distributed at Commencement, and eagerly scanned by the assembled graduates. It was a major thrill in a Harvard man's life to see his name in the Triennial for the first time, or the first honors inserted after his name; and it was a comforting thought that, after his death, his name would live on forever among the *stelligeri*, who, as the quaint Latin note informed you, *e Vivis cesserunt*.[2] Everyone loved and laughed over the old Triennials, with their *pastores literis Italicis exarati*,[3] and their extraordinary efforts to latinize and abbreviate such titles and achievements as 'Speaker of the House of Representatives' (*Congr. Rerumpub. Fœd. Repr. Prolocutor*); 'President of South Carolina College' (*Coll. Carol. Meridional. Præses*); 'Fellow of the Royal Society of Antiquities of Copenhagen' (*S. Reg. Antiqq. Septentr. Hafn. Soc.*); 'Hancock Professor of Hebrew and Other Oriental Languages' (*Heb. cæt. q. Lingg. Orient. Prof. Hancock*); and 'Envoy Extraordinary to Conclude a Treaty with China' (*ad Sinensium Imperat. de Fœd. pangendo Legat. Extraord.*).

The club catalogues imitated them; class reunions and the Med. Fac. burlesqued them. But as the University swelled in numbers and became more complicated in organization, the Quinquennial grew so thick and unwieldy as to call down upon its editors a very small measure of those blessings that President

1. F. J. Stimson, *My United States* (1931), p. 45.
2. This asterisking of the dead first appears in the Catalogue of 1698, as printed in *Magnalia*, book iv. 136–39. See Barrett Wendell's charming essay and poem, in his *Stelligeri and Other Essays* (1893).
3. This practice of italicizing ordained ministers lasted only a century, from the Triennial of 1782 to the Quinquennial of 1885, inclusive. Note the jokes on it in doggerel Latin in Quincy, ii. 684. The practice is still kept up in the Yale Quinquennials.

Hoar invoked for its original.[1] Hence, in 1934, the Corporation decided that the Quinquennial of 1930 should terminate this long series, so valuable for preserving the record of Harvard graduates, and for fostering a worthy emulation in academic honors.

So, having buried the Harvard Quinquennial, let us wish a longer life to others from the same parent stock, and return for a moment to their progenitor, Leonard Hoar's Catalogue of 1674. The dedication, signed with the President's initials, one may, with much loss of sonority, translate:

To John Leverett, Esquire, Governor of the Colony of Massachusetts; and to the other dicæarchs [2] of the New England Colonies most worshipful; to Deputy-Governors and Magistrate Assistants of the same, men no less adorned with than honored for their Authority, Judgment, and true Religion; to the Overseers of Harvard College, most kindly vigilant; to Patrons and Benefactors, most munificent; to all Ministers of the Churches, for learning, worth, and genuine piety most deservedly reverend; to all, moreover, who in that famous Lycæum [3] are rightly and faithfully teaching and ruling; this Catalogue of the Sons of Harvard who, over a space of three and thirty years have been admitted to some Degree in Arts, both as a Memorial and a votive Tablet of Honor, Gratitude, and Love, now most devotedly dedicates,

L. H.

President Hoar's purpose, one infers, was two-fold: to revive the somewhat drooping pride of Harvard men in their House; and to impress, by the number and distinction of our graduates, possible benefactors in England. That he sought an audience overseas is clear from his Latin verses at the end. The dignified and touching sentiment of these verses, with the ringing appeal

---

1. The Quinquennial of 1930, the best and most accurate of the long series, contains 1463 pages, of which 250 are the index. Yet it is still true of the Catalogue of 1930 what Cotton Mather wrote of the Catalogue of 1698, 'If *Harvard* be now asked, as once *Jesse* was, *are here all thy Sons?* It must be answered, *no*.' With few exceptions (such as early students in the Divinity School), only graduates are included. For names of *alumni non graduati*, one must seek the slowly advancing Sibley, and, for recent times, the *Harvard University Directory* (first edition, 1910). The latest edition (1934) of the *Directory* includes necrology since the 1930 Quinquennial appeared.

2. 'Just ruler'—*N. E. D.* Did not the President intend a pun, since *dicaearchi* also means the pupils of Aristotle?

3. Sibley's reprint makes a bad misprint here: *lycao* (animal of the wolf tribe) for *lycæo*. The original has the ligature.

to *pii iuvenes* at the end, is best read in the original Latin; but
the verses are too good to leave untranslated: [1]

> En regis magni diploma insigne *Jacobi!*
>   Quo data in *Hesperiis*, terra colenda piis.
>
> Regum illustre decus, premat ut vestigia patris
>   *Carolus* innumeris regibus ortus avis,
> Supplicibus diploma novis dedit: unde Coloni
>   Protenus arva colunt, et sata læta metunt.
>
> Sed neque cura minor juvenum cultura: et alumnis
>   Musarum *Harvardi* est munere structa domus,
> Patroni, patres, et cum rectoribus almis,
>   Curâ, consiliis, muneribusque fovent.
>
> Unde favente Deo, in sylvis Academia surgit;
>   Heu quàm non similis matribus Anglicolis
> Non matrona potens, ut vos: sed sedula nutrix:
>   Vivet in obsequiis matribus usque suis.
> Si nos amplecti, prolemque agnoscere vultis,
>   Quæ vestræ soboli gaudia! quantus honos!
>
> Pingitur his tabulis studiorum messis, honores
>   Pro merito juvenum munere, more dati.
>
> Inter victrices lauros tibi *Carole* serpat,
>   Quæ spica est segetis, quam tibi sevit Avus.
>
> *Macti estote pii juvenes; atque edite fructus*
>   *Condignos vestro semine, Rege, Deo.*

Behold the Charter of the great KING JAMES,
whence broad estates for pious men to plough
were granted forth in this Hesperian land.

That he might press the footsteps of his Sire,
KING CHARLES, illustrious ornament of kings,
descendant of unnumbered royal line,
a Charter hath vouchsafed to suppliants new
whereby his Colonists from that day forth
might till their fields, and reap abundant crops.

---

1. The text is in Sibley, i. 250–51 and *Proc. M. H. S.*, viii. 14–15, with a translation
which is the basis of the one here given.

The culture of our youth is no less charge:
JOHN HARVARD's bounty here hath built a House
for nurslings of the deathless Muses nine.
Patrons and fathers, kindly governors,
tend it with counsel, gifts, and loving care.

Whence riseth by God's will, in wilderness,
a University. Ah! how unlike
her mothers, rooted to Old England's soil!
No potent matron she, but heedful nurse
loyal to these her mothers shall she live.
If ye embrace us, and your offspring own,
what joy, what honor, to your progeny!

Upon these tablets fair engrossed, behold
honors conferred by custom on our youth
for labors well-deserved, their studies' yield.

Among thy conquering laurels twine, O CHARLES,
this stalk of cornfield that thy grandsire sowed.

*Advance then, pious youth! And put forth fruits
worthy your ancestry, your King, your God.*

XX

'A LOW AND LANGUISHING STATE'
1675–1684
Academia Instaurata

President Hoar 'made a resignacion of his Presidentship of the College' to the Board of Overseers on March 15, 1674/75; and at the same meeting the Corporation was restored almost to its full strength by confirming the reëlection as fellows of Urian Oakes and Thomas Shepard (who had resigned two years before as a protest against Hoar), and of Increase Mather, minister of the Second Church in Boston.[1]
On April 7, there was a joint meeting of both Governing Boards, under the presidency of Governor Leverett:

> Mr Vrian Oakes was desired to give his Answer to a former motion of the Overseers to accept of the place of the President of the Colledge pro tempore.
> In Answer wherto, he declared a deep sence of his unfitness for the work; yet considering the present Exigency the Society was now in, and confiding in the Overseers seasonably to endeavour the settling a fitt person for that work, manifesting his willingness to accept of that place for a time God enabling by health and strength, and so far as his church consented.[2]

This was the first presidential election in which the Corporation took part, as it was entitled to do by the Charters of 1650 and 1672. Oakes' qualified acceptance as President *pro tempore* was irregular; but nothing could be done about it. The College was actually closed in April 1675, and the main thing was to see that it did not stay closed. Indeed, for the next fifteen years we find the fear frequently expressed that the College

---

1. *C. S. M.*, xv. 231. If Samuel Sewall had already resigned, as seems probable, this left but one vacancy.
2. *Id.* 232.

was 'sinking' to the point of extinction; and, although it never came so near being snuffed out as in the last winter of Hoar's presidency, conditions were so unsettled that no man dared predict that Harvard College would long continue.

Yet it was in this 'Low and Languishing State,' as the Synod of 1679 described the condition of the College,[1] that Harvard nourished some of her most distinguished alumni. Thomas Brattle, shortly after taking his second degree in 1679, made observations with the college telescope that were favorably noticed by Newton;[2] Cotton Mather, the amazing fount of erudition, graduated in 1678; John Leverett and William Brattle, the one to be a great President of Harvard, and both fellows of the Royal Society, were of the Class of 1680; John Williams, whose account of his captivity became a colonial best-seller, took his first degree in 1683, and Gurdon Saltonstall, a distinguished Governor of Connecticut, in 1684.

As long as the Harvard President's salary was paid by the Colony, the confirmation of his election by the General Court was a practical necessity. On May 12, 1675, the General Court declared 'their hearty approbation of the election of Mr Oakes to that place, and doe . . . earnestly desire his acceptanc thereof and continuance therein, that there may be a revivall of that society vnto the glory of God and the publick weale of these churches so much concerned therein.' And they settled on him the salary of £100, which was what Chauncy had received, and Hoar, in his last year of office.[3]

> 'Twas done! The gloomy fear
> Of a *lost Colledge* was dispell'd! The Place,
> The Learning, the Discretion, and the Grace
> Of that *great Charles*, who long since slept and dy'd,
> Lov'd, and Lamented, worthy *Oakes* supply'd.[4]

President *pro tempore* Oakes held his first Corporation meeting at Cambridge on April 19, and provided for the prompt reopening of the College by reappointing the tried and trusted

---

1. *Magnalia*, book v. 94.
2. See above, Chapter X.
3. *Mass. Bay Recs.*, v. 31. On October 13 the Court appointed a committee under Major-General Denison to thank Oakes for 'carrying on that worke' and pray him 'to continue his labours as praesident.'
4. Cotton Mather, *Poem to the Memory of Urian Oakes* (1682, *Early American Poetry*, iii, Club of Odd Volumes, 1896), p. 8.

Thomas Danforth as Steward, William Bordman, the former
Steward, as cook, and Edward Payson, a sophomore, as butler.
At the next Corporation meeting, on April 26, it was evident
that the late animosities were not wholly quelled. On Samuel
Danforth's (A.B. 1671) being elected to a vacant fellowship,
Increase Mather, who had cast his ballot for Ammi Ruhamah
Corlet (A.B. 1670), predicted that Danforth's confirmation
would be opposed by the Overseers, on the ground that he had
subscribed to a petition against President Hoar. 'But Mr.
Shepard's spirit was raised; and he said that he was resolved
more for Mr. D., and against Mr. C., than before'; and President Oakes pronounced that unless the Overseers would declare
an amnesty against Dr. Hoar's enemies, he would resign forthwith. Danforth was duly confirmed; and Mather was again
defeated when he proposed that those students who stayed by
the ship might have preference in allotment of studies over
those who had deserted. Hence, he concluded, 'the hopes of
the college's reviving are at present dashed.'[1]

Nevertheless, the students began to trickle back: 'This day
my Cotton went to live at the Colledge,' notes Increase Mather
on June 22 — and shortly thereafter, 'Much hinderd by Trouble
at Cottons being abused by John Cotton, and some other
Scholars at the Colledge.'[2] We may feel confident that normal
college life was completely restored, if that insufferable young
prig Cotton Mather was being kicked about, as he so richly
deserved.

The Mathers, father and son, were not good coöperators.
Cotton's trouble was due, in part at least, to his objecting to
the ancient college custom that freshmen run errands for their
seniors.[3] And Increase was soon making trouble on his own
account. Cotton had reported to him a choice bit of buttery
gossip, to the effect that Increase was trying to get Harvard
College moved to Boston,[4] when he would take the presidency.
So Mather senior rode out to Cambridge, complained to President Oakes, and proposed to resign his fellowship. Oakes

1. Belknap copy of Increase Mather's diary, *Proc. M. H. S.*, III. 318.
2. Diary, June 22 and July 16, 1675. 2 *Proc. M. H. S.*, XIII. 348–49.
3. Diary for July 17, *ibid.*
4. That there was some talk of this is evident from an entry in the records of the
First Church in Boston. When subscriptions were being solicited for the new building
in 1672, many showed 'their desire to haue it at Boston' by offering to give three-,
five-, or ten-fold if the College were so moved. A. B. Ellis, *Hist. of First Church*, p. 132.

smoothed him down, but Mather flared up again after hearing
that the tutors had been grilling the students in order to discover the tale-teller. He wished to resign from the Corporation, so he told them, but if that would be grievous to Mr.
Oakes, he would continue to 'practise selfe denial.' And 'so we
parted very lovingly.'[1] It was always thus in Mather's relations
with the College, for a quarter of a century. His self-esteem
required frequent proffered resignations, followed by assurances of his indispensability, and renewed 'self-denial.' Shortly
after, in his periodical dichotomy of rewarding and chastening
providences, Mather confided to his diary that the College
was 'again likely to Fall.'[2] That is what he and his son always
predicted when their own desires were thwarted.

URIAN OAKES

Urian Oakes' career and parts gave every promise of a brilliant presidency, even if his health did not. Born in England
about 1631, he had been brought to Cambridge by his parents
as a small boy. His father, Sergeant Edward Oakes, was a
prominent citizen of the middle class: selectman for twenty-nine
years; representative in the General Court for seventeen years.[3]
Urian graduated from Harvard in 1649, and became a teaching
fellow shortly after. Diminutive in stature, as we know from
an epigram on his Almanac for 1650,[4] he had a ready wit and
abundant grace. 'His English,' wrote Moses Coit Tyler, 'fur-
nishes the most brilliant examples of originality, breadth, and
force of thought, set aglow by flame of passion, by flame of
imagination, to be met with in our sermon-literature from the
settlement of the country down to the Revolution.'[5]

Returning to England in the summer of 1654,[6] the young
man obtained an important church at Titchfield, Hants, where
he became noted for lively preaching and holy living.[7] He re-

---

1. Diary, May 28, June 18, Sept. 6, 1675. 2 *Proc. M. H. S.*, XIII. 346, 347, 351.
2. *Ibid.* 353 (Oct. 7, 1675).
3. Paige, p. 616.
4. 'Parvum parva decent: sed inest sua gratia parvis.' Cf. Horace, *Ep.*, I. vii. 44.
5. *History of American Literature*, II. 16; and cf. p. 164.
6. He signed a diploma at Cambridge on July 1, 1654 (above, p. 16 n.), but on
November 16 President Dunster refers to him as having left the country. Appendix
A, below, doc. 5.
7. *Magnalia*, book iv. 186. It was probably in England that Oakes married, as his
eldest son Edward (A.B. 1679) was born about 1657. His wife died before he returned
to New England.

signed or was ejected for non-conformity after the Restoration, and became for a time headmaster of the Southwark Grammar School; he then returned to Titchfield and ministered to the unreconstructed members of his former flock. Thence he was recalled to New England by Cambridge Church in 1671; on his arrival he was thus greeted with an ode by Cotton Mather:

> Welcome, Great Prophet, to *New England* Shore,
> The Fam'd *Utopia* of more famous MORE,
>
> .   .   .   .
>
> That for the *New-Jerusalem*, there may
> A *Seat* be found in Wide *America*.[1]

Oakes' sermon upon the Ancient and Honorable Artillery Company, preached in 1672,[2] was so eloquent and energetic that in 1673 he was asked to give the annual election sermon,[3] in which he vigorously supported the ruling class, declaring 'an unbounded Toleration as the first born of all Abominations.' This oration earned him, from Cotton Mather, at least, the title of 'the *Lactantius* of *New-England*';[4] and Oakes' elegy on the death of his friend and colleague, Thomas Shepard,[5] reached the highest point touched by colonial poetry between the death of Anne Bradstreet and the American Revolution. 'Considered as a *Scholar*, he was a Notable *Critick* in all the Points of Learning; and well Versed in every Point of the *Great Circle*.'[6]

Oakes' Commencement orations fully bear out his contemporary reputation as the greatest 'Master of the true, pure, Ciceronian Latin and Language' in America.[7] He uses Latin as a living language, following the prevailing academic mode of working in quotations from and paraphrases of classical authors, yet not hesitating to make up words, and perpetrating a succession of puns and quips that must have brought bursts of laughter from an appreciative audience. The impression of the

1. Quoted in *Magnalia*, book iv. 187.
2. *The Unconquerable, All-conquering, and more-then-Conquering Souldier* (Cambridge, 1674).
3. *New-England Pleaded With* (Cambridge, 1673).
4. *Magnalia*, book iv. 191.
5. *An Elegie upon The Death of the Reverend Mr. Thomas Shepard* (16 pp., Cambridge, 1677); reprinted in J. F. Hunnewell, *Elegies and Epitaphs* (Club of Odd Volumes, 1896); selections in Tyler, *op. cit.*, II. 17–18, and S. E. Morison, *Builders of the Bay*, pp. 210–11.
6. I.e. the Encyclopaedia of the Arts. *Magnalia*, book iv. 187.
7. Cotton Mather, *Just Commemorations* (1715), p. ii.

man is not so favorable. Whole pages, in the closely written script of these orations taken down by John Leverett, are devoted to his ill health, his unwillingness to take the permanent presidency, the cares and burdens of the office, and the outrageous imputations that he had intrigued to get it; to the evil times, the low state of the College, disrespect for eminent men, and want of veneration for learning — remarks ungracious if not untrue, in view of the recent popular subscription for building Harvard Hall.

In his first presidential oration, at Commencement 1675, Oakes describes himself wittily as *praeses umbraticus ac personatus, praeses pro tempore, pro tempore quidem difficili, atque adverso, quo . . . ἀμετρία ἀνθολκῆς Academicis rebus multum calamitatis importarunt.*[1] Grave and sinister rumors of him and his are spread about among the vulgar, but *Regium est cum bene feceris male audire.* He cares naught for what ungrateful and ignorant men, malevolent and unjust judges of affairs, may feel and think; he is persuaded with that clever and ingenious comedian Plautus that he who does right has enough applause. And he can scarcely contain his anger with the most worthy Overseers for thrusting, in such grave times, this insupportable burden on him, sick, weak, and almost dead and buried; exposing him in the academic arena to the bites of ravening beasts, his calumniators. If this be to love him, he wonders what it might be to hate him! Alma mater, too, is in the lowest stages of life, almost in the last agony. He is sorry for her; she cannot expect much restorative from so feeble a physician as himself.

Oakes pays his respects to certain men (otherwise unknown to local history), fanatical haters of the Tongues and the Arts, who 'like wolves and ugly bears that skulk about dying men' promise themselves mountains of gold (the college property?) if eternal night should reign over our Republic of Letters.

After employing almost every known funereal adjective to describe the state of Harvard the previous winter, the new President makes an eloquent plea for the seceding scholars,

---

1. 'A president shaded [a play on his name] and masked, president for the time being, a time difficult and unfavorable indeed, in which lack of moderation imports much calamity to academic affairs.' 'Oratio Secundo. Cantabrigiæ Nov-Anglorum in Comitiis Academici Habita, a.d. 4. Id. Sextil. 1675.' H. U. Archives, 'Leverett's Book of Latin Orations, 1688.' See above, p. 396 n., for the manner in which I have abstracted translations of Oakes' orations.

which lends some credibility to the charge that they were instigated by him:

Heed not the hateful gossip of the women's quarters, the street corners, or speeches of the vulgar. If there were mistakes, imprudence, or rashness of youth on the part of the scholars, if they acted inadvisedly or irregularly, we beg you, O nursing fathers of the University, assume toward your children the disposition and feeling of parents, pardon those humbly seeking refuge; it is not fair for old men, not prone to those things that youth do, to censure boys.

He begs the Overseers to do their best to build up and foster the restored College, and thus disappoint her enemies,

wretches who know no language but ill-speaking, and no liberal science, unless liberally and drunkenly attacking *bonae litterae* and educated men. Knowledge comes from suffering.[1] Cast all suspicions and resentments of former times into oblivion; elect a permanent president, able and worthy of the office; look kindly on these youths, candidates for the baccalaureate, who are about to give you an excellent specimen of their erudition. If my oration shall have shown any biting, bitter, or acrimonious quality, expect not in this iron age to obtain such a miracle:

That the tough Oaks distill dew-dropping honey.[2]

At length this oration so long, rambling, and repetitious, querulous of course, apologetic, salutatory, deprecatory, gratulatory, persuasory, valedictory, and in a word (with Cicero's indulgence I wish it said) anything-you-like-ary [3] has come to an end; nor will I consume any more of your time, not even *pro tempore*. I thank you auditors all for your patience and attention. And in conclusion, I humbly beseech Almighty God, the Father of Our Lord Jesus Christ, that He may be pleased to shatter that very barbarity, whence ariseth our greatest peril of destruction; that from the barbarians who impend and expend our lives, His boundless lovingkindness will deliver us sound and whole; that He who hath refreshed our afflicted and almost destroyed University, shall deign to sustain her restored, to adorn her sustained, and to make her flourish; and that He will make this festive day, adorned by your presence, happy and propitious [4] to the scholars, to you (most splendid auditors), to us, and to the entire Commonwealth.

---

1. Παθήματα μαθήματα — quoting Aeschylus, not the Bible.
2. A paraphrase of Virgil, *Ec.*, iv. 30: Et durae quercus sudabunt roscida mella.
3. *Quodlibetaria.*
4. An elaboration of the Ciceronian phrase (de Divinatione, i. 45), *Quod bonum, faustum, felix, fortunatumque esset, præfabantur*, the initials of which still appear at the head of each Harvard Commencement programme.

KING PHILIP'S WAR

President Oakes' prayer for deliverance from the barbarian enemy was not amiss; for on Commencement Day (August 10, 1675) King Philip's War, the most dangerous and deadly conflict in all New England history, was already on. Hundreds of militiamen, clothed in leather jerkin and breeches and steel helmet, armed with four-foot musket, bandolier, 'one pound of powder, twenty bullets, and two fathoms of match,' accompanied by fighting chaplains with Harvard degrees,[1] were scouring the woods from Dunstable to the Berkshires in search of King Philip's elusive warriors. During the summer and fall of 1675 the Indians had it all their own way, passing their pursuers unseen to surprise and sack the frontier towns, ravaging the Plymouth back-country and the Connecticut Valley. In the following spring and summer a dozen settlements in Massachusetts were partially or wholly destroyed — one of them, Sudbury, barely twenty miles from Cambridge. It was only after the United Colonies drew out their resources to the last man, keeping the Indians constantly on the move, and destroying the food supplies, that the enemy was finally beaten. King Philip was killed in August 1676, and by autumn the war had ended everywhere except in Maine.

The College kept in session throughout these hostilities, for the time was far distant when college students would be expected to fight for their country.[2] But it could not help being affected. King Philip's War was a terrific drain on New England. Almost half the settlements had been attacked; an enormous property loss had been sustained; a tenth part of the men of fighting age had been killed; in Massachusetts an expense had been incurred equal to the value of all personal

1. See *Harv. Grads. Mag.*, XXVI. 559–62, for Harvard graduates in this war. To names there found should be added that of Major William Bradford, who had been a Harvard student some thirty years before, commander of the Plymouth forces, and wounded at the Swamp Fight. See also above, Chapter XVII, for the part of Harvard Indians in this war. Among those who led marauding parties of his own race was James the Printer, who had assisted Green and Johnson in printing the Indian Bible at Cambridge.

2. Apparently they were expected to write for their country, however:

'What meanes this silence of *Harvardine* quils
While *Mars* triumphant thunders on our hills?'

asks Benjamin Tompson (A.B. 1662), in his epic poem *New England's Crisis* on King Philip's War (Club of Odd Volumes ed., 1894, p. 22).

property in the Commonwealth; the only assistance received by New England from without her borders was a shipload of provisions from Ireland, collected by Nathaniel Mather (A.B. 1647), Congregational minister in Dublin. Obviously, there would not be much money to spend on education, for years to come. The average size of graduating classes at Harvard from 1676 through 1683 was a fraction over four. 'When *New England* was poor, and we were but few in Number Comparatively, there was a Spirit to encourage Learning, and the College was full of Students,' wrote Increase Mather in 1679.[1] 'But it is deeply to be lamented that now when we are become many, and more able than at our Beginnings, that Society, and other Inferior Schools are in such a Low and Languishing state.' Yet in these times of poverty and discouragement, the community provided Harvard with a new building.

OLD HARVARD HALL [2]

In the disparaging and inaccurate account of Harvard College that Edward Randolph, the royal agent, sent home in 1676,[3] was one statement for which college historians are grateful. 'New-colledge, built at the publick charge, is a fair pile of brick building covered with tiles, by reason of the late Indian warre not yet finished. It contains 20 chambers for students, two [4] in a chamber; a large hall, which serves for a chappel; over that a convenient library. . . .' A popular subscription for this building had been started, as we have seen, in 1671.[5] The work had been entrusted by the Overseers to a

1. 'The Necessity of Reformation' (report of Synod of 1679), in *Magnalia*, book v. 94. Cf. T. J. Holmes, *Increase Mather Bibliography*, II. 369–73.

2. More often called 'Harvard College' or 'New College' or 'Old College' (after Stoughton was built) by contemporaries. On the first edition of the Burgis 'Prospect' it is labelled 'N. Harvard.' Throughout this history I have called it Harvard Hall, the name used on the second (1743) edition of Burgis' 'Prospect,' and have added 'Old' to distinguish it from the present Harvard Hall, which was built on the same site in 1764.

3. Thomas Hutchinson, *Collection of Papers* (1769), p. 501; dated September 20 and October 12, 1676; cf. *Calendar of State Papers, Colonial, 1675–76*, pp. 467–68. As an example of Randolph's attitude and accuracy, this may suffice: 'their commencement is kept yearly on August 2d in the meeting-house at Cambridge where the Governor and Magistrates are present, attended with throngs of illiterate elders and Church members who are entertained with English speeches and verses.'

4. The version in the *Calendar* inserts the word 'studies' here.

5. See above, Chapter XVIII. Some of the documents are in Mass. Archives, LVIII. 74–81.

committee of their own number, headed by Deputy-Governor Leverett, and to

Deacon John Cooper and Mr. William Manning of Cambridge, to be Agent and Stewards to mannage that work, both in hiring and paying workmen and Artificers, in procuring and purchasing materialls and in doing all other matters and things, referring to the building and finishing the said Colledge.[1]

The place chosen was on the very northern edge of the Betts lot, the site of the present Harvard Hall;[2] and this choice begins a reorientation of the college buildings toward the west, and the building up of a new quadrangle without any reference to this original quadrilateral grouping of President's Lodge, Old College, Indian College, and Goffe. Considerable sums were at once subscribed throughout the colony, but actual payments were slow. The materials were mostly on hand by the beginning of Hoar's administration, and the frame was raised on August 7, 1674;[3] but it was impossible to finish the building before the war began. Probably the state of the College under President Hoar led many people to suppose that it would soon be given up. Early in Oakes' administration the General Court issued an 'Order for the quickning of the seuerall tounes, as well those that haue subscribed and are behind as those that haue not, to bring in, etc, their contribution to further and finish the new buildings, etc, at the colledge.'[4] Selectmen were requested to see that half each town's subscription was paid immediately, 'and the remayning part as soon as may be,' and that elders and ministers in non-subscribing towns be required 'to stirr vp the inhabitants to so pious and necessary a worke.' The following month, King Philip's War broke out and the building 'during the warr hath stood at a stay for want of mony to finish it.'[5] But in February 1675/76, when the war

1. *C. S. M.*, xv. 220–21. Deacon Cooper's house on Linnean Street is probably the oldest standing in Cambridge. Manning, a merchant, had a warehouse and wharf at the southwest corner of Dunster and South Streets.

2. This site, as we have conjectured earlier, was originally a part of the town grant to Eaton (II) in 1638, but afterwards secured by Betts; it certainly was part of the lot that Betts conveyed to the College in 1661. The Sweetman-Spencer lot north of it (VI) was conveyed to the College in 1697, not in 1677 as the map in Eliot's *Sketch* states. Old Harvard overlooked Spencer's garden on the north.

3. See above, pp. 405–06.

4. *Mass. Bay Recs.*, v. 32.

5. *Id.* 143.

was far from finished, the Council of Magistrates ordered 'that
the Stewards for the new brick Colledge, doe forth with finish
up the place appoynted for the Coll: library, that so they may
be imediately secured therein.'[1] The building must have been
walled and roofed and at least one pair of stairs built by the
summer of 1676, when Daniel Gookin moved the books from
the Old College into the new Library.[2]

On May 29, 1677, the stewards reported the Library to be
complete, and the outside almost finished; but the rest of the
house 'for the present vselesse,' few floors laid, three flights of
stairs wanting, no plastering or ceiling 'withinside,' at least
twenty tons of lime and ten or twelve thousand foot of boards
wanting, and no money 'to purchase them withall'; part of
the Old College, besides the turret, fallen down, 'and mens
eyes generally vpon vs to get the new building finished, but wee
have not the wherewithall.' Most of the subscribing towns
were behind, and no subscriptions were as yet obtained from
Salem, Ipswich, and most of Essex County.[3] This report procured prompt action from the General Court. A sharp circular
letter was sent to all towns whose subscriptions were not yet
paid in full. The selectmen of non-subscribing towns were
invited to read and ponder 1 Chronicles xxix. 10–17, 'wherein
David and the people of Israell gaue liberally vnto a good
worke, . . . acknouledging that all their substance came from
God, and that of his oune they had given him,' and to bring
in their communities to join their helping hands 'in a free contribution for finishing the new bricke colledge at Cambridge.'[4]
The building was 'so far finished' by the summer of 1677 that
Commencement was celebrated in the new college hall;[5] but
it seems doubtful whether the General Court's efforts to cash
in on former promises were so immediately successful as to get
the whole building ready for students' use that winter. Most
of the twenty-five or so students then in residence could have
been accommodated in the Indian College while waiting the
good pleasure of the towns to make chambers and studies
ready for occupancy.

It will be interesting to discover, if we can, just what Old

1. Mass. Archives, LVIII. 92.
2. See above, Chapter XIV.
3. 2 *Proc. M. H. S.*, IX. 100–01. Also printed in *N. E. H. G. R.*, XXXV. 361.
4. *Mass. Bay Recs.*, V. 143–44.
5. William Hubbard, *History of New England*, in 2 *Coll. M. H. S.*, VI. 610.

Harvard did cost. On October 10, 1677, the General Court appointed a committee of one member from each county, consisting of Captain Thomas Brattle of Boston, chairman,[1] Major Samuel Appleton of Ipswich, Captain Laurence Hammond of Charlestown, Captain Nathaniel Saltonstall (A.B. 1659) of Haverhill, Lieutenant David Wilton of Northampton, Mr. Samuel Wheelwright of York and Wells, and Mr. Elias Stileman of Portsmouth,[2] to take account of the stewards of the 'new bricke building,' ascertain what remained unpaid, and report to the Governor and Council, who were to decide what to do.[3] In the Massachusetts Archives there is a return of this committee, dated April 24, 1678, with a precise list of subscriptions paid and unpaid.[4] Although the Committee reports a total subscription of £3028 9s 2d, an earlier list adds up to but £2277 5s 8d.[5] Cotton Mather places the amount actually collected and paid to the College at £1895 2s 9d, including £800 from Boston; 'and of that, there was *One Hundred Pounds* given by the One Hand of Sir *Thomas Temple*, as True a *Gentleman*, as ever set foot on the *American* Strand.'[6] And, as the detailed accounts show, the auditing committee of the General Court in 1682 approved a final account of £1969 14s 9d received, and just 11d more spent.[7]

The committee's report states clearly enough why it was difficult to collect everything promised before the war. And we have detailed evidence in an actual return to the committee from Medfield, dated April 15, 1678. There are sixty-three subscribers, of whom twelve 'sence their subscription to the new Collidge were burned out by the Endians.' The largest subscription is £2 from the minister, John Wilson (A.B. 1642); the smallest, of which there are several, are one shilling each. Among those who promised a bushel and a half of 'Endian,' but fell victim to the scalping knife before he could make good, was Thomas Mason. His descendant in the seventh generation, more than two centuries later, became a loyal son of Harvard, and a devotee of music. The Medfield donation list (which

1. The father of Thomas Brattle (A.B. 1676) and William Brattle, F. R. S. (A.B. 1680).
2. New Hampshire had not yet been separated from Massachusetts.
3. *Mass. Bay Recs.*, v. 156–57.
4. See Appendix D.
5. *C. S. M.*, xv. 222–23.
6. *Magnalia*, book iv. 129; noted in the college list.
7. See Appendix D, doc. 2.

by that time had been printed) troubled his New England conscience; and he wondered how a descendant in 1895 could make amends for a very pardonable ancestral failure in 1675. The compound interest on the value of Thomas Mason's subscription for 220 years ran into astronomical figures; so Daniel Gregory Mason compromised for the six pecks of corn by presenting the College Library with the scores of the four symphonies of Brahms.[1]

The Court did not abate its efforts to recover unpaid balances, for the stewards had run in debt for the building, and were clamoring for money. In October 1678 they authorized 'some meete person or persons in each toune' to levy unpaid subscriptions 'by distresse, as any constable may doe in respect of gathering in of rates.'[2] The order was renewed a year later, and printed;[3] and in May 1680 the selectmen of certain specified towns were ordered to make return, under penalty of £20.[4] The following October one Job Lane, who did 'all the timber worke for the said Colledge,' declared that £100 had been owing him for five years; the Court invited him to sue for it.[5] And John Francis of Cambridge presented a lengthy bill for doctoring, 'wines and other nesesitys,' occasioned by breaking his leg when the frame was raised; he was given 100 acres of land.[6] It was not until October 1682 that the stewards, Manning and Cooper, presented their accounts for Harvard Hall to a committee of the Court, which approved of them 'as faire and honest,' and recommended that the Court 'consider' the stewards 'for their pains.'[7]

Several bills were still unpaid; and as late as 1684 Manning and Samuel Gookin were authorized to sue subscribers for arrears, Manning and Cooper to retain respectively £35 and

1. *N. E. H. G. R.*, x. 49–50; story told me by Mr. Mason's roommate, Mr. Pierre la Rose.

2. *Mass. Bay Recs.*, v. 195. A stronger order that did not pass the deputies is in Mass. Archives, LVIII. 99. The selectmen of Topsfield were ordered to rate the inhabitants of that town for their balance. *Id.* 96.

3. *Mass. Bay Recs.*, v. 255.

4. *Id.* 268.

5. Mass. Archives, LVIII. 105.

6. *Id.* 101.

7. Appendix D, doc. 2. In the meantime, Harvard Hall was threatened from a chimney fire; 'great gobs of fire came out and ligh't upon the College but the Rooff being wetted and scholars standing with water to extinguish it was easily secured.' Diary of Noadiah Russell. Another fire in 1704 was extinguished by the students. *C. S. M.*, xv. pp. xcii–xciii.

£15 out of the total collections.[1] That is the last we hear in the records of this very tedious business. Altogether, the building cost about £2000.

Fortunately, we have a good picture of Old Harvard in the Burgis 'Prospect of the Colledges' of 1726, taken after the Corporation had ordered 'the top of the Colledge be guarded with Ballisters.'[2] On the basis of this view, and contemporary descriptions, Mr. Harold R. Shurtleff has provided the annexed front elevation and floor plans. In a newspaper description (probably by President Holyoke) immediately following the fire of 1764, the dimensions are given as 42 by 97 feet.[3] The master builder was Samuel Andrew of Cambridge, a master mariner in early life, and 'well skilled in the mathematics.' [4] No hint as to the architect has come down to us; probably a rough plan was drawn by some one of the Overseers' committee who had a taste for that sort of thing.[5] Doubtless their long experience with the E-shaped design of the Old College, difficult to heat and wasteful of space, led to the choice of a rectangular plan, and the design was sufficiently normal from the English point of view to please the carping Randolph. Until the Wren building was completed for the College of William and Mary, in 1695, Old Harvard was the most imposing structure in the English Colonies, and except for the roof, it was successful. The twelve gables, ten dormers, and two gambrels made such a number of rain and snow pockets that the roof timbers began to rot before many years. In 1712, the Overseers urged the Corporation to take off the roof, 'and to raise a third Story

1. *Mass. Bay Recs.*, v. 445–46. Cf. Archives, LVIII. 124–28.

2. *C. S. M.*, xvi. 832.

3. *Boston News Letter*, February 2, 1764, p. 2/1, quoted in *C. S. M.*, xv. p. xciv. Thomas Pemberton, writing about 1814, in 2 *Coll. M. H. S.*, I. 87, gives the dimensions as 42 by 99; but the other is the better source.

4. Paige, p. 480; cf. Sewall, *Diary*, II. 357.

5. The committee (*C. S. M.*, xv. 221) consisted of Deputy-Governor Leverett, Daniel Gookin, Thomas Danforth, William Stoughton, John Sherman, and Urian Oakes. Of these, Stoughton had lived several years in New College, Oxford; and later donated a building to Harvard College; but Old Harvard Hall was totally unlike anything in New College, or in Oxford. John Sherman (see *F. H. C.*, p. 400) was an alumnus of St. Catharine's Hall, Cambridge, but it is probably only a coincidence that the building at Cambridge which most resembles Harvard Hall is the north range of the new quadrangle at that College, begun after long planning in 1674, and completed in 1675 (Willis and Clark, *Arch. Hist. Univ. Cambridge*, II. 98–102, IV. plate 16; David Loggan, *Cantabrigia Illustrata*, plate xxiii). Cf. the windows and strapwork on the Bishop's Hostel, Trinity College (Willis and Clark, *op. cit.*, II. 552–60 and Loggan, *Cantab. Ill.*, plate xxxi), designed probably by Wren, and built in 1670.

OLD HARVARD HALL
From the Burgis Prospect of 1726

OLD HARVARD

1677 ~ 1

SCALE $\frac{3}{16}" = 1'- $

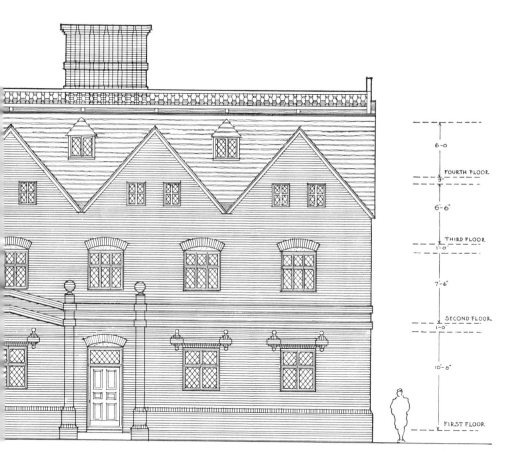

6-0

FOURTH FLOOR
9"

6-6"

THIRD FLOOR
1-0

7-6"

SECOND FLOOR
1-0

10'-8"

FIRST FLOOR

LL

0   5 ft.   10   15   20   25

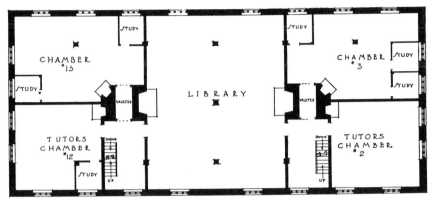

SECOND FLOOR

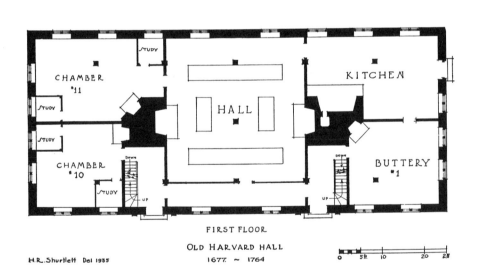

FIRST FLOOR

OLD HARVARD HALL

1677 ~ 1764

H.R. Shurtleff Del 1935

CONJECTURAL FLOOR PLANS OF OLD HARVARD
By H. R. Shurtleff, Esq.

upright in stead of the two Storys which are now under the roof, with a flat roof well shingled; with a Coving or Mondillions on each Side of it, and a battlement of Brick at each End,'[1] which was not done, as the Burgis 'Prospect' proves.

From the 'Chamber Settlement' lists in the University Archives, and several descriptions of the building after it was burned, we can reconstruct the interior arrangement with reasonable accuracy.[2] We know that the hall, which served for chapel, assemblies, lectures, and meals, was the middle room on the lower floor. And as there was no use in building through passages into Goodman Spencer's garden, the hall screen and entry were parallel to the front of the building. There was no hall dais. The usual table arrangement is shown on the plan: a head table near the fire for the Fellows; another, if needed, for Masters and Bachelors; and the long tables for undergraduates; chairs at the head table, and backless forms at the others, as in the English colleges today.

In the northeast corner, entered from outside, was the kitchen, and in the southeast corner the buttery, with its racks of bottles and barrels of beer, and 'tables' where Paine Wingate (A.B. 1759) remembered the freshmen crowding about to see how their names were placed in the order of seniority.[3] The butler and his roommate slept in this cervisial atmosphere.

Suppose we trudge upstairs with the Honorable and Reverend the Board of Overseers, to attend a meeting in the Library.[4] We shall not fail to stop for refreshment in Tutor Flynt's chamber (no. 2); every Royal Governor does that, on his first ceremonial visit to the College. The chamber in the rear, with its three studies, has to be entered by a vaulted passage through the chimney stack. Until 1761, chamber no. 12, in the sunny southwest corner of this floor, was occupied by a tutor; that year the partition was taken down between 12 and 13, and the whole room turned over to Professor Winthrop for his philosophical and mathematical apparatus. Descending the stairs, and passing through the hall, we may visit chamber no. 11,

---

1. Sewall, *Diary*, II. 357; *C. S. M.*, xv. p. xc.
2. Faculty Records, I (1725). 2–3; Chamber Settlements, 1748–64, H. U. Arch. I. 70.20.41; *C. S. M.*, xv. p. xciv, quoting *Columbian Magazine*, II (1788). 673; Sibley, II. 525, quoting Pemberton in 2 *Coll. M. H. S.*, I (1814). 87; reminiscences of Timothy Pickering (A.B. 1763) in his life by Octavius Pickering, I. 9–12, note.
3. B. Peirce, *Hist. of H. U.*, p. 311.
4. See Chapter XIV above.

which in 1724 was assigned to 'Mr. Monis for the managing of his Hebrew Instructions,' and named the 'Hebrew School,' an interesting survival of medieval usage.[1] The third floor contained six chambers for students, and eighteen studies within them, according to the list of 1725; the front one over the Library was called the long chamber.[2] On the fourth floor were three more chambers, described as 'inconvenient on account of the form in which the roof was constructed.'[3] For twenty-two years Old Harvard was the only building (except the decaying Indian College) that the College owned; until its destruction seventy-five years later it was the centre of college life; and the Harvard Hall that succeeded it performed the same function until University Hall was built in 1814.

COMMENCEMENT ORATION OF 1677

A good part of Harvard history during the next thirty years is comprised in the quest for a President. At a slimly attended Corporation meeting on May 14, 1677, John Rogers (A.B. 1649) of Ipswich was chosen 'President of the Colledge, nemine contradicente.'[4] Master Rogers, so far as we can discover, was free to accept. Although for some years he had been assisting the pastor of Ipswich, he had never been ordained, and was not bound to the Church. Possibly his medical practice, which 'caused him to abate of his Labours in the *Pulpit*,'[5] seemed more interesting than the Harvard presidency. For several months he would neither accept nor decline, as appears in the Commencement oration of 1677[6] by President *pro tempore* Oakes, the first delivered in Old Harvard Hall.

1. *F. H. C.*, p. 21; *C. S. M.*, XVI. 512. But in 1739 Judah Monis was moved up to no. 7 on the third floor, the north chamber over the Library (Faculty Records, I. 117–18).

2. *C. S. M.*, XXXI. 453; undated schedule, probably 1746, in Chamber Settlement Lists (H. U. Arch., 1.70.27.41). The long chamber in the Old College had probably been a freshman dormitory.

3. *Columbian Magazine*, II (1788). 673, quoted in *C. S. M.*, XV. p. xciv. This description of Old Harvard makes the same mistake as Randolph, in stating that there were 20 chambers for students besides the public rooms. The Faculty Records and Chamber Settlement Lists show conclusively that from 1725 to the fire the building never contained more than 13 students' chambers, including the buttery.

4. *Id.* 65.

5. Sibley, I. 167, quoting *Magnalia*.

6. 'Oratio Cantabrigiæ Nov-Anglorum in Comitijs Academicis habita postrid: Idus Sextilium [Aug. 14]. 1677.' H. U. Archives, 'Leverett's Book of Latin Orations, 1688.'

If anything, this was wittier than Oakes' earlier orations. He was positively gay at the prospect of relinquishing the presidency; his only fear was lest Rogers refuse. After paying his respects to the *furor fanaticus* that carps at Commencement ceremonies, he praises the exercises as a means of stimulating the strength and ambition of *ingenui adolescentes*, and affording pleasure to everyone in that large gathering but his unfortunate self. This is the fourth time he has delivered the Commencement oration.[1] The Thracians couldn't count beyond four; he can scarcely go that far; his mental furniture is so exhausted, used up, absolutely impoverished, that he really has nothing to say. Anticipation of this day has given him a worse paroxysm than the quartan ague that periodically shakes his limbs. Long he has shuddered, grown stiff, kept vigil, spent tossing and laborious nights, at the very thought; objurgated the Board of Overseers; and as the critical day approached, the κρίσις (as the disciples of Hippocrates like to say) has come on. At length the distinguished *medicus* John Rogers has been summoned by the Overseers to prescribe for his *morbus comitalis*:[2]

If he won't take pity, it's all up with me. Three words to thee, most worthy Rogers: in Roman and Praetorian manner *do, dico, addico* [3] to thee my Presidency. Come on then, Morning Star, render day to the scholars; why postpone our joy? Why delay and procrastinate? — it is my right to address my ancient classmate [4] familiarly and boldly.

And then, paraphrasing Cicero against Catiline in a way that must have convulsed the audience:

Quousque tandem abutere, Humanissime Rogersi, patentia nostra? Quamdiu must thy dalliance keep us in anxiety and suspense? *Quem ad finem* wilt thy modesty or prudence stretch itself out? Will not the shade of John Harvard; the embraces, kisses, tears of *Alma Mater Academia;* the most earnest prayers of the scholars; the urgent entreaties of the Commonwealth and Churches; the consensus of all good men; the votes of the College Corporation; the faces and looks of these Overseers, move thee? Struggle thou may'st; escape thou

---

1. He moderated in 1672, before Hoar's installation; his oration for 1676 is lost.
2. One of Oakes' best puns. The phrase in Latin means epilepsy; *Comitia* was the Latin name for a university assembly, such as Commencement.
3. 'I give, bequeath, hand over' — the formula when a Praetor gave way to his successor.
4. *Sodalis* — they were both of the Class of 1649.

canst not. And so, most desired man, be not deaf to the Academic Senate demanding, to the scholars imploring, to God Himself wishing and calling; tergiversate not, I beg thee; evade not the academic burden; make no evasive excuses; but gird thyself for this scholastic task, and give thyself completely, we implore thee, to the University.

A humorous exhortation to Rogers' father-in-law, Major-General Daniel Denison, follows:

To thee most splendid Denison I come, asking hope, safety, help; with the entire band of scholars I cast myself a suppliant at thy feet! Father thou art, not only of the President designate, but to Commonwealth and Churches; nursing father of the University. To a parent we speak, not a hard, harsh, difficult, morose parent, no Demea, but a mild, affable, easy, kind parent, bearing humanity in his very look and countenance. Correct therefore, we beseech thee, thy laggard son, goad him on, thrust him forth; if necessary, drag him with a rope around his neck to his appointed province! If he scorns parental authority, bring him willy-nilly by the whole force of your militia, into our power!

Not the least interesting feature of these Commencement orations are the comments on current events and tendencies. The Latin text lends itself to superlatives; but the orators, speaking to their own social class, in a language incomprehensible to the vulgar, were able to speak their full minds. A scandalous incident of the Quaker invasion of Massachusetts is thus related by Oakes:

That prodigious creature with dishevelled hair appeared not only on the Lord's Day, but even while the sacred rites were being performed, presenting herself, to the terror of spectators, like a Medusa or Gorgon, or a comet or wandering star — not bearded indeed, but hairy,[1] portending something dreadful, unless God avert the omen. The most heretical of heretics with unparalleled boldness are making their advance, and go about in unbridled fury, and more widely every day creeps the contagion of heresy (which is nothing else than a disease of the Commonwealth, the downfall of religion, the pyre of all

---

1. *Cometae . . . non barbatae quidem, sed tamen crinitae* — the ancients used these adjectives to describe different kinds of comets. The incident is described in Increase Mather's diary: 'July 8, 1677. A Quaker woman dressed herself up after a horrid manner, and came into [   ] meeting-house. Many women thought she had been the Devil; were frightened into fits. One miscarried, and died.' *Proc. M. H. S.*, III. 320. The Quakers had also been making trouble in Cambridge; one Benanuel Bowers, who kept up for years a contest with Danforth and Gookin (Paige, pp. 347, 350), is possibly the demagogue mentioned shortly after by Oakes.

good laws), until New England shall become a sewer and stinking cesspool of all sordid heresies.

After noticing prominent deaths of the year, the gratulatory part begins with compliments to Governor Leverett. The presence of Daniel Gookin, who had been reëlected to the magistracy that spring after being defeated in 1676, as a punishment for his defence of Indian converts in war-time,[1] gives Oakes an opportunity to pay his respects to the democratic principle:

I admit that this distinguished man seems to be ill fitted in character or experience for catching [2] popular favor. He does not sell himself to the public, as do some leaders and standard-bearers, whose 'public-assembly' minds and spirits we know, and who in their arrogant desire to uphold the Commonwealth, as Atlas the heavens, desire exclusive popularity. But, if to be truly popular is to consult public advantage rather than the public's wishes, Master Gookin has a popular mind. Your restitution (Master Gookin) *qua* magistrate and *qua* Overseer, we congratulate as grateful to God and happy and auspicious for the Commonwealth.

After compliments to some of the other Overseers present, Oakes returns to his favorite complaint — the growing contempt for learning:

The Emperor Nero, during his famous *quinquennium*, when advised to sign a death warrant, used to say, 'How I wish I knew not letters!' I'm afraid that no small number among us *eruditi*, men most highly deserving of State and Churches, condemned to a laborious life, exposed to the injuries and mockeries of artisans and workmen who are leading a profitable and pleasant existence, will say with Nero, 'How *we* wish we knew not letters!' If there be one thing more lamentable in these times than aught else, it is that foolish fellows, good-for-nothings, mad nobodies, haranguers at street-corners, have more influence with the populace than reverent men, filled with singular gifts of the divine spirit. It was a Roman orator who said to the judge, 'If you make me angry, I shall promote myself jurisconsult in three days' time.' And there are those among us who, despising all academic training, think they can make themselves noted orators,

---

1. 'His taking the Indians' part so much hath made him a by-word both among men and boys.' *The Present State of New England*, quoted in J. G. Palfrey, *History of New England*, III. 201 n. It was quite unprecedented for anyone so near as Gookin to the head of the list in seniority to be defeated. Joseph Dudley (A.B. 1665), a veteran of the war, was elected in his place.

2. *Aucupandam*, lit. 'bird-catching.'

and (as if by a leap) Doctors of Theology, in three days. They consider us unworthy, men prepared through much labor, great expense, long experience. Consult I pray you, that golden (not to say *Gouldean*)[1] offspring of Anabaptists and fanatics: so many theologians as there are men; all professors, and no students. And it's no better in medicine. Not only young women medicasters,[2] but all manner of mechanics and workmen rush into this most worthy profession; it has come to such a point that the sons of Vulcan rather than Apollo profess the noble art.

It is a subject of congratulation that the University is not yet extinct or fallen down, but preserved by grace of God. Indeed it cannot fall without the State's falling too. Rescue learning from contempt, not only on its own merits, but to combat the vanity, vice, and fanatical evil genius and ingenuity of the century. We beg you not only to save this our *Athenæum* from calamity, but to put it out of danger of calamity. As it was glorious for your ancestors to leave Harvard University[3] in a flourishing condition, so it should be shameful for you not to preserve and sustain that charge.

The tropes with which the President introduces the graduating class would have been startling in a more delicate century:

The fecundity of Mater Academia seems a happy omen, since this year she has brought forth six sons, whom she offers to be adorned (with degrees) by your testimonials and suffrages. Alma Mater does not grow barren while she grows old; every year she grows big with a new foetus. Behold your sons, not unworthy of such a mother, whom she has brought forth in this turbulent year. Alma Mater is like Cornelia, who since she is poor, shows neither heaped-up wealth, nor Attalian garments, nor silver vessels, nor carved reliefs, nor Augustan buildings and magnificent structures, nor libraries crowded with books; but useful sons, children trained up to honest disciplines, gentlemen educated like gentlemen,[4] of whom she produces six today, and presents them to your gaze — not merely to look at but to be adorned with academic laurel or crowned as Bachelors, if they deserve it. They themselves will shortly show forth their praise, and what strength they have, in the literary arena.

1. Thomas Gould of Charlestown, the godly but unlearned organizer and first pastor of the First Baptist Church in Boston, died in 1675.

2. *Mulierculae medicastrae;* probably a reference to women herb doctors. There follows some punning about *Faber aliquis* — probably a quack doctor named Smith under whom Oakes had suffered. There is also an allusion to the Spagyrics, or alchemical doctors. It may be remarked that if Harvard College had undertaken to train or even (like the English universities) to license physicians, these conditions need not have arisen.

3. *Harvardina Academia.*

4. *Liberi liberaliter educati.*

What is now left for me but to step down, and wish you all things joyful and prosperous, most worthy auditors? I won't ask you to applaud. It is not so much my concern whether you applaud or hiss as that you let me escape from this office in which I am like Prometheus with the vulture tearing at his liver. My saying farewell to the office will be to me like a Roman triumph.

But it was not farewell. Rogers did not accept; and on May 21, 1678, the Overseers desired Mr. Oakes 'to continue his care over the Colledge and to officiate in the place of President at the next Commencement.'[1] It seems that after Hoar's experience, nobody cared to undertake the task, while the mordant intellect of Oakes was in Cambridge. His Commencement oration of 1678[2] was brilliant as usual. The opening paragraphs must have made his audience glad indeed that Rogers had declined:

They say that the famous orator Marius Porcius Latro when he first spoke in public was so embarrassed that he began with a solecism. I am afraid I shall be equally unfortunate to-day. Indeed, it wouldn't be strange if I should be confused from start to finish,[3] for my whole oration to-day, from head to heel,[4] is just a continuous and absolute solecism. For what can be more like a solecism, what can be more absurd, than for me — who at the last commencement solemnly handed over my rectorate to the then lately chosen president and uttered my last farewell — should now rise to address you, as if I'd repented or had been attacked by voluntary forgetfulness? And some may suspect (if they don't accuse me of insincerity — as if I were like rowers, who look one way and make the boat go the other) that I am more changeable than Proteus. It seems to be my fate to get myself worse entangled in this business the more I struggle to free myself. Like Hercules, I must have been born on the fourth of the month — an unlucky day. This is my fifth labor of Hercules. I hope I shall not have twelve of them, as Hercules did! When shall I reach the columns of Hercules so that I shall not have to run *plus ultra* in this academic track?

A year later, the Governing Boards were so desperate as to give William Stoughton, then absent on a mission in England, full

1. *C. S. M.*, xv. 237.
2. 'Oratio Quinta Cantabrigiæ Nov-Anglorum habita in Comitijs Academicis. Idib. Sextil. 1678.' Ms. in John Leverett's hand, H. U. Archives. 'Leverett's Book of Latin Orations, 1688.'
3. *A carceribus ad metam.*
4. *A capite ad calcem.*

powers to procure a President over there.[1] But none was forthcoming. The Harvard graduates in London and their dissenting
friends knew well enough what had happened to Brother Hoar.

OAKES ACCEPTS

On February 2, 1679/80, after almost four years of him as
President *pro tempore*, the Corporation unanimously chose
Urian Oakes President of Harvard College without any qualification. The Overseers approved the choice on February 9, and
appointed an impressive joint committee 'to present their desires to mr Oakes and the Church at Cambridge, for his acceptance of said trust and their concurrance therin.'[2] A few days
later the General Court held out additional bait, in the shape
of a £50 increase to his salary 'in country pay' (provisions, etc.),
'prouided he accept.'[3] Oakes had often protested that he
never could or would accept the full presidency; but by some
means his resistance, and the natural reluctance of the Cambridge Church to part with him,[4] were overborne; and by May
28, 1680 he had accepted.

On that date, the General Court took into consideration his
request to provide 'Lodging nearer the Colledge than wher he
now liues in order to his more constant and conuenient Attendance of his place.'[5] He was then living in the parsonage especially built for his reception in 1670, within the present Yard,
on the site of the eastern entry of Wigglesworth Hall, nearly
opposite Plympton Street.[6] To us, that would seem to be a
not unreasonable distance for the President to live from Harvard Hall; but the master of a college, according to English
notions, should live where he might see and hear everything
that went on. The Lodge built for Dunster in front of the Old
College was now left high and dry by the transfer of all collegiate activities to Harvard Hall; and having lain empty since

---

1. *C. S. M.*, xv. 66, 238.
2. *Id.* 67, 239.
3. *Mass. Bay Recs.*, v. 263; Mass. Archives, LVIII. 102.
4. It does not appear that Oakes' pastoral relations with the church were ever
severed; but the church, when Oakes became President, gave Nathaniel Gookin
(A.B. 1675), then teaching fellow, 'a call to be helpfull in the ministry,' with the idea
of breaking him in; and he was ordained pastor after Oakes' death.
5. *C. S. M.*, xv. p. cvii.
6. Paige, p. 270 n. (who, I think, has it a little too far east); map in Eliot, *Sketch*.

SIR MATTHEW HOLWORTHY

LADY HOLWORTHY

President Hoar's departure, it was reported to be 'so defectiue' as not to be worth repairing. The Court on June 9, 1680 ordered 'that there be new Lodgings Built and finished with all con- uenient speed . . . as neare as may be to the New Colledge.' A committee was appointed to see it done; £100 was voted toward the cost, 'the rest to be paid out of the Colledge stocke.'[1] Payments totalling £260 were made by the College Treasurer between July 1 and September 23; and the follow- ing April, 1681, the Governor and Council ordered Manning and Cooper, the stewards for Harvard Hall, to provide 'such out-houses and Fenceing as is necessary yet to bee done about the Presidents Lodgeing.' This new President's Lodge was on the site of Massachusetts. It was used for only a few years, by Oakes and Rogers; in 1684 it was fitted up for students, the study rents going to Presidents Mather and Leverett,[2] and in 1719 it was removed to make way for Mas- sachusetts Hall.

'The Reverend Mr Urian Oakes was Installed President of Harvard College by Governor Bradstreet in the College-Hall on the Commencement day' (August 10, 1680), read the college records.[3] Unfortunately his inaugural address has not been preserved.

Only one Corporation meeting is recorded during the eleven months of Oakes' permanent presidency. It had the pleasant duty of empowering Treasurer Richards 'to dispose of the money sent out of England, either by letting it out, or makeing some purchase therewith, as hee shall Judge, will be most conduceing to the advantage of the Colledge.'[4] This was the most valuable gift that the College had as yet received — a thousand pounds sterling from Sir Matthew Holworthy.

Sir Matthew was the eldest son of Richard Holworthy, merchant and mayor of Bristol, and a staunch supporter of the Parliamentary cause. Matthew graduated from Brasenose

1. *C. S. M.*, xv. p. cviii. The Deputies had already authorized the use of 'part of the Colledge State or Stocke . . . provided, they meddle not with any thing that is giuen to particular Vses' (p. cvii). The only College stock known to be then in the Colony treasury was the Mowlson-Bridges scholarship fund (*F. H. C.*, pp. 310–11). Probably the balance of £160 over the £100 granted was paid out of this fund; but fortunately the General Court did not discover that when they settled accounts with the College in the next century.
2. *C. S. M.*, xv. pp. cix–cxiv; Mass. Archives, LVIII. 103a.
3. *C. S. M.*, xv. 239.
4. *Id.* 68.

College, Oxford, in 1629. His interest in Harvard College may have come through friendship with James Noyes, minister of Newbury, Massachusetts, who was of the same year at Brasenose, or from the fact that Holworthy married twice into the West-Country family of Henley, who were friends of Harvard College.[1] A merchant-shipowner in London under the Protectorate, Holworthy prospered, purchased a country estate in Norfolk, conformed at the Restoration, and was knighted by Charles II in 1665. Sir Matthew died in 1678, and by will bequeathed

vnto the Colledge or vniversity in or of Cambridge in New England the summe of one Thousand pounds to be paid and made over to the Governors and directors thereof to bee disposed of by them as they shall judge best for the promoteing of learning and promulgation of the Gospell in those parts. The same to be paid within Two yeares next comeing after my decease.[2]

The legacy was promptly paid, and fetched £1234 2s 6d in New England currency. This sum, it appears from Treasurer Richards' accounts, was let out at 8 per cent in twenty or more mortgages and short-time loans secured by personal bonds, the 'profitts improved towards maintenance of Fellowes, Schollars of the House, etc.'[3] No Holworthy fund was established, and the principal seems to have been gradually dissipated as the loans fell due, and moneys for current expenses were urgently needed.[4] But Sir Matthew Holworthy was not forgotten. In 1812, when a new building was erected by the College out of the proceeds of a lottery, the Corporation voted to name it Holworthy Hall after 'one of the earliest and most generous patrons of our Society'; and from that day to this Holworthy has been a favorite residential hall of Harvard men.[5]

1. Henry Henley of Lyme gave £27 to the College in 1669.
2. Albert Matthews, 'Sir Matthew and Lady Holworthy,' C. S. M., XIII. 153–80; will on p. 177.
3. C. S. M., xv. 224, 246–47; letter of Treasurer Richards, 1688, in 4 Coll. M. H. S., viii. 502.
4. It was ordered drawn upon for salaries as early as December 1683. Sibley, II. 458–59.
5. C. S. M., XIII. 153–54, 160. In 1909 the portraits here reproduced were purchased from a descendant and presented to the College. They are undoubtedly by Sir Peter Lely; but considerable doubt has been expressed by experts on costume that they represent Sir Matthew and Dame Susanna Holworthy.

Another good English friend of the College who remembered her at this time was Henry Ashurst, merchant and alderman of London, Treasurer of the New England Company, and a close friend of William Pennoyer and of Richard Baxter, who preached his funeral sermon. Mr. Ashurst had been one of the trustees 'for the Enlargement of University Learning' in 1659. In 1672 he transmitted £100 to the College 'as a benevolence of sundry in England' (doubtless including himself), and left the same amount to the College by will. It was sent over unusually quickly, and produced £128 in New England currency.[1]

Urian Oakes did not long survive to enjoy the new President's Lodging — if there was anything connected with the presidency, except lamenting its burdens, that he could enjoy. In July 1681, in his fiftieth year, he was seized with a malignant fever, died on the twenty-fifth, and was buried the next day; the College expended £16 16s 6d for scarves and gloves, and £8 14s for twelve mourning rings. Young Cotton Mather, whose pride had been flattered when Oakes conferred the first degree on him in 1678, wrote an elegiac poem in the President's honor which proved that Cotton Mather was not destined to be a poet; he also preserved the stately Latin epitaph on the President's tombstone in the Old Burying Ground, which has long since disappeared.[2]

Hastily the College made preparations for the impending Commencement. Increase Mather, after twice refusing, consented to manage the ceremonies, and presided on August 9.[3] In view of the recent bereavement, the Overseers put a check on the customary festivities. Samuel Andrew (A.B. 1675) was 'appoynted to execute the office of a Proctor for the commencement week,' and to clear all strangers out of College; he and Daniel Gookin (A.B. 1669), the other teaching fellow, were

1. *D. N. B.*; C. B. Clapp, in *C. S. M.*, xx. 199–203. Henry Ashurst is often confused with his son Sir Henry Ashurst, agent of Massachusetts in London and friend of Increase Mather.

2. Sibley, i. 180–83; *A Poem Dedicated to the Memory of the Reverend and Excellent Mr. Urian Oakes* (Boston, 1682), by Cotton Mather; his first published work. Reprinted in *Early American Poetry*, iii (Boston, Club of Odd Volumes, 1896). Cf. Sibley, i. 181, ii. 529. Daniel Gookin (A.B. 1669) also wrote a very lame elegy on Oakes (*C. S. M.*, xx. 249–52). Funeral sermons had not yet come into fashion in New England.

3. Ms. Diary (A. A. S.), July 26, 28, Aug. 8, 9, 1681; *C. S. M.*, xv. 241.

given charge of the College by the Overseers, pending the election and installation of a new President.[1]

It was a sad Commencement; no Bachelors, and but four Masters, confirming the general impression that Harvard's best days were over:

> That rare Society, which forth
> Hath Sent Such Gems of greatest worth,
> Its Oaks and pleasant Plants by death
> Being pluckt up, it languisheth;
> Thus dye our hopes, and Harvard's glory
> Scarce parallel'd in any Story.[2]

MATHER DECLINES, ROGERS ACCEPTS

Increase Mather was the logical candidate for the presidential succession. On August 25 the Corporation met in the Town House in Boston, on the site of the Old State House, and a ballot was taken. Treasurer Richards voted for Samuel Hooker (A.B. 1653), minister of Farmington, Connecticut. Increase Mather voted for 'Mr Collins.' John Sherman of Watertown and the two young teaching fellows voted for Mather; and this election was confirmed by the Overseers on September 8. 'I told them,' wrote Mather, 'that except the church to which I am related should consent to my leaving them, I was not free to doe it, and I thought they could not consent thereunto.'[3]

They consented not — Mather could always manage that. Although Treasurer Richards, the Reverend James Allen, and the Worshipful Richard Saltonstall, Esq. were appointed a committee of the Governing Boards to treat with the Church,[4] and although the General Court voted Mather a salary of £100 in money and £50 'country pay' if he would accept,[5] the

1. *Id.* 240–41. Gookin was succeeded as teaching fellow by John Cotton (A.B. 1678), on August 9, 1681. *Id.* 68. Andrew was the son of the master builder of Old Harvard. He and Cotton were granted £50 between them by the General Court on May 24, 1682, for 'having took much paynes and vsed much diligence in ‚carrying on the praesidents worke, since Mr Oakes death, to good sattisfaction.' *Mass. Bay Recs.*, v. 352. The College paid them £50 apiece, and £45 the next year, when Rogers was President. *C. S. M.*, xv. 245, 254.

2. Verses on the death of John Foster (A.B. 1667), in Sibley, II. 225.

3. Increase Mather, Ms. Diary, Aug. 25, Sept. 8, 1681. The Collins he voted for was probably John Collins (A.B. 1649) of London.

4. Mass. Archives, I.VIII. 109.

5. *Mass. Bay Recs.*, v. 34.

Church refused, in an unconsciously humorous document,[1] to release its Teacher:

Wee See no satisfactory ground to apprehend that our Reverend Teacher may in Likelihood be more serviceable to Christ, and to his people, by his removal to Cambridge, then by his Continuance in Boston . . . the Jerusalem of this land. . . . Wee doe not see the ruine of the Colledge wrap't up in our unwillingnes that he should remove to Cambridge; but tis too plain to be dissembled, that if mr Mather goe, this Church is a broken Church, and this end of the Town is a ruined place — wee know not where to find another so suited to teach, and guide, and goe in and out before us. Wee would prize, and encourage Schollars; And our affections have bin, and still are, toward one of them, namely, our Reverend Teachers son,[2] hoping that he may be setled among us with his father; but for the Church to give up their Interest in their Teacher, is a likely way to be deprived of them both . . . so that though wee could be glad to help a Sister that has no Breasts, yet wee see not what Rule of Charity or reason, requireth us to cut off our own Breasts, that our Sister may be Supplyed. . . .

And that was that.

Samuel Torrey, minister of Weymouth, a classmate of Increase Mather but not a graduate, was next offered the presidency; but he declined.[3] On April 10, 1682 the Corporation met at Increase Mather's house in Boston, and, after dining with Treasurer Richards, elected John Rogers President. Increase Mather at once offered to resign his fellowship;[4] either he considered Rogers an unsuitable choice, or, as is more likely, wished to be reassured of his indispensability. The other fellows, who were used to these manoeuvres, produced the expected flattery, and Mather did not resign. Rogers' election was duly confirmed by the Overseers; and the General Court voted him £100 per annum in money, and £50 'in other pay.'[5]

1. Mass. Archives, xi. 16–17; draft in lviii. 110–12, both dated October 15, 1681.
2. Cotton Mather, although not yet Master of Arts, had been Assistant Teacher of the Second Church since February 23, 1680/81; ordained Pastor on May 13, 1685. Diary, i. 98; Samuel Mather, Life of Cotton Mather (Boston, 1729), p. 27.
3. Mather, Ms. Diary, January 5, 1681/82; Sibley, i. 565; C. S. M., xv. 243. Mather's petition to the elders of Weymouth to release Torrey is in 4 Coll. M. H. S., viii. 99–100.
4. Mather, Ms. Diary, April 10, 1682.
5. Mass. Bay Recs., v. 352. On May 12, 1684, President Rogers petitioned the Court that 'by reason of the unseasonable and Dilatory payment thereof he is much discouraged, and almost incapacitated to subsist . . . is forced to take up money upon Interest beforehand to maintein his Family for the greatest part of the year,' and begs that his salary be paid quarterly and regularly. Mass. Archives, lviii. 129. The Court

John Rogers belonged to a family prominently identified with puritanism since the reign of Elizabeth. He was the son of Nathaniel Rogers, pastor of Ipswich; grandson of 'Roaring John' Rogers of Dedham in England; and cousin of Ezekiel Rogers, the pioneer pastor of Rowley.[1] Born in England in 1630, he was brought to New England with his parents at the age of six, and graduated from Harvard first in the Class of 1649. After taking his second degree, Rogers assisted his brother-in-law William Hubbard (A.B. 1642) in the ministry at Ipswich, without being ordained,[2] and practised medicine on his parishioners, without having had a medical training. A charming gentleman, it appears, whose character and personality might well have made him a successful president despite want of 'teaching experience' and 'evidence of scholarship.' Although in 1677 he had resisted the witty importunities of his classmate Oakes, he now accepted.

The new President's Lodging was vacant and ready; but the Rogerses and their large family of children took their time about moving in. After all, as they had to spend the rest of their lives in Cambridge, why hurry?

Increase Mather managed Commencement in 1682. Rogers came to Cambridge without his family on October 24 'to make a Little Trial of what it is to be president,' as Cotton Mather (who hoped before many years to try it himself) wrote. Apparently the trial was satisfactory, for after a few months the President returned to Ipswich for his family, and moved into the Lodge on May 23; but he was not 'solemnly inaugurated' until August 14, 1683.[3] A year later he was dead.

---

so voted (*Recs.*, v. 445); but on Sept. 12, 1684, nearly three months after his decease, two years' salary was still due, and was ordered paid to his widow (*id.* 451).

1. See *F. H. C.*, pp. 397–98 and index; Sibley, I. 166–67; M. M. Knappen, *Two Elizabethan Puritan Diaries*; *D. N. B.*; *D. A. B.*; President Rogers' grandfather John Rogers (1572?–1636), of Dedham, is often confused with John Rogers the martyr (d. 1555), and John Rogers (1627–1665?), Fifth-monarchy man. Neither was any relation to the New England family.

2. Hence it is claimed that Rogers was the first layman to become President of Harvard. Never having been formally ordained, he was a layman in the technical Congregational sense; but as preaching had been his principal occupation, he was not a layman in the ordinary meaning of the word. President Leverett, although he had preached sermons as a young man, came to the Harvard presidency after many years' service as college tutor, deputy, and judge.

3. *C. S. M.*, xviii. 371 n., xv. 72, 253; Mather's Ms. Diary, July 27 and Aug. 8, 1682 and August 14, 1683; heading of Quaestiones, in Appendix B, below; Diary of Noadiah Russell, in *N. E. H. G. R.*, vii. 57–59; 4 *Coll. M. H. S.*, viii. 388.

Cotton Mather briefly characterized Rogers, and tells an anecdote of his short presidency, in the *Magnalia:*

He was One of so sweet a Temper, that the Title of *Deliciæ humani Generis* might on that Score have been given him; and his Real *Piety* set off with the Accomplishments of a *Gentleman,* as a Gem set in *Gold.* In his *Præsidentship,* there fell out one thing particularly, for which the Colledge has cause to remember him. It was his Custom to be somewhat *Long* in his *Daily Prayers* (which our *Presidents* use to make) with the *Scholars* in the Colledge-Hall. But one Day, without being able to give Reason for it, he was not so *Long,* it may be by Half as he used to be. Heaven knew the *Reason!* The Scholars returning to their Chambers, found one of them on fire, and the Fire had proceeded so far, that if the Devotions had held three Minutes longer, the Colledge had been irrecoverably laid in Ashes, which now was happily preserved.[1]

The time of his death offered another curious coincidence, which must have set superstitious heads a-wagging throughout New England. Late in 1683, the Corporation decided that in the future Commencement would be held on the first Wednesday in July. A few days later President Rogers observed that on that date there would be a total eclipse of the sun. 'How obstructive the Eclipse whilbee as to the business of the day, is very obvious,' he and the tutors wrote to Mather. 'Wee are not superstitious about it, but reckon it very inconvenient.'[2] One can imagine the effect of a total eclipse on attention to the exercises. Accordingly, Commencement was set one day ahead, for July 1. On that very morning, Rogers was taken suddenly ill, and on July 2 he died, just as the sun was 'begining to emerge out of a Central Ecclyps.'[3]

As there is little we know of President Rogers, we may reproduce the epitaph which, according to Cotton Mather, 'to *Immortalize* this their Master, one of the Scholars in *Harvard-Colledge* gave to the Great Stone of *ROGERS*':[4]

Mandatur huic Terræ et Tumulo,
Humanitatis Ærarium,
Theologiæ Horreum,
Optimarum Literarum Bibliotheca,

---

1. Book iv. 130.
2. *C. S. M.,* xviii. 329; Sibley, i. 168 n.
3. *C. S. M.,* xv. 255.
4. *Magnalia,* book iv. 130.

Rei Medicinalis Systema,
Integritatis Domicilium,
Fidei Repositorium,
Christianæ Simplicitatis Exemplar,
πασῶν τῶν ἀρετῶν θήσαυρος.

Sc. Domini Reverendissimi,
D. JOANNIS ROGERSII,
Rogersij Doctissimi Ipsuicensis in
Nov-Anglicâ, Filij,
Dedhamensis, in Veteri Angliâ, per
Orbem Terrarum Clarissimi, Nepotis,
Collegij Harvardini
Lectissimi, ac Merito dilectissimi Præsidis,
Pars Terrestior.
Cœlestior, a nobis Erepta fuit,
Julij 2°. A.D. M.DC.LXXX.IV
Ætatis suæ, LIV.
Chara est pars restans nobis, et quando cadaver.

Within three weeks of Rogers' death, the Corporation voted
the presidency to Joshua Moody (A.B. 1653), the minister of
Portsmouth, New Hampshire, who had been instrumental in
obtaining the 'Piscataqua benevolence' for alma mater some
years before.[1] Moody's name was then on everyone's lips, for
he was stoutly resisting the efforts of Governor Cranfield and
the entire group of royal officeholders in New Hampshire to
Anglicize him or break him. At that moment he was renewing
his strength by a visit to Boston. He had already declined a
call to the Church of New Haven, feeling it his duty to see
his persecuted people through the wilderness.[2] Probably for
the same reason Moody refused the Harvard presidency, in
October 1684, after his election had been confirmed by the
Overseers.[3] Michael Wigglesworth, author of 'The Day of
Doom,' was then approached; but he declined 'to undertake or
manage such a weighty work.' [4] And so the Corporation was
again at a standstill for a President — its chronic condition for
ten years past and twenty-three years to come. New England
parsons, and their congregations, did not follow Maimonides

1. *C. S. M.* xv. 256. July 21, 1684.
2. Sibley, i. 370–75.
3. *C. S. M.*, xv. 257.
4. 4 *Coll. M. H. S.*, viii. 645.

in believing that 'the sanctity of a school is greater than that of a synagogue.' [1]

During the academic year 1684–85, the College was presumably in charge of John Cotton (A.B. 1678), the senior tutor; and a gay season of rowdiness and turkey suppers it appears to have been.[2] Perhaps, after all, this would be the last winter of Harvard College. The Colony Charter had been vacated, and nobody knew what the King might do next: suppress the College, as Governor Cranfield advised,[3] or, even worse, Anglicize it.

1. See *F. H. C.*, p. 221 and n. The Maimonides quotation (*Mishneh Torah, Tefillah*, xi. 14) was probably derived by our Commencement orator from Thomas Godwyn, *Moses and Aaron*, lib. ii. chap. ii (1641 ed., p. 72).

2. See next Chapter.

3. See Chapter XXII, below.

XXI

THE STUDENTS AND THEIR LIFE
1673–1707 [1]

 Jasper Danckaerts and Hendrik Sluyter, two Dutchmen of the Labadist sect, visited Harvard College on July 9, 1680, shortly after Urian Oakes accepted the permanent presidency. Jasper's remarks on Old Harvard Hall, the Indian College, and the students, are the earliest detailed observations we have by an outsider.[2]

9th, Tuesday. We started out to go to Cambridge, lying to the northeast of Boston, in order to see their college and printing office. We left about six o'clock in the morning, and were set across the river at Charlestown. We followed a road which we supposed was the right one, but went full half an hour out of the way, and would have gone still further, had not a negro who met us, and of whom we inquired, disabused us of our mistake. We went back to the right road, which is a very pleasant one. We reached Cambridge about eight o'clock. It is not a large village, and the houses stand very much apart. The college building is the most conspicuous among them. We went to it, expecting to see something unusual, as it is the only college, or would-be university [3] of the Protestants in all America, but we found ourselves mistaken. In approaching the house we neither heard nor saw anything mentionable; but, going to the other side of the building, we heard noise enough in an upper room to lead my comrade to say, 'I believe they are engaged in disputation.' We entered and went up stairs, when a person met us, and requested us to walk in, which we did. We found there [4] eight or ten young fellows, sitting around,

1. Dr. Clifford K. Shipton has helped me obtain material for this chapter.

2. Translation in *Journal of Jasper Danckaerts, 1679–1680* (B. B. James and J. F. Jameson, eds., 1913), pp. 266–68. Also in *Memoirs of the Long Island Historical Society*, 1 (1867). Edward Randolph's description (see previous chapter) is earlier, but much less detailed.

3. Translated 'academy' in the editions quoted; but the Dutch word was undoubtedly *Akademie*, which means university as well as academy, and in this connection certainly meant university.

4. This smoking room was probably one of the west chambers on the middle floor, whose windows are clearly shown in the Burgis 'Prospect,' as the visitors would natu-

smoking tobacco, with the smoke of which the room was so full, that you could hardly see; and the whole house smelt so strong of it that when I was going up stairs I said, 'It certainly must be also a tavern.' We excused ourselves, that we could speak English only a little, but understood Dutch or French well, which they did not. However, we spoke as well as we could. We inquired how many professors there were, and they replied not one, that there was not enough money to support one. We asked how many students there were. They said at first, thirty, and then came down to twenty; I afterwards understood there are probably not ten.[1] They knew hardly a word of Latin, not one of them, so that my comrade could not converse with them. They took us to the library where there was nothing particular. We looked over it a little. They presented us with a glass of wine. This is all we ascertained there. The minister of the place goes there morning and evening to make prayer, and has charge over them; besides him, the students are under tutors or masters. Our visit was soon over, and we left them to go and look at the land about there. We found the place beautifully situated on a large plain, more than eight miles square, with a fine stream in the middle of it, capable of bearing heavily laden vessels. As regards the fertility of the soil, we consider the poorest in New York superior to the best here. As we were tired, we took a mouthful to eat, and left. We passed by the printing office,[2] but there was nobody in it; the paper sash however being broken, we looked in, and saw two presses with six or eight cases of type. There is not much work done there. Our printing office is well worth two of it, and even more.

This pleasant picture of student life requires a few observations. As Danckaerts' latest editor remarks, the Dutchman 'viewed his surroundings through the eyes of a fanatical self-satisfaction. For this reason his criticisms or strictures upon persons and conditions are to be received with much discount.'[3] How fortunate that the unknown student produced wine! Although the statute as to speaking Latin in college may well have been relaxed during Oakes' *pro tempore* presidency, it is hardly conceivable that the Harvard student body 'knew

---

rally have taken the west staircase, nearest the highway from Charlestown. The earlier restriction on smoking to students who had their parents' permission and a physician's certificate was dropped from the College Laws of 1686; and Josiah Cotton (A.B. 1698) writes of his life at college, 'I learnt (among other arts) to smoke it.' Sibley, IV. 399.

1. The Classes of 1680, 1681, and 1683 (there were no B.A.'s in 1682) numbered 17. Probably a few resident Bachelors were also on hand at this time, a month before Commencement. Four members of 1677 took their second degree in 1680.

2. In the Indian College. See Chapter XVII.

3. *Journal*, 1913 ed., p. xviii.

hardly a word of Latin,' the language of most of their text-books.[1] Much more likely is it that Sluyter, an alumnus of the University of Leyden, used the Continental pronunciation, which Harvard students had never heard. And Sluyter's surmise that the students were 'engaged in disputation' is likely enough correct. The visit took place about a month before Commencement; and the 'eight or ten young fellows' may well have been the graduating class of five, practising Commencement exercises with their tutor and some of the junior sophisters. We may surmise that among the smokers who entertained the disparaging Dutchmen were two future founders of Yale (James Pierpont and Samuel Russell, 1681), two future Fellows of the Royal Society (John Leverett and William Brattle, 1680), and John Williams, the 'Redeemed Captive' of Deerfield.

SOCIAL STATISTICS

The Harvard student body of the Classes 1673–1707 was more provincial than that of the Dunster and Chauncy administrations (Classes 1642–1671), but covered a wider social range.[2] Dunster's dream of establishing a national university for the English empire had vanished. Harvard has become a New England college,[3] and another century and more will elapse, a political revolution take place, and an industrial revolution begin, before she can hope to be anything else. No more 'exorbitant children' come from England, where the dissenters now have academies giving the equivalent of a university education; nor planters' sons from the Chesapeake, where the College of William and Mary is flourishing. Of New England, apart from Maine and Rhode Island,[4] Harvard is fairly repre-

1. The Latin-speaking requirement is retained in the College Laws of 1686 (C. S. M., XVI. 849, § 8), but not in the Laws of 1692 (Magnalia, book iv. 132–34). As late as 1688 two students of the Class of 1690 were admonished for using English within the College precincts. Proc. M. H. S., XIV. 225; Sibley, IV. 42.

2. See beginning of Chapter V. The graduates for the later period of thirty-four years number 362, as against 290 for the first thirty years of Harvard history. This includes non-graduates for the Classes 1690–1707, when Aaron Bordman's quarter-bill book gives us a complete list of Harvard alumni; their lives are included with those of the degree holders in Sibley, vols. IV and V. But we have so few names of non-graduates for the Classes 1673–1689 that I have counted the graduates only.

3. A number were born in England to New Englanders sojourning there during the interregnum, but only Pelham (1673) was sent out from England.

4. Melyen (1696) was a New York Dutchman, but his parents resided at Boston for several years before he entered college. We also have one from Jamaica, one from New Jersey, and one from Long Island; but their parents were New Englanders.

sentative. We know the homes, at the time they entered college, of 324 out of the 360 students in our period (1673–1707). Of these, fifty-two came from the Connecticut Colony and Valley,[1] eight from New Hampshire, seventeen from the Plymouth Colony,[2] and but one from Rhode Island;[3] the remainder were from Massachusetts Bay.[4] Of this Bay contingent, 241 strong, about half came from Boston, Roxbury, and Cambridge.[5] Or, taking a sectional analysis, there were 152 from the tidal valley of the Charles, forty-nine from the coast towns of Essex County,[6] fifteen from the South Shore of Massachusetts Bay,[7] and twenty-five from the easternmost belt of inland towns that stretched from Dedham to Dunstable.

These figures reflect, as in the earlier period, the relative excellence of grammar schools. If Boston, with sixty-eight students in college, has pulled far ahead of her rival towns as a seed-bed for scholars, it is due less to her wealth and numbers than to Ezekiel Cheever, who took charge of the Boston Latin School in 1670, and missed not a day of attendance until just before his death in 1708. Ipswich and Charlestown, which rivalled Boston when Cheever was there wielding the official birch, send but seventeen and nine scholars respectively, in this period. Roxbury, second to Boston with thirty, reflects the able supervision of her young Harvard-trained schoolmasters by John Eliot, and the endowment that he obtained for the Roxbury Latin School. At Newbury, the ambition for learning inculcated by Thomas Parker (d. 1677) continues to bear fruit with twelve Harvard students. Dedham, which Wheelock and Allin [8] started well on the road to learning, is first of the inland farming towns, with eleven Harvard scholars. Salem, though generous in contributions to Harvard Hall, and still the second seaport in New England, sends but five boys

---

1. Ten from Hadley, Hatfield, and Northampton.
2. Annexed to Massachusetts in 1692, but students entering later from that area are included with the Plymouth Colony.
3. Ebenezer Brenton, 1707; Samuel Niles, 1699, sometimes called a Rhode Islander, was born in Block Island, but entered from Braintree.
4. Excepting 5 from England, the West Indies, New Jersey, and Long Island, and all but one of these (Maxwell, 1699) were of New England families.
5. The numbers are respectively 68, 30, and 21, including Muddy River (Brookline) with Boston.
6. Including the Merrimac River.
7. Braintree (10), Hingham, Weymouth, and Hull.
8. See *F. H. C.*, Appendix B.

to college over this term of thirty-four years; and Watertown, maintaining (with some years blank) a grammar master within a mile of the College Yard, presents but two *pii iuvenes* to mother Harvard. Distant Hadley and Northampton do better than that.

With a native-born student body coming from New England towns where vital records were kept, we have more accurate statistics of the ages of entering freshmen than before:

AGES OF ENTERING FRESHMEN

Taken at Commencement preceding Freshman Year *

Classes	Total No. Students	Number whose ages are known	Ages in years and months		
			Lowest	Highest	Median
1673–1689	105	94	11.6	18.5	15.0
1690–1696	93	91	10.10	21.4	15.9
1697–1702	95	87	12.0	22.1	15.5
1703–1707	67	54	12.0	23.1	15.7
1673–1707	360	326	10.10	23.1	15.7–15.8

* The ages of those who entered a class higher than freshman are stepped down for freshman year. For comparison with the earlier period, and an explanation of median age, see above, pp. 75–76.

This table indicates that the median age at entrance fell off after Chauncy's administration, but rose quite sharply under President Mather; whether this indicates any corresponding slump and recovery in standards of admission is doubtful. An infant prodigy like Paul Dudley or Cotton Mather could commence freshman at the age of eleven; but the usual age of entrance was still that of the English universities in 1600, from fifteen to sixteen.

In order to afford a basis of comparison of students' parentage with the hundred Harvard students under Dunster and the equal number under Chauncy, I have grouped those of this period in hundreds, the first ending with the Class of 1689,[1] the second in the middle of the Class of 1696, and the third in the middle of the Class of 1703. Beyond that point the Sibley continuation has not yet proceeded far enough to afford reliable social statistics.

1. It must be remembered that there are no non-graduates among this first hundred.

PROFESSIONAL OR SOCIAL STATUS OF FATHERS OF
HARVARD STUDENTS

	First Hundred (1673–89)		Second Hundred (1689–96)		Third Hundred (1696–1703)	
	Harv.	Non-Harv.	Harv.	Non-Harv.	Harv.	Non-Harv.
Ministers	29	6*	14	2	27	1
Magistrates and Lawyers	2	9	1	8	2	12
Merchants, Shopkeepers, Master Mariners	—	14	2	17	—	12
Physicians and Schoolmasters	1	2	—	2	2	—
Wealthy Farmers, Militia Officers, etc.	—	8	—	10	—	10
Ordinary Farmers	—	1	—	8	—	2
Artisans, Seamen, Servants	—	10	—	11	—	10
Unknown	—	18	—	25	—	22
Total	32	68	17	83	31	69

* Including five Oxford or Cambridge alumni.

This table seems to indicate that the social status of the student body until 1689 remained much as it had been in Chauncy's administration, received a considerable middle-class dilution in the next seven years, and then returned to normal. Ministers and magistrates together fathered forty-six of the first hundred students, twenty-five of the second, and forty-two of the third; and, if we add the sons of merchants, physicians, schoolmasters, and the better sort of farmers (large landowners, militia officers, representatives in the General Court), 64 per cent of the student body from 1673 to 1703 came from the gentry and the propertied classes. Of the unknown fathers, it is safe to assume that almost all were plain farmers or artisans. Any attempt at a comparison with the more fluid and infinitely more complicated social structure of today would mislead; but it does seem that the College was fairly successful, after 1654, in recruiting boys of scholarly ambition from the plain people of New England. It also appears that Harvard alumni, ministers for the most part, were supplying about one-quarter of the student body.

The same system of 'placing' students in an order of seniority, kept posted on a 'table' or bulletin-board in the buttery, continued through the period under review. A social analysis of the students' parents in the Classes 1690–1700 [1] suggests a possible drift toward a purely social ranking; but the discrepancies are still so great that other factors as well, such as piety and scholarship, must have entered into seniority. Indeed, the admission of Josiah Cotton (A.B. 1698) that 'through favour, not merit I happened to be placed second in the Class,' [2] suggests that personal merit normally had considerable weight in placing. Fellow-commoners, as in the earlier period, paid extra tuition and were placed first. Major-General Wait Winthrop had his son John (A.B. 1700) raised to the top of his class at the least expense, by having him made fellow-commoner the last term of senior sophister year. [3]

STUDENT LIFE

The routine and pattern of student life from 1672 to 1708 differed little at the end of the century from what it had been in Dunster's and Chauncy's day. [4] The same early-to-bed and early-to-rise schedule; the same want of lawful recreations, except swimming in summer and skating in winter; [5] the same practice of taking breakfast and afternoon luncheon (no longer called bevers) in one's chamber or in the Yard; same meals, student waiters, dignified Steward, cider added to beer as a buttery staple; 'parts' of Commons raised and lowered as the currency inflates and deflates. Payments are now supposed to be in specie, but unfortunately we have no steward's book extant to show what actually was paid in; the accounts of one student of the Class of 1674 were partially discharged 'in goods, Porke, and money.' [6] Two statements of the cost of a Harvard education in our period have come to my notice; just under £50 for a member of the Class of 1674, and £140 for a member of the Class of 1697. [7]

A pleasant picture of the informal manner of admitting a

1. Sibley, IV. 18–23; *Proc. A. A. S.*, n. s. XLII. 388–90.
2. Sibley, IV. 22.
3. *Id.* 536; and see illustration of Steward's Quarter-Bill book.
4. See Chapter V.
5. See the account of the drowning accident in Fresh Pond on November 30, 1696, in Sibley, IV. 521, 480.
6. Middlesex Court Files, account rendered by President and Fellows in suit against widow Alice Thomas for expenses of her son 'Ebenezer Cartland' (Kirkland), December 23, 1673. Cf. Pulsifer transcript, III. 79.
7. *Ibid.*, and Sibley, IV. 366.

freshman is given in Sewall's diary.[1] The Judge drove his son Joseph to Cambridge from Charlestown in a calash on June 28, 1703, and heard him examined orally by Tutor Remington in the presence of Tutor Flynt and Vice-President Willard. 'He Answer'd well to Mr. Remingtons Critical Examination.' Mr. Willard gave him, as subject of a theme, the Aeneid, i. 646:

> Omnis in Ascanio chari stat cura Parentis.

He then advised Joseph and three other sub-freshmen to be studious, thus paraphrasing Horace's *Ars Poetica*, lines 412–13:

> Qui Cupit optatam cursu pertingere metam
> Multa tulit fecitque puer, sudavit et alsit.

Joseph had a week to write his theme. On July 5 his father took him back to Cambridge, paid Steward Bordman the statutory £3 caution money, and walked into Tutor Flynt's chamber in Old Harvard, where examinations were being conducted. While the tutors were quizzing other candidates, Vice-President Willard read Joseph's theme and found it acceptable; presently he signed an *admittatur* at the end of a manuscript copy of the College Laws which Joseph had provided,[2] saying to the Judge, 'Your Son is now one of us, and he is wellcom.'

This was two days before Commencement, which a freshmen like Joseph Sewall, who had no elder brother to entertain him, probably did not witness. Immediately after that exhausting event came a summer vacation of a month or more, as we learn from President Mather's writings. 'After the vacation Time was over' in 1685, he 'revived the disputations of the graduates';[3] in 1696, the President visited the College a month after Commencement, and noted 'the Scholars not returnd.'[4] Wait Winthrop wrote to his brother Fitz-John on July 11, 1698 (five days after Commencement):

Tis vacation time at Cambridg, and I know not but it will be better to take John with me if I go into the country; twill keep him out of harmes way. The scolars are all gon for fiue or six weeks, which is their custom every year....[5]

---

1. II. 80–81.
2. Several copies of these Laws so signed are noted in *C. S. M.*, xxv. 247.
3. Ms. Autobiography, A. A. S. By the graduates, he meant the resident B.A.'s.
4. Ms. Diary, A. A. S.
5. 5 *Coll. M. H. S.*, viii. 532.

This was not the only vacation that Harvard students enjoyed. From the diary of Josiah Cotton (A.B. 1698), we learn that in his time, as earlier, it was customary for 'many of the scholars to draw off in the winter.' Josiah spent the winter of his freshman year studying under Eliphalet Adams (A.B. 1694) at Taunton; the next winter he kept school at Plymouth in his father's parsonage, but at the town charge; the winter of senior sophister year, he 'dwelt and studied at Home.' [1]

Joseph Sewall was such a model student that we hear little of him in the next four years, save through the medium of his father's diary. Commencement, as we have seen, came in 1703 on July 7. On the twenty-fourth, 'Joseph takes leave of his Master and Scholars' at the Boston Latin School 'in a short Oration,' which the proud father doubtless heard. On August 11 the Judge went to Cambridge to see that Joseph got a study in Tutor Remington's chamber.[2] On August 15, Joseph celebrated his fifteenth birthday; [3] and the next day his freshman year began. The Judge drove him and his little trunk 'with a few Books and Linen' from Charlestown to Cambridge in a calash. 'Went into Hall and heard Mr. Willard expound the 123 [Psalm]. 'Tis the first exercise of this year, and the first time of Joseph's going to prayer in the Hall.' A week later the Judge 'went to Cambridge to see Joseph settled in his study, help'd to open his Chest.' Joseph went home over the Sabbath, and returned to Cambridge by the Charlestown ferry, and on foot. A month later he had another week-end visit to Boston, and was given a lift back as far as Muddy River (Brookline). About every month during his college course, Joseph managed to go home for a day or two, often on the excuse of a wedding or funeral, or having a 'Tooth pull'd out'; and in the vacation he went fishing with his father at Pulling Point. But 'he keeps his Thanksgiving at Cambridge' in senior sophister year.[4]

Students bought books, and copied extracts from those that they had no means of buying, as in the earlier days; but there was less writing of original poetry; it was a period of silence between love lyrics and the heroic couplet. John Dunton the

1. Sibley, iv. 399.

2. Samuel Sewall, *Diary*, ii. 83, 84.

3. *Id.* i. p. xviii. Joseph was the Judge's sixth son, but his first to enter Harvard, all but one of the others dying young.

4. *Id.* ii. 87–89, 134, 170.

bookseller managed to do considerable business at the College, whither Librarian John Cotton invited him in 1687.[1] Edmund Quincy (A.B. 1699) entered in his notebook a list of the books which he owned in his sophomore year, about a hundred in number, containing 'some of the Greek classics.'[2] The commonplace book of John Leverett (A.B. 1680), the future President, shows a taste for the same sort of poetry and pithy maxims that Elnathan Chauncy was writing down twenty years earlier:[3]

Henry Bourbon, Prince of Condé on his Death-bed recommended two things to the practice of his Sonn, the Duke of Enguien; *Never to revenge a private Injury; and Freely to hazard his life for the Publick Good.*

If any Speaketh against mee, saith Sir W[alter] R[aleigh], to my face, my tongue shall give him an answer; but my back-side is good enô to return to him, who abuseth mee behind my backe.— Ful.[4]

Copied at length are two specimens of contemporary poetry, both elegies on his grandfather the Governor (who died when he was in college); one is by Benjamin Tompson (A.B. 1662) and the other by Lawrence Oakes, a son of President Oakes who died in college. More interesting to us are some extracts from Cowley's *The Mistress*, such as:

My Dyet

Now by my Love, the greatest Oath that is,
None loves you half so well as I:
I do not ask your Love for this;
But for Heavens sake believe me, or I die

Returning to Joseph Sewall, we find that on April 8, 1707, the Judge brought him at Cambridge 'a small piece of Plate to present his Tutor with, Bottom mark'd March 5, 1706/7 which was the day his Tutor took Leave of them; price 39s 2d. View'd his Chamber in the President's House, which I like.'[5]

---

1. Dunton in his *Life and Errors* (1705), p. 157, says that he sold books 'to the Students there'; in his ms. *Letters* (printed by the Prince Society, 1867), p. 156, he says 'to the Colledge.'
2. *N. E. H. G. R.*, XXXVIII. 150. I have been unable to locate the books.
3. 'John Leverett His Booke 1682' (but some extracts are dated earlier), ms. in the M. H. S. For Chauncy, see above, Chapter XVI.
4. Thomas Fuller, *Worthies of England* (1840), I. 420.
5. Sewall, *Diary*, II. 183. The President's Lodging built for Oakes had long before

Tutor Remington's farewell speech to the Class of 1707 has been preserved:

1.   You know how you have spent your time; if idley redeem the little that remains, for the eyes of your Parents are upon you; learning will be of use to you in every condition.

2.   See you carry it decently and as becometh you, without haughtiness.

3.   Come into Prayers duly; this will set an example to your Juniors; show that you do it for conscience sake.

4.   Beware of Drinking and Card Playing. These make the Colledge stink.

5.   Subordinate all other studies to that you especially apply yourself to. Get some Author's Scheme perfect.

6.   Above all Study Christ; there is great sweetness and profit in this Study.

Conclusion.   I shall rejoice at your Prosperity and Welfare.[1]

The tutors in this period were comparatively well paid — £50 a year and the tuition fees, when there were only two;[2] but that meant that each had to take entire responsibility for teaching two classes. 'Mr. Pemberton is very kind to our Class,' wrote Theophilus Cotton (A.B. 1701) in 1699, 'on faith that we will carry Like men he'll carry Like one to us, but he doth Clink[3] the freshmen.' One freshman would have run away, had not his parson visited the College to calm him down; and another 'was amost going, but he has got more courage now.'[4]

A few weeks after March 5, when the senior sophisters' tutorials ceased and a sort of reading period began, Joseph Sewall started a diary of his soul's state, or *Ephemeris Sacra*, as he called it.[5] The document proves that, in spite of the charges of irreligion and liberalism that were being circulated against Harvard (to the profit of the rising Collegiate School in Connecticut), pious students like Sewall were able to acquire

---

been fitted up for students' chambers and studies, since Presidents Mather and Willard lived in Boston. The Presidents received the rents as a compensation for providing their own lodging.

1. Sibley, IV. 301.
2. *Id.* 107.
3. 'To beat smartly, to strike with smart blows' — *N. E. D.*
4. M. H. S., Misc. Mss., 71. H. 157.
5. 'Joseph Sewall His Book April 27, 1707. *Ephemeris Sacra.*' Ms. in Prince Collection, B. P. L. Thomas Prince was Sewall's classmate, and later his colleague in the ministry of the Old South Church, Boston.

JUDGE SAMUEL SEWALL

THE REVEREND JOSEPH SEWALL

the spiritual attitude that the early puritans thought right and proper. Sewall's *Ephemeris* might have been written by an Elizabethan puritan like Richard Rogers[1] or by Michael Wigglesworth or Cotton Mather; and even the last was his senior by a quarter-century. There is the same moaning over spiritual shortcomings, the same weekly balance-sheet of 'mercies' and 'sins,' the same ideal of a constant, unwearying obedience to God's will, the same yearning to attain a Christ-like perfection in thought, word, and deed. It was not fear of hell that prompted this minute soul-searching.[2] Joseph was free from all fear of future damnation. Being of the regenerate, the twice-born, he felt a solemn obligation to live consistently the New Testament life. It is a matter of regret to him if his thoughts are vain and worldly on a horseback journey to Boston, a source of woe if his mind wanders during divine service; and the biological urge, intruding visions of Venusberg on his hours of meditation, seems proof of an irrepressibly carnal nature. 'O wretch! full of sin. Lord show me my wretchedness' — 'Some holy desires, yet alas! not humbled enough for my horrid carnality' — 'Monstrously ingulpht in sin. Lustfull' — such ejaculations are frequent. After recovery from illness, 'Dear Father, grant me more mercy, that I may never forget thy mercies.' Unconscious egoism appears in his comment on the defeat of the provincial forces at Port Royal. 'Lord let not my sins prevent thy People's good!' But by May of senior year he has attained 'a comfortable holy state,' which lasted until Commencement. 'Now God hath heard my prayers. O set up the Ebenezer and praise the Lord. O for a thankfull heart!' And he is not alone in this attitude. There are frequent mentions of prayers and holy discussions with classmates and junior sophisters, with whom Sewall formed a society — the first college club on record — for social prayer and mutual edification.

Despite Sewall's preoccupation with his spiritual state, he does afford us a few details of college life. Twice in the summer vacation, he 'goes a-gunning. The Lord preserved and return'd me. Bless his name!' And from his diary we find evidence of

1. Cf. M. M. Knappen, *Two Elizabethan Puritan Diaries* (1933). Mr. Knappen's remarks on the diary of Rogers apply equally well to that of Sewall, a century and a half later.

2. Only once in the *Ephemeris* does Joseph mention hell: 'I confess I deserve Hell, but Lord what ever thou doest with me, grant that I may love thee,' p. 5. Nor is the devil once mentioned.

the first rudimentary Class Day — a senior treat by the Fellows on May 27, 1707.[1] It came just after the senior sophisters had finished 'sitting their solstices'[2] in hall, to practise disputations and answer questions put by President and Overseers. For one week before 'the Fellows treated us,' Sewall notes, 'The President gave us our Questions. Did not examine us. I make the Oration and hold a question. Lord help me, for without thee I can do nothing! . . . I too much indulged vain proud thoughts.'

'Pride and Licentiousness'

If Sewall's attitude was not exceptional, it was certainly no longer typical of Harvard undergraduates. He was destined from early childhood for the ministry, and a majority of his Class chose that profession; indeed, of all periods in Harvard history, this was the one in which the largest proportion of graduates entered the Church. But there is plenty of evidence that many of the students, including some future ministers, reflected the tendency of the age, and chose Harvard College as a place to sow their wild oats.

According to local clergymen and poets, this was a sad, degenerate, demoralized era compared with that of the founding fathers. Increase Mather's report of the Synod of 1679 painted a gloomy picture of backsliding and licentiousness: a 'great and visible decay of the Power of Godliness,' 'Pride in respect of Apparel,' notoriously among servants and the poorer sort, profane swearing and irreverent behavior at meeting, Sabbath breaking, undue indulgence of children and servants, tale-bearing and promise-breaking, drunkenness, idleness, 'mixed Dancings, light Behaviour,' and wanton women with 'naked Necks, and Arms, or which is more abominable naked Breasts.'[3] Apparently the manners and customs with which

1. P. 24 of ms. Benjamin Wadsworth (A.B. 1690), who became President in 1725, wrote in his Diary of the seniors' getting together in March before their Commencement for valedictory orations, a custom that had evidently grown up since his undergraduate days. *C. S. M.*, xxxi. 455–56, 463. This, or the treating mentioned by Sewall, was the senior gathering which developed into Class Day in the nineteenth century. Cf. A. Matthews, in *Harvard Graduates' Magazine*, xxii. 580–81.

2. See above, p. 68. This practice continued through the century. President Rogers wrote to Increase Mather, April 26, 1684, 'the yong men that are this yeer to commence Bachelors are ordered these next three weekes, to attend the two first days of every the said weeks, in the Hall, the pleasure of such Gentlemen whom it concernes to make tryal of their sufficiency, according as is appointed.' 4 *Coll. M. II. S.*, viii. 522.

3. *Magnalia*, book v. 88–90.

Mr. Pepys was familiar were beginning to be practised behind the puritan hedge. And, if the experience of recent wars is any guide, King Philip's War must have been followed by a moral reaction.[1]

Although no Harvard students took part in the war, the College could not avoid reflecting the manners of the community. A good instance of this may be found in Thomas Danforth's record of certain goings-on at Cambridge in 1676–77.[2] It seems that a number of lads and wenches of the servant class were meeting at people's houses without their parents' or masters' permission, drinking rum and cider, and dancing together until after midnight. Although this was considered very bad indeed by the Magistrates, most of us will sympathize with one of the culprits, who was fined 40s and costs for 'sundry expressions tending to sedition and breaking down the pal[e]s of government,' the expressions being these:

It was a sad thing young persons could not meet together w[hen] they were come home from the warr but they must be thus requited, and he did beleuiv if the young men of watertown should be dealt with in the manner they would go negh to burne the towne over their eares that should so serve them. and it was a pitifull thing that a young man and a mayd could not be together but such reports must come of it, and he did beleuiv ere long the young men must pass by the mayds like quakers and take no notice of them, lest they should [   ] be taken notice of: and if there were any Service to be done for the Country it must be the young men that must do it, and let them do all they could a young man could neuer be made an old man and if a man were but in a by corner and heard the confession the young persons made before mr Danforth he aloues it would be a parcell of such blind stuffe as was not worth the hearkening unto, or words to the purpose

---

1. A perusal of the printed records of the Suffolk County Court from 1671 to 1680 (*C. S. M.*, xxix–xxx, see esp. index, pp. 1189–90) does not suggest that breaches of the moral code were more frequent in Boston and the neighborhood after the war than before; but enforcement may have been lax. Numerous entries in Increase Mather's Diary indicate that he believed it was lax. He relates (ms. in A. A. S., entry for Jan. 27, 1675/76) how Governor Leverett took him to task for saying in a sermon that strangers reported more drunkenness in New England in six months than they had seen in England in a lifetime: the Governor 'sayd that they that sayd so Lyed, And that there was more drunkeness in N. E. many years agoe then there is now, yea at the first beginning of this Colony.' Mather retorted (in his Diary) that the Governor was responsible for the enormous number of liquor licences in Boston. The court records certainly sustain him as to the number.

2. 'Disorders Papers, 1676,' H. U. Archives.

No students were accused of taking part in these gatherings, but some of them were getting altogether too intimate with one of the nocturnal revellers, a certain Onesiphorus Stanley, aged nineteen. After the close of one of these parties, near daybreak in midwinter, Onesiphorus 'went to the Colledge, and there knoct at the doore of one of the students chambers. and after often knocking got in and went to bed with the said student.' A few days later he spent several hours in the chamber of James Allen, a student seventeen years old,[1] another student fetching in 'a pint of Rumme from Mr Angier's,' when the supply on hand gave out. The monitor reported that he heard company 'drinking and carousing' in Allen's chamber, and heard Stanley 'swear sundry times by his faith.' Onesiphorus, convicted of 'frequenting the College and drawing the students from their studyes,' was fined 40s and costs, and ordered to procure himself a master 'on Penalty of being committed to bridwell.'[2] But nothing was done to the leading citizen of Cambridge who sold the rum to the boys.[3]

Another unwholesome village character with whom the college rakes became intimate proved too smart for the authorities. This was Samuel Gibson,[4] glover by trade, entertainer of students by choice, suspected of burglary, pound breach, cutting town timber, and other crimes and misdemeanors. The first case in which Gibson was involved incidentally gives us our first glimpse of a Harvard student's wardrobe. Edward Pelham (A.B. 1673), a wild younger son of the first Treasurer of the College, sold to Gibson, without parent's consent, '1 pair of

1. Neither he nor the other students mentioned in the record are found in the Catalogue of Graduates. Probably they were expelled for this or some similar party.

2. Later, in 1679, he was sentenced to be whipped and to be bound out to service by the County Court, for drunkenness and 'publishing false reports to amuse the people.' Middlesex Court Files, Docket Book, Pulsifer transcript, iii. 290.

3. Edmund Angier, who is sometimes described as a gentleman, and who married a daughter of the great William Ames, had a licence to sell strong waters from his shop on the southeast corner of Dunster and Mt. Auburn Streets, the site of the Signet Club. This was the nearest groggery to the College. In 1676 the Blue Anchor Tavern, on the northeast corner of Boylston and Mt. Auburn Streets, was being run by the widow of Andrew Belcher, father of Governor Jonathan Belcher (A.B. 1699); there was a second tavern at the northwest angle of Brattle Street and Brattle Square; on the opposite corner John Stedman, who had been Mrs. Jose Glover's steward, had a licence to sell liquor from his shop; William Manning, the steward for Old Harvard Hall, had a similar licence for his shop near the town landing. Paige, pp. 224–28, 481, 486, 601, 661.

4. The story of Samuel Gibson's relations to the College is told, with copious documentation, by John Noble in C. S. M., III. 448–70.

new breeches conteyneing 3 yards Devonshir Kersie' costing
£1 4s, and one broadcloth greatcoat, which had stood his
father £3 6s. The same month (September 10, 1672), young
Pelham induced a Cambridge schoolboy, Percival Green (afterwards A.B. 1680), to shoot with Pelham's fowling piece a turkey
belonging to the worthy Daniel Gookin, sitting on the fence
between his property and that of paterfamilias Green. Percival
then conveyed the turkey to Gibson's house, where the goodwife
baked it in the oven, 'and in the night following it was eaten'
by Pelham, his classmate John Wise (of later political fame),
and a sophomore named Jonathan Russell, another future
minister. The Gibsons confessed and got off with admonition
and a forty-shilling fine. How the students were dealt with
does not appear in the college records.

We next hear of Samuel Gibson in 1678, when he was summoned before President Oakes and the Board of Overseers, 'and
solemnly cautioned of entertaining any of the Students in his
house, frequenting the Colledge or drawing them otherwise into
his company.' And the students were given a similar caution
not to frequent the house of Gibson.[1] No doubt other Cambridge turkeys had been disappearing from time to time, but
in the winter of 1684–85 the college poultry fanciers made the
mistake of stealing a fine bird that belonged to Madam Danforth, wife of the worshipful Magistrate. Two Cambridge boys
testified that they had attended a turkey supper in the chamber
of Francis Wainwright, a fellow-commoner and junior sophister,
and that Sam Gibson was a member of the party. Wainwright
was forced to make a public confession of this and other offences
in college hall.[2] But the matter was not allowed to rest there.
Magistrate Danforth decided that this was the long-wanted
occasion to put Gibson away. He was prosecuted 'for frequenting the colledge contrary to law,' and apparently found guilty.
He promptly appealed on the ground that 'no law of the Massachusetts estableshed by a Generall Court prohibits me or any
else fraquenting the Colledge much less going to the Coledge . . .
being invited.' This was true enough. There was a law for-
bidding people to entertain minors, servants, 'schollers belonging to the Colledg, or any Latine school'; but it was no crime
to accept an invitation from these youths, and an order of the

1. *C. S. M.*, xv. 237–38.
2. *Id.* 78.

Overseers was not a law, although Danforth endeavored to induce the Court to find it so. The 'Answer' to Gibson's 'Reasons of Appeal,' probably by Danforth, alleged that since President Rogers' death Gibson

and sundry others that were his companions in disorder did make it their opportunity to play their Reaks in the Colledge more than formerly some of them staying there the whole night, and they continued so to do untill a discovery was made of their wicked doings; and their manner was this winter last past there to meet together night after night and theyr mispence of time was not all but they did drive a Trade of stealing Turkies, Geese and other fowle untill they had so cloyd themselvs that they left them stinking in some of the chambers and studies of the students before they could get them dressed. And one of them so smelt into the Towne, as it occasioned sundry persons to be examind, when it appeared that Samuel Gibson was one of sd Company feasting in one of the Students chambers more than once and that he was partaker with them in their stollen Turkyes.[1]

Considering that the seventeenth century was not an era of sensitiveness to foul odors, the reek from Gibson's stolen poultry must have been something terrific to have carried from Old Harvard to the village houses. But the worshipful Court of Assistants had to let Gibson off, for he knew the law.

By the 1670's 'rumme' was becoming a prevalent and popular drink in New England; naturally it got into the College, and made trouble. Drunkenness was not a sufficiently serious offence to get into the Corporation records; but in John Leverett's 'Diary' there are the exact words of a public admonition that he delivered to John Ballantine (A.B. 1694) about the year 1691.[2] The 'single and sorrowfull object' of this assemblage, he tells the students, is 'that this person stands before us convict of the sin of excessive drinking,' a violation both of the Divine Laws and the Statutes of this House. He then reads statute 11 (*atrociora delicta*) of the Dudleian code of college laws, and concludes:

Wherfore, you *Ballantine*, we are now to admonish you; and wish to Almighty God that you may receive our Admonitions with Endeavours like to our designs, which are that they may be for your good: for we have no other designs as you nor desires, then that you

1. *C. S. M.*, III. 467–68.
2. *Proc. M. H. S.*, XIV. 226.

may so see the no profit of that thing wherof we trust you are now so ashamed, as never to repeat it, or any other so unprofitable, so ill a thing.

Even the most serious misdemeanours were generally pardoned upon the student's giving evidence of repentance. Such was the puritan way with breaches of their ethical code that involved no harm to others. For instance, Nathaniel Welch (A.B. 1687) was upon his own confession expelled from college for theft and notorious lying, but was readmitted six months later on public acknowledgment thereof and promise of reformation.[1] Joseph Webb (A.B. 1684) as a junior sophister was expelled by the Corporation 'for his abusive carriages, in requireing some of the freshmen to goe upon his private errands, and in strikeing the sayd freshmen,' but was readmitted within two months.[2] John Wade (A.B. 1693) was expelled for 'abominable lasciviousness' at the beginning of his senior sophister year, but was readmitted in time to graduate with his Class, upon due confession and testimony of two ministers as to his reformed habits.[3] Benjamin Shattuck (A.B. 1709), expelled for the 'Atrocious Crime' of 'committing fornicacion' in the December before he was to graduate, after suitable confession and testimony from two ministers as to good conduct was restored to the bosom of alma mater a year later, 'And the Buttler was Order'd to put up his Name in the Buttery according to his Standing.'[4] Both Wade and Shattuck, despite these breaches of the seventh commandment which were confessed before the entire College, became ministers of New England churches. This does not mean that the puritans held such offences of slight consequence — far from it. But they did believe that no sin was too great for God's grace, after a genuine repentance; and unlike some who profess and call themselves Christians, they followed the example of forgiveness that their Master had enjoined.[5]

Since the Corporation records mention only the most serious

1. *C. S. M.*, xv. 78–79.
2. *Id.* 70–72. Cf. Diary of Noadiah Russell, *N. E. H. G. R.*, vii. 53–54.
3. *C. S. M.*, xv. 346, 349.
4. *Id.* 384, 387, 390. In the Catalogue of Graduates, he appears with his original class, although he cannot have taken a degree before 1710.
5. Daniel Henchman (1696), a student expelled for theft just before his Commencement, was never readmitted; but there is no record of his confessing and petitioning. Sibley, iv. 297; *C. S. M.*, xv. 354. Increase Mather's Diary shows that the date given in the records, July 15, is a mistake for June 15.

offences in this period, we know of the petty misdemeanors only through the fines in Steward Bordman's quarter-bill book after 1686; and this seldom gives the reason for the fines — unless for breaking window glass, for which the fines and damages were so numerous that hardly a student was exempt.[1] Of course many things went on of which the college authorities knew nothing. For instance, it is from the diary of Joseph Green (A.B. 1695), whose subsequent ministry in the hag-ridden Salem Village was the most courageous and successful in the annals of New England, that we hear of his misspending precious time at college in fowling, fishing, profanity, Sabbath breaking, card playing, dancing, and roistering.[2] George Curwin (A.B. 1701) is said to have sat up all night over punch and cards. Apparently there was plenty of fun going on toward the turn of the century. There is still preserved the impromptu paraphrase of the first Psalm by Harvard's first Irishman, Hugh Adams (A.B. 1697), when he was the victim of a trick chair in a classmate's chamber:

> Blest is the man who hath not lent
> To wicked *Reed* his ear;
> Nor spent his life as *Collins* hath,
> Nor sat in Southmayd's chair![3]

And an entry in President Mather's diary, 'visited the College . . . examined several of the Scholars about the Comedy etc.,' strongly suggests that some of the young hellions had actually performed a stage play.[4]

In the summer of 1689 tutors Leverett and Brattle took two of their pupils, John Emerson, who had just graduated, and Thomas Maccarty, a junior sophister, on a trip to New York, which like many later visits by Harvardians was full of unexpected thrills. They happened to arrive at a time when Jacob Leisler, who had seized the government from Andros' henchman as soon as he heard of the Bostonian revolt, was in a state of jumpy nerves, expecting Sir Edmund (who had lately escaped from Boston in disguise) to come back at him with force. Informed by a busybody that some strangers had arrived, who did

1. See Sibley, IV, *passim*.
2. *Id.* 229.   3. *Id.* 322.
4. Ms. Diary, A. A. S., October 10, 1698. By 1762 the College authorities permitted the acting of plays by students as an 'academical exercise' (*C. S. M.*, XXXI. 358).

not answer a sentinel's challenge, Leisler jumped to the conclusion that Leverett and Brattle were Sir Edmund Andros
and Lieutenant-Governor Nicholson in disguise, and that the
two students were their orderlies; he promptly had all four
Harvardians taken to the fort and locked up in the calaboose
for the night. Wild rumors spread about nervous Manhattan
to the effect that Andros and Nicholson were in town with an
army to surprise the fort, five hundred militiamen turned out,
Dutchmen and Englishmen suspected of hankering for Andros'
return were seized and thrown into the fort with the college
contingent, and the whole town buzzed with excitement. In
the morning a friend of Leisler's received a letter from Boston
telling who the visitors were, and they were released; but the
other unfortunates who had been seized by reason of the alarm
stayed in confinement for some time.[1]

COMMENCEMENT

In this period Commencement began to take on the popular
character that it definitely assumed in the next century. It
had always been a festive occasion for graduates at the expense
of those taking degrees. The display of classical wit that
President Oakes provided, coming just after the war when
people wanted a little mirth and recreation, attracted such large
numbers of graduates and their families to Cambridge that
hucksters and cheap-jacks came too, in order to cater to the
crowd in its lighter moments. Thus a purely literary occasion
evolved into a sort of puritan midsummer's holiday.[2] It seems
significant that in 1681, when, by reason of President Oakes'
death shortly before Commencement, the authorities desired a
sober ceremony, they should find it necessary to restrict degree-
takers to a provision of three gallons, and other students to one
gallon of wine per man; and that a proctor was appointed to
clear strangers out of the college 'at or before 9 a clock at

1. Letter of George McKenzie to Lieut.-Gov. Nicholson in Public Record Office,
C.O. 5/1081 (calendared in *Calendar State Papers Col., Am. & W. I., 1689-92*, p. 128).
Also letter of Governor Leisler to Governor Bradstreet, printed in T. Hutchinson,
Massachusetts Bay (second edition), I. 392-93 n., and Sibley IV. 106-07.
2. According to the Triennial Catalogue of 1698 (*Magnalia*, book iv. 136-39) there
were about 225 graduates living in New England; and probably at least 150 of these
could have attended Commencement with no great difficulty. Adding the non-
collegiate element in Boston and neighboring towns, it seems probable that several
hundred persons would be in Cambridge at Commencement time.

night . . . and to signifye to them that the usual recourse of any
to the Colledge the following days of the week, excepting
Schollars is displeasing to the honoured and Reverend Overseers, and that they are required accordingly to forbeare.' [1]

> Commencement's come, but (friendly) I advize
> All sorts of Rabble now their Homes to prize,
> For if to it they come, so Blind they'll bee,
> That Really no Body will see. [2]

Increase Mather puts down to his credit in his Autobiography
that he 'endeavord the Reformation of those excesses and
abuses which were wont to be of later years on the Commencement day and weeke, and therefore did my selfe stay that weeke
at the Colledge, that so I might pr[e]vent disorder and pro-
faneness.' [3]

Our principal authority on Commencements in this period is
Samuel Sewall, who managed to attend about every other one.
Generally he crossed by the ferry to Charlestown and drove
thence to Cambridge in a calash, coaches being reserved for
the ladies, so that their toilettes would not become dusty or
disarranged. Once he had the honor of being rowed to Cambridge in the official barge with Governor Bradstreet, Major-
General Winthrop, and other dignitaries; [4] once he went to
Malden to meet Governor Dudley on his return from Maine,
and conduct him to Cambridge. [5] On another occasion he and
a group of neighbors chartered a sailboat, but ran into head
wind and tide off Captain's Island, [6] and so had to 'get over the
Marsh to the Upland; and go into the Rode' and walk to the
College Yard.

Commencement exercises began at eleven in the morning.
As long as the Old College stood, and for a few years after Old
Harvard was built, they were held in the college hall. By 1687,
probably in order to have more space for the audience, the
exercises had been transferred to the meetinghouse in the
southwest corner of the present Yard; and in that building,
and its successors on the same site, they continued until 1833. [7]

1. *C. S. M.*, xv. 241. There is also a reference (p. 242) to former abuses.
2. *C. S. M.*, xviii. 335, quoting William Brattle's *Ephemeris* for 1682.
3. Ms., A. A. S. (1684).
4. Sewall, *Diary*, I. 323 (foot).   5. *Id.* II. 81.
6. *Id.* II. 133–34. Captain's Island is the nucleus of the present playground at
the foot of Magazine Street.
7. *C. S. M.*, xviii. 375–77.

The first time the new meetinghouse was used, in 1707, the desks were decorated with green cloth, at the expense of the family of one of the commencers.[1]

As earlier in the century, morning was devoted to the Bachelors, afternoon to the Masters of Arts. In 1685, 'besides Disputes' Sewall notes four orations: one in Latin by Thomas Dudley, the Governor's son, two in Greek, and one in Hebrew by Nathaniel Mather; and President Mather, after conferring degrees, 'made an Oration, in Praise of Academical Studies and Degrees. . . .'[2] As the numbers of the graduating classes increased, there were fewer orations and more disputations.

President Oakes always opened the exercises with one of his witty orations; but the salutatory, in which the commencers were congratulated, normally came after the disputations and before the conferring of degrees.[3] In his 1678 oration[4] Oakes combined both functions and introduced — or perhaps revived — a pleasant custom of addressing each candidate personally. It so happened that all four graduates that year bore historic names:[5]

JOHANNES COTTONUS, est *Magni illius* . . . JOHANNIS COTTONI *Nepos non indignus*. This sweet and memorable name would be enough to recommend this youth most highly to New England. May God bring it to pass that he not only follow after his grandfathers, the honored Bradstreet . . . and the illustrious Cotton, . . . but catch up with them.[6]

The next is called COTTONUS MATHERUS. What a name! I made a mistake, I confess; I should have said, what names! I shall say nothing of his reverend father, Overseer of the University most vigilant, since I wish not to praise him to his face. But if this youth bring back and represent the piety, learning, graceful ingenuity, sound judgment, prudence and gravity of his reverend grandsires John Cotton and Richard Mather, he may be said to have done his part well.[7] And I despair not that in this youth Cotton and Mather shall in fact as in name coalesce and revive!

Cotton Mather never did recover from that.

---

1. Sewall, *Diary*, ii. 190. 2. *Id*. i. 85.
3. See Appendix B, 1687, 1689, and 1693. But in 1688 the *oratio salutatoria* precedes the Quaestiones, and in 1708 it precedes the Theses.
4. 'Leverett's Book of Latin Orations, 1688,' H. U. Archives.
5. This section of the Oration here quoted is reproduced in Cotton Mather's *Just Commemorations* (1715); in Sibley, ii. 2, 6–7, 159; and the *Magnalia*.
6. 'Non insequatur Solum, sed tandem etiam assequatur.'
7. 'Omne tulisse Punctum dici poterit' — cf. Horace *Ars Poetica*, 343.

Third, sounding something grand,[1] is GRINDALLUS RAWSONUS, born also of noble race, for his father holds high office in the Commonwealth; the most pious and orthodox John Wilson, an apostolic man to be sure, was his great-uncle; and Edmund Grindall, sometime Archbishop of Canterbury, a most holy man and almost a puritan archbishop, was his great-great uncle. May God express in him the learning, holiness, and highest *mores* of Wilson and Grindall — but I neither wish nor prognosticate for him an Archiepiscopal see.[2]

Poor little Urian Oakes, Jr., already suffering from a 'languishing consumption,' came next, and last. But there were no compliments for him. 'For wouldn't it be ridiculous, and make even Heraclitus laugh, if a father openly and before an assembly should praise his son? But I wish him to be commended today if he deserve it, for that quality and rank, for which Caesar Augustus commended his sons to the people.'

Mather seems to have continued Oakes' practice of making himself the principal feature of Commencement;[3] but the more modest Vice-President Willard (one infers from Sewall) was content to deliver an opening prayer, moderate the disputations, and confer degrees. A Commencement oration or disputation was naturally a very important event in a young man's life; for in the absence of other academic honors or extracurricular activities, his elders who had jobs to give were apt to judge him on his public performance that day. Samuel Sewall was much concerned for his pious son Joseph, who on Commencement morn was 'weak and something discouraged,' 'but God helped him,' his cousin Parson Moody of York 'had pray'd earnestly for it the night before,' and 'it was accepted above what I could reasonably expect. Thy power is shown in weakness!' In fact, young Sewall did so well as to respond to a quaestio that afternoon in place of an absent inceptor, who had gone with the fleet to Port Royal.[4] The afternoon exercises began with an *oratio gratulatoria*, and closed with an *oratio valedictoria*, which at this period seems to have been given by one of the inceptors.[5]

1. 'Grande quiddam Sonans.'
2. 'Neque verò Archiepiscopalem ei Sedem vel opto vel ominor.' This joke was omitted by Cotton Mather.   3. *Magnalia*, book iv. 131–32.
4. Joseph Sewall, Ms. Diary (*Ephemeris Sacra*), Prince Collection, B. P. L., p. 51; Samuel Sewall, *Diary*, ii. 190.
5. *Id*. ii. 134; cf. Quaestiones in Appendix B, especially 1675, 1678–80, and from 1682 on. But in 1689 the *oratio gratulatoria* precedes the morning exercises (see Theses).

ORDER OF SENIORITY IN 1700
From Steward Bordman's Quarter-Bill Book

THE STOUGHTON CUP
By John Coney of Boston. Presented to the College by
William Stoughton, *c.* 1700

Between the two halves of the exercises, Commencement dinner was served in college hall, at the expense of those taking degrees, to both Governing Boards, returning graduates, and distinguished strangers. A vote of the Corporation several months in advance of Commencement in 1691, to the effect that Steward Bordman 'find Wood, Candles, Cooks, Turn-Spitt Indians and things of the like Nature,' [1] indicates preparations for a heavy feast. The President opened the feast by 'craving a blessing,' and at the end 'gave thanks.' Next, the company sang a psalm — the third part of the one hundred and third, in 1685.[2] Finally, there came the pleasant old ceremony of handing around the loving cup, or grace cup, as it was then called. It was the Governor's privilege to start it on the rounds, with a little speech. In 1701 Lieutenant-Governor Stoughton, who was on his deathbed, deputed Judge Sewall and 'Mr Nelson, Secretary' 'to present his Bowl.' [3] 'After dinner and singing,' records the Judge,

I took it, had it filled up, and drunk to the president [Mather] saying that by reason of the absence of him who was the Firmament and Ornament of the Province, and that Society, I presented that Grace-cup pro more Academiarum in Anglia The Providence of our soveraign Lord is very investigable in that our Grace Cups brim full, are passing round; when our Brethren in France are petitioning for their Coup de Grace.[4]

His Excellency Governor Dudley was wont to linger over Commencement dinner until well after the Masters' exercises had begun. Judge Sewall followed him into the meetinghouse in 1704 just in time to hear the last quaestio being argued. But he had the pleasure of witnessing an impromptu performance by Jeremy Dummer (A.B. 1699), who had not yet recovered from

1. *C. S. M.*, xvi. 830.
2. Sewall, *Diary*, i. 85. I do not imagine that the same one was sung at every commencement. When the 78th Psalm, 'Give ear, O my people,' became standard and traditional on these occasions, I have not discovered. John Pierce (A.B. 1793) speaks of 'singing the usual hymn' at Commencement, 1803; and of Commencement, 1806, he notes 'We sung St. Martin's to the usual psalm, "Give ear, my people," etc.' 2 *Proc. M. H. S.* v. 169, 171.
3. 'Bowl' was then used, as in Shakspere and the phrase 'flowing bowl,' for any kind of drinking vessel.
4. *C. S. M.*, xviii. 330–31. The last clause is probably an allusion to the sufferings of the Huguenots. The two-handled cup with cover, ten inches high, by John Coney of Boston, presented by the Lieutenant-Governor to the College, is here depicted in the belief that it is the very vessel that Sewall used as grace cup.

his Utrecht Ph.D. Dr. Dummer 'rose up and in very fluent good Latin ask'd Leave, and made an opposition; and then took Leave again with Commendation of the Respondent.'[1]

Wine was dispensed at private parties in the students' chambers, by themselves and their parents. Apparently the traditional accompaniment was plum cake, which seems innocent enough. But a kill-joy Corporation, President Mather in the chair, put a stop to this in 1693:

> The Corporation having been informed that the Custom taken up in the Colledge, not used in any other Universities,[2] for the Commencers to have Plumb-Cake, is dishonourable to the Colledge, not gratefull to Wise men, and chargable to the Parents of the Commencers; do therfor[e] put an End to that Custom, and do hereby order that no Commencer or other Schollar shall have any Such Cakes in their Studies or Chambers, and that if any Schollar shall offend therin, the Cakes Shall be taken from him, and he shall moreover pay to the Colledge twenty shillings for each Such offen[ce].[3]

We may close this chapter as we began it, with a description. Thomas Story, an English Quaker, visited Cambridge in the summer of 1704, in the course of a visitation during which he had many unpleasant experiences. The local Friends arranged for him to hold a meeting at a Cambridge inn— probably the Blue Anchor; but the Reverend William Brattle threatened to have the innkeeper deprived of his licence, if his property were used for a purpose so unpleasing to the established faith. So the Quakers decided to meet outdoors, and the little company of the faithful, with others who were merely curious, wandered up Brattle Street to the Square. There, the tall meetinghouse offered a grateful shade; but Story refused to take shelter under the shadow of persecution. 'Some of the students,' wrote Story, 'would have us sit down in the College Orchard, which was dry and sufficiently shaded.[4] I acknowledged the Civility; but not having License from their Superiors, we might have been

1. *Diary*, II. 111. Such intrusions by any learned member of the audience were the custom at the Continental and Scottish universities (see *F. H. C.*, p. 135). I have noted no other instance of it at Harvard before 1709, when Colonel Samuel Vetch tried his hand at an opposition.

2. President Mather had lately returned from England.

3. *C. S. M.*, xv. 343.

4. They probably meant the Sweetman-Spencer lot, the site of Holden Chapel, which was often called the Spencer orchard; I do not suppose that they would have ventured to invite the company into the Fellows' Orchard (III).

liable to Disturbance, and so declin'd it.' The Friends proceeded to the Common, where the ancient oak from which John Wilson had harangued the multitude in 1637 was still standing, and under its spreading branches sat them down.

And many of the Students of the College being there, they were sent for by the President, and some of them went to him; but others of them remained in the Meeting, and several of those who went out returned before the Meeting was ended. . . . And I must say this for these young Students, that they did behave themselves better, and much more like a moral Education at least, nay more like Christians too, than at *Cambridge* or *Oxford*, in *Old England*, or at *Edinburgh*, *Glasgow*, or *Aberdeen*, in *Scotland*; some of them being very solid, and, generally, very attentive: Whereas those others commonly behave like the Scum of the Earth, the Refuse of Mankind, from whom little can be expected, other than the Depravity of a Nation. I hope this Meeting was of some Service among them; and that was all we desired there.[1]

A very different impression from that of Danckaerts; but the Dutch Labadist and the English Quaker at least agreed that Harvard students were well mannered.

1. *A Journal of the Life of Thomas Story* (Newcastle-upon-Tyne, 1747), pp. 341–43. Several of the students later attended his meeting in Boston, 'and were very sober and attentive.' The site of this oak is marked by a tablet on Cambridge Common; cf. map in *F. H. C.*, p. 193.

XXII

INCREASE MATHER AND THE DOMINION
1685–1692 [1]

 With the election of Increase Mather as President, in 1685, we enter a confused period in the political history of the College. During the next twenty-two years Harvard had but two presidents, neither of whom resided in Cambridge or had much influence on the College, the constitution of which was changed no less than eight times.[2] One after another the new charters and arrangements faded away, leaving the government in 1708 exactly what it had been in 1685—Presi-

1. For the College Archives at this period, see Appendix F. The *Mass. Bay Recs.* end in 1686; the records of the short restoration of the Old Régime after 1689 have not been printed; such records of the Council and Dominion of New England under the Dudley and Andros régimes as are printed, will be found in 2 *Proc. M. H. S.*, xiii. 222–86 and *Proc. A. A. S.*, n. s. xiii. 237–68, 463–99. After 1692 we have the *Acts and Resolves of the Province of Massachusetts Bay*, with Abner C. Goodell's voluminous notes; but no printed House Journals, except as calendared in the *Calendar of State Papers, Colonial, America and West Indies*. For the best modern account of the Andros régime and bibliography of the contemporary pamphlet literature, see Viola F. Barnes, *The Dominion of New England* (1923). Increase Mather's Diaries and Autobiography still remain in ms. in the A. A. S. (with two in the M. H. S.); I have used a typed copy made by Mr. Allyn B. Forbes, who hopes to print them before long in *C. S. M.* Cotton Mather, whose *Magnalia Christi* (1702) is a contemporary authority for this period, and whose printed Diary (7 *Coll. M. H. S.*, vii–viii) is an important source, drew on the Autobiography for his *Parentator* (1724). The Mather mss. in the Prince Library, B. P. L., are printed as *The Mather Papers* in 4 *Coll. M. H. S.*, viii (1868). K. B. Murdock, *Increase Mather, the Foremost American Puritan* (Harvard Univ. Press, 1925) is the best biography of the President; T. J. Holmes, *Increase Mather, A Bibliography* (2 vols., Cleveland, 1931), opens up much contemporary printed literature. The *Diary of Samuel Sewall* (5 *Coll. M. H. S.*, v–vii) is by far the best guide to the social background, and affords many facts on the College not found elsewhere. For this period Josiah Quincy's *History of Harvard University* (2 vols., 1840) becomes really useful. The different charters, and extracts from the Mather's diaries, are printed (not very accurately) in his appendices, and in the text he gives a full and detailed account, not always fair to the Mathers, of the political struggles between conservatives and liberals; a subject which Quincy described with great zest, since in his administration (1829–45) the liberals, securely entrenched in the Corporation, were being continually sniped at by the defeated conservatives, from both political and religious ambushes.

2. Summary of the eight changes: (1) Rector and Tutors, 1686; (2) Charter of 1650

dent and Fellows and Board of Overseers acting under the Charter of 1650. And through it all the College serenely went her way, 'calm rising through change and through storm.'

After Joshua Moody declined the presidency and Wiggles-worth refused to be considered, the Governing Boards knew not where to turn. When Commencement of 1685 was so near that something must be done, they persuaded Increase Mather to 'act as *Praeses pro Tempore*, till such Time as a settlement could be procured.' [1] As in the case of Oakes, this presidency *pro tempore* lengthened out into a presidency without qualification; yet Increase Mather never resided more than a few months in Cambridge during the sixteen years of his incumbency. He could have had the presidency at any time after Hoar's resignation, at the cost of giving up his Boston church, but that he never would do, at least for the College. In 1685 the Governing Boards were glad to have him on any terms; and he served the College as well as a commuting president could. His house in the North End of Boston was not far from the ferry to Charlestown, where a horse was maintained for him at college expense; [2] and it was a pleasant recreation in a busy minister's life to ride over to Cambridge every so often, 'vntil the extremity of the winter came on,' to moderate disputations in college hall.[3] President Mather generously allowed the £100 voted by the General Court as his first year's salary to be spent by the Corporation: half to discharge the last debts to William Manning for building Old Harvard, and the rest to the tutors who were conducting the College, John Cotton (A.B. 1678) and John Leverett (A.B. 1680).[4]

---

restored, 1690; (3) Charter of 1692; (4) Temporary Settlement of October 12, 1696; (5) Charter of 1697; (6) Temporary Settlement of July 25, 1699; (7) Temporary Settlement of 1700–02; (8) Charter of 1650 restored, 1708. For a brief account of these changes, and the personnel of the successive corporations, see Mr. Matthews' Introduction to *C. S. M.* xv., pp. xxv, xxxiv–lxiii; but see also footnote at beginning of Chapter XXIV, below.

1. Mather's Autobiography (ms., A. A. S.), under date March 19, 1684/85; probably this records an informal invitation from the Corporation. College Book I records only an invitation from the Overseers on June 11, 1685 (*C. S. M.*, xv. 78).

2. Treasurer Richards' accounts, H. U. Archives, ff. 11, 12, 14.

3. Autobiography, March, 1684/85.

4. *C. S. M.*, xv. 79.

Dudley, Cranfield, and Morton

 Over all these doings, even in the dry records, there appears a feeling of apprehension that great changes would be forced on the College, as on the Colony. Massachusetts Bay had lost her Royal Charter, under which an autonomous and well-nigh independent Commonwealth had been built up. The Colony Charter was formally vacated and voided by judgment in the Court of Chancery in October 1684; but it was not until May 14, 1686 that Edward Randolph arrived on the *Rose* frigate bearing a commission to Joseph Dudley (A.B. 1665) as President of the Council for New England. Sewall tells us in his Diary of the General Court's assembling for the last time on May 21; how Mr. Nowell prayed that God would pardon each Magistrate's and Deputy's sins, and gave thanks for past mercies vouchsafed to the Colony; how Sewall moved to sing Habukkuk iii. 17–18, 'Although the fig tree shall not blossom . . . yet I will rejoice in the Lord, I will joy in the God of my salvation'; and how the Marshal-General in tears declared the General Court of the Governor and Company of the Massachusetts Bay in New England adjourned *sine die*. And then (May 25, 1686) a proclamation of President Dudley, published 'by beat of drumme and sound of trumpet,'[1] to the effect that Massachusetts was henceforth to be governed by His Majesty's immediate representative and an appointed council.

All this boded ill for the College. Whatever lawyers might say as to vested rights, it was generally assumed that the College Charter perished with its parent; or, as plain-speaking people expressed it, 'the Calf died in the cow's belly.'[2]

Governor Cranfield of New Hampshire had written to the Lords of Trade three years before:

When the Charter shall bee made void it will bee necessary to desolue their Vniversity of Cambridge for from thence all the seuerall Colonys of New England are supplyed the people Lookeing upon their Teachers little less then Apostles, it is incredible what an influence they haue ouer the Vulgar and do make it their business dayly to

---

1. 2 *Proc. M. H. S.*, XIII. 227–28.
2. Letter of President Leverett, Aug. 28, 1721, in Ewer Mss. (N. E. H. G. S.), I. 59. Increase Mather in 1708 accused Dudley of coining the phrase. 1 *Coll. M. H. S.*, III. 126.

Excite and stirr them up to Rebellion being profest Enemies to the Kings Gouernment and Church, it is to bee feared this people will neuer bee reclaimed untill the Vneuersetys of England supply there Colonys, the not nipping them in the budd may proue of great inconueniencies; by takeing away their Vneversity (which will also be forfited with their Charter) the Effect will cease, for all other waies will bee uneffectuell the fountaine being impure.[1]

On the same date Cranfield wrote to Sir Leoline Jenkins, His Majesty's principal Secretary of State:

I haue obserued, That there can bee no greater evill attend his Majesties affaires here, then those pernicious and Rebellious principles which flowes from their College at Cambridge which they call their Vniuersity from whence all the Townes both in this and the other Colonys are supplied with factious and Seditious Preachers who stirr up the people to a dislike of his Majestie and his Gouverment and the Religion of the Church of England terming the Liturgy of our Church a precident of Superstition and picked out of the Popish Dunghill so that I am humbly of opinion this Country can neuer bee well settled or the people become good Subjects, till their Preachers bee reformed and that Colledge supressed and the severall Churches supplied with Learned and Orthodox Ministers from England as all other his Majesties Dominions in America are.[2]

Fortunately, Cranfield enjoyed no great credit in England, and President Dudley and three or four members of his Council were Harvard men.[3] But this change in régime, a revolution in New England government, did prevent Harvard from obtaining a distinguished teacher as her head.

While President Dudley was building new political fences, the Reverend Charles Morton, sometime master of a famous dissenting academy at Newington Green, was on the ocean. He had left England to escape persecution,[4] and emigrated to

1. June 19, 1683. Public Record Office, C. O. 1/52.35.

2. P. R. O., C. O. 1/52, 33; printed in H. W. Foote, *Annals of King's Chapel*, 1. 54–55.

3. Wait Still Winthrop (1662), Peter Bulkeley (A.B. 1660), and William Stoughton (A.B. 1650). Nathaniel Saltonstall (A.B. 1659) also received an appointment to the Council, but declined to serve. C. S. M., XVII. 30–31. The Councillor John Pynchon was father of the Harvard student of that name who belonged to the Class of 1666.

4. Under Charles II, the government began to prosecute for perjury graduates of Oxford and Cambridge who were teaching in dissenting academies, on the ground that they had violated their oath at commencing M. A. not to lecture except at Cambridge and Oxford. H. McLachlan, *English Education under the Test Acts* (Manchester, 1931), pp. 76–77. See also above, pp. 236–37.

New England with the hope and expectation of becoming President of Harvard College,[1] whither he had already sent a pupil and nephew, Nicholas Morton (so he wrote Increase Mather), 'as a pledge of my good will in your affairs.'[2]

Morton's candidacy and arrival at Boston were noted on July 1 by Edward Randolph, who on the seventh wrote to the Archbishop of Canterbury that the New Englanders were all 'more taken up in puting in one Morton of Neventongreen, a rank independent, to be theire precident, than to shew any respect which is due to your graceouse present.'[3] But of course it would have been unwise for the 'dead calf' to have attempted to elect any president, folly to have chosen a *persona non grata* to the English government. Before the month was ended, President Dudley and his Council settled the matter themselves.

The College under Rector and Tutors

At a Council held in Boston on July 20, 1686, it was decided that 'The Colledg of Cambridge being in an unsetled posture by the late alteration of the Government, and Mr. Increase Mathers dismissing himself from further care and service there,' the Council would deal with that question in three days' time, on the spot. And a new set of College Laws drafted by Mather was ordered to be submitted to John Leverett 'and the

---

1. Henry Horsey of Newington Green wrote to his brother, April 12, 1686, '*Mr. Charles Morton* . . . is a person of great learning, and piety, and moderation, and of an excellent sweet natural temper, of a loving and generous spirit, who will be well worth your acquaintance and friendship in anything you can serve him in, especially in that he goes over in prospect of; viz., to be president of your college at Cambridge.' He adds that Morton is well known to Dudley and Stoughton. Copy by Thomas Prince in his mss. at the M. H. S., p. 51; printed in W. I. Budington, *Hist. of First Church, Charlestown* (1845), p. 221. With Morton came his pupil and disciple Samuel Penhallow (see *D. A. B.*), who was recommended to Increase Mather by Nathaniel Mather, and by a London merchant of his acquaintance, 'in getting a place in your Vniversity.' 4 *Coll. M. H. S.*, VIII. 59, 649. And Penhallow in his autobiography says that Morton 'was invited and courted . . . to take upon him the presidentship of the college, being a gentleman of universal learning.' 2 *Coll. M. H. S.*, I. 161. On the other hand, Morton's reply to a letter of Increase Mather's written in August 1685 proves that Mather conveyed an invitation to be pastor of Charlestown, although he may also have held out the alternative of being President of Harvard. R. Frothingham, *Charlestown* (1845), p. 195.

2. Sibley, III. 367.

3. R. N. Toppan, *Edward Randolph* (Prince Society, 1909), VI. 186; T. Hutchinson, *Collection of Papers* (Prince Society ed.), II. 293. Later Randolph wrote that Morton had been 'welcomed by our president' (Dudley) and 'designed to be Master-head of our colledge,' but did not dare to proceed 'by such large steps.' *Id.* II. 287.

other Principall Schollars (now upon the place)' for their ad-vice.[1] On July 23, President Dudley with the Harvard members of his Council and two others duly met in the college hall at Old Harvard. 'It was unanimously Agreed upon and declared,'

1. That the Reverend Mr Increase Mather be desired to accept of the Rectorship of the Colledge, and make his Usuall Visitations.

2. That Mr John Leverett and Mr William Brattle be the Tutours, and enter upon the Government of the Colledge, and manage the publick reading in the hall,

3. That Charlestown ferry and Mr Penoyers Legacy. i.e. one Moïety of it, as it falleth be settled upon the said Tutours as their Sallary.

4. That their Pupills each of them pay to their Respective Tutours ten Shillings, per Quarter for their Tuition.

5. That Andrew Boardman the present Cooke of the Colledge do hence forward manage the Office of Stewarde in the Manner as of late.[2]

Randolph, who evidently shared Cranfield's views on the College, was furious at this settlement, put over by Dudley and the Harvardians during his absence.[3] Rector and Tutors were but President and Fellows writ small. The College could not have been put in better hands, unless Morton had been substituted for Mather. The change of title from President to Rector was doubtless made in order to avoid confusion with Dudley's title — there was not room for two presidents in Massachusetts.

At the same meeting of the President and Council on July 23, 1686, a Latin code of College Laws which Rector Mather had drafted was adopted and promulgated. This Dudley code, as we may call it,[4] was the first set of College Laws since the Chauncey code of 1655. It was the shortest and simplest set of Harvard College statutes between 1642 and the Eliot admin-istration.

Shortly after, the Rector and Tutors issued a new set of 'Rules and Orders respecting the Steward Cook and Butler of

1. 2 *Proc. M. H. S.*, XIII. 257.
2. *C. S. M.*, XVI. 827–28.
3. R. N. Toppan, *Edward Randolph* (Prince Society, 1909), VI. 245.
4. Printed from College Book IV, in *C. S. M.*, XVI. 848–50; in *Proc. M. H. S.*, XIV. 226–28, from a ms. copy that belonged to John Leverett; and reprinted in a pam-phlet *Rules, Orders, and Statutes of Harvard College . . . 23d July, 1686* (Cambridge, 1876).

Harvard College.' [1] The Steward must provide 'all Necessarys and meet Provisions,' and 'for his Cost and Pains' was to receive what the students and tutors paid for commons and sizings, provided the total exceeded not £60 per quarter; of the excess he could retain five-sixths, and of any defect of £60, the Treasurer [2] should allow him one-third. He must pay over to the Treasurer all sums received for study rents, detriments, fines, gallery money, and glass mending, and to the tutors all tuition fees. 'The Steward shall deliver in unto the Butler his Bread at five Shillings per Bushell and his Beer at four per Barrell each Barrell consisting of 16 Gallons of Beer measure allowing thereto two pecks of Barley Malt.' The butler and cook have the onerous duty of making an inventory of 'all the College Utensils and Vessels great and small,' with notes of damages, every quarter. They must deliver table utensils and wooden trenchers clean to the servitors, who are responsible for their return to the 'Buttery Hatch and Kitching.' The old rules against removing vessels 'out of Doors from the Sight of the Buttery Hatch,' and frequenting the kitchen, are renewed; the butler is allowed to advance 10d on the bushel of bread, and 16d on the barrel of beer; [3] the cook is to advance 50 per cent on the cost of provisions, when cooked.

Certainly the Rector did not intend to let the college standards down. As we have already observed, the Commencement Theses in Grammar and Rhetoric show some signs of depression in these years; [4] but Astronomy and Physics were greatly stimulated by the adoption of Charles Morton's *Compendium Physicae*. [5]

Morton, after failing to obtain the Harvard presidency, accepted the pulpit of Charlestown, where his father's sometime protégé John Harvard had once held forth. For two young men (Samuel Penhallow and another) who had come over with him, Morton proceeded to set up in his Charlestown parsonage an informal academy, which, says Penhallow, attracted 'several from the college.' This caused 'uneasiness' at Harvard. [6]

---

1. *C. S. M.*, xv. 259-62.

2. Nothing was said about a Treasurer in the settlement made by President Dudley, but Treasurer Richards resumed office in 1686, after a three-year incumbency by Samuel Nowell. *C. S. M.*, xv. p. clvi.

3. *Id.* 259-62.   4. Above, Chapter VIII.

5. Above, Chapter XI.

6. 2 *Coll. M. H. S.*, i. 162.

PRESIDENT INCREASE MATHER

GOVERNOR SIR EDMUND ANDROS

On December 15, 1686, after John Emerson of the sophomore class had been punished for negligence in studies, and removed by his father to this incipient tutoring school, the Rector and Tutors addressed a sharp letter to Master Morton. They declared that it would be 'very offensive' to them if he continued to 'enterteyn any of the scholars without the approbation' of themselves; and that if such as Emerson were allowed to take refuge with him, it would be 'no small reflection' on him.[1] The reflection, one would think, was rather on a college that could not suffer the competition of one gifted Englishman; but upon that hint, Mr. Morton amiably gave up his private academy, and at the first opportunity was suitably rewarded by being taken into the Harvard fellowship.

THE DOMINION OF NEW ENGLAND

A few days after this letter was sent, Sir Edmund Andros landed in Boston, with a royal commission (replacing Dudley's) as Governor of the Territory and Dominion of New England.[2] It was within his power to undo what Dudley had done; and the Rector and Tutors feared lest he suppress or anglicize the College. Uncertainty and even dread appear in John Leverett's address in Latin (with a bit of Greek and Hebrew) when Governor Andros pays a ceremonial visit to Harvard College not long after his arrival.[3] Leverett was probably chosen to present this complimentary effusion because he was known to be more or less sympathetic to the new régime.[4] Certainly no out-and-out partisan could have found more compliments for this *Miles Insignissimus*, the fame of whose *humanitas, sapientia, clementia* is constantly increasing, so that the clouds hardly measure the height of his merits. The college authorities are grateful to His Excellency for trusting the loyalty of

1. 4 *Coll. M. H. S.*, VIII. 111–12.
2. December 20, 1686. *C. S. M.*, XVII. 7.
3. H. U. Archives, 'Leverett's Book of Latin Orations, 1688,' pp. 99–104. It is in Leverett's hand and headed simply 'Oratio. 1686.' From internal evidence it would seem to have been delivered shortly after Andros' arrival on December 20. Another copy, undated but endorsed 'Sr. Ed. And. per J. L. — V. D.' is in Leverett's ms. Notebook at the M. H. S.
4. The pamphlet *The Deplorable State of New England* (London, 1708, probably by Cotton Mather) referred to Leverett on p. 24 as a 'Tory'; and Leverett's letters to Governor Dudley and others suggest that he belonged to the royal prerogative or 'tory' party.

his New Englanders, in spite of evil rumors circulated by idle fellows. They are grateful to him for deigning to notice his scholars and *alma nostra Cantabrigia*, seat of the Muses, seminary of good Arts, stronghold of religion and loyalty.

Your Excellency, whom a few days ago your Bostonians saluted when disembarking, like the rosy-fingered dawn arising from the sea (since Aurora is also friend to the Muses); in like manner we your Harvardians would worship, as the risen sun giving light to this sphere of Letters (were it not that the Persian rite is not practised by us, nor would it be grateful to a Christian knight). And by your benign influence whatever fear possessed our hearts is dissipated, and every hope seems to grow afresh. For, as Manoah's wife once said with faith in God, 'If the Lord were pleased to kill us, he would not have received a burnt-offering and a meat-offering at our hands, neither would he have shewed us all these things.' [1] So also by proper analogy we may say that every sinister interpretation of your presence is absent (and behold, O you who hold the place of Caesar among us, what licence, what audacity your humanity giveth us!), if we had been doomed to ruin, if Your Excellency had determined on the subversion of Harvard, you would not have listened with such patience and candor to these our congratulations and thanks; nor would you have deigned to bless us and our University with your presence. . . .

The favors of Joseph Dudley and Wait Winthrop, of Stoughton and his *fidus Achates* Bulkeley, members of the Governor's Council who apparently accompanied him on this visitation, are bespoken; their ancestry and their Harvard education are recalled; Rector Mather is praised for his wisdom, care, learning, and good administration.

It is not likely that Andros was moved by, or even that he understood, this tactful adulation; but there is no evidence that he or the English government seriously contemplated the 'subversion of Harvard.' He could well afford to let the little college go its own way for a time; and although he may have observed, as had Governor Cranfield a few years earlier, that his stoutest opponents were Harvard-trained ministers, they were offset by Harvard-trained councillors. There were many more immediate and pressing matters for the Governor's attention. It does appear, however, that Sir Edmund took some interest in the college estate. Treasurer Richards, in order to secure the property of the defunct Corporation to the living College,

1. Judges xiii. 23.

called in all loans and issued new bonds and leases, payable to Dudley, Stoughton, Mather, and their heirs. This prudent measure seemed outrageous to Edward Randolph;[1] and it was probably at his instance, although at the Governor's orders, that Richards, in August 1687, drew up a neat balance-sheet of 'Stocke belonging to Harvard Colledge att Cambridge.'[2] From this account, it appears that the College was in relatively flourishing financial condition. In the previous eight months the Treasurer received £130 11s interest (mostly on loans made from the Holworthy bequest), a few rents, and £50 from the Charlestown ferry. The Mowlson fund, however, had disappeared with the Colony Charter, and no Pennoyer rents had come in for some time. Even so, this was sufficient to give Leverett and Brattle much higher stipends than any earlier tutors had received.[3] Disbursements include investments (£20 lent on a mortgage note, which cost 28s to record); the Treasurer's and tutors' salaries, care of the presidential horse at Charlestown, and stipends of £5 each to three Scholars of the House, one of whom was Paul, the precocious son of the wealthy Joseph Dudley—a disposition which Randolph thought highly reprehensible.[4] The balance, a modest £19 11s, was paid over to Rector Mather.[5] And, in spite of Leverett's fears for the subversion of Harvard, the public had sufficient confidence in the stability of the College and the abilities of Messrs. Leverett and Brattle to enter twenty-two freshmen, a record-breaking class, in the summer of 1686.

The following Commencement passed off very well. Sir Edmund Andros graciously attended in his scarlet laced coat

---

1. R. N. Toppan, *Edward Randolph*, vi. 245, 225.

2. *C. S. M.*, i. 205–06, with facsimiles of pages covering summary of accounts through 1691.

3. See above, p. 52.

4. This obvious political favor to a ruler was construed by Randolph as evidence of the intention of Dudley, Mather, and Stoughton to divide up the college property among themselves! Toppan, *op. cit.*, vi. 245.

5. *C. S. M.*, i. 206, facsimile. This pocketing of the balance is curiously interpreted by Mather's biographer as showing that the Rector 'was ready to shoulder, as an individual, the task of defending Harvard's property' (K. B. Murdock, *Increase Mather*, p. 179). That this was all the salary received by Mather is doubtful. Probably he received something from the Governor and Council; but in the absence of financial records of the Dominion, one cannot be certain. Treasurer Brattle's accounts (College Book V, H. U. Archives) show that he received the rents from students' studies in the President's Lodging, which he did not occupy: £26 10s in November 1693, and £13 5s in May 1694, for instance.

and wig of the latest fashion; and to him, as 'Knight, Member of the Privy Council, Governor and Captain-General of Our Sovereign Lord the King over his Territory and Dominion of New England in America,' the graduating class dedicated their theses.[1] The disputations on up-to-date scientific subjects, of which there are eight on the programme, such as 'Gravity is the Attractive Force of the Earth,' and 'Rays of Light are Corpuscular,'[2] are derived from Charles Morton's informing textbook. Indeed, the only note that jarred on Samuel Sewall that day was Sir Edmund's insistence that his Anglican chaplain sit in the pulpit during the ceremonies, as a symbol of the newly established church.[3]

Mather apparently feared lest Andros turn him out in the autumn of 1687;[4] but there is no evidence that the Governor had any such intention. He did not even take advantage of Mather's going to England in April 1688, for the express purpose of undermining him, to appoint a loyal man as Rector. Sir Edmund invited Samuel Lee,[5] an eminent dissenting clergyman who had lately come over, to preside at Harvard Commencement; and when Lee hesitated to accept, the Governor appointed William Hubbard of Ipswich, puritan historian and senior Harvard graduate in the Dominion, to manage the ceremonies.[6] Yet Hubbard was a ringleader in the opposition at Ipswich against paying taxes. Andros certainly played fair and square with Harvard, although he might have handed her over to the Anglicans, or even suppressed her, by executive fiat.[7]

1. See below, Appendix B.
2. *Id.* 1687, theses physicae, nos. 14, 21.
3. Sewall, *Diary*, I. 181. Robert Ratcliffe, the chaplain, was an Oxonian of Exeter College; his son John (d. 1775) became Master of Pembroke College. *C. S. M.*, xxiv. 35.
4. 'The Colledge state (should you desert it, or be, as you say, dismissed from it, . . .) is much to be lamented and feared.' John Bishop of Stamford, Conn., to Mather, October 18, 1687. 4 *Coll. M. H. S.*, viii. 315.
5. See above, pp. 250–5.
6. The warrant appointing Hubbard 'to exercise and officiate as President of the said College at the next Commencement' is printed in 3 *Coll. M. H. S.*, i. 83. Sewall notes in his diary that Hubbard compared Sir William Phips, in his oration, to Jason. Sibley, I. 59.
7. Increase Mather complained, in a memorial presented to the King shortly after his arrival in England, that the impending Anglicanization of Harvard was 'commonly discoursed' at Boston (4 *Coll. M. H. S.*, viii. 700). But I have searched the Public Record Office in vain for evidence of policy toward Harvard on the part of any government board, or Andros; and Professor Viola F. Barnes, who has combed the records of this period with much greater thoroughness, tells me that she has found nothing

MATHER IN ENGLAND

Rector Mather was absent in England for four years (1688–92), during which tutors Leverett and Brattle were the sole teaching staff, and (with Treasurer Richards) the governing board of the College. The Rector modestly admitted that he 'could not do much for the Colledge' from such a distance;[1] and his mission was primarily political; but he never forgot to put in a good word for alma mater on suitable occasions. At one of his several interviews with James II, Mather remarked 'that it would be an obligation beyond all expression great, if his Majesty would grant them a charter for their Colledge: That if the Church of E[ngland] men would build a Colledge for themselves no one would object against it; but they thought it hard, that the Colledge built by Nonconformists, should be put into the hands of Conformists.' The King replied, 'Thats unreasonable, and it shall not be.'[2] Again on October 16, 1688, the King assured Mather 'that property, liberty, and our Colledge should all be confirmed to us.'[3] His Majesty had apparently read a petition presented by Mr. Mather, urging that the Charter of 1650 be confirmed, and the Corporation ousted in 1686 reëstablished.[4]

There is at least an even chance that James Stuart would have been as good as his word; but he had not the opportunity. Within three weeks of this interview William of Orange landed in Torbay; and within two months James II was a refugee from his kingdom. As soon as the news of this 'Glorious Revolution' reached America, the Dominion of New England, which by this time stretched from the Penobscot to the Delaware, fell apart into its constituent colonies. At Boston, Sir Edmund Andros was overthrown on April 18, 1689; a self-appointed

---

on that subject. Mather, when racking his memory for charges against Andros (see pamphlets in *Andros Tracts*, II), found nothing to say about his attitude toward the College. Randolph did, however, drop a hint in a letter of March 29, 1688, to Sir Nicholas Butler, a recent Roman convert, that might well have been dangerous: to use the 'publick Stock' of the College to maintain an English Roman Catholic mission to the Indians, and thus counteract French influence. Toppan, *Edward Randolph*, VI. 245–47.

1. *Andros Tracts*, II. 295–96.
2. Mather, Ms. Autobiography, July 2, 1688. Cf. Murdock, *op. cit.*, pp. 197–98.
3. Autobiography, October 16.
4. 4 *Coll. M. H. S.*, VIII. 113–14.

'Council for Safety' took charge, a convention consisting of members of the last General Court was summoned, and, with old Governor Bradstreet in the chair, resumed the government of Massachusetts Bay as if nothing had happened. Now that the cow had come to life, the calf revived too; on the tutors' motion the present and surviving members of the College Corporation met on June 2, 1690, under the presidency of Treasurer Richards, and elected Nathaniel Gookin (A.B. 1675) and Cotton Mather (A.B. 1678) to fellowships. Ten days later the Board of Overseers assembled for the first time in four years, to confirm these elections.[1] Mather now automatically became President, as he had been before the overturn of 1686. But Leverett and Brattle carried on as the sole tutors and actual government of Harvard College, so long as the President remained in England.

It was well understood that these restorations of colonial and college governments were temporary measures, awaiting the good pleasure of Their Majesties to make a permanent arrangement. At this juncture, President Mather did effective work at Whitehall. He procured an exemption for the New England Colonies from an Order in Council that James' colonial governors should continue in office;[2] and when the news of the Boston rebellion arrived, he took care that William and Mary should interpret it as a gesture of loyalty toward them, rather than of revolt against lawful authority. But Sir Edmund Andros soon came to London to present his side; and among the permanent officials of the English government, Massachusetts had a bad reputation. Mather needed all his diplomacy to prevent a virtual restoration of the Stuart régime, such as took place with bloody consequences in New York. Elisha Cooke (A.B. 1657) and Thomas Oakes (A.B. 1662), who were sent out to act as joint agents with Mather, lost their provincial heads amid the intrigues of the court, and proved a hindrance rather than a help. The restoration of the Colony Charter soon appeared to be hopeless; but although Mather did not obtain exactly the charter he wanted, the Province Charter of 1691 gave Massachusetts Bay a greater measure of home rule than any other royal or proprietary colony in America enjoyed. And Mather was allowed to nominate the first Royal Governor

1. *C. S. M.*, xvi. 828.
2. Murdock, *op. cit.*, p. 215.

(Sir William Phips), Lieutenant-Governor (William Stoughton, A.B. 1650), and Council.

Nor did Increase Mather forget his academic office. He received some of the Pennoyer rents—although he was later unable to remember how much; [1] and he cultivated the friendship of Robert Thorner, a wealthy dissenter of Baddesley, Southampton, who had known Increase's brother Nathaniel many years before, and formed the intention of leaving a legacy to Harvard College. 'Deare Sir, I shall not forgett that Nursery of Lerning and piety, upon which God, I hope, haue set my harte for meny yeeres past,' he wrote Mather early in 1689.[2] Mr. Thorner was as good as his word. By his will £500 was bequeathed 'unto Harvard College in New-England whereof Mr Increase Mather is now President,' [3] after the expiration of certain specified leases. Mr. Thorner died in 1690, and although the legacy was not wholly paid until 1775, the donor's nephew and executor Thomas Hollis, who also met Mather in England, had in the meantime outdone all our English benefactors.

Two legacies or donations of £100 and £50 respectively,[4] from Nathaniel Hulton, with whom Increase Mather stayed on his first arrival in London, and from Thomas Gunston of Newington Green, where he preached, were given to him personally, for the College. The income from the Hulton bequest, £6, was used during Mather's lifetime and after to supply exhibitions for his grandson and other young kinsmen.[5]

President Mather also obtained a bequest for Indian education at Harvard from the Honorable Robert Boyle,[6] who as

1. See above, p. 385.

2. 4 *Coll. M. H. S.*, VIII. 678. In his diary Mather mentions Thorner's showing him his will on Sept. 13, 1688.

3. H. F. Waters, *Gen. Gleanings*, I. 478. Cf. K. B. Murdock, *op. cit.*, pp. 276–79; Quincy, I. 185–86. Thorner had undoubtedly decided to leave Harvard a legacy before he met Mather; but the President, by making a good impression on Hollis, may have helped to bring later donations from that quarter.

4. £130 and £65 in New England currency. *C. S. M.*, XVI. 415.

5. *Id.* index under Hulton, especially pp. 438, 446–47, 514; Waters, *op. cit.*, I. 509. The Gunston bequest seems to have been swallowed up by current expenses. Mather preached at Newington Green on December 27, 1691, and on the 31st 'visited [*undecipherable*] to sollicit for the Colledge in N. E.' Ms. Diary, M. H. S.

6. 'The donation was obtained by my meanes' — Mather to President Leverett, November 6, 1710, in collection of the Hon. Leverett Saltonstall. It is not clear whether Mather refers to the clause in Boyle's will, or to the subsequent allotment of £45 annually to Harvard.

Governor of the New England Company had long been interested in that interrupted aspect of the college work.[1] Dying in 1691, the noted philosopher created by his will a fund of £400 to be employed as a stock for the relief of poor Indian converts.[2] At that time the energetic Dr. James Blair was seeking funds and interest for the Virginia institution which received a royal charter in 1693 as the College of William and Mary. He persuaded Boyle's executors to invest the £400 and more in the manor of Brafferton in Yorkshire; and, after allotting £45 from the annual rents to the New England Company for the salaries of two Indian missionaries, and £45 more to the President and Fellows of Harvard College, 'to be by them Employed and bestowed for the Salary of two other Ministers, to teach the Natives, in or near His Majesties Colonies there, in the Christian Religion,' [3] to give William and Mary the balance for educating Virginia Indians. It required much time and trouble before Harvard could persuade the New England Company to pay the £45 due. Nothing was received until 1712, when elaborate regulations were drawn up by the College Corporation in order to insure that the scholars who had the benefit of it would learn the Indian language and go into the local mission field.[4] But the same blight settled on this as on all other attempts at Indian education in New England. The first payment on account of the Hon. Robert Boyle's legacy provided a scholarship for Benjamin Larnel (Class of 1716), the last Indian to enter Harvard in the colonial period, and the next payment was for Benjamin Larnel's funeral. A scholarship was granted to Calvin Galpine (A.B. 1715), who declined to do what he had promised after graduating, when his father was requested to refund the money. Oliver Peabody (A.B. 1721), the next recipient, actually fulfilled his promise, and for many years ministered to the dwindling remnant of the Apostle Eliot's praying Indian town at Natick.[5]

1. See above, Chapter XVII.
2. Thomas Birch, *Life of Robert Boyle* (London, 1744), p. 339.
3. Transcript of Sir W. Ashurst's letter, in *C. S. M.*, xv. 386; Increase Mather's ms. Diary, A. A. S., March 3, 1698.
4. *C. S. M.*, xv. 393–94, 400–01.
5. *C. S. M.*, xvi. 401, 407, 423, 577–80, and index under Boyle and Peabody; H. U. Archives 1.20.720. The connection of William and Mary College with the Boyle bequest gave rise to the cock-and-bull story (printed in Rutherfoord Goodwin, *Brief History of and Guide to Williamsburg*, ed. 1930, p. 15) that the Virginia college

At one time, Mather hoped to obtain a royal charter for Harvard College. Elisha Hutchinson and Samuel Nowell (A.B. 1653), who were then in London, joined with him in petitioning the King for 'Liberty of Conscience and Property' for New England and 'a Charter for their Colledge confirming the Government of that Society in such hands as layed the Foundation thereof, they taking Care that Persons of all Parswasions relating to Religion, that may desire to be admitted among them, shall be instructed in Academicall Learning.'[1] Their Majesties proclaimed liberty of conscience gladly; but Mather was advised by 'some great Ministers of State' with whom he discussed the question of a college charter 'that a better way would be for the General Court of Massachusetts Bay to Incorporate their Colledge; and to make it an University, with as ample privileges as they should think necessary; and then transmit that Act of the General Court to England, for the Royal Approbation, which would undoubtedly be obtained.'[2] By that method there was more likelihood of the College's obtaining such a charter as she wished than by direct application to the Crown. In his last interview with William III, on January 3, 1692, President Mather said:

'There is one thing which I would humbly put your Majesty in mind of. Wee have in New England an Academy, a Colledge. Many an excellent protestant divine has had his education there.' The king sayd, 'I know it.' I thereupon added, 'If your Majesty will cast a

---

helped to support 'the infant College of Harvard in Massachusetts.' An earlier version will be found in Charles F. Thwing, *History of Higher Education in America* (1906), p. 55. No payments to Harvard on account of the Boyle or any other bequest came from Virginia. A correct, brief account of the Boyle bequest as respects William and Mary College will be found in Lyon G. Tyler, *Williamsburg, the Old Colonial Capital* (1907), p. 119; and Mr. Goodwin has graciously corrected his statement, to which I advert only because I have had so many inquiries about it. Harvard College received no Boyle money after the Revolution. The fund from which the College still pays the salary of the minister to the Indian church at Mashpee on Cape Cod is not the Boyle, but a very similar fund created from unexpended balances of an annuity left to the College by the Rev. Dr. Daniel Williams of London in 1716, for 'the blessed work of converting the poor Indians.' *C. S. M.*, xvi. 840, and see index.

1. *Proc. M. H. S.*, xii. 112. Note that even at this period, when puritanism appeared to be slipping, Mather did not purpose to confine the benefits of a Harvard education to a single sect, as Oxford and Cambridge had been forced to do by the Test Acts.

2. Mather's *Brief Account Concerning Several of the Agents*, in *Andros Tracts*, ii. 295-96. Cf. iii. 138, 142.

favorable aspect on that society, it will flourish more than ever.' The kings return to me was, 'I shall willingly do it.' [1]

Shortly after, His Majesty's favorable aspect was cast toward a new college in Virginia named for him and his consort, and organized on principles more to his liking. But Mather did at least get a clause into the Province Charter of Massachusetts Bay, confirming the titles of all grants and donations formerly made to 'Colledges' and 'Schooles of Learning.' [2]

Rector Mather had acquitted himself well on his foreign mission, and honored his alma mater. Without sacrificing his dignity, or compromising principles, he had cultivated all sorts of people, from peers and court ladies to the humblest dissenters, who might be of some assistance to his cause and to the institutions he represented. He had proved himself an ecclesiastical statesman, a Yankee Mazarin. It is no wonder that churches and College, on his return to Boston in May 1692, competed for his undivided attention, or that the most they could offer seemed uninteresting after a four years' residence in the capital of the Empire.

NOTE ON THE MAP FACING THIS PAGE

This is a section of the *Carte de la Ville, Baye, et Environs de Baston, par J. B. L. Franquelin, hydrographe du Roi, 1693. Verifée par le S[ieu]r de la Motte.*[3] From internal evidence, this map seems to have been made in 1688 or early in 1689, in anticipation of King William's War. Is the large building with wings at Cambridge meant for the Old College, abandoned but not yet in ruins, and the one with the belfry meant for Old Harvard; or are they merely conventional representations of college buildings?

The key reads as follows: A. Le Fort d'Andros (Fort Hill); B. Temple du Sud, Presbyteriens (Old South Meeting); C. Renegats Français (Boston Latin School, where the French Huguenots met); D. Temple de Calvinistes (King's Chapel — but why Calvinist?); E. Grand Temple Presbyterien (Meetinghouse of First Church); F. Maison de Ville (Town House); G. Batterie de Canons; H. Petit Temple d'Anabaptistes (First Baptist Church); I. Pont Fixe; L. Pont Levis; M. Petit Temple des Coäcres (Quaker Meeting); N. Temple du Nord, Presbyteriens (Second Church); O. Maison de Guillaume Phips; P. Deux Moulins; Q. Trois Moulins; R. Reservoir d'Eau pour les Moulins (Mill-pond); S. Place D'Armes (Training Field); T. Le Phare (on Beacon Hill); a. Deux Moulins à Charleston; b. Maison de Ville (Town House); c. Le Temple (First Church in Charlestown); d. Embarquement (Ferry Landing); e. Drydock ou Havre Sec pour la Batisse de Vaisseaux; f. Batterie de 11 Pieces de Canon.

1. Ms. Autobiography, Jan. 3, 1691/92.   2. *C. S. M.*, II. 17.
3. Original in Dépôt des Cartes de la Marine, Paris; this is from a tracing made in 1879 for the B. P. L., which has reproduced the entire map in heliotype. Cf. I. N. Phelps Stokes, *The Iconography of Manhattan* (1915), pp. 233-34.

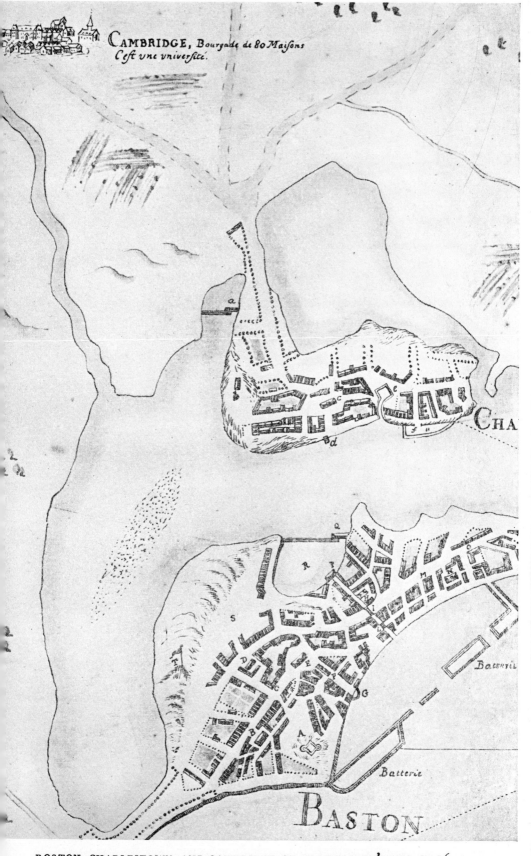

CAMBRIDGE, Bourgade de 80 Maisons
C'est une université.

CHA

BASTON

Batterie

Batterie

BOSTON, CHARLESTOWN, AND CAMBRIDGE ON FRANQUELIN'S MAP OF 1693

XXIII

CHANGING CHARTERS AND MATHERIAN MANOEUVRES
1692–1701

CHARTER OF 1692

Just before candlelight on Saturday the fourteenth of May, 1692, Increase Mather and Governor Sir William Phips disembarked from the *Nonsuch* frigate at Long Wharf, Boston. In the sabbath hush of a Lord's Day eve there were no cheers or cannon salutes to greet the returning heroes; but eight companies of foot turned out to escort His Excellency home, and after leaving him at his brick mansion near the Charlestown ferry, they 'waited on' Mr. Mather to his modest parsonage on Middle Street. On Monday the sixteenth Sir William was inaugurated Captain-General and Governor-in-Chief in and over Their Majesties' Province of the Massachusetts Bay in New England, Increase Mather standing by. Lieutenant-Governor William Stoughton and several of the new Council, all of whom owed their seats to Mather's nomination, were Harvard graduates. The omens seemed favorable for a new era of friendly coöperation between State, Church, and College.

Increase Mather, who had acquired a keen sense for political atmosphere, struck quickly for what he wanted. A process which contemporaries called 'rebuilding the hedge'[1] began with the passage of laws through the General Court reëstablishing the Congregational churches, local government, and the school system.

A large and important gap in the puritan hedge was apparently filled on June 27, 1692, when an 'Act for Incorporateing of Harvard Colledge at Cambridge in New-England' passed both houses, and received the signature of Governor Sir William Phips.[2] This Charter of 1692 was little more than the Charter

---

1. *N. E. Q.,* I. 533.
2. Printed in Appendix E, below.

of 1650 redrafted with reference to the times and to President Mather's wishes. His guiding principles in the several college charters that passed the legislature during this decade were independence of government and dependence on the orthodox puritans, or Congregationalists, as we may now begin to call them. If the Board of Overseers as organized in 1642 had been reëstablished, substituting Their Majesties' Councillors for the old Bay Colony magistracy, a few Anglicans or even Baptists might obtain ex officio seats. Hence, in the Charter of 1692, the functions of both Governing Boards are combined in a single corporation of President, Treasurer, and eight Fellows. Increase Mather and John Richards were named to the first two offices; and the fellows, doubtless selected by Mather, were James Allen (B.A. Oxford 1652) of the First Church in Boston; Samuel Willard (A.B. 1659) of the Third (Old South) Church, Boston; Nehemiah Hobart (A.B. 1667) of Newton Church; Nathaniel Gookin (A.B. 1675) of Cambridge Church; Cotton Mather (A.B. 1678) of the Second Church in Boston; John Leverett and William Brattle (A.B. 1680), the two experienced tutors; and Nehemiah Walter (A.B. 1684) of Roxbury Church, the President's son-in-law [1] — altogether a very close and clerical corporation.

Acts of the provincial legislature, such as this college charter, went into effect as soon as approved by the Royal Governor; but they might be disallowed at any subsequent date by the King in Council. Accordingly the new Corporation created by this act met on July 26, 1692, hoping that their Majesties would be graciously pleased to let the new Charter stand.

University Gestures

Although the Charter of 1692 calls Harvard a 'Colledge or Academy,' it was President Mather's intention to give Harvard full university status, without further delay. The Charter of 1650 had said nothing about granting degrees, which is a university rather than a collegiate function; but the Charter of 1692 declares:

---

1. Hobart declined to serve, and at the first meeting of the new Corporation the Reverend Charles Morton (M.A. Oxford 1652) was elected to fill the vacancy. Gookin died after attending one meeting, but his place does not appear to have been filled. Mr. Matthews' Tables of Attendance, C. S. M., xv. p. cxlix.

And whereas it is a laudable Custome in Universities whereby Learning has been Encouraged and Advanced to confer Academical Degrees or Titles on those who by their Proficiency as to Knowledge in Theology, Law, Physick, Mathematicks or Philosophy have been Iudged Worthy thereof. . . . the President and Fellowes of the said Colledge shall have power from time to time, to grant and admit to Academical Degrees, as in the Universities in England, such as in respect of Learning and Good Manners, they shall find worthy to be promoted thereunto.[1]

At the second meeting of the new Corporation, on September 5, it was voted

That the Reverend President be desired to accept Gradum Doctoratus in Theologiâ, and that A Diploma be drawn up by the Corporation and Presented to him.

2. That Mr John Leverett and Mr William Brattle be by the President admitted ad gradum Baccalaureatus in Theologiâ, they first making each of them A Sermon in Latin in the Colledge Hall, and Responding to A Theologicall Question.[2]

These were not honorary degrees, although listed as such in the Quinquennial Catalogue; nor were they empty gestures of academic pride.[3] The new Mather code of College Laws, adopted in 1692, followed out the charter provision respecting 'Academical Degrees as in the Universities in England' by adopting regulations for obtaining the Baccalaureate and Doctorate in Divinity or Theology.[4] For until Harvard granted degrees in at least one of the higher faculties of Law, Medicine, or Theology, she could not, by any definition of university known to the learned world, claim university status.[5] It was

---

1. Appendix E, below.   2. *C. S. M.*, xv. 340.

3. An honorary degree or *gradum honoris causa*, according to ancient usage, is one granted to persons whom the University wishes to honor, or whose incorporation in the University is deemed an honor to the institution. A degree conferred by special vote on persons who have followed the equivalent studies elsewhere, or otherwise qualified themselves for that particular degree, is not an honorary degree; nor is an *ad eundem* degree, which is simply an inter-university courtesy, relic of the ancient *ius ubique docendi*. These distinctions, which are still observed at Oxford and Cambridge, were lost sight of at Harvard in the eighteenth century. For instance, in 1765 the Corporation voted that four men, at least three of whom were incorporations from Yale, 'be admitted to honorary second degrees . . . this year.' The first honorary degree in the European sense conferred by Harvard was Benjamin Franklin's M.A. in 1753.

4. *Magnalia*, book iv. 133–34, nos. 19, 20, 21; also printed in *C. S. M.*, xxxi. 344–46.

5. See *F. H. C.*, p. 6; and dedications of quaestiones after 1692 in Appendix B.

now made possible at Harvard, as at Oxford and Cambridge, for a Master of Arts to proceed Bachelor of Divinity (S.T.B.) after waiting five years, engaging in two disputations and delivering two orations *vel in Templo vel in Aula Academiae*. And after another quinquennium had elapsed, the Bachelor, by performing another 'Act' and publishing a tract 'against Heresy or some current error, or on some useful topic assigned by the President and Fellows for the profit of the community of Churches,' might proceed Doctor of Divinity (S.T.D.). Now, as the Oxonian James Allen may have reminded his fellows, it was an immemorial academic principle that only a doctor could create a doctor, and only a member of a theological faculty could confer a theological degree. Hence, if Harvard was to grant divinity degrees in proper form, there must be a nucleus of grantors. As Increase Mather had not been laureated doctor in England,[1] it was necessary to make him one. The text of his diploma, which Cotton Mather piously preserved, proves that the degree was not granted to him *honoris causa*, but because of his many books, which proved him to be highly versed 'not only in the Tongues and Liberal Arts, but in the Holy Scriptures and Theology,' and 'because he had rendered himself for his Learning and Merits, the object of highest commendation, not only among the American, but among the European Churches.'[2]

After Increase Mather had become an almost self-created Doctor of Divinity, he was able to admit Leverett and Brattle as Bachelors of Divinity; but they had to perform an 'Act' first, so there can be no question of their degrees being anything but degrees in course.

After all these preparations, as Cotton Mather sadly remarks, Harvard found no more takers for the new degrees. 'Partly from the *Novelty* of the Matter it self . . . and partly from the *Modesty* of the Persons most worthy to have this Respect put upon them, there was yet never made among us any of these *Promotions*. . . . But I see not, why such Marks of Honour may not be properly given by an *American* University.'[3] Not until 1771 did Harvard grant another doctorate;

1. As a dissenter he was ineligible for a Divinity degree at Oxford or Cambridge.
2. *Magnalia*, book iv. 134.
3. *Ibid*. This is one of the earliest uses of 'American' in the English colonies, a word of which Cotton Mather was fond.

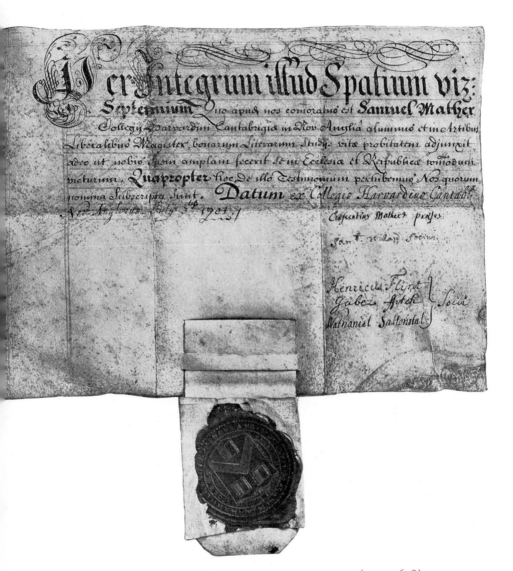

MASTER OF ARTS DIPLOMA ISSUED TO SAMUEL MATHER (A.B. 1698) IN 1701

With an Impression of the Seal of 1693

THE CHRISTO ET ECCLESIÆ SEAL

not until 1870 were degrees in Theology granted as the result of study and examination.

Another university gesture was made in designing the new Harvard seal. The Charter of 1692 authorized the President and Fellows to 'have forever one Common Seale to be used in all causes and occasions of the said Corporation, and the same Seale may alter, change, breake and new make from time to time at their Pleasure.' Accordingly in 1693 a new die was designed and sunk by John Coney the Boston silversmith, at a cost of £2 2s 6d.[1] This was the third seal used by Harvard College.[2] The shield, nicked and eared, contains a chevron separating three open books with blank leaves. On the outer border is the inscription SIGILLVM: ACADEMIÆ: HARVARDINÆ: IN: NOV: ANG: and between the shield and the border is the motto CHRISTO ET ECCLESIÆ.

This motto of the University of Franeker very likely was suggested by the use of it in William Ames' *Disceptatio Scholastica*.[3] President Mather did not discard *Veritas*, for unless he looked into College Book I, he had no reason to suppose that it had ever been adopted. Nor did *Christo et Ecclesiæ* portend any change of policy. It was appropriate in an era of declining religious interest to emphasize the dynamic motive in founding Harvard College, to provide learned ministers for the Church of Christ in New England and elsewhere.

Coney's handsome seal appears to have made the College heraldically-minded. Henry Newman (A.B. 1687), who at that time was making voyages as supercargo between Boston, Barbados, and Spain, proposed in 1694 to have the college arms carved in stone at Bilbao, to adorn Old Harvard Hall. The Treasurer paid him £5 'to procure the Colledg arms to be cut in Freestone or in marble.' But for some unexplained reason, Newman invested the sum at Barbados in a parcel of cane-joints for walking-sticks. Most of them, the College Treasurer notes, 'being short, scabby, and of no Substance,'

---

1. Treasurer Richards' Records, quoted in *Proc. M. H. S.*, VI. 341.

2. For the first, or Overseers' Seal of 1643, see *F. H. C.*, pp. 328–29; for the second, or *In Christi Gloriam* seal of 1650, see above Chapter I; for Coney's, and the seals of 1843 and 1885, see S. E. Morison, 'Harvard Seals and Arms,' *Harvard Graduates' Magazine*, XLII (1933). 1–15. A sixth seal, designed by Pierre la Rose (A.B. 1895), was adopted by the Corporation on May 20, 1935, and used for the first time on diplomas at the following Commencement.

3. *F. H. C.*, pp. 330–32.

had to be sold at half price; and as the result of Newman's 'adventure' the College barely recovered her £5 and obtained no achievement of arms.

WITCHCRAFT

Although the Salem witchcraft frenzy of 1692 was in full swing at the time when Harvard was receiving her new charter and making a plea for university status, it affected the life and history of the College no more than does a great strike or 'crime-wave' of the present century. Nevertheless we cannot pass over in silence an event that shook the whole community, and in which so many prominent Harvardians were involved. It is typical of the place of the College in our history that the chief justice and prosecutor of the witch trials (William Stoughton, A.B. 1650), the judge who left the bench rather than stain his hands with innocent blood (Nathaniel Saltonstall, A.B. 1659), and the judge who openly confessed the wrong that he had done (Samuel Sewall), one of the twenty victims (George Burroughs, A.B. 1670), the most active minister among the witch-hunters (John Hale, A.B. 1657), the minister who braved mob fury in helping some of the accused to escape (Joshua Moody, A.B. 1653), the two men who did most to bring the prosecutions to an end (President Mather and Thomas Brattle), the minister who initiated the movement for indemnity to the victims' families (Michael Wigglesworth), and the young minister who restored peace to the distracted Salem Village (Joseph Green, A.B. 1695); all were Harvard graduates.

The notions on witchcraft prevalent in New England in 1692 differed not from those of educated men in England at that day and generation. Nobody doubted its existence; everyone believed that people could confederate with the devil, and in so doing justly incurred the penalty of death. Since the appearance of Professor Kittredge's work, it is not necessary to argue that a man of learning, cognizant of the new experimental philosophy, could take this attitude honestly, and (so far as he himself could judge) consistently. Witchcraft was a phenomenon, like the phenomena of motion, heat, and light, which should not be ignored, but must be faced and investigated.

The evidence of its existence was quite as strong, so far as men of that time could judge, as the evidence for planetary motion, or the molecular structure of matter; much stronger than the evidence for spiritualism, in which so many well-educated people have faith today. It is difficult, with our modern pre-possessions, to avoid the feeling that men like President Mather, who had just returned from England, and Charles Morton and William Stoughton, who had been residents at Oxford in the days of Wilkins, Wallis, Hooke, and Wren, should have quenched the superstitious zeal of their New England brethren with the cold water of scientific scepticism. Actually, the converse is true. Robert Boyle, and doubtless most of the English men of science who founded the Royal Society, believed in witchcraft; and the man responsible for the revival in witch-craft literature near the end of the century was a Fellow of the Royal Society, Joseph Glanvil, who was known as a sceptic in respect of all science not tested by experiment and observation. Glanvil's *Sadducismus Triumphatus* (1681) 'was thought to have put the belief in apparitions and witchcraft on an un-shakable basis of science and philosophy.'[1] Indeed it was the people who composed what one might call the Harvard scien-tific group of that day — Morton, Willard, Stoughton, and the Mathers — who took the keenest interest in witchcraft. If the Boston and Salem clergy had been more old-fashioned, and less curious respecting phenomena, we might never have had the hangings of 1692. The fatal expansion of a neighborhood quarrel into a popular panic occurred when the 'afflicted' girls of Salem Village discovered that their antics obtained attention and publicity from the leading intellectuals of the Province.[2]

The prelude to the Salem frenzy was the Goodwin witchcraft case in Boston, in 1688. Charles Morton, James Allen, Joshua Moody, Samuel Willard, and Cotton Mather undertook to cure the 'afflicted' children by fasting and prayer; and the first four signed the preface to Cotton Mather's *Memorable Providences relating to Witchcrafts and Possessions*, describing the Goodwin case and others, which was printed at Boston in 1689.[3] We

---

1. G. L. Kittredge, *Witchcraft in Old and New England*, pp. 335–36.
2. See Edward Wyllys Taylor, *Some Medical Aspects of Witchcraft* (the nearest to a rational explanation of the frenzy that we have), and Upham, *Salem Witchcraft with an account of Salem Village* (1867), II. 112.
3. 4 *Coll. M. H. S.*, VIII. 367–68; *Magnalia* (1702 ed.), book VI. pp. 71, 74, 75; G. L. Burr, *Narratives of the Witchcraft Cases* (1914), p. 97. Willard had already

have already seen the effect of this tract on the Harvard theses
physicae of that year. No causal connection between Cotton
Mather's publication and the outbreak of 1692 can be proved,
but there is reason to suspect that Ann Putnam and the other
young exhibitionists of Salem Village had heard the Goodwin
case talked about, and that the Reverend Samuel Parris,[1]
whose bungling contributed greatly to the spread of the disease, supposed that he was playing the rôle of exorcist so
successfully assumed by the ministers of Boston and Charlestown. By the middle of May, when Increase Mather and
Governor Phips arrived, neighborhood scandal had already
become a provincial tragedy. It was one of those moments
(becoming more rather than less frequent in recent history)
when a madness runs through the people, infecting all ranks
and classes; when civilized raiment is stripped off and man lies
revealed in his naked depravity. At such moments, it takes
unusual courage and superior wisdom to stand up for justice
or simple decency; and unfortunately the higher degrees of
these qualities are seldom found in the same man, even in a
President of Harvard College.

On August 1, 1692, after six women had been hanged as
witches at Salem, the Cambridge Ministerial Association, of
which President Mather was a prominent member, met in the
library of Old Harvard Hall and debated the question of 'spec-
tral evidence,' the use of which had been largely instrumental
in these judicial murders. They agreed that no court should con-
demn a person to death on the basis of such evidence alone. In
their opinion the devil could so possess one of his victims as to
accuse a totally innocent person of being a witch;[2] yet it was
persons so accused who had been executed. Quick action to
impress that doctrine on the Salem court would have saved
fourteen lives and untold suffering, but the mob, whipped up
by Stoughton's judicial brutality, was howling for more blood,
and even ministers had to watch their steps very carefully in
order not to find themselves treading the path that ended on
Gallows Hill.

---

successfully handled the case of an 'afflicted' girl at Groton a few years before by this
method. *Memorable Providences* was reprinted at London with a preface by Richard
Baxter in 1691, and at Edinburgh in 1697.
    1. Parris was not a Harvard graduate, but may have attended the College around
1672–74, when we have no record of students who failed to take a degree.
    2. *Proc. M. H. S.*, xvii. 268.

As a result of the ministerial meeting of August 1, Increase Mather composed his *Cases of Conscience concerning Evil Spirits*. It was read in manuscript and endorsed by the Ministerial Association on October 3, promptly laid before Governor Phips, and printed before the end of the year. This tract had a strong if not decisive influence in inducing the muddle-headed Governor to stay the proceedings, release the fifty or more persons then in jail (seven of them already condemned to die), and reprieve the three whom Stoughton tried to rush to the gallows. After this new lead had been given to public opinion by the ministers and by intelligent laymen like Thomas Brattle, the frenzy, which if unchecked might well have numbered its victims by the hundreds, subsided.[1] Nor did President Mather consider his responsibility at an end until he had visited in prison some of the persons who under terror had confessed witchcraft, and obtained recantation from eight of them.

A curious aftermath of the witchcraft trials is said to have been the ceremonial burning in the Harvard Yard, at President Mather's orders, of Robert Calef's *More Wonders of the Invisible World*, a virulent attack on Cotton Mather's share in the tragedy. If this book-burning actually took place, it was the unique instance of that nature in Harvard history; but the earliest date to which we can trace the story is 1809.[2] Of course this does not necessarily discredit the tale. Official book-burnings were common in Europe, and the Mathers doubtless knew that in 1692 Anthony Wood's *Athenae Oxonienses* had been publicly burned at Oxford for an alleged libel on a defunct chancellor of the University. The same method of dealing

---

1. See T. J. Holmes's able discussion of Increase Mather's *Cases of Conscience concerning Witchcrafts*, in his *Increase Mather Bibliography*, 1. 115–38. Thomas Brattle's Letter to a minister in Connecticut, which was probably circulated in ms. copies, is printed in G. L. Burr, *op. cit.*, pp. 169–90. Note especially his remarks on p. 171 respecting the misunderstood Cartesian philosophy by which the judges defended some of their idiotic 'tests.' There is no ground for the distinction that some modern writers have drawn between the respective attitudes of Mather and Brattle toward the Salem outbreak. Brattle in fact mentions Mather (p. 180) as one of those who saw eye to eye with him. Cotton Mather is more blameworthy, both for his reluctance to speak out when he knew that things were going wrong (*Diary*, 1. 150–51) and for urging the execution of George Burroughs (A.B. 1670), condemned largely on the basis of phenomenal feats of strength. But he made partial reparation by treating and curing the two Boston wenches who attempted to start a witch-hunt in the capital.

2. John Eliot, *Biographical Dictionary* (Boston, 1809), p. 95. Calef's book arrived in Boston in November 1700, when Increase Mather was still President.

with the slanderous 'Calf book' would naturally have suggested itself to Matherian megalomania.[1]

INCREASE MATHER

It would probably have been better for the College if some other person had been named President in the Charter of 1692. For Mather not only refused to reside in Cambridge and give his entire attention to the College; he was a storm-centre in provincial politics, and this naturally involved the College. Mather's diplomatic finesse seemed to slip away at the water's edge. In England he was willing to compromise and even intrigue to obtain what he wanted; but in Boston he was accustomed to giving orders, and it was too late for even a distinguished cleric to dictate to politicians. Mather had been allowed by the Crown to choose the first Governor's Council named in the Royal Charter. A statesman would have made up the slate in such a way as to placate and win over opponents. Mather not only passed over his colleagues in the agency, Elisha Cooke and Thomas Oakes, who had opposed him in London, but left out all the members of the old House of Assistants who were known to be in favor of Cooke's absurd policy of 'the Old Charter, or none.' These included several important people, such as Thomas Danforth, who had served the College long and well, and William Browne, a wealthy Salem merchant who was one of the college benefactors.[2] Cooke, the cleverest and most unscrupulous politician in the Province, was not one to take it lying down. He circulated the story that Massachusetts could have had her Old Charter restored, but for Mather's desire to control the Province through a puppet Royal Governor; and when elected to the lower House so stirred up his fellow representatives against the President of Harvard 'that they'll allow him no sallary at the Colledge unlesse to be resident and desire and advice that another be chosen.'[3] On Febru-

1. Cf. G. Peignot, *Dictionnaire des principaux livres condamnes au feu* (Paris, 1806), pp. 185 ff., for list of Voltaire's works burned, and C. R. Gillett, *Burned Books* (New York, 1932), esp. p. 591 for the burning of J. A. Froude's *Nemesis of Faith* in an Oxford college in 1849. One of Increase Mather's own works, together with tracts by Benjamin Colman, Joseph Sewall, and Charles Chauncy, was publicly burnt on the town wharf at New London on March 6, 1743, at the instigation of the Rev. James Davenport (A.B. Yale 1732). *Boston Evening Post*, April 11, 1743.

2. K. B. Murdock, *Increase Mather*, p. 252.

3. Letter from a Bostonian to the Lords of Trade, March 23, 1692/93. P. R. O., C. O. 5/857, no. 41; *Calendar State Papers, America and West Indies, 1693-1696*, p. 63.

ary 16, 1693, the House of Representatives voted Mather a salary of £100 with the proviso that 'it is desired for the Future that the Presidents Shall be Resident at the Colledge.' Mather's hand-picked Council declined to act on this resolve, but initiated another bill for £100 salary without the rider. The House came back in November with a vote 'that the President of Harvard Colledge for the time being shall Reside there as hath bin accustomed in times past.' Finally, in October 1694, the House voted £50 to Mather, not as President, but as a gratuity

for his paines and Labour he hath taken the Last year at the Colledge in the absence of a setled president there ... and That he be Requested to setle there or Els be serviceable as formerly untill the Corporation or this Court shall agree with some person that they shall call to setle there who will attend said Work.

The Governor and Council concurred in the grant, but not in the innuendo; and in January 1695 Mather was paid his first salary, a pitiful £50 in lawful money of New England.[1]

The demand that Mather either reside at Cambridge or quit the presidential office was perfectly reasonable; but he had no intention of doing either. He was conscientious in making frequent visits to Cambridge;[2] and the Corporation provided him with a new horse at the cost of £10, paid for its board and shoeing at Charlestown at the cost of about 6s 8d a week, and voted £3 12s for a new saddle and bridle, in the hope that he would be tempted to visit Cambridge more often.[3] Mather doubtless believed that he could serve the College just as well by 'commuting' as by residence, for he was curiously blind to the social aspects of academic life. He set no value whatever on that 'collegiate way of living' for which the founders of

1. These documents are printed in *Acts and Resolves of the Province*, VII. 452–53.

2. According to his diary for 1693–94, Mather either 'visited the Colledge' or attended a ministers' meeting at Cambridge or preached there on March 29; April 2, 3, 7, 14, 18, 19, 26; May 5, 7, 8, 17, 24, 28; June 7, 11, 12, 19, 23, 28; July 4, 5 (Commencement), 7, 10; August 2, 9, 14, 20, 23, 30; September 3, 4, 6, 13, 17, 20, 29; October 1, 2, 4, 11, 15, 25, 29; November 6, 12, 22; December 3, 6, 12; January 3, 7, 10, 16, 21; February 4, 27; March 4, 5, 18. This was doing well for a busy minister and author, fifty-four years old. In subsequent years, his visits to Cambridge were less frequent; but, except in the dead of winter or the summer vacation, he seldom let a fortnight pass without a visit.

3. Treasurer Richards' accounts, H. U. Archives, fols. 14 (verso), 15, 59 (verso), 60 (verso), *et passim*.

Harvard had made such great sacrifices, through which the scholars obtained a social education in addition to book learning, and to which (having come full circle) American and European universities are now paying homage in the establishment of new 'houses,' 'residential units,' and *cités universitaires*. As an undergraduate, Mather had lived less than a year at Cambridge;[1] at Dublin he lodged with his brother instead of in Trinity College, where he took his second degree; his son Cotton's social experience at Harvard had been unhappy. When asked for advice by the organizers of the Collegiate School in Connecticut, Increase Mather pointed to the example of the Continental universities, where the students 'do not live a Collegiate life, but board in the Town'; he denounced Harvard Commencements as 'very expensive' and 'occasion of much sin,' stating (quite falsely) that the English universities had no such 'publick Acts'; he advised the gentlemen who were eager for university learning in Connecticut simply to hire a 'Large room,' engage a 'President and two or 3 Tutors' — and there's your college![2] Fortunately the founders of Yale rejected this pallid plan, as had the founders of Harvard over sixty years earlier.[3]

Mather was a curious compound of ambition, emotion, and cold intellect. He professed to be actuated solely by a desire to serve God; yet he could not see that to take active charge of the only college in New England would be a far more effective way to preserve those principles that the puritans believed to be the most perfect expressions of God's will, than to serve the largest and richest church in Boston. His excuse, repeated *ad nauseam* whenever it was proposed that he move to Cambridge and properly perform his presidential duties, was the refusal of his church to release him. The Old North was deeply devoted to Dr. Mather; but his assumed obligation to serve

1. Autobiography, and *C. S. M.*, xxxi. 139–40. The rest of the four years he studied with John Norton at Ipswich and Boston, returning to Cambridge only to take his degree.

2. Franklin B. Dexter, *Documentary History of Yale* (1916), pp. 6–7. The similar but anonymous advice from Boston, *ibid*. pp. 1–6, is I think from Cotton Mather; compare the first two paragraphs under heading vi with his remarks on the University of Upsala in *Magnalia*, book iv. 126, which had been written but not printed when the letter was sent.

3. Precisely the same advice had been sent by Emmanuel Downing to Governor Winthrop when Harvard College was being planned (*F. H. C.*, pp. 171–72, 251–52), and flatly rejected.

it until death would have been brushed aside very lightly if the call for which he was hoping and praying had come from England.

Increase Mather had passed in the British Isles the most impressionable period of his young manhood; and Boston seemed very flat after four brilliant years in London. He who had had 'Access to 3 crowned heads, and a frequent conversation with nobles, and other persons of Quality,' and preached 'the Gospell in many congregations in and near London'; [1] he who had enjoyed the lively and learned conversation of Englishmen like Sir John Maynard and Sir Henry Ashurst, and listened, with Dr. Bates, to the dying words of the great Richard Baxter,[2] was now doomed to live in a provincial town on the edge of the wilderness, where few people were his intellectual equals. Within a few months of his return, Increase began to confide to his diary intuitions of a coming call to England; [3] 'A strange Impression' at prayer 'that I should yet have an opportunity to glorify God, and the Lord Jesus Christ in England.' [4] Every ship that entered Boston Harbor, Mather hoped and prayed would bring him a call to a dissenting chapel in the happy isle; and though God often spread that enticing vision before him, only to whisk it away, Mather never ceased to trust in God and hope for England. The good Lord whom he had served so long and faithfully would surely not let him down; would grant him one more taste of England before he died; would allow his poor body to be laid below green English sod, instead of under the mangy turf of Copps' Hill Burying Ground. Hence all his feverish activity in publication, in order that some dissenting congregation in the old country, wanting a parson, would read his books and declare with one voice, 'Our man is Dr. Mather.' Even if there were no call to a congregation, he must get to England somehow, as agent for the Colony or the College. This emotional nostalgia is the key that unlocks all Mather's intrigues and inconsistencies about college charters,

1. Ms. Diary, Aug. 22, 1696. A. A. S.

2. *Id*. Feb. 7, 1690/91, May 30, 1691. M. H. S.

3. Ms. Diaries, June 17, Aug. 12, Sept. 3, 9, Oct. 7, 29, Nov. 4, Dec. 30, 1693; Jan. 27, Feb. 24, March 13, 24, 1693/94; Jan. 19, 27 and March 3, 23, 1694/95; April 20, June 15, 29, July 13, 27, Aug. 4, 10, Oct. 5, Nov. 2, 7, 30, Dec. 6, 1695; Jan. 16, Feb. 22, March 21, 1695/96; April 9, 18, 19, 26, May 2, 9, 16, 24, June 13, 18, July 11, Aug. 8, 9, Sept. 5, 12, 13, Oct. 3, 11, 31, Nov. 21, 28, Dec. 11, 26, 1696; Jan. 23, Feb. 20, March 20, 1696/97; etc., etc.

4. Jan. 19, 1694/95.

procrastination and tergiversations about the Harvard presidency, for an entire decade.

It is transparently clear from the diaries that if the long-desired summons to England had come, Mather would hardly have waited to change clothes, much less allowed his church to keep him in Boston. In the meantime, preaching to a great urban congregation that adored him, advising in the intimate concerns of a thousand or more people, meeting the Philosophical Society, and dining out with His Excellency the Governor and His Honor the Lieutenant-Governor in that kindly provincial society depicted in Judge Sewall's diary, was several degrees better than being pocketed in Cambridge, preaching to boys, and keeping watch on the college servants.

It also needs explaining why Mather frequently offered to resign the presidency, why the Corporation always beseeched him to stay, and why he did remain President until forced out by the General Court in 1701. Mather enjoyed the prestige of the office. 'President of Harvard-Colledge at Cambridge in New-England' looked well on the title pages of those tracts with which he hoped to impress English dissenters. It served God to have a hand in training up, even if largely by absent treatment, the future ministers of New England. And he thoroughly enjoyed the showy aspects of the presidential office, such as moderating disputations and presiding at Commencement. He generally spent several days coaching the degree candidates and gave up all other engagements in preparation for the great academic festival. And although there is no positive evidence to be cited, it seems very probable that Increase Mather had very much at heart being succeeded in the presidency by his son Cotton. Certain it is that no notions of duty to the Old North (where for some years he had been his father's colleague) would have prevented Cotton from snapping at such an opportunity; for it was one of his major griefs that he was repeatedly passed over in the several presidential elections during his lifetime.

The same ambition of the junior Mather probably explains the consternation of the Harvard Corporation whenever the elder Mather proposed to resign. For the membership of the Corporation between 1692 and 1700 was such that the election of Cotton might have easily been managed — indeed, could hardly have been prevented. Those who disliked the father had no reason to desire a change to the son, and even a Mather partisan would have found service under the heir apparent a heavy cross. For Cotton Mather was a typical infant prodigy grown up, pedantic and conceited, meddlesome and tactless, unsympathetic to the aspirations of youth and intolerant of their failings. Cotton as President would have emptied Harvard College even faster than Leonard Hoar.[1] Leverett and Brattle were born the same year as he, and graduated two years later; they knew Cotton through and through. After all, Increase Mather let them pretty much alone; he was a dignified and effective presiding officer, and the best known clergyman of New England.

Increase Mather held the College so at arm's length that it is difficult to put one's finger on his influence upon the society. From one Commencement oration reported by his son we know that he commended the 'liberal mode of philosophizing' that was already traditional at Harvard. On the other hand, he introduced an illiberal method of study for the resident Bachelors who were intended for the Church. Under his predecessors, Harvard M.A. candidates studied Theology; Increase Mather wished them to study Calvinist Theology. 'I caused the masters of Art,' he boasts in his Autobiography, 'to begin disputations in Theological Questions, with a design to dispute down Arminianisme.'[2] Not that it did his cause any good in the end; for a strong minority at least of the students whom he thus caused to debate petty sectarian issues later went far along the road to that Arminianism which he fondly hoped to 'dispute down.'

Toward the scientific leaven that was working in Harvard College, Mather's influence was undoubtedly friendly and benevolent;[3] for the 'New Philosophy' was one of his major interests; and Charles Morton, author of the *Compendium Physicae*, was his friend. But it is too much to assert that the

1. Cotton, aged twenty-two, had no sooner been ordained his father's colleague, and thus become *ex officio* an Overseer of the College, than he proposed to suggest to the Rector 'many profitable Things. Especially, as to settling the Students in good Principles.' *Diary*, I. 105. His *Paterna* ms. (Chicago Historical Society) reveals that for several years previous Cotton had been taking pupils through university learning; conducting a private academy, as it were. Cf. *Diary*, I. 72.

2. Ms. Autobiography for 1692.

3. See end of Chapter XI, above. Mather probably brought over the second Harvard telescope in 1692. His diary in London mentions visiting an instrument-maker's shop.

public 'Proposals made by the President and Fellows of Harvard College' on March 5, 1693/94, the only corporate intellectual enterprise of Mather's presidency, showed a spirit of inquiry 'essentially scientific.'[1] If these 'Proposals,' directed to the ministers of New England, had stated for their object the collection of vital statistics and data on natural history, plants, animals, fishes, Indians, and meteorological phenomena, the results might well have been exceedingly valuable for scientists of that day, and for historians of science today; even without results, the attempt would have been praiseworthy. But instead, all that the Harvard Corporation called for was 'notable Occurents,' 'Unusual Accidents,' 'Mercies to the Godly,' 'Judgments on the Wicked,' and 'Glorious Fulfilments of either the Promises or the Threatnings, in the Scriptures of Truth' — the same sort of tall stories and old wives' tales that made up the bulk of Mather's 'Illustrious Providences' in 1684. Indeed, there is reason to suspect that the 'Proposals' were intended for no greater object than to provide Cotton Mather with material for his *Magnalia Christi Americana.* If so, he was disappointed. The New England parsons either cared no longer for such stuff, or were not yet questionnaire-conscious; for Cotton Mather complained that 'not half ten considerable histories' came in.

Leverett and Brattle

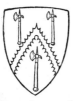
Beyond this, and his valiant efforts to abolish Commencement plum cake as stimulant to sin at that festive season,[2] it is difficult to find any positive achievement of Mr. Mather's on behalf of his alma mater. Such excellence as the College enjoyed between 1686 and 1697, and whatever progress it made, should rather be attributed to the two devoted tutors, John Leverett and William Brattle, who carried on the entire instruction during those twelve years, and governed the College as well during Mather's absence in England.[3] Each was born in Boston in 1662 and to a mercantile and magisterial family; they went through Latin School together, at Harvard

1. Murdock, *op. cit.*, p. 343. The 'Proposals' are printed in *Magnalia*, introduction to book vi.
2. See above, p. 470.
3. Note the headings to quaestiones, 1686-91, in Appendix B.

were classmates, and became tutors and fellows of the Corporation in 1685 and 1686, respectively. They were not only learned and pious, but young men of the world (such world as Boston afforded) with private means that enabled them to live comfortably in college and entertain guests suitably. Both remained bachelors during their teaching careers, and then married in the same month; both were elected Fellows of the Royal Society at the same meeting in 1713. A more talented, sympathetic, and devoted pair of tutors Harvard College has never had. Brattle endeared himself to the students by staying with them during the small-pox epidemic of 1690–91, and 'ministring both to their *souls* and *bodies*; for he was a skillful *Physician* to both.' He caught the disease himself, insisted on making one more round of his patients, 'and then chearfully went into his own *bed* to live or die as God should please,' but recovered, and became known as the 'Father of the College.' [1]

Impressive tributes to Leverett and Brattle are found in the letters of some of their pupils. Henry Newman (A.B. 1687), when Secretary of the Society for the Promotion of Christian Knowledge in London, was accused of corresponding only with Boston 'dissenters.' Indignantly he wrote to an English friend (March 29, 1714):

Two of my three Correspondents at Cambridge have made more Proselytes to the Church of England than any two men ever did that liv'd in America, nor am I asham'd to own that I am one of their Proselytes. These Gentlemen are Mr. Leveret the President of the College and Mr. Brattle the Minister of Cambridge who have had the Government of the College there in whole or in part for about thirty years past in which time 350 Gentlemen of that Country whose names I have by me have been educated under their Care. I could produce several Letters from these Gentlemen to prove their affection to the Church of England. . . . 'Tis above 25 years since I had the happiness to be Mr. Leverett's Pupil and then I can bear him and Mr. Brattle witness the only Tutors at that time in the College that they recomment to their Pupils the reading of Episcopal authors as the best books to form our minds in religious matters and preserve us from those narrow Principles that kept us at a Distance from the Church of England and this at a time when there was a President that thunder'd out anathemas upon all that went to the Church of England as apostates from the Primitive Faith. The 1st time that I presum'd

---

1. Sibley, III. 201; Benjamin Colman, Funeral Sermon on Brattle, as reprinted in Ebenezer Pemberton, *Sermons and Discourses* (1727), pp. 298–99.

to go to the Church of England I should have been publickly admonish'd for it or expell'd if these Gentlemen had not generously interpos'd and protected me. Imagine the 350 Gentlemen educated by them and their Pupils to be dispers'd in all parts of the Country either as Clergy, Schoolmasters, Physicians, merchants or Gentlemen and consider the influence they would have on others it will not be wonder'd at that the Number of friends to the Church of England in that Country is at least 10 times I may say 20 times more since these Gentlemen govern'd the College than they were before, and this very thing they are daily reproach'd with by some austere Gentlemen that they have poisn'd the Youth throughout the Country so that the Rising Generation seem prepar'd for a general apostacy (as they call it) to the Church of England. It may be added that this was the principal thing objected to Mr. Leveret when he stood Candidate for the Presidents Chair that he was too well affected to the Church of England to be trusted with such a charge. . . .

And to another correspondent Newman wrote of William Brattle:

I have been intimately acquainted with this Gentleman above 20 years and he has more than once declar'd to me so long ago that he was so much in Love with the Beauty and Order of the Church of England and the Learned Men at the head of it that if it were possible to take Holy Orders without the hazard of going 1000 Leagues for them he would do it. . . .[1]

'Mr. *Brattle* was all *calm* and *soft* and *melting*,' wrote one of his pupils, Benjamin Colman (A.B. 1692). He was 'wise and discreet; humane, affable, courteous, and obliging; free, open, sincere and upright, tender, compassionate and bountiful to the needy, . . . a known peace-maker to persons or societies.'[2] And an 'enlarged *Catholic* Spirit' was cherished in Colman by Mr. Leverett.[3] As an instance of their liberal policy, Newman recalled that 'instead of studying Theology' for his Master's degree, he was allowed to learn French and 'read chiefly Mathematical Books and Travels.'[4] Brattle, as we have al-

1. Newman to Mr. Taylor, Secretary of the S. P. G., and to Dr. Smalridge, Dean of Christ Church, Archives of the Society for the Promotion of Christian Knowledge, London. Mr. Allyn Bailey Forbes has kindly given me copies.

2. *A Sermon at the Lecture in Boston, after the Funerals of Mr. William Brattle and Mr. Ebenezer Pemberton*. Boston, 1717, pp. 29, 34. Also printed in Pemberton's *Sermons and Discourses* (1727), pp. 274, 306.

3. Ebenezer Turell, *Life of Benjamin Colman* (1749), p. 123.

4. Ms. Autobiographical letter to Thomas Prince, July 16, 1729, in Archives of S. P. C. K., London.

ready seen, wrote an excellent manual of Cartesian Logic that
was used as a textbook at Harvard for many years after his
death. Even Cotton Mather, writing before the breach, praised
the 'Prudent Government' of these two tutors.[1]

Indeed, so genial was the College at this time, and so con-
ducive to learning and study, that several of the more intellectual graduates such as Paul Dudley and Ebenezer Pemberton
continued to reside after taking their second degrees or resumed residence after spending a few years elsewhere. Fellows'
table in Old Harvard Hall must have been very pleasant toward the end of the seventeenth century with Leverett presiding, Brattle at the opposite end, four or five witty young
Masters of Arts, several divinity students, and a sprinkling of
young *domini* who simply stayed on because they had nothing
better to do.[2]

There seems to have been outward harmony at least between
Mather and the tutors for several years. When Treasurer
Richards resigned from the Corporation in 1693, Thomas
Brattle, William's astronomically-minded brother, was unanimously elected in his place. But in 1696 this excellent team
began to break up. William Brattle received a call from the
Cambridge Church in the summer of 1695, and was ordained
on November 25, 1696. Leverett, who at the age of thirty-four
probably felt it was time for him to marry and settle down,
made preparations for a new profession by reading Law, and
in the spring of 1696 was elected to the lower House as representative from Cambridge. Josiah Cotton (A.B. 1698) remembered that in his junior sophister year his 'Class did some
penance . . . for some of their faults being obliged to recite at
five o'clock in the winter mornings that Mr. Leverett might
seasonably attend the General Court at Boston.'[3] In spite of
their other occupations, Leverett and Brattle continued to reside in Old Harvard and to tutor undergraduates until after
the summer quarter of 1697,[4] when they were succeeded as

1. *Magnalia*, book iv. 131.
2. Steward Bordman's Quarter-bill book (ms., H. U. Archives) shows that in
1695 and 1696 Sir Saltonstall, Sir Vaughan, Sir Remington, Sir Estabrook, and Sir
Melyen, who were studying for the M.A., were living and taking their meals in College,
together with Sir Fitch, Mr. Paul Dudley (A.B. 1690), Mr. Nathaniel Williams (A.B.
1693), Mr. Caleb Cushing (A.B. 1692), and Mr. Ebenezer Pemberton (A.B. 1691).
See Sibley, iv. for sketches of these men.   3. Sibley, iv. 399.
4. Steward Bordman's Quarter-bill book proves that they remained tutors until
after October 8, 1697.

tutors by two friends and former pupils, Ebenezer Pemberton and Jabez Fitch, who had resided in college almost without a break since their graduation. Leverett and Brattle promptly married in the first month of their release from tutorial duties (November 1697),[1] and continued to live within the present precincts of the Yard; Leverett on the old Shepard property which he had purchased from the Mitchell heirs, and Brattle in the parsonage originally built for Oakes, opposite the present Plympton Street.

Pemberton was well fitted to carry on the liberal tradition, so recently founded. He and William Brattle (writes Colman in his funeral sermon on them)

were exceedingly one in friendship and mutual affection, and that affection founded on best and strongest basis, scil. the gifts and graces of the *Holy Spirit* which they saw in one another. Their opinion and value of each other was very great and just, and in proportion to that esteem was their delight in one another. They had a long and full opportunity of knowing one another, and their soul clave to each other like the soul of *Jonathan* and *David*. Great was the confidence they had in each others integrity, and equal the freedom they us'd with one another: they reverenc'd as well as lov'd one another, and never fear'd nor suspected any thing of evil one from the other. . . . Indeed there was a great likeness in these servants of *God:* I mean not in face and feature . . . nor in their way of preaching; but they were alike men of great parts and learning, alike Philosophers and Divines, masters of the best literature, and very thorow and general scholars; they had read books and men, and were good judges of both, for they had an uncommon strength of mind, and searched every thing to the bottom, as far as the ordinary attainments among men, may allow me to say so. . . .[2]

Pemberton was probably too high-strung and passionate to be a first-class tutor. He was a terror to freshmen, and some of his later (and quite pardonable) outbursts against the Mathers are recorded in Sewall's diary.[3] On his early death, in 1717, Cotton Mather wrote very judiciously, 'He was a man of greater Abilities than many others: and, no doubt, a pious man:

1. Brattle to Elizabeth Hayman on November 3, 1697, and Leverett to the widow Berry, daughter of President Rogers, on November 25. Cotton Mather performed the latter ceremony; Charles Morton and the Andros régime had accustomed the New Englanders to ministerial marriages.

2. Ebenezer Pemberton, *Sermons and Discourses* (London 1727), pp. 293–94.

3. See p. 456, and Sibley, IV. 109.

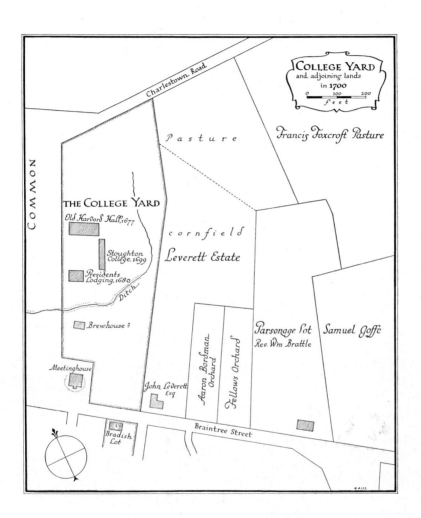

COLLEGE YARD
and adjoining lands
in 1700
0   100   200
feet

Charlestown Road

Francis Foxcroft Pasture

Pasture

COMMON

THE COLLEGE YARD
Old Harvard Hall, 1677

cornfield
Leverett Estate

Stoughton
College, 1699
Presidents
Lodging, 1680

Ditch

Brewhouse?

Meetinghouse

Aaron Bordman
Orchard

Fellows Orchard

Parsonage Lot
Rev. Wm Brattle

Samuel Goffe

John Leverett
Esq

Braintree Street

Bradish
Lot

R AISL

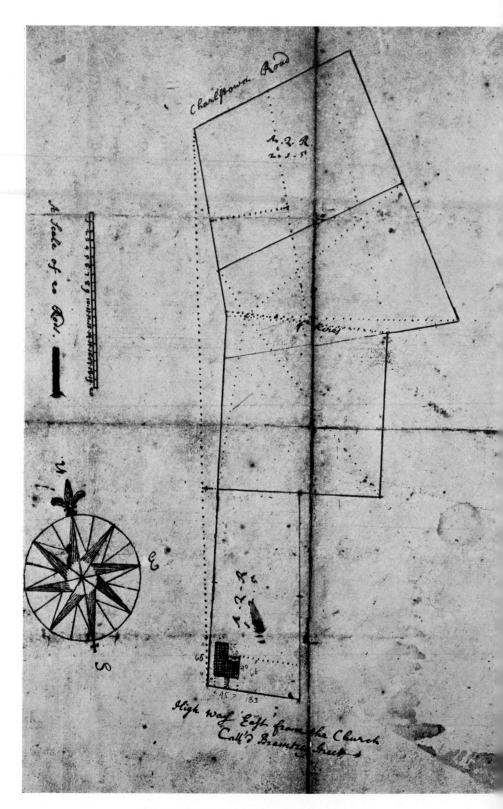

PLAN OF THE LEVERETT ESTATE, 1700

but a man of a strangely choleric and envious Temper, and one who had Created unto me more Trials of my Patience, and more Clogs upon my Opportunities to do good, than almost any other Man in the World.' [1]

CHARTER MONGERING, 1696–97

In the summer of 1695, following the repeated motions of the House of Representatives that he should reside in Cambridge if he continued President, Dr. Mather made two separate motions to resign, and urged the Corporation to 'think of another president.' Unanimously they requested him to lay aside 'Such thoughts and not too deeply resenting the Matters of Discouragement layd before him in said Vote . . . continue his care and conduct of this Society as formerly.' And, as the General Court refused to grant him a salary for a part-time job, the Corporation voted him £70 from the college treasury, and 'such mony as he should need to purchase a horse with, for the better Capacitating him to make his Visits etc. at the Colledge.' [2]

Later in the year 1695, Mather became wrought up over a new scheme to visit England as agent for the Province. Just what he expected to accomplish is not clear, but some proposal to that end had been made to the General Court. On November 30 his diary records a prayer that God 'Overrule the Hearts of those in the General Assembly [3] in that matter relating to an Agency'; and on December 6 the Assembly is still backing and filling about sending him over. Probably his object or excuse was to urge the allowance of the College Charter of 1692, apparently lost in the circumlocution office at Whitehall. But on July 12, 1696, news arrived that the Privy Council had disallowed the College Charter on the ground that 'it reserves no power to the King to appoint a visitor, which power should be reserved to the King and to the Governor.' [4] 'A special Rebuke

---

1. Sibley, IV. 111. For 'Opportunities to do good,' read 'The Harvard Presidency.' It was Pemberton's son of the same name (A.B. 1721) who became a founder of the College of New Jersey.

2. Ms. Diary, August 5 and September 2, 1695; *C. S. M.*, xv. 351, 353. A copy of the Corporation vote of August 5, and of Mather's querulous answer, both in his hand, are in the University Archives, 1.15.860. Mather states parenthetically, 'I had not received the Least pennyfarthing for all my paines.'

3. It was becoming customary to call the provincial legislature the General Assembly, rather than the General Court, which was its official title.

4. *C. S. M.*, xv. p. xlii and note 1.

of providence to my endeavors,' recorded Mather. The business of obtaining a charter had to begin again. But there was consolation in this: 'being sent to E[ngland] begins to be again discoursed.' [1]

Unfortunately this visitation matter complicated the charter question by intruding the issue of royal prerogative against provincial autonomy. The power of visitation, as understood in England, meant the right of an official Visitor (such as every college had) to intervene upon extraordinary occasions in order to smooth out difficulties and adjust disputes; sometimes the Visitor's consent was necessary to new college statutes. The Crown asked for nothing more in respect of Harvard than it already possessed directly, or indirectly through a bishop or other magnate, in every collegiate foundation of the British Isles. The most that a Visitor of Harvard College might have done would have been to serve as umpire in controversies, to see that members of the Anglican Church were not discriminated against, and perhaps to veto the election of a fellow who was *persona non grata* to the Crown. Increase Mather, who knew something about English colleges, saw no objection to this, in spite of his desire to keep the College pure from Anglican taint. But to the General Court, the power of visitation seemed one of those subjects, small enough in themselves, that must be made an issue on principle. If the King got his foot in the college door, he might similarly insist on supervising the New England churches. Furthermore, they connected the power of visitation with the late Board of Overseers (which exercised that power among others under the Charter of 1650), and so conceived the Visitor as a constant meddler in college affairs who might, if 'a violent man and an Enemy to their Religion,' smash things up,[2] and not merely play a club behind the door, as the Crown intended. Consequently, after the Privy Council had raised the issue of visitation, the question of what form the College Charter should assume was tied up with the major political issue of colonial liberty against imperial control. No doubt Elisha Cooke and his friends were ready to tease Dr. Mather and force him to resign; but this personal issue merely

1. Ms. Diary, A. A. S., August 8, 1696.
2. Lord Bellomont's letter, quoted below. And Thomas Danforth, the former College Treasurer, declared in his will (1699) that 'if any Prelatical Injunctions shall be Imposed on' Harvard College, his bequest to that Society shall revert to his heirs. *C. S. M.*, xv. 282.

added venom to the constitutional one. And it was perfectly reasonable for the Court to insist that the President of Harvard College reside at Cambridge. He has to do that even today, when Cambridge is ten minutes from Boston by subway, instead of two hours by horse and ferry.

In September 1696 the House prepared a bill for a new charter, which the Council rejected and replaced by another.[1] Although the substituted text followed, in general, that of the 1692 Charter, there were a few important differences. The Corporation was to consist of President, Treasurer, and fourteen Fellows, of whom ten were necessary for a quorum. 'The President and all Fellows receiving salary shall dwell and reside at the College; and no one shall enjoy a Fellowship with salary for more than ten years, except continued by new election.' Tax exemptions and property-holding limits were reduced. The power of visitation was vested in the Governor and Council.

Although this charter bill was approved by the Governor on December 17, 1696, it never went into effect, because the officers named in it (who were much the same as in the 1692 Charter), and who had not been consulted, stoutly protested against the terms, and declared they would not serve. Several points against it were made, but the real reason was the residence requirement, which would have thrown out President Mather. A letter from the two Mathers, Allen, and Willard, declaring their names must be omitted if the General Court insisted on this charter,[2] reached the Council at an inopportune moment, shortly after that honorable body had been subjected to a characteristic tirade from Cotton Mather about its partiality for vice and immorality. 'I doe not know that ever I saw the Council run upon with such a height of Rage before,' wrote Judge Sewall. 'The Lord prepare for the Issue . . . And the Ministers will go to England for a Charter, except we exclude the Council from the Visitation. Allege this Reason: because the K. will not pass it, and so shall be longer unsettled.'[3] A more lengthy and reasoned protest, signed by most of the

1. Mass. Archives, LVIII. 157–60; printed in Quincy, I. 597–99. Anyone interested in the minutiae of the charter bill of 1696 should consult *Calendar of State Papers, Colonial, Am. & W. I., 1696–97*, pp. 158, 223, 231; and *C. S. M.*, xv. pp. xlii–xlvii and notes.

2. Mass. Archives, LVIII. 161; printed in *C. S. M.*, xv. pp. xliii–xliv.

3. Sewall, *Diary*, I. 441–42. December 18–19, 1696.

members of the 1692 Corporation, was sent to Lieutenant-Governor Stoughton on January 6, 1696/97.[1] And by common consent the 1696 Charter was dropped.

Already, Increase Mather was straining at the leash. Far from wishing to stand by until something definite was decided about the College, he recorded, when the 1696 bill was before the House, that he simply must return to England, 'there to do Service for Christ.'[2] At that time, if not earlier, he had the bright thought that it would serve Christ for him to visit England and procure a royal charter for Harvard College; and he so far prevailed with the College Corporation,[3] that on November 9, 1696, while the General Court was still debating its charter bill, they voted to petition the King for a royal charter.[4] On December 11, Mather informed the Representatives that he proposed to go to England and secure it. By the time the politicians had digested this threat, they determined at all costs to prevent its execution. For Mather's charter-procuring abilities at Whitehall they had a healthy respect, and a royal charter for Harvard College they wished to avoid at all costs. A charter issued by the Crown out of its sovereign power would be unalterable by the General Court, and irrepealable; whilst a legislative charter, even if accepted by the Crown, could be altered or repealed by the provincial legislature at any time. So the law-makers decided to capitulate, and invited Mather to draft his own charter and present it to the General Court. He accepted; and his draft, somewhat altered, was signed by Lieutenant-Governor Stoughton on June 4, and became the short-lived Charter of 1697.[5]

1. *C. S. M.*, xv. pp. xliv-xlvii. Rough draft of another protest among Holmes-Mather mss., M. H. S.

2. Ms. Diary, A. A. S., October 3, 1696.

3. I.e., the Corporation as organized under the Charter of 1692, which Lieutenant-Governor Stoughton ordered to continue to function until the King's pleasure about a new charter be known. *C. S. M.*, xv. 355.

4. *Id.* 356. The Corporation's wishes to that effect are also recorded in Mather's ms. Diary for December 6 and 26, 1696 and March 25, 1697.

5. Mather's ms. Diary, Jan. 4, 1696/97: 'discourse with Livt Governour [Stoughton], and Corporation dè Colledge — drew up Charter'; Jan. 5, 'wrote Charter.' Cf. *Calendar State Papers, Col., Am. and W. I., 1696–97*, pp. 242, 255, 402, 406, 494. The engrossed and sealed Charter of 1697 is printed in Appendix E, below. For other copies see *C. S. M.*, xv. p. xlvii, note 2. Mather's original draft is not preserved.

CHARTER OF 1697

This, again, was very similar in terms to the Charter of 1692, with a larger Corporation: President Mather, Vice-President Morton, Treasurer Thomas Brattle, and fourteen Fellows, including tutors Leverett and Brattle;[1] nine to be a quorum; fellowships to be automatically vacated every seven years. The amount of real estate that the College could hold was limited to £3000 (a compromise between the Charters of 1692 and 1696); similar tax exemptions and immunities for college servants to those of 1692; the same provisions as to advanced degrees; President and all fellows receiving salaries to reside 'att the Colledge,' 'after this Act shall be confirmed' — the last clause a compromise between Mather's friends and Cooke's, since it would enable the President to continue commuting until the new Charter was accepted by the Crown. But the power of visitation was again vested in Governor and Council. This can hardly have been in Mather's draft, since he had gone on record a few months before to the effect that such a provision in any college charter would mean rejection in England.

Prospects for a presidential passage to England again seemed bright, since the General Court had risked rejection by disobeying instructions from England about the power of visitation. Obviously, the proper way to get the Charter allowed was to send over President Mather as its advocate! On June 7, three days after the Charter received Lieutenant-Governor Stoughton's consent, Mather summoned a meeting of the new Corporation created by it at his house in Boston; and as an upshot of that meeting, Vice-President Morton on behalf of his colleagues bespoke the 'concurrence, countenance, and assistance' of the General Court in Mr. Mather's undertaking 'a voyage for England, in order for the obtaining the Royal approbation' of the new Charter, 'or in case that cannot be, then to endeavour the obtaining such a charter from his

---

1. Quincy (i. 87) sees evidence of Matherian intrigue in Sewall's remark (*Diary*, i. 450) about the Council's leaving Leverett's name out of the draft, and wondering 'how the Deputies will resent it.' Obviously, if the Council left it out, Mather must have put it in; probably the Council objected to two Representatives (John White, A.B. 1685, was the other) being on the College Corporation when none of the Council were, and Leverett's 'tory' reputation may have counted against him.

Majesty as will be consistent with the constitution of the people and churches in this country.'[1]

If there was ever any chance of the General Court's appropriating money for Mather's projected voyage, this last suggestion wrecked it. They naturally feared that the Reverend President, instead of working for *their* Charter of 1697, would procure *a* charter more to his liking from the fountain of sovereignty. Although the Corporation again petitioned the General Court, 'We utterly despair of attaining our establishment without a personal application to His Majesty,' the heartless House of Representatives, on the very next day, voted down a motion to pay the President's return fare to England out of the public treasury.[2] And the Corporation had no funds for such a purpose.

Poor Mather, who had assumed that the General Court would follow the Corporation's wishes, was reduced by this vote to a state of extreme depression. The pertinent extracts from his diary are these:

July 3, 1697. The Colledge is in a Ticklish State, because of an ill spirit in the General Court the Representatives there having voted and unvoted what concerns the settlement of that society. . . .

Humble Requests to God in Jesus Christ

. . . 4. The Lord send reviving Tidings from E. and order the matter which concerns mine and my Samuels Returning to that Land in mercy. . . .

July 17. . . . I am distressed about the Colledge, inclined to resign my presidency — The Lord help me to sett aside all selfish respects, and to do what shall be most pleasing to him.

Memorandum.

A special Ground of my setting apart this day, by Fasting and prayer to seek the Lord, was, bec. of my being much distressed in my spirit, lest my Faith as to an opportunity to do service and promote the Interest and glory of Christ in England, should suffer a disappointment, since it has bin for so long a Time delayed. But in the last prayer

---

1. Quincy, i. 495–96. Cf. Mather's diary, June 7, 1697, 'the Corporation unanimously desired me to undertake a voyage for E. on the Colledges account.' That this was the new Corporation created by the Charter of 1697 is shown by the presence of Samuel Torrey and Peter Thacher, who were not fellows of the former Corporation.

2. Petition of June 14, 1697 and memorial of June 9, 1698, printed in Quincy, i. 496–98; also *Cal. S. P., Col., Am. and W. I., 1697–98*, p. 272. The Corporation probably did not help their case by a tactless reminder that the General Court owed the College 'money, not repaid unto this hour' — the Mowlson-Bridges scholarship fund (see *F. H. C.*, pp. 310–11).

as I was before the Lord, I was melted with hope of reviving Tidings
Coming from England. . . .

August. 7. 1697 . . . I am determined (with the Lords Leave) to
Resign my Relation to the Colledge this next weeke, having desired
a Corporation meeting for that end — The Lord provide and supply
the Colledge with a better than I am; pardoning my many defects,
and in that I have done no more good for the poor Colledge.

August 12. . . . Corporation meeting at mr Allens about Colledge
affairs, when I desired to Resign the presidentship, but they urged
me to continue still to preside, expecting a Governor from E[ngland].[1]

September 4. 1697. Grounds for Humiliation before the Lord. . . .

In the Colledge matters are uncomfortable. There is difficulty as
to the chusing of new Tutors.[2] My discouragements are such, as that
I am fully purposed to Resign the presidentship.

On September 15, President Mather went to Cambridge with
another resignation in the pocket of his riding coat; but it
being a stormy day, there wanted one to make a quorum for
a Corporation meeting. Eleven days later the 'heart-melting
persuasions' that he was about to 'glorify the Lord Jesus Christ'
in England returned for the first time in many moons. It is
unkind, but not unfair, to infer that this change of mood was
due to Mather's turning over in his mind that pregnant in-
sinuation of someone at the Corporation meeting on August
12, that the new Governor expected from England might promote Mather's ambition for a pleasure cruise.

This new angel was Richard Coote, Earl of Bellomont, a hearty Irish peer, the best born and one
of the most popular among the Royal Governors of
Massachusetts Bay. But His Lordship was an un-
conscionable time a-coming. Commissioned Governor as early as June 1697, he began a leisurely
progress toward New England late in that year. Dr. Mather,
whose 'heart-melting persuasions' of an approaching voyage had
been returning at discreet intervals, was in a fever of apprehen-
sion lest the Privy Council take action upon the Charter of 1697
before he had an opportunity to visit England on its behalf.
To that end, he wrote to William Blathwayt (one of the
principal Lords of Trade) on March 28, 1698:

---

1. A holograph of Mather's plaintive resignation of August 12, and four fair copies,
are in H. U. Arch. 1.15.860.

2. To replace Leverett and Brattle.

. . . I know you have your Hands full of weighty Occasions; and therefore I would not take up any of your Time with Impertinences. But you will give me Leave to beg your Favour in an Affair, wherein the Welfare of all the Countrey is concerned. It is with Respect to the College. I suppose I had been with you before this; but that it is necessary, that the Governour should arrive before my Going to England, that so I may have his Countenance and Concurrence in what I am to sollicit for. Wee are the Last week assured of his being at Barbados, the Winter Norewest Winds have forced him from these Coasts.

I leave only to entreat, that you would please to Improve your Interest at Court, that the Law for Incorporating Harvard-College, which was sent over this Winter, may not come under Consideration until such Time, as I can be with you, which I hope may be in July or August next. In the meane Time, if I can any way serve His Majesties Interest here, you may Command,

Sir

Your Humble Servt.

INCREASE MATHER [1]

The actual effect of this missive was to prevent the Charter of 1697 from being accepted! A few days before the letter reached Blathwayt, the Solicitor-General of the Crown reported to the Board of Trade and Plantations that he saw no objection to the Charter.[2] If nothing else had occurred, the Charter would have gone up to the Privy Council with a sheaf of other acts of colonial assemblies, and would have stood.[3] Sir Henry Ashurst wrote Mather that it 'had passed the solicitor without any amendment and would certainly pass the Council.'[4] But Mr. Blathwayt, on receipt of Mather's letter, produced it before the Board of Trade on May 30, and moved that consideration of the Harvard Charter be postponed.[5] Perhaps he did this merely to be courteous to Mather; but the effect of it was

1. *C. S. M.*, xix. 149–50; *Calendar S. P. Col., Am. & W. I., 1697–98*, p. 148.
2. *Id.* 219.
3. It was not necessary for the King or Council to sign or accept an act of a colonial assembly, such as were the Harvard Charters of 1692 and 1697. The royal governor gave assent. But the King in Council could, and often did, disallow a colonial act after it was already law; and (with few exceptions) all colonial acts had to be submitted to the Privy Council for inspection. The Board of Trade and Plantations (commonly called the Lords of Trade) established in 1696 investigated colonial acts, and its advice was generally followed by the Privy Council. So as long as the King in Council did not disallow the Charter of 1697, it was law.
4. *Acts and Resolves of the Province of Mass. Bay*, vii. 609.
5. *Calendar S. P. Col., Am. & W. I., 1697–98*, pp. 258, 563.

to subject the Charter of 1697 to a new and more careful scrutiny. The Lords of Trade then saw the little joker about the visitation, and recommended that the Act be disallowed. Mather's craze for a trip to England simply called attention to a feature of the Charter which would otherwise have passed unnoticed among the mass of documents coming in from all parts of the Empire.

Lord Bellomont appeared to be in no hurry to visit his Province of the Massachusetts Bay, where the Mather family was so eagerly expecting him. Magnificently received on April 2 at New York, over which also he had a governor's commission, His Excellency tarried there week after week, and month after month. By May 1698, Increase Mather could wait no longer. On the twelfth, the Corporation consented to send an address to New York, bespeaking the Governor's aid and countenance to the President's projected mission; and one of the younger fellows of the Corporation, John White (A.B. 1685), was chosen as messenger. On the same day the Council received a letter from Sir Henry Ashurst in London, urging that the President be sent over if the College ever expected to get a charter allowed. The visitation matter had now been noted, and wanted explaining. Mather's cup of happiness overflowed. 'These things are astonishing to me. . . . What shall I do for God, and for Jesus Christ?' [1]

John White executed his mission to New York at the cost of £25 to the College Treasury — time and money wasted.[2] Lord Bellomont replied, when he was ready, that it was perfectly useless to send an agent to England; the Charter of 1697 was certain to be disallowed, for its manner of arranging the visitation. 'The Lord overrule this affair, To his owne glory,' recorded Mather.[3]

Bellomont was quite right. When they finally got around to it, the Lords of Trade recommended that the Charter of 1697 be disallowed, and disallowed it was by the King in Council.[4] The Board wrote to Lord Bellomont, desiring him to inform the General Court in very plain language that no college charter would be allowed unless the 'power of visitation' were 're-

1. Ms. Diary, May 12, 1698.
2. C. S. M., xv. 360.
3. Ms. Diary, June 11, 1698.
4. Cal. S. P., Col., Am. & W. I., 1697-98, p. 563. November 24, 1698.

served to his Majesty and the Governor in Chief of that Province.'[1]

Mather had one more string to his bow. On June 9, 1698, James Allen, in the name of the Fellows of Harvard College, presented an address to the General Court, begging that they send Mather over to secure confirmation of the 1697 Charter, 'or, if that cannot be obtained, then to Endeavor for Such a further Settlement, as may be judged proper for Us, Considering the Constitution of our Churches and of the Countrey.' This last phrase was, of course, a euphemism for a royal charter. Every argument Mather could think of was employed. Without a charter, Harvard 'will Indeed be no Reall Colledge, but quickly come to be Nothing at all' (although it had got on pretty well without one since 1686). Donations are being lost because there is no legal Corporation (but the existing Corporation had ample powers over property, and Judge Sewall had lately given the College a farm of 500 acres in the Narragansett Country).[2] Governor Bellomont says that the President should go to England to solicit a royal charter (he had said no such thing). Sir Henry Ashurst urges the same thing (he had not); and (this, thought Mather, would clinch the matter), if you want a resident president, you must have a charter, and if you want a charter, who has more experience in getting one than our Reverend President?[3]

In four days' time, this second bowstring snapped. 'In Council. 14 June 1698, Read and Voted in the Negative' is endorsed on the memorial; and on the same day is written in the President's diary, 'The will of the Lord be done.'

STOUGHTON COLLEGE

We may now take a recess from this protracted affair of the college charters, to glance at the new building erected by the bounty of Lieutenant-Governor William Stoughton. There was a gradual but steady upturn in the number of students from 1686, with no accommodation save thirteen chambers in Old Harvard, and the President's Lodging.[4] At a Corpora-

1. *Id. 1699*, p. 38.   2. *C. S. M.*, xv. 272.
3. Mass. Archives, LVIII. 175; printed in Quincy, I. 497–98. Cf. Sewall's remarks in *Diary*, I. 480–81.
4. The Indian College was still standing, but apparently had been uninhabited, if not uninhabitable, since 1680. See Chapter XVII.

LIEUTENANT–GOVERNOR WILLIAM STOUGHTON
Stoughton College in the Background

STOUGHTON COLLEGE

tion meeting in October 1693, Charles Morton brought in a report on the question 'How may the Colledge be made greater and better?' and was appointed chairman of a committee, with Leverett and Brattle, 'to draw up Som proposalls for the Enlargement of the Colledge by new buildings.'[1]

Nothing more happened until 1698, unless the purchase in 1697 of the Sweetman-Spencer lot (VI), just north of Old Harvard, was intended to provide a site for immediate expansion.[2]

Some time before March 3, 1697/98, Lieutenant-Governor Stoughton came forward with a proposal to provide a new building; for on that date the Corporation appointed a committee consisting of the two Mathers, Leverett, Allen, and Willard 'to treat with The Honourable Lievt. Governour about the additional building to the Colledg.'[3] William Stoughton (A.B. 1650), one of the most prominent, wealthy, and unpopular of Harvard alumni, died an unrepentant witch-hanger. Increase Mather loved him as an exemplar of early puritan virtues; and by the President's favor he had been named Lieutenant-Governor in the Province Charter, which made him acting governor between Sir William Phips' departure in 1694 and Lord Bellomont's arrival in 1699. Samuel Willard declared in a funeral sermon that with Stoughton 'much of New England's glory' was entombed; but a more realistic contemporary described him as 'pudding faced, sanctimonious and unfeeling.'[4] However, he was the first Harvard alumnus to provide alma mater with a building; and Stoughton College, as it was called, was the first Harvard building to be completed promptly, without long-drawn-out trouble about payment. 'Mr. Stoughton's eight hundred pound new colledge goes on livelyly,' wrote a gossipy graduate on June 22, 1698. 'It is to

1. *C. S. M.*, xv. 345.

2. See maps of Yard in this volume, and in *F. H. C.* No owner of this northwest corner of the present Yard can be found in the Cambridge records until about 1645, when Thomas Sweetman, weaver, settled there, built himself a house, and somehow acquired a good title. He sold the lot in 1677 to his son-in-law Michael Spencer, subject to a life interest of himself and wife. Sweetman died in 1683, and on June 12, 1697, Spencer sold the lot to the College, reserving the use of a third part to his mother-in-law, who died about 1709. There is no record of what the College did with the dwelling house on the lot; Holden Chapel (1744) was the first College building erected on it. Paige, pp. 659, 668; *C. S. M.*, xv. 265–66, 385; original deed in H. U. Archives. The Treasurer was authorized to pay 'not above four score pounds' for the house and lot.

3. *C. S. M.*, xv. 357–58; and see pp. xciv–c, where Mr. Matthews has collected most of the known facts about this building.

4. Sibley, I. 203; C. K. Bolton, *Portraits of The Founders*, II. 484.

be four storys high, and in length about 100 foot, in bredth 23 or 24.'[1] The site chosen was southeast of and at right angles to Old Harvard. The worshipful Lieutenant-Governor, who very likely had to pay out one or two hundred pounds over the estimated cost of £800, omitted to provide a cellar; but master builder Willis consented to dig one for an additional £10.[2] This was divided up into compartments, where each occupant of the building, for an annual rental of 6s, could keep his wine.[3]

Stoughton College appears to have been ready for occupancy by Commencement 1699, if not earlier.[4] Burgis' Prospect gives an excellent front elevation of the building; and it is also shown, against a background of lofty mountains (probably intended to represent the donor's native Blue Hills), in the portrait of William Stoughton owned by the College. In the centre of the façade the arms assumed (without right) by the Lieutenant-Governor were carved in stone; and underneath, the inscription[5]

DEO. OPT. MAX. BONISQ. LITERIS S.
GULIELMUS STOUGHTON ARMIGER PROVINCIÆ
MASSACHUSET. NOV-ANGLORUM VICE-GUBERNATOR
COLLEGII HARVARDINI OLIM ALUMNUS
SEMPER PATRONUS FECIT
ANNO DOMINI 1699

The building was but one room deep, and the plan was simple.[6] In accordance with the medieval tradition that was followed in all our college buildings previous to Holworthy,

1. John Danforth, in 5 *Coll. M. H. S.*, I. 447. Elsewhere described as 100' x 20', and 97' x 22' 10'' (*C. S. M.*, xv. p. c.); I think that the last, being based on actual measurement, is probably correct.

2. *C. S. M.*, xv. 360, 363.

3. *Id.* 364. Occupants of Stoughton could also have a section of the garret; for Joseph Sewall, on returning to Harvard after his Commencement, noted in his ms. Diary (B. P. L.) that his garret, study, and cellar had been broken into.

4. A curiously garbled report of building activity at Harvard, based probably on Stoughton College, appeared in the London *Flying Post* of October 1, 1700 (Burney Collection, British Museum): 'Letters from Boston in New England say, that they are about raising Money to build a Publick Library and Theatre at their University of Cambridge, for the Encouragement of the Students, and the conveniency of their performing their Publick Exercises, at their Commencements and Terms, &c.'

5. *C. S. M.*, xv. p. c.

6. There is a rough ground-floor plan facing *C. S. M.*, xv. 260.

corner studies (indicated in the façade by the narrow windows) were provided, two or three in each of the sixteen chambers.[1] One of them, called 'the painted Chamber,' was reserved for the donor's kindred; and one of the studies, or its occupant, was especially endowed by Thomas Danforth.[2] In return for using the bricks of the dilapidated Indian College for the walls of Stoughton, a study and chamber space were promised gratis to any Indian that might show up. The redskins did not show any alacrity to obtain this privilege.

Master builder Willis appears to have scamped his work; for as early as 1714 the Corporation had to repair the roof, and in 1721 the Overseers represented 'the desperate and Dangers Condition of Stoughton House.' A survey showed the building to be 'so exceedingly bow'd and broken' that the Overseers recommended it be taken down and rebuilt. Nothing was done, however; and the walls became so bulgy and wobbly that everyone expected the Lisbon earthquake of 1755 to shake them down into a heap of bricks — instead of which, *mirabile dictu*, the walls were shaken back 'to their perpendicular direction.' After serving as a dormitory for twenty years more, as barracks for the American army in 1775–76, and as printing shop for a refugee patriot newspaper, Stoughton became too dilapidated to be reoccupied by students; and in 1781, after a part of the rear wall had fallen, the Corporation allowed Deacon Aaron Hill to demolish it, in return for 'half of the Bricks.'[3] The site was never built upon again; but Stoughton Hall (1805) was so named to perpetuate the Lieutenant-Governor's memory.

COLLEGE POLITICS OF 1698–99

In the meantime, Ebenezer Pemberton and Jabez Fitch had succeeded Leverett and Brattle as tutors, and the College was being carried on as though the Charter of 1697 were valid; the news of its official disallowance did not reach Boston until April 26, 1699.[4] During the winter of 1698–99, Increase Mather managed to evade another presidential crisis. The first move came from the Corporation, which on November 29, 1698 proposed to the General Court that it establish the office of a

---

1. Ms. Faculty Records, I. 3–4. For the medieval chamber-and-study arrangement, see *F. H. C.*, pp. 280–81. 2. *C. S. M.*, xv. p. xcv.

3. *Id.*, pp. xcvi–c. 4. *C. S. M.*, xv. p. xlviii.

salaried Vice-President to reside at the College and do the President's work 'under the continuall assistance and Countenance of the Reverend President (the continuance of whose relation to the Colledg is on all Accounts needfull) and in his absence, to have the full power of the President.' [1] The Court naturally did not see why Harvard should have two presidents, one to do the work and the other to enjoy the honor; and on December 7 the Lieutenant-Governor approved a resolve 'for encouragement unto the Reverend Mr. Increase Mather, president, to remove and take up his residence there,' offering him £200 per annum 'from the time of his removal, during his residence at the colledge.' [2]

This vote nearly brought a show-down, but not quite. On December 8, 1698, Judge Sewall and a committee of the General Court called on Increase Mather; and of the interview that ensued, both men have left accounts, the close agreement of which confirms their truth.[3] The committee's object was to engage Mather to accept the salary, and move to Cambridge. The President began by finding fault because his name had been left out in one of the drafts, and because the proffered salary had been reduced from £250 to £200. Speaker Byfield replied that the House was unanimously in favor of Dr. Mather's being President — that was what the committee had come to secure. The President declared unwillingness to give up his weekly sermons, 'which he prefered before the Gold and Silver of the West-Indies.' Judge Sewall observed that he could preach to the students twice daily; but Mather replied that that was not the same thing. Or, as he expressed it later, in a sentence of a letter that demonstrates his attitude toward the College better than any amount of description, 'Should I leave off preaching to 1500 souls . . . only to Expound to 40 or 50 Children, few of them capable of Edification by such Exercises?' [4] The committee plied him further; he replied, 'I could not go till the charter confirmed,' etc.

What Mather meant by this last condition is explained by the next entry in his diary:[5] 'I therefore sett apart this day to cry to Heaven for direction in this particular, and that God

---

1. *Acts and Resolves of the Province*, VII. 609, quoting Mass. Archives, LVIII. 179.
2. *Acts and Resolves*, VII. 202.
3. Mather's ms. Diary, December 8, 1698; and Sewall, *Diary*, I. 487–88.
4. Sewall, *Diary*, I. 493.   5. December 10, 1698.

will incline my Heart to do what shall be pleasing in his sight. but oh that God would accept of Service from me in England, according to my Faith!' No trip to England; no move to Cambridge. Six days later, Mather formally declined the Court's offer in a letter of amazing frankness, confessing 'a strong Bent of Spirit to spend (and to end) the remainder of my few days in England.' For that privilege, but not to serve the College or train up the younger generation, he would break his pastoral relation.

So things were back where they had been for thirteen years. On February 6, 1698/99, Mather took a straw vote of the brethren of his church on the Court's proposition. Naturally they did what was expected of them and voted unanimously against his leaving. On the ninth he craved a 'Loving dismission' from the Corporation. But 'None seemed willing.' Oh, if a call would only come from England![1] On February 23 there was a joint meeting of Council and Corporation on the subject. Mather fell back on the last excuse of a weak man, his wife's wishes. He would move only if the church and his wife would let him, quickly adding 'except some tidings from England did prevent.' At that, blunt old Samuel Torrey blurted out what everyone must have been thinking, 'All you say is nothing. . . . Your pretending to resign is but a flourish.'[2]

CHARTER BILL OF 1699

His Excellency the Earl of Bellomont finally tore himself away from Manhattan, and arrived in his long-expectant Province of the Massachusetts Bay near the end of May 1699. He was preceded by news that the College Charter of 1697 had been disallowed at London;[3] and so the tedious business of charter-making had to begin all over again.

In his first speech to the General Court, the Governor offered 'very gladly' to join with them in petitioning His Majesty for a royal charter;[4] but, as he wrote home a few months later, 'the sour part of the Council, who make a majority, would not hear of a [royal] charter.'[5] It must be their own charter, or none.

---

1. Ms. Diary, Feb. 6, 9, 18, 1698/99.
2. *Id.*, February 23, 1698/99. Torrey apologized the next day.
3. *C. S. M.*, xv. p. xlviii.   4. *Ibid.*
5. *Cal. S. P. Col., Am. & W. I., 1699*, p. 413. August 28, 1699.

Accordingly, another charter bill, the fourth in seven years, was agreed to by both Houses on July 13. This so-called 'Charter of 1699' followed, in general, the earlier drafts.[1] It broke the deadlock about the visitation by an ingenious compromise: the power was reserved exclusively to 'his Majesty and his Governor'; but five Councillors were appointed to the Corporation, which was to consist of President, Vice-President, and fourteen Fellows. The new feature of this charter, and the one that wrecked it, was an illiberal safeguard to 'our holy religion' which was inserted at the express desire of the two Mathers and six other ministers:[2]

Provided, that no person shall be chosen, and continued President, Vice-President, or Fellow, of said Corporation, but such as shall declare and continue their adherence unto the principles of Reformation, which were espoused and intended by those who first settled this country, and founded the College, and have hitherto been the profession and practice of the generality of the churches of Christ in New England.[3]

This was decidedly a step backward. No such provision had been in the Charter of 1650, or in any of the bills or disallowed charters of the years 1692–97. It was contrary to the principle of religious toleration contained in the Province Charter, and would have made Harvard College definitely sectarian, as it never had been before, or was destined to become. Governor Bellomont very properly took exception to so crude an attempt to exclude forever 'all members of the Church of England,' or even of a Congregational church which the Mathers did not approve, from the government of the College.[4] On July 18, 1699, he refused consent to the charter unless the sectarian clause were expunged; and the Council declined to delete it. 'Your Lordship was much in the right . . . in refusing to pass

1. C. S. M., xv. p. xlix; text printed in Quincy, i. 602–07, from Mass. Archives, lviii. 188–90.

2. James Allen, Samuel Torrey (Class of 1656), Samuel Willard (A.B. 1659), Peter Thacher (A.B. 1671), John Danforth (A.B. 1677), Benjamin Wadsworth (A.B. 1690), the future President of the College. Their Address, dated July 7 (before the bill passed), is printed in Quincy, i. 99. See next Chapter for discussion whether or not the 'Manifesto Church' affected this.

3. Quincy, i. 604.

4. Bellomont to the Lords of Trade, August 28, 1699, Cal. S. P. Col., Am. & W. I., 1699, pp. 413, 416; cf. pp. 301, 340, 350. See, however, Professor Murdock's apology for this clause in his Increase Mather, pp. 353–55.

the Bill about Harvard College,' wrote the Lords of Trade in reply.[1]

This fateful 18th of July had been set aside by Cotton Mather as a day of fasting and prayer for the passage of the bill, that the parental 'Voyage to *England*, might bee well-ordered.' At noon his prayers were rewarded by a direct assurance from Heaven that Increase should 'bee carried into *England*.' At that very moment, the Governor was writing his veto message. 'Lord, preserve my Faith,' beseeches poor Cotton in his diary for that day, 'and assist me to wait with an holy and humble Patience, for the Issue of these mysterious Things!'[2]

On advice of Council, the Governor now ordered the Corporation as of the Charter of 1697 to continue; and under this 'temporary settlement' of July 25, 1699, the College was governed until July 1700.[3] The only important act of the Corporation during this short régime was the tutorial appointment of Henry Flynt (A.B. 1693), who was destined to serve the College without promotion for fifty-five years, and to be a living link between the age of the Mathers and the age of revolution.[4]

DRAFT CHARTER OF 1700

In his speech opening the next session, May 30, 1700, Lord Bellomont again renewed his recommendation that the General Court put a stop to charter-mongering, and join him in petitioning the King for a 'Royal Charter of Priviledges.'[5] The House apparently agreed,[6] but later thought better of it. Fearing lest His Majesty grant them such a charter as they would not care to accept (which would have been exceedingly awkward), they decided to write their own 'draft charter' and present it to the King as the sort of college charter they hoped he might grant.

1. *Cal. S. P. Col., Am. & W. I., 1700*, p. 164. April 11, 1700.
2. Cotton Mather, *Diary*, I (7 *Coll. M. H. S.*, VII.). 308–09.
3. *C. S. M.*, XV. pp. l–lii.
4. Sibley, IV. 162–67, with portrait. Flynt was probably elected tutor as a conservative balance to Pemberton, who was of the liberal party. Leverett objected to the appointment (*C. S. M.*, XV. p. li note) on the ground that a third tutor was unnecessary, and that Flynt's salary was found by docking Pemberton's £10 and Fitch's £15.
5. *C. S. M.*, XV. p. lii.
6. June 11, 1700. *Cal. S. P. Col., Am. & W. I., 1700*, p. 329. If any reader still has appetite for details of what even Quincy, who wrote of all this with the zest of a seasoned politician, calls a 'tedious drama,' he may find them in Quincy, I. 104–08, and in the references to the Calendars given in *C. S. M.*, XV. p. lii, note 3.

So for the last time (rejoice with me, reader!) the legislative mill started grinding out a college charter.

By June 1700, when debates on this last of the futile attempts at chartering began, Increase Mather was much exercised over the possibility of the College's falling into the hands of his local theological enemies. His growing antagonism to the very mild liberalism of John Leverett and the Brattles — detailed consideration of which is postponed to the next chapter — had now reached a high point, owing to the provocative manifesto of the new Brattle Street Church. It was obvious that the Crown would never accept a college charter containing a test of puritan orthodoxy. Yet, if the new charter contained no such test, how could Mather prevent young innovators, or even heretics, one day controlling the Corporation?

Faced by this dilemma, President Mather decided that, rather than risk a liberal Corporation, he preferred no charter at all. He would sacrifice the proud prerogative of conferring degrees (for which a charter authority was necessary), and allow Harvard College to sink into an unincorporated divinity school for orthodox puritanism of the primitive New England pattern. Such, at least, is the conclusion that I have drawn from this paper in the President's handwriting, which from internal evidence was written in June or early July 1700:

Queries Worthy of Consideration [1]

Q. 1. Did not the general Court Nominate the persons whose Names were inserted in the act for incorporating the Colledge,[2] with a design that the Government of that Society might be kept in hands who would endeavour that the young scholars might be seasoned with principles agreeable to the order of the gospell professed in these churches?

Q. 2. If any succeeding general Court should Consent to haue it otherwise, will not God be displeased?

Q. 3. If they consent to haue a clause in the Colledge Charter expressly declaring that the Corporation may if they will Chuse such to be Presidents and Fellows as are known to espouse those principles which our Fathers Came into this Land for no other reason but that so they and their posterity might not be Corrupted therewith, will there not be sin in it?

---

1. H. U. Archives, 1.15.860.

2. The bill of July 13, 1699, from which the names of Thomas Brattle as Treasurer, and John Leverett as Fellow, had been dropped at the last minute.

Q. 4. In case a Considerable number of those members of the Corporation who are known to be well affected towards that Church State which has bin the profession of N. E. shall be remoued and others disaffected thereto placed in their stead, will not that which has bin the Religion of the Countrey be endangered thereby?

Q. 5. Is it not much more eligible to haue the Colledge turned into a school for Academical Learning without priviledge of Conferring degrees, as in Geneva it has bin where many Eminent divines haue had their education, than to consent to such fatal alterations in the government of the Colledge, as some would haue?

If this paper was presented to one of Mather's friends in the General Court, it had no effect. The 'Draught of a Charter of Incorporation for Harvard Colledge at Cambridge in New-England, *agreed* by the Council and House of Representatives . . . to be humbly Sollicited for to his Majesty,'[1] dated July 12, 1700, contained no religious test, but attempted to secure the same result by creating a nearly all-clerical Corporation consisting of President Mather, Vice-President Samuel Willard, and twelve fellows, all but three of whom were clergymen and not one of whom was identified with the liberal movement. It repeated, with some change in phraseology, the association of the Council in the visitatorial power, to which the Crown had already twice indicated a decided objection.

Increase Mather's diary for 1700 has not been preserved; but from his son's diary it appears that the father was promptly consoled for want of a religious test by a revived expectation of visiting England. On June 16, 1700, when the draft charter was still under debate, there occurred to Cotton Mather 'one of the most astonishing Things, that ever befel.' After a few hours' prayer, prostrate on his study floor, he felt an afflatus as 'if an *Angel* from Heaven had spoken.' He arose, opened his Bible at random; and his eyes fell slap on Acts xxvii. 24 — 'Fear not, Paul; thou must be brought before Caesar!'[2]

'And now what shall I say?' concludes Cotton. For the voyage to London promptly faded out! 'Some of our Tories, had so wrought upon the Governour' that he gave up the idea of recommending a Matherian mission; and even pious Stoughton, who once had been for it, 'appeared with all the little Tricks, imaginable to confound it.'[3]

1. *Acts and Resolves*, vii. 257–60; for other copies, see *C. S. M.*, xv. p. lii, note 3.
2. Cotton Mather, *Diary*, i. 353–56.
3. *Id.* 356. And what made the pill more bitter was that Cotton Mather had

And this, as it turned out, was the last chance of Increase Mather's being sent to England. Not again was he to stand before Caesar; nevermore to preach in the dissenting chapels at Newington Green, Holborn, and Hackney; never again to hear the soft, well-bred voices of dear Sir Henry Ashurst and kind Lady Sutherland; no more to rummage in the bookstalls of St. Paul's Churchyard, or read the Gazettes in the coffee-houses of Fleet Street; never again to breathe that sweet, smoky, titillating, dirty, divine atmosphere of London. Dust and ashes — a provincial church or a little brick college — were his portion now and henceforth, until death brought release to a Heaven that must (if God were good) be something like London.

It was not the wicked 'tories' who created the last and worst of this series of disappointments, but the kind Governor. Despite the General Court's stubbornness about the visitatorial power, Lord Bellomont, like the good fellow he was, decided to urge Whitehall to accept their draft and make a royal charter of it. And as he promised to 'improve' his 'interest for the obtainment of his Majestys grace and Favour,' there was no sense or reason in the General Court's paying good money to give Dr. Mather an English holiday.

On July 15, 1700, Lord Bellomont fulfilled his promise by writing this hearty letter to the Lords of Trade: [1]

[I] will now proceed to say something about the settlement of Harvard College, which seems to Involve the ardent desires and affections of these people beyond all other things in this world; for as they have an extraordinary zeal and fondnesse for their Religion, so any thing that disturbs 'em in that, touches 'em in their Tenderest part. I join'd with the Assembly in this addresse, not because I approve at all of their Church government; but out of a principle of moderation, for thô I have all my life been of the Church of England, yet I have ever Thought the Protestant Churches in the wrong to quarrel about the modes of worship, and the externals of it; when the essentials of

---

publicly declared in his election sermon, *A Pillar of Gratitude*, only a month before, that 'Except we . . . take the Advice of our Excellent Governour, for the Establishment of this our Colledge, it is much to be fear'd it will presently be broken up; without his Direction and Countenance we can do nothing to purpose' (p. 28).

1. Public Record Office, C. O. 5/861, no. 53; *Cal. S. P. Col., Am. & W. I., 1700,* pp. 415–16. A copy of the 'Humble Address' of the General Court to the Governor, signed by Isaac Addington and John Leverett (probably the 'tory' Cotton Mather alluded to), follows the letter; as well as an Address of Governor, Council, and Assembly to the King, on the same subject.

Religion were the same; therefore I have long since Concluded in my own mind, that we ought to bear with our Protestant brethren in their way of worship and leave the rest to God Almighty whose prerogative it is to govern the Consciences of men and whoever goes about to abridge Protestants of the exercise of their Consciences, does not rightly distinguish between the quarrel of some hot-headed Churchmen, and the Cause of God. your Lordships Know very well I have not spar'd to acquaint you with the faults of these people, and I am as plain with them; but then I reprove 'em with Temper, and not with passion, and I endeavour to reason 'em out of their errors, by which means I have gain'd upon 'em; and I flatter my selfe much, if I have not a good Interest in the people here of all sorts and ranks; which Interest I labour to Improve for the King's service, and Interest of England.

I have desir'd Sir Henry Ashhurst to wait on your Lordships from time to time, and receive your directions towards Carrying on the Colledge-Charter. The General Assembly do not desire there should be any Clause in the Charter exclusive of Members of the Church of England, but they desire the power of visitation may be lodg'd in the Governor and Council, and not in the Governor singly, and they give this reason for it viz: That as this Country is very remote from England, a Governor that were a violent man and an Enemy to their Religion, might probably vex and disturb the whole people of this Province by an attempt upon their Colledge in order to Innovate in matters of discipline or Religion, and that before they could make their Complaint to the King, and be reliev'd against such a Governor. I hope your Lordships will gratifie 'em in this point, which I humbly Conceive is reasonable enough, as it is consonant with the liberty of Conscience which the Act of Tolleration allows, with his Majesties generous Temper, and singular moderation; and with the wisdom of the Government, of England, which I am apt to believe will thinke it safest and best to Cramp these people (as often as they deserve it) in their Trade, rather than to abridge or disturb their Consciences. If it be objected that the lodging of the visitation in the Governor and Council is derogatory to the King's prerogative; I answer 'tis not so great a condescention in the King, as the Constitution of his Majesties Council in this Province, who by an expresse Clause in their Charter are annually chosen by the House of Representatives. there is this to be consider'd too, that whenever these people abuse the King's Grace and favour, a writt of Quo warranto, or an act of Parliament will reach 'em.

Strangely enough, the Draft Charter of 1700 had the ignominious fate of getting lost in the files of Sir John Hawles, Solicitor-General of the Crown, whither the Lords of Trade had sent it for an opinion.[1] Not that it mattered. Harvard College got along very well under another 'Temporary Settlement' made by the General Court.[2] The persons named to the Corporation in the draft were ordered to carry on the government of the College, and this they did until the end of 1707, when the ancient Charter was revived. The document of 1700, acme of nine years' charter-mongering, object of bitter recrimination between House and Council and occasion of many prayers and tears in the Mather family, was forgotten as completely as an empty bottle after a picnic.

Mather Tries Cambridge

For Increase Mather the time had come at last when he must make up his mind to be President in Cambridge or Minister in Boston. All parties were agreed upon that; and the Charter of 1700 was plain and explicit, 'That the President of the said Corporation, as also all the Fellows and Tutors, thereof receiving salary shall reside at the Colledge. ...'[3] On July 10, 1700, a resolve passed both Houses voting £220 out of the public treasury 'to the President of Harvard Colledge, already chosen, or that shall be chosen by this Court.' There was a threat in this language. And at the same time it was voted 'That the Person chosen President of Harvard Colledge Shall reside at Cambridge.' A committee was appointed 'To wait on the Reverend Mr Increase Mather, and acquaint him, that this Court hath chosen him President of Harvard Colledge, and Desire's, him to accept of said office and so, Expect's, that he Repair to and reside at Cambridge, as soon as may be.'[4] That very day Judge Sewall waited on President Mather, prefacing his remarks with a quotation from a life of St. Athanasius: *Maluit sedem quam Fidei syllabam mutare.*[5] Mather might have replied that he saw no such alternative; but he was too broken in spirit to do more than mumble the old excuse about his church, and to declare that even if it consented he could not move his family without the charter of 1700 being accepted in London —

1. Mr. Matthews's note in *C. S. M.*, xv. pp. liii–liv.
2. See next Chapter.
3. *C. S. M.*, xv. p. lv, n. 1.
4. *Acts and Resolves*, vii. 255; cf. 644.
5. 'He chose the Chair rather than change a syllable of his Faith.' Sewall, *Diary*, I. 19.

a last pathetic hint that the Court should send him over to urge it. Sewall reported back this answer the next day;[1] the Court brutally required Mather to call a church meeting that very evening, and sent a delegation thither to argue for consent. The church so voted the next day; and the long-sustained Matherian bluff that the church would never release him was called at last.

Then what scurrying was there to receive the King in his capital! On July 13, 1700, the Court appointed a committee 'to take Care that a suitable Place at Cambridge be Provided for the Reception and Entertainment of the President of Harvard Colledge, And to see and Consider what is meet to be done with respect to' the President's Lodging, where no president had lodged since the death of Rogers.[2] The committee found the Lodging 'much out of repair,' and so 'procured Sutable Entertainment' at the house of honest Aaron Bordman, College Steward.[3] President Mather, deeply offended, complained to Stoughton of the 'great hardship' of not having a house to himself; but in the recess of the Court it was impossible to do anything about repairing the official Lodging until next March, when it was ordered done.

At Cambridge Dr. Mather resided during the stifling summer. To Stoughton he reported on October 17, 1700:

I have been three months (and some days more) residing in Cambr.: my Work there has bin a dayly Inspection of the colledge. Sometimes 2 or 3 times in a day I have stept into the Colledge, to enquire if any thing were amiss amongst the students. Seldom a day but I have called one or other of them into the Library to advise them about their studdys and also about their Soul Concernment. I have moreover preached to the Schollars every Lords day in publick and given them an Expository Lecture in the Colledge Hall once a week and have moderated the disputacions of the Graduates once a fortnight.[4]

And some months after returning to Boston he made the further report:

The Colledge is like to be in a languishing State as to Learning, through the Defect of Grammar Schooles, otherwise it is in a better

---

1. *Acts and Resolves*, VII. 644.
2. *C. S. M.*, XV. p. cx.
3. *Ibid*. His house was on the west corner of Dunster Street and Massachusetts Avenue; no. 21 on Dr. Norris's map of Cambridge, in *F. H. C.*, pp. 192–93.
4. 'Extract of a letter' from Mather to Stoughton, October 17, 1700, H. U. Archives, 1.15.860.

and more hopefull Estate than it was a few years since. For the Scholars (I hope) are not so much tainted with some unhappy Principles (which it is the Interest of N. England that the Students there should be preserved from) as they were some years ago.[1]

It was some satisfaction to have felt he had rooted out these 'unhappy Principles' of liberalism that Leverett and Brattle had introduced;[2] but life in Cambridge was boring at best. The presidential steed no doubt made frequent journeys in the reverse direction to his usual habit, carrying the Reverend President to Charlestown where he might sniff the east wind that he loved, and sadly watch the ships setting sail for England, and cross the ferry to spend a night or two with his dear Maria. By the middle of October the prospect of spending the winter in Cambridge 'alone in a Cold Room' is too horrible to contemplate. 'Altho' I have beene in the world 61 years,' he writes to Lieutenant-Governor Stoughton, 'this has been the most uncomfortable 3 months that ever I saw . . . either the aire or the diet of Cambridge not agreeing with me.' He is returning to Boston forthwith; and although he cannot 'refuse to take the care of the Colledge' as in '19 years past,' he desires 'that another president may in the mean time be thought of.'

Nothing could be done about it until the Court met again, in February 1700/01. Stoughton then read Mather's letter to the Council, which communicated it to the House; and on March 14 they passed the order under which the College was governed for the next seven years.[3] The clause of immediate interest is this:

forasmuch as the constitution requires the president to reside at Cambridge, which is now altered by his removal from thence . . . it is therefore,— Ordered, . . . in case of Mr Mather's refusal, absence, sickness or death, that Mr Samuel Willard, nominated to be vice-president . . . before named, be and hereby are invested with the like powers and authority aforesaid . . .

---

1. Mather to Stoughton, March 4, 1700/01, ibid.; Acts and Resolves, VII. 644–45.

2. Inspection of the biographies in the forthcoming Sibley, vol. v. for the classes in college in 1700, suggests that the Reverend President was somewhat overconfident in this matter; and it was in 1701 that a visiting Englishman wrote home, 'here is a great many young men Educated at the Colledge at Cambridge, who differ much in their principles from their parents.' Sibley, IV. 3.

3. Acts and Resolves of the Province, VII. 271–72. See next Chapter, and Appendix E for text.

Plain words again! So Increase Mather wearily packed up his things, kissed Maria good-bye, and returned to Cambridge in that repulsive season of the year when winter was breaking up, and the village streets were knee-deep in mud and slush.[1]

It was no use. The President could not endure Cambridge. No Philosophical Society, no dinners with wealthy merchants and distinguished strangers, no calls on Lady Phips, no devoted, eager congregation fifteen hundred strong to greet him every Lord's Day and to admire the beauty of his diction and the unction of his prayers. Only a parcel of gangling hobbledehoys called (by courtesy) scholars, three college tutors, and a few nobodies, the village nabobs. So, on June 30, 1701, he wrote Stoughton that as soon as Commencement was over he would return to Boston, 'and no more to return to reside in Cambridge'; for it was unreasonable to expect him to remain longer absent from his family, or to break up his Boston home and move the family to Cambridge, 'when the Colledge is in such an Unsettled state.' He earnestly desired that the Court would 'think of' another president; and remarked that it would be 'fatal' if they should choose a person (such as John Leverett, if you please) 'disaffected to the Order of the Gospel professed, and practised in these Churches.'[2]

On July 2, 1701, Dr. Mather presided at Commencement; and thereafter Cambridge saw his distinguished figure no more. The Second Church in Boston had kept his seat warm; so he simply slipped back into the old life — and so delightful did Boston seem after Cambridge, that even England was forgotten for a time.

Yet, such was Mather's persuasion of his indispensability, that he still expected to hold the presidency; what presently occurred gravely offended him. 'The Colledge was through the malice of dr Cooke and Byfield put into the hands of mr Willard as vicepresident, who readily accepted the offer without so much as once consulting with me about it,' he complained in his Autobiography. Willard had been his own creature on the College Corporation, a safe man!

No doubt it was the political sagacity of Elisha Cooke that brought this to pass. Lieutenant-Governor Stoughton died

1. As repairs to the President's Lodging were authorized only on March 15 (*id.* 275), Mather must again have taken private lodgings at Bordman's, or elsewhere.
2. *Acts and Resolves*, VII. 645. Mather's own copy is in H. U. Arch. 1.15.860.

five days after Commencement, which made the game much easier to manage; for Stoughton had been a friend of Mather's, and the executive power, according to the Province Charter, now devolved upon the Council.[1] On August 1, 1701, the letter that Mather had written to Stoughton a week before his death was read to the General Court, which immediately resolved to invite Vice-President Willard to accept the presidency. Willard delayed a definite reply, and the matter went over during the summer recess. On September 5 and 6 a counter-resolve renewing the many-times-repeated invitation to Mather to reside and rule was negatived; and Willard then replied that he would 'do the best service he could for the College, and that he would visit it once or twice every week, and continue there a night or two, and perform the service used to be done by former Presidents.' [2] At this point, if not earlier, it evidently occurred to Cooke or some such political genius that, while the draft charter of 1700 and various votes of the General Court declared that the *President* must reside in Cambridge, nothing had been said as to where the *Vice-President* should live. And so it was resolved by both Houses, on September 6, 1701:

That the Reverend Mr. Samuel Willard nominated for Vice President of the Colledge, (together with the Gentlemen named for the Corporation in the order of this Court) be desired to take the care and Over Sight of the Colledge and Students there according to the late Establishment made by this Court and to manage the affairs thereof, as he has proposed in his answer to this Court. Vizt. to reside there for one or two days and nights in a week, and to perform prayers and Expositions in the Hall and to bring forward the Exercise of Analisying.[3]

Thus Increase Mather's presidency of sixteen years came to an end, brutally cut off by a legislative resolve; and another commuting president succeeded.

The manner in which the Mathers received this result throws considerable light on the sincerity of the President's frequent offers to resign. Both were unspeakably grieved, wounded, and angry. Increase wrote in his Autobiography that the Council resolve accepting Willard's conditions was passed by a snap

1. *C. S. M.*, XVII. 50.
2. *Id.* xv. pp. lvi–lvii, notes.
3. *Acts and Resolves*, VII. 312. Cf. p. 703, and *C. S. M.*, xv. p. lvii.

vote of eleven to ten, when one of the Mather party had stepped out; and that it was sent down to the Representatives at the noon hour, by arrangement with Cooke, when the Mather partisans in the lower House were unsuspectingly eating dinner. 'Thus pittifully did mr W[illard] succeed. Hee managed the Commencement there in 1702, but so as to expose himselfe to contempt and the Colledge to disgrace.' [1] Cotton Mather, meeting Judge Sewall in a Boston shop, roared at him loud enough for passers-by to hear, that the Judge 'had used his father worse than a Negro.' Placid Sewall then sent Increase a haunch of venison, and expostulated with Cotton from 1 Timothy v. 1, 'Rebuke not an elder, but intreat him as a father.' Cotton replied, 'he had consider'd that,' and 'charg'd the Council with Lying, Hypocrisy, Tricks, and I know not what all.' [2]

On July 1, 1702, Increase Mather wrote in his diary, 'The Colledge is in a miserable state. This day is the Commencement, where I have for many years bin honord, but am now layed aside. The Lord pardon me in that I did no more good whilest related to that society.'

Harvard College has more reason for gratitude to President Mather for what he forbore than for what he accomplished.[3] A closer attention on his part to the students would have cramped that rising generation of 'young men educated at the Colledge at Cambridge, who differ much in their principles from their parents.' Yet nobody, in the seventeenth century, wrote a finer tribute to his alma mater than that which came from the pen of Increase Mather in 1688: [4]

---

1. These vindictive feelings of Increase Mather toward Willard lasted for some time. In October 1702 he wrote to the Speaker of the House that unless the College were under a learned head, 'the Colledge and whole Country will be exposed to disgrace, as of late it has bin.' He proposes that William Brattle, whom he rates as 'sincerely pious, and fully as orthodox as the person who has had the Name of vicepresident since Mr Mortons death,' be made vice-president, as he is 'too young [40!] for president,' and that Nehemiah Hobart of Newton, 'the Repairer of Breaches,' be made President. H. U. Archives 1.15.860.

2. Sewall, *Diary*, II. 43–45; cf. *Letter-Book*, I. 263, 266, for the reconciliation.

3. After he ceased to be President, Mather made a very sound and forward-looking suggestion, in a letter to Governor Dudley, of about 1704/05, signed 'Increase Mather. Late president' and 'James Allen,' that Jeremiah Dummer (A.B. 1699), who had lately returned to Boston with a Utrecht Ph.D., be made Professor of Philology at Harvard; but nothing came of it. Harvard College Papers, I. 76; Sibley, IV. 455.

4. *A Narrative of the Miseries of New-England* (London, 1688), as reprinted in *Andros Tracts*, II. 25.

A *Colledge* that has sent forth Able and Faithful Pastors to more than 100 Christian Congregations, in that Country, besides the help they have afforded to some other parts of the World. A *Colledge* that has been supplyed with Students from *free Schooles* ordered to be setled in Every Considerable Town of the Collonies. . . .

On all this, the *Colledge* by Ingenuous and Civil Education hath had its proper Influence. The *Colledge* which *we* say was a *Noble* and *Necessary* Work, and therefore deserves all Encouragement and Promotion. *Noble*; for where is the Like in all the English America? where, even among those that in wealth do far Exceed the poor Laborious New-Englanders, is there any such thing? And *Necessary* too; for else the Rising Generations would have soon become Barbarous; because neither would their Estates reach to seek Education in *England*; neither would any person of worth goe from hence (unless driven by Persecution) so far off to seek Employment when he might have it nearer home. 'Twas therefore a brave and happy thought that first pitched upon this *Colledge*. . . .

XXIV

WILLARD TO LEVERETT

1701–1707

TEMPORARY SETTLEMENT OF 1700

For six years after Mather's dismissal, Harvard College was ruled by a commuting president and a scratch corporation, under a 'Temporary Settlement' consisting of three resolves of the General Court of Massachusetts Bay.[1] The first, dated July 13, 1700, placed the College in charge of those persons named in the draft charter of 1700, who to all intents and purposes were the Corporation from that time until October 28, 1707.[2] After Willard had replaced Mather, one of the latter's partisans must have raised in Council the constitutional point whether this so-called Corporation had the power to confer degrees. The Council voted that it had.[3] The Mather code of College Laws (1692) was still in force,[4] and the College was conducted in the usual manner; for the forms, customs, and institutions worked out under the early presidents were too well grounded, and the temper of the Corporation was too conservative, to make or even desire a change.

1. The 'Charter of 1700,' as we have seen, was only a draft, never an act or a charter. It was agreed to on July 12, 1700; the next day, the General Court brought the 'Temporary Settlement' of 1699 to an end, and made a new 'Temporary Settlement' (the eighth successive régime since 1685), with the 'Order' (i.e., Resolve) of July 13, 1700, for the text of which see Appendix E. The distinction, to be sure, is one without a difference; but it is not correct to say that the College was ever 'under' the draft charter of 1700, which never had the force of law. Increase Mather realized this, as may be seen in the postscript to his letter of March 4, 1700/01 to Stoughton (H. U. Archives 1.15.860), in which he remarks that he has never seen the 1700 draft charter.

2. The records of their infrequent meetings are in *C. S. M.*, xv. 364–81. See below, p. 549, for changes of personnel.

3. Order of April 28, 1702, in Appendix E. Increase Mather had already raised this point in his 'Queries worthy of consideration'; see above, p. 527.

4. So declared in 1697 until further notice. *C. S. M.*, xv. 356.

We may, however, notice a new and informal governing board which had grown up since 1692, as it was the embryo of the Faculty of Arts and Sciences. This board consisted of the President or Vice-President and the resident teaching fellows. The 'President and Tutors,' or 'Immediate Government,' as the new board was soon called,[1] came into existence because the large and unwieldy corporations in the successive constitutions from 1692 to 1707, meeting infrequently, could not handle ordinary cases of House management and student discipline. When important disciplinary matters, such as expulsion, were decided by the President and Tutors, they were entered in the college records between Corporation meetings.[2] This term 'Immediate Government' was used until 1825, when it was superseded by 'Faculty.'

VICE-PRESIDENT WILLARD [3]

Samuel Willard lacked the brilliance of the Mathers, but was fully competent to this new collegiate task at the age of sixty-one. John Barnard (A.B. 1700), who knew the Vice-President well, described him as 'an hard student, of great learning for that day, of a clear head, solid judgment, excellent both in preaching and in prayer, an exemplary Christian, pleasant in conversation. . . .'[4] Born in 1640 to the stout planter, fur trader, and Indian fighter of Concord, Simon Willard, Samuel

1. Mr. Matthews's first note of the phrase 'Immediate Government' is in a memorial of the fellowship controversy of 1720; but it was probably used in conversation long before. I find the abbreviation 'Iᵃ Gᵒ' in a letter of Peter Oliver (A.B. 1710) to John Denison, April 16, 1708; ms. owned by Hon. Leverett Saltonstall (A.B. 1914).

2. Such entries may be found in C. S. M., xv. 346 (Wade), 354 (Henchman), 367 (Devotion), 384 and 390 (Shattuck), 385 (Nutting — this case decided by 'President and Resident Fellows, with the Advice and Concurrence of the Non-Resident Fellows'), 391 (Nutting), 398 (Waldron), 402 (Hussey), and xvi. 425 (Moody and Gray). The systematic recording of 'Acts and Agreements of President and Tutors' begins in Wadsworth's administration, C. S. M., xiv. 315-16.

3. Sibley, ii. 13-36, with bibliography; Sidney Willard, *Memories of Youth and Manhood* (1855), i. 4-13; Ebenezer Pemberton, *Funeral Sermon on the Death of the Reverend Mr. Samuel Willard* (Boston, 1707). Samuel's father subsequently married, as second and third wives, a sister and a niece (or second cousin) of President Dunster (*N. E. H. G. R.*, LXXX. 93-94). Samuel, a child of Simon Willard by his first wife, Mary Sharpe, married (1) Abigail, daughter of the Rev. John Sherman of Watertown, and (2) Eunice, daughter of Edward Tyng, and sister of Governor Joseph Dudley's wife Rebecca Tyng. By his first wife he had, among other children, John Willard (A.B. 1690), the father of Samuel Willard (A.B. 1723), the father of Joseph Willard (A.B. 1765), President of Harvard College, 1781–1804.

4. 1 *Coll. M. H. S.*, x. 168.

The Reverend
Mr. SAMl. WILLARD.

Quantæ Pietatis imago!

Rev.^{dus} D. Ebene^r Pemberton
nuper V.D.M. apud Bostonienses
in Nova Anglia.

graduated with the Class of 1659, and a few years after began preaching at Groton. When that frontier settlement was partially destroyed and the inhabitants scattered by King Philip's warriors, Willard was called to the Third (Old South) Church in Boston, and there ministered from 1678 until his death. Once in Boston, there began to flow from his pen a succession of sermons and tracts, less numerous than those of the Mathers, but written in a clear and vigorous prose that reflected his youthful study of classical rhetoric. He was the leading exponent among Harvard graduates of the New England 'Covenant' theology, and his 'Compleat Body of Divinity,' a compilation of expository lectures on the Assembly's Shorter Catechism, covering a thousand folio pages, was published by subscription after his death.

While all New England knew what the Mathers thought on almost every subject, few people knew what Willard thought on any subject save his particular business of theology: 'He always affected that learning, which was least for *pomp* and *ostentation*, and most for service,' [1] until asked for an opinion, when he consistently showed the power of making a just estimate or wise decision in an emergency. By keeping his head and holding his tongue, when the Anglicans seized the Old South, he saved his people from a futile and bloody rebellion against Governor Andros; and his intelligent handling of a witchcraft case at Groton undoubtedly prevented a serious outbreak in Middlesex County that might have rivalled the tragedy of Essex.[2] When the Salem frenzy broke in 1692, Mr. Willard did his best to instill common sense in the heads of the witchcraft judges, three of whom were his parishioners; but he was not heeded in time.[3]

Vice-President Willard presided at the fourteen Corporation meetings held during his incumbency,[4] and moderated regularly at Commencement, probably to somewhat better effect than Increase Mather thought. He enjoyed the confidence and respect of his brother-in-law Joseph Dudley, who became Governor of Massachusetts Bay in 1702; and as the Mathers

1. Ebenezer Pemberton, 'The Author's Character,' preface to Willard's *Compleat Body of Divinity*, p. 1.
2. 4 *Coll. M. H. S.*, VIII. 555–70.
3. Thomas Brattle's letter, in G. L. Burr, *Narratives of the Witchcraft Cases* (1914), pp. 186–87.
4. *C. S. M.*, xv. 366–77.

promptly quarrelled with Governor Dudley, Willard's position, and that of the College, became the more secure. He left behind him in manuscript 'Brief Directions to a Young Scholar Designing the Ministry,' which was eagerly perused by divinity students in his day and printed long after his death.[1] A mere stop-gap until some permanent settlement of the college constitution could be made, he seems to have accepted this rôle amiably, and filled it to satisfaction.

Willard inherited from the Mather régime three tutors: Henry Flynt (A.B. 1693), who had served but one year of his record term of fifty-five, Jabez Fitch (A.B. 1694), and Nathaniel Saltonstall (A.B. 1695), who, after endeavoring for a year and a half to instruct the small but unresponsive Class of 1704, went to England to care for his father's property. Fitch obtained a pulpit the next year. The two junior fellowships 'of the House' were then filled by Jonathan Remington (A.B. 1696), who held the post eight years, subsequently entering the law, and Josiah Willard (A.B. 1698), the Vice-President's son. According to his pupil Thomas Prince, young Mr. Willard 'shined in the Politeness, Freeness, Openess and Pleasancy of his Conversation, and in a very generous and manly sort of Conduct.'[2] He resigned in 1706 to follow the sea. Twice already he had almost been drowned when sailing in Boston Harbor;[3] but he escaped the fate of many Boston seafarers, and rose to command his own ship. After sailing the triangular route between Boston, Europe, and the West Indies for fifteen years and undergoing sundry hardships and adventures, Captain Willard returned to Boston and obtained a commission from George I as Secretary of the Province, a post which he held until 1756. Obviously, Harvard students were now having a different type of young man for tutor from the clerical fellows of the last century. Or, to put it another way, the high scholars chosen to be tutors no longer regarded a ministerial career as inevitable.

The average graduating class in Samuel Willard's administration was twelve, slightly less than the average for the previous decades.

1. Pemberton, *op. cit.*, p. 135; Sibley, II. 35.
2. Sibley, IV. 426.
3. 'This is the second time Sam has been neer drown'd with Josiah Willard.' Samuel Sewall, *Diary*, II. 13 (April 29, 1700).

THE LIBERAL CONGREGATIONAL MOVEMENT

In our lengthy discussion of changing charters and presidential manoeuvres, in the previous chapter, we said nothing about the split in the puritan (or Congregational) party between the Mathers and the Brattles, since to us it seems to have had slight influence on charter-mongering and none on the result. We must now look into it, in reference both to the next presidential election and to the founding of Harvard's first, oldest, and dearest rival, Yale University.

There is no outward evidence of hostility between the Mathers on the one side and Leverett and the Brattles on the other until 1699; but we can discern signs of a growing coolness about two years earlier. On the witchcraft question in 1692 they were united, not divided.[1] Thomas Brattle was elected Treasurer of Harvard College in 1693, when Increase Mather was President; and his name, with those of his brother and of Leverett, appears in the list of fellows in the College Charter of 1697 and in the bill of 1696; Leverett and William Brattle were fellows in the 1692 Charter as well. Neither in Increase Mather's diary, nor in Cotton's, nor in Cotton's account of Harvard College in the *Magnalia*,[2] is there any hint of coolness. Leverett and both Brattles fell in with the Corporation's 'Proposals' of 1694 respecting the collection of marvellous providences,[3] and joined the Mathers in defeating the proposed Charter of 1696. Increase Mather later declared that he 'advised the precious Church in Cambridge' to elect William Brattle their pastor; and he took part in Brattle's ordination, although the form thereof was distasteful to him, as we shall see presently.[4] If the liberal and 'Catholic spirit' of Leverett and William Brattle as tutors, their friendly attitude toward the Church of England and recommendation of Anglican writings to their pupils,[5] had been suspected by Increase Mather, no doubt he would have felt differently about them; one of

---

1. See above, pp. 494, 497 n.
2. The *Magnalia* does not mention the disallowance of the Charter of 1692, hence book iv on the history of the College must have been written before July 1696; the 1698 triennial catalogue was doubtless added after the rest of the work was finished in 1697. Cf. *F. H. C.*, p. 289 n., and *C. S. M.*, xxi. 170 n.
3. See above, p. 504.
4. Sibley, iii. 201.
5. See above, pp. 505–06.

the advantages of his Olympian attitude toward the College was ignorance of what was going on.

The first evidence that Increase Mather suspected something amiss is found in his 'Epistle' addressed to Church and Scholars of Cambridge, in Cotton Mather's 'Life of the Reverend and Excellent Jonathan Mitchel.'[1] The preface is dated May 7, 1697, and the book came out in Boston the same year. Mather's general drift was to praise orthodox Congregationalism, and to denounce any deviation therefrom as contrary to the Word of God. The first part was addressed to Cambridge Church, over which William Brattle had been ordained the previous November without the traditional 'laying on of hands,' and where he had promptly introduced a few small changes in the order of the service.[2] Mather described in loving detail how things had been done under 'blessed Mr. Mitchel,' and bluntly informed the Cantabrigians that if they allowed anything different they would be no better than degenerate apostates to God's truth.

The following passages were addressed to William Brattle in his tutorial capacity and to John Leverett:

A few Words let me further speak to you, who belong to that *Nursery*, for Religion and Learning, which has for a long time been the *Glory*, not of *Cambridge* only, but of *New-England*. . . . There is no One Thing of Greater Concernment to these Churches, in present and after-times, than the Prosperity of that *Society*. They cannot subsist without a *Colledge*. There are at this day not above Two or Three of our Churches but what are supplyed from thence. Nor are the Churches like to continue *pure Golden Candle-sticks*, if the *Colledge*, which should supply them, prove *Apostate*. If the *Fountain* be corrupted, How should the *Streams* be pure, which should *make Glad the City of God?* How should *Plants of Renown* spring up from thence, if the *Colledge* it self become a *Degenerate Plant?* You that are *Tutors* there, have a Great Advantage put into your Hands (and I pray God give you Wisdom to know it!) to prevent it. The Lord hath made you *Fathers* to many *Pupils*. You will not deny, but that He has made *me* a *Father* to *you*. It was my Recommendation, that brought you into that *Station*. And therefore, as my *Joy* will be Greater to see you Acquit your selves *Worthily*, so my earnest Sollicitudes for it must needs be the more, on *that* Account. There are many

---

1. T. J. Holmes, *op. cit.*, I. 231; reprinted in *Magnalia*, book iv. 158–65, whence my quotations are taken. I do not find it mentioned in Cotton Mather's *Diary*. He published eight other tracts the same year (Sibley, III. 64–65).

2. Sibley, III. 200.

(I believe, you wish you could say so of all of them) who were once under your *Tuition*, that do worthily in *Ephratah*, and are like to be famous in *Bethlehem*, for which you ought to (and I doubt not but you do) humbly Bless the Lord, That *you* (and they who shall succeed you) may be yet *Greater Blessings*, Let me commend unto you the Example of this Blessed Man, whose *Life* is here described. When *Jerom* had considered the Life of *Hilarion*, he Resolved *Hilarion shall be the Champion, whom I will follow!* Say each of you, 𝕸𝖎𝖙𝖈𝖍𝖊𝖑𝖑, (once a *Tutor* in *Harvard-Colledge*) *shall be the Example, whom I will imitate!* You will see in the Story of his Life, that he did not only Instruct his *Pupils* in the Knowledge of the *Tongues* and *Arts*, but that he would sometimes discourse them about the *Spiritual Estate* of their Immortal Souls.

In other words, I made you what you are, take care that you do my bidding!

Language such as this, addressed to the two veteran Fellows who had had entire charge of the House during Mather's absence of four years and who had been the sole instructors for twelve years, was imprudent as well as offensive. On May 27, 1697, about three weeks after Mather's preface was signed, the local association of ministers met in college hall and declared 'that they were made sensible of the tendencies which there are amongst us towards Deviations from the good Order wherein our Churches have . . . been happily established and continued.'[1]

Did Increase Mather's preface cause Leverett and Brattle to resign as tutors? Probably not. Brattle as minister of Cambridge and Leverett as representative for Cambridge were obviously remaining as tutors merely until successors could be agreed upon; but there is much reason to believe that the question of their successors was a bone of contention between the liberals and conservatives. Increase Mather's diary for September 4, 1697 mentions trouble about electing tutors. Leverett and Brattle resigned after October 8, 1697.[2] Ebenezer Pemberton (A.B. 1691), who was certainly a liberal, and Jabez Fitch (A.B. 1694), who probably was not one at this time,[3] 'were chosen to be Tutours in Harvard Colledge' at a Corporation

1. T. J. Holmes, *op. cit.*, II. 390, 397 n. 2.
2. See above, pp. 507–08.
3. Note their rival candidacy for the assistant ministry of the Old South; Sibley, IV. 108, 202. But Fitch later signed the address in favor of President Leverett.

meeting on November 15.[1] A few days later Samuel Willard, who had been present, told Judge Sewall 'of the falling out between the President and him about Chusing Fellows last Monday. Mr. Mather has sent him word, He will never come to his House more till he give him satisfaction.'[2] Obviously it was the election of Mr. Pemberton that produced these unchristian sentiments from Mr. President Mather.

For two years this latent controversy smouldered, and then it burst into flames. A group of Boston merchants, among whom Treasurer Brattle and John Mico were prominent, proposed to found a liberal Congregational church.[3] William Brattle, John Leverett, Ebenezer Pemberton, and Simon Bradstreet (A.B. 1693) were openly sympathetic to the movement, and joined in urging Benjamin Colman (A.B. 1692), a favorite pupil of the two Harvard tutors, to accept the pastorate.[4] Colman was then in England; and the organizers of the new church, knowing that the Mathers and their sort would make difficulties about his ordination in the usual Congregational way, played a smart trick by having him obtain Presbyterian ordination in London before coming over. Colman did not receive the invitation until June 19, 1699, at Bath. But the Mathers must have suspected what was afoot. Nothing else can explain the President's effort to have a religious test inserted in the charter bill that passed both Houses July 13, 1699, or dropping the names of Thomas Brattle and John Leverett from the proposed corporation in that charter, at the last minute.[5] Lord Bellomont had a good mind, so he wrote Judge Sewall, to restore the names of at least one of these men to the draft; he wondered 'whether it be best to humour Mr. Mather's Selfishnesse and pedantick pride,' or to honor 'the vertue, Learning and merit of Mr. Brattle and Mr. Pemberton.'[6]

Colman arrived in Boston on November 1, 1699; and before the month was out his church issued a 'Manifesto' of its principles that threw the fat in the fire.[7]

1. C. S. M., xv. 357. Mr. Matthews shows on p. lii n. that the inclusion of White's name was a 'clerical error.'

2. Sewall, Diary, I. 464.

3. 'The germ of the society . . . was formed as early as January, 1698.' S. K. Lothrop, History of the Church in Brattle Street (1851), p. 43.

4. Id. 47-50.

5. C. S. M., xv. p. xlix n.

6. N. E. H. G. R., XIX. 236.

7. Printed in Lothrop, op. cit., pp. 20-26.

The innovations adopted by this Brattle Street or 'Manifesto' Church were all in matters of ecclesiastical polity; there was no dissent from the orthodox puritan theology professed by the New England churches. The practice of public confession of religious experiences before admission to the Lord's Supper was abandoned; the Lord's Prayer was used; the Bible was read without comment; all children of professing Christians, whether communicants or not, were admitted to baptism.[1] These changes in 'Gospel order,' trivial and innocent enough as they seem to us, were really a significant challenge to the New England Way. The Mathers by this time were reconciled to tolerating other sects, they could understand wolves trying to break down the puritan 'hedge,' but they had no patience with sheep trying to eat their way out. And the 'Manifesto' was provocative, almost truculent, in tone. Increase Mather replied to it in 'The Order of the Gospel' (1700). Colman retorted the same year with 'Gospel Order Revived,' and Cotton Mather came back with 'A Collection Of Some Of the Many Offensive Matters Contained in a Pamphlet Entituled, The Order of the Gospel Revived' (1701), prefaced by his father.[2] The Mathers were not used to having people answer them back; and Colman's retort had the further offence of being witty at their expense. That was the unforgivable sin. As a popular ballad of the period put it:

> Relations are Rattle with Brattle and Brattle,
>   Lord Brother mayn't command,
> But Mather and Mather had rather had rather
>   The good old way should stand.
> Saints Cotton and Hooker, Oh look down and look 'ere
>   Where's Platform, Way and the Keys?
> Oh Torrey with story of Brattle Church Tory
>   To have things as they please.
> Our Merchants *cum* Mico do stand *sacro vico*
>   Our Churches turn genteel;
> Our Parsons grow trig with Wealth, Wine and Wig,
>   And their heads are covered with meal.

As this doggerel suggests, the Brattle Street movement was not popular, but 'high-brow,' one which the ordinary New

---

1. Williston Walker, *The Creeds and Platforms of Congregationalism* (New York, 1893), pp. 473–74.
2. T. J. Holmes, *op. cit.*, II. 386–97; Sibley, IV. 129.

Englander regarded with conservative repugnance tinged by social envy. In a small puritan community, any religious controversy is the subject of unending conversation, and news travels fast. So it can readily be appreciated that around 1700 or 1701 many conservative church members may have regarded Harvard College as a place where young men were trained up to novel and dangerous principles, in spite of Mr. President Mather's efforts. And in 1701 Dr. Mather was turned out and replaced by Mr. Willard, who had befriended one of the young radicals.[1] There is no evidence or even probability that Leverett and the Brattles had any influence on the presidential crisis of 1700-01. Mather was dropped by the pious and orthodox majority in the General Court. But one can easily see how he might be represented as a victim of rash innovators. His reference to a 'person disaffected to the Order of the Gospel' in his letter of June 30, 1701,[2] was a clear hit at Leverett, Colman, and their friends.

THE FOUNDING OF YALE

'The first Movers for a College in Connecticut alledged this as a Reason, because the Colledge at Cambridge was under the Tutorage of Latitudinarians,' wrote, twenty years later, the Reverend Moses Noyes (A.B. 1659).[3] The Mathers, and other conservative Bostonians such as Samuel Sewall, at once showed an interest in the Connecticut college movement that to Harvardians has sometimes seemed over-friendly; but we must not read later rivalries into this affair, or place too much emphasis on the fear of a budding Harvard liberalism. A collegiate establishment had been talked of at New Haven since 1648 and earnestly promoted by John Davenport and James Pierpont (A.B. 1681), pastors of that town.[4] Connecticut Colony and the Connecticut Valley of Massachusetts were full of Harvard graduates and others who wished to send their boys

---

1. Sibley, IV. 108, 202.   2. See above, p. 533.
3. To Samuel Sewall, 6 *Coll. M. H. S.*, I. 15. Noyes was commenting on Rector Cutler's apostasy to Anglicanism. Also in Franklin B. Dexter, *Documentary History of Yale University*, p. 242.
4. Franklin B. Dexter, *Biographical Sketches of the Graduates of Yale College with Annals*, I. 1; Edwin Oviatt, *Beginnings of Yale*.

to a college nearer home. Many good people in this region believed that Harvard was too expensive and infested with idle sons of wealthy merchants, 'rakehells' and 'blades.' For instance, the Reverend Solomon Stoddard (A.B. 1662) of Northampton sent two sons to Harvard, who graduated respectively in 1697 and 1701. His election sermon preached at Boston in May 1703 plainly gave notice that the 'pope of the Connecticut Valley' was not pleased with current customs at alma mater:

Places of Learning should not be Places of Riot and Pride: wayes of profuseness and prodigality in such a Society, lay a foundation of a great deal of sorrow; fond and proud Parents should not be suffered to introduce evil customes; 'tis not worth the while for persons to be sent to the *Colledge* to learn to Complement men, and Court Women; they should be sent thither to prepare them for Publick Service, and had need to be under the over-sight of wise and holy men.[1]

The founders, the early rectors, and almost all the first trustees of Yale were Harvard men; the meeting organizing the College took place in the parlor of the Reverend Samuel Russell (A.B. 1681); and several loyal Harvardians of Boston, notably Judge Sewall, aided the movement with advice and prayer.[2]

The first Yale graduate was Nathaniel, grandson of President Chauncy and son of Nathaniel Chauncy (A.B. 1661). Chauncy inherited so large a share of the family intellect that Abraham Pierson (A.B. 1668), first rector of the Collegiate School, was able to prepare him not merely for the A.B. but the A.M. in the surprisingly short space of four months; he took both degrees at Commencement 1702. No evidence of unfriendliness at Cambridge toward the rising institution has been detected. There was, perhaps, some jealousy at the propensity of the new College to dress up her early Commencements by granting M.A.'s to Harvard graduates in Connecticut, and thus deprive Harvard of their Commencement fees. On the other side, the

---

1. *The Way for a People to Live Long in the Land that God Hath given them* (Boston, 1703), p. 13.

2. F. B. Dexter, *op. cit.*, p. 8. Samuel Sewall's letter is most amusing. He conceived that the mission of the Connecticut college was to reëstablish the Harvard of his undergraduate days; to do everything 'as the late Reverend and Godly Learned Mr. Charles Chauncey was wont to doe at Cambridge.' The draft for a charter prepared by Sewall and Addington (*id.* 18) even proposed to insert a provision that William Ames's *Medulla Theologiae* should be 'diligently read in the Latin Tongue, and well studyed by all Schollars educated in the said School.'

Connecticut Trustees objected to sending 'to cambridge' for a tutor.[1] When President Leverett in 1709 'proposed the Desires of three Young Gentlemen,' graduates of Yale, to take the Harvard A.M., the Corporation advised 'that it is not advisable to admit the Persons above mentioned to their Degrees the Commencment now approaching.'[2] But the Corporation soon relented, and from 1714 it was common for Yale graduates resident in or visiting Massachusetts to be admitted *ad eundem gradum* at Harvard.[3] It is true that the Mathers, after 1701, and Jeremiah Dummer (A.B. 1699), who failed of obtaining a coveted professorship at Harvard, later threw their influence in favor of the Collegiate School; and it was Cotton Mather who, after being twice balked of the Harvard presidency, had the bright thought of writing to a certain East India nabob of Boston birth and former New Haven residence that 'if what is forming at New Haven might wear the name of YALE COLLEGE, it would be better than *a name of sons and daughters*.'[4] But Harvard friendliness to Yale was not confined to the conservatives. When Tutor Elisha Williams (A.B. 1711) led off a secession of Yale students to Wethersfield and proposed to lead them still further, to Cambridge, it was the liberal Benjamin Colman, then a Fellow of Harvard College, who declined to 'weaken and dishearten your Accademy' by encouraging the seceders.[5] It may well be a matter for congratulation and pride that Harvard men not only founded, governed, and supported Yale in her infancy, but even obtained for her a patron, a library, and a name.

THE ELECTION OF LEVERETT

Governor Joseph Dudley, who took office as Lord Bellomont's successor in 1702, was an old friend of Leverett's and a brother-in-law of Vice-President Willard. He quickly became embroiled with the popular branch of the General Court; and it was probably to strike the Governor through Willard, rather than to champion the 'evangelical Interests,' that the House on March 12, 1703 resolved unanimously 'That the Reverend Mr Cotton Mather be treated with, in Order to be Obtained, for

---

1. F. B. Dexter, *op. cit.*, p. 53.   2. *C. S. M.*, xv. 387.
3. *Quinquennial Catalogue*, 1930, pp. 1146–47.
4. Quincy, I. 525.
5. Colman to Timothy Woodbridge, June 4, 1718. *C. S. M.*, vi. 184.

a resident President of Harvard Colledge.' Cotton was willing enough; but this impending calamity, the worst that had
threatened Harvard in thirty years, was averted the next day
when the Council negatived the order and informed the Representatives in no uncertain terms that they would accept no
president 'Named by that House.' [1]

Increase Mather attempted to revive charter-mongering in
1705. On receipt of a letter from William Blathwayt of the
Board of Trade that the College could have a royal charter
if the General Court would see reason in the matter of the
visitation, he wrote to Governor Dudley proposing that His
Excellency initiate the business and officiously enclosing a list
of names for the fellowships, 'all except the president.' The
Governor appears to have been unwilling to stir up the General
Court unnecessarily, and nothing was done. [2]

The *de facto* Corporation directed by the Court's order of
July 13, 1700 to govern the College 'until his majestie's pleasure
shall be known' had already undertaken to fill its own vacancies.
In this way the conservative slate of Fellows arranged by Increase Mather gradually became diluted with liberals. Cotton
Mather and Nehemiah Walter attended no more meetings after
the elder Mather was dropped, and were considered as having
'abdicated' in 1703, when the Brattle brothers were elected to
their seats. [3] Leverett and Pemberton were chosen to fill other
vacancies on August 6, 1707.

They were just in time. Vice-President Willard, now in his
sixty-eighth year, was taken seriously ill on August 11, when
visiting Cambridge to expound Scripture to the students; the
next day he requested Judge Sewall to submit his resignation
to the Governor and Council, as he 'believ'd he was near his
end.' [4] The Judge did as he was asked on the fourteenth, where-
upon the General Court appointed a committee to visit the
Vice-President and express their thanks for his services. (The

1. *C. S. M.*, xv. pp. lvii-lviii, notes; Cotton Mather, *Diary*, I. 472.
2. Blathwayt to Mather, June 1, 1704, Mather's drafts to Dudley of Jan. 2 and
Feb. 20, 1704/05, Mather's draft of proposed address to the Governor by 'severall [?]
belonging to Harvard College in Cambridge,' Mather's draft to Blathwayt, March
6, 1704/05; in H. U. Archives 1.15.860.
3. *C. S. M.*, xv. pp. liv note 1, cli.
4. Sewall, *Diary*, II. 193. Willard had evidently been in poor health for some time,
since on May 8, 1707, William Brattle sounded Increase Mather as to his accepting
an invitation from the Corporation to preside at Commencement. H. U. Archives I.
15.860.

lower House took this occasion to nominate the Reverend
Nehemiah Hobart as a new acting Vice-President, but were
properly snubbed by the Council.) On September 7 Mr. Willard had sufficiently recovered to baptize a child and admin-
ister the Lord's Supper at the Old South; but on the twelfth
he 'cut his finger while eating oysters' and fell into a convulsion.
Friends and neighbors rushed in, and Judge Sewall saw his
'dear Pastor Expire.' 'There was a dolefull cry in the house.'
At the funeral next day, the two Mathers, Benjamin Colman,
Benjamin Wadsworth, James Allen, and Thomas Bridge bore
the body from the Old South parsonage to the ancient burying
place by King's Chapel; fellows and students of Harvard College led the procession. The Vice-President's body was laid
next that of his old college tutor, Joshua Moody, in the Sewall
tomb. 'Very Comfortable Day,' concludes the Judge.[1]

On October 28, 1707, the Corporation met at Cambridge and
proceeded to a ballot for President. John Leverett had eight
votes, Increase Mather three, Cotton Mather one, and William
Brattle one.[2] The Corporation drafted an Humble Address to
Governor Dudley announcing the election, praising Leverett as
a 'very Faithfull and able Instrument to Promote the Holy
Religion here practised,' commending him to His Excellency's
'Favourable Acceptation,' and praying His Excellency to present his name 'to the Honourable Generall Assembly, and move
for His honourable Subsistance.'[3] It was voted that the Reverend Mr. Allen as senior fellow present this to His Excellency
in the name of all, and 'Mr. Treasurer with the Fellows, living
in Boston are desired to Accompany the Reverend Mr. Allen,
when He waits upon the Governor with the said Address.'[4]

John Leverett, Esquire, sometime tutor and fellow of Harvard College, had learned a good deal of human nature in the
course of the last ten years, during which he had practised
law, represented Cambridge in the General Court, served as
Speaker of the House, Councillor, and Judge of the Superior
Court, and gone on a mission to the expedition against Port
Royal. He and his friends well knew that the Mathers would
bring all their influence to bear in order to prevent the General

1. C. S. M., xv. p. lix n.; Sibley, ii. 23; Sewall, *Diary*, ii. 193–95.
2. C. S. M., xv. 379; Sewall, *Diary*, ii. 196. 'Mr White did not vote, and Mr.
Gibbs came when voting was over.'
3. C. S. M., xv. 379.
4. *Id.* 380.

Court from accepting Leverett's election and voting him a
salary. Governor Dudley's favor they could count on; but
they anticipated that the Mathers would cry down Leverett
as a 'Manifesto' liberal, which would prejudice the country
members. Accordingly, Leverett's friends drafted an address
to the Governor from the ministers, and circulated five identical copies in different parts of the Province to obtain signatures.
They were so far successful that thirty-nine ministers' signatures were obtained, from all parts of the Province except the
Islands, Maine, and the Connecticut Valley, which it was impossible to reach in time.[1]

The address is an impressive tribute to Leverett's character
and competence:

May it please your Excellency.

We have lately with great Joy understood the great and Early
care, that Our Brethren, who have the present Care and Oversight of
the Colledge at Cambridge, have taken in Supplying the Place of the
Late Reverend and Learned Mr. Samuel Willard deceased, by their
Unanimous Choice of Mr. John Leverett, A Worthy Member of that
Society, to be President of that Colledge. And we humbly take the
freedom to Acquaint and Assure your Excellency, That no person
whatsoever could be more Acceptable to us in that Station. Your
Excellency personaly knows Mr. Leverett So well, that We Shal Say
the Less of him, however we cannot but give this Testimony of our
great Affection to and Esteem of him, that We are abundantly Satisfied and Assur'd of his Religion and Learning and other Excellent
Accomplishments for that Eminent Service, A Long Experience of
which we had while he was the Seniour Fellow of that House, for that
under the Wise and faithfull Government of him and the Reverend
Mr. Brattle of Cambridge the greatest part of the now rising Ministry
in New England were happiely Educated, And we hope and promise
ourselves, through the blessing of the God of our Fathers to See
Religion and Learning thrive and flourish in that Society under Mr.
Leverett's Wise Conduct and Influence as much as ever yet it hath
done

Wee Accept with all Thankfullness your Excellency's great, Sincere

---

1. The originals are in Mass. Archives, LVIII. 254–60, and are printed in *Acts and
Resolves of the Province*, VIII. 796, and, inaccurately, in Quincy, I. 504–05. The Address
is also copied into President Leverett's ms. Diary (H. U. Archives), pp. 3–5, which is
the text used here. The oldest signer was Samuel Whiting of Billerica (A.B. 1653),
and the youngest, Nathaniel Pitcher of Scituate (A.B. 1703); 19 or 20 had been Leverett's pupils in College. I am indebted to Mr. Matthews for an analysis of the
signatures.

and Constant care and respect to the Colledge, and doubt not but you will now readiely give an Instance of it, not onely in Approving the Choice made, but also in procuring and Encouraging as much as in you Lyes an Honourable Support and maintenance (for the President) the Granting of which we doubt not but that our Great and General Court will Chearfully and readiely take Effectual Care of. Your Excellency will Easiely excuse the freedom we take, when you consider how very near and Dear both to yourself and us the Interest of that Society is, and that the Support and encouragment of Religion and Learning in the Colledge is of the Last Importance to the Church and State of New England: Wee Shall add no more, but pray for the Divine blessing on your Excellency's person, family and happy Government, and Subscribe ourselves

Your Excellency's
Sincere and humble Servants

The Mathers promptly wheeled their batteries into action, as may be seen from an unsigned and undated letter in Cotton Mather's unmistakable handwriting, addressed to William Denison (A.B. 1681), Representative of Roxbury in the General Court:[1]

Sir —

Now there is a Violent Essay, to betray the College, and to destroy all the Ch[urche]s of N. E. happy will be the man, that shall appear effectually at this critical Time in the cause of God.

I know no man in the Assembly but Mr *Denison* to be in this Cause relied upon. And give me Leave to say, *If thou altogether hold thy peace at this Time!* —

Sir, You ought to lett the House know, That the best men in the Countrey are very ill satisfied in the *principles* of the *person*, who is now *commended unto you for a praesident.*

That, to make a lawyer, and one who never affected the study of Divinity, a praesident for a College of Divines,[2] will be a very preposterous thing, a thing without a precedent. That the same Reasons, which moved your House to judge him unfitt for the Council, may argue his unfitness for the Colledge.[3]

And, whereas there will be brought you, a sham-recommendation of him, from the ministers of the countrey, — you ought to inform

---

1. This letter was among the family papers of the late Justice Oliver Wendell Holmes, given by him to the M. H. S. It is endorsed '7br or 8er 1707.'

2. This is the earliest instance that has come to my notice of Harvard's being called a divinity college.

3. Leverett was elected to the Council in 1706, to represent Sagadahoc, where he owned land; but was not elected in 1707.

them, (the care of Truth required in the 9th Commandment, will oblige you to it,) that it has been procured in the most fallacious and fraudulent manner, that ever was heard of.

The very first clause of their Instrument (*That he was unanimously chosen by the Fellows*) is a notorious Falsehood in matter of Fact. There were but seven or eight that voted for the man.[1] They who have cyphers before their Names, in the enclosed catalogue, declare, that they voted for another. They who have stars, voted not at all. And it is certain that the Fools which went unto the ministers about the countrey, obtained their Hands with other Insinuations, which were as False as the clause now complained of.

Hitherto, the Governor pretended the Nomination must not come from you, but from him. It now comes from neither, but from seven or eight men, some of whom, you never thought fitt to be brought in to the Corporation.[2]

If you vote an Approbation of what these men have done, you are trick'd into the snares of a former vote, that obliges you to give him 220*lb* a year.

Certainly your desire, that your old praesident, would, (until you can take further order) act as formerly, and as lately you have allow'd a vice-praesident to do, would be (with less money thrown away) more for the [*blot*] and Honour and welfare: and some Reparation for the Indignities that have been offered him.— But, of that as you please.

If any one man of your prudence and Courage, would boldly insist on these things, the Churches might yett be saved.

Sins of omission will be accounted for.

The Governour has tried many wayes to obtain a Subsistence for a Needy Lawyer. On the failing of other wayes, must the Gen[eral] Ass[embly] and all our Churches be thus putt upon.

If you vote this matter, I would pray, that the vote be fairly expressed; And the Colledge be directly Voted into the hands of the Bishop of London.[3]

Syr, you will pardon my Freedom. You will conceal my Letter. You will consider the matter.

Nothing but a vast concern for our Holy Religion, and a beleef of your Discretion and Fidelity could have extorted this, from,

Syr, your sincere

Fr[ien]d and Servt.

---

1. True, as we have seen from Judge Sewall's Diary; but the Corporation may well have made the choice unanimous, before they adjourned.

2. This constitutional point was well taken. The Corporation had no right under the Court Orders creating the Temporary Settlement of 1700–02, to fill vacancies; and from what other source could they derive that right?

3. A hit at Leverett's kindly feelings toward the Church of England.

Leverett had plenty to say on the subject in a letter that he wrote to his friend Henry Newman in London the following year. Unfortunately his rough draft, which is all we have, is partly in his own system of shorthand, and cannot all be deciphered: [1]

Cambridge, New England, August 26, 1708.

Sir

... I cannot but inform you that notwithstanding the great Industry that Mr. M[ather] has used to bring me into disgrace with my Countrey, & to put every body into Terrour that I have led the voyaging Israelites back to Egypt, as their phrase is, Alm[ighty] God has not smiled upon their attempts. And they have been equally frustrated in the effect of their insolent treatment of his Excellency; as to the body of the people, by their rudeness, they have lost most of their reputation and Interest. The Ministers do so generally resent their temper and orders that they ... those who have do not nor cannot run to the same excess of Insolence, and sedition, and dispight to Government ... I hope that the Loyalty and deference to Superiors by which the Ministers of this Countrey ... Non Nobis, Non Nobis, Sed Nomini tuo Sit Omnis Laus et gloria integra. Amen. ...

The address of the thirty-nine ministers was the most effective answer that could have been devised to Matherian representations that Judge Leverett was a renegade, an apostate to the true Word, who would train up a generation of religious perverts and lead the country 'back to Egypt' (the Church of England). But it did not answer the serious doubt whether the scratch Corporation of 1700 had any right to elect a President of Harvard College; and from two mischievous little resolves found among the Mather papers, it seems probable that some of the lower House were disposed to take that line.[2] Nor had the ministers answered the charge that Leverett was a 'tory,' that is, a friend to Governor Dudley and the royal

1. Ms. owned by the Hon. Leverett Saltonstall; Mr. D. H. McPherson has kindly deciphered such part as can be deciphered.

2. 'Voted. That it belongs to the General Assembly to nominate and appoint the President of the Colledge as well as to state His salary, and that the denial hereof is an invasion on the Privilege and Power of this Court.'

'Voted, That it is the opinion of this House that the Colledge ought to be forth with settled with a President residing there, Chosen by this Court, and that if any Person shall presume to act as President not chosen by this court, no salary shall be allowed to Him out of the publick Treasury.' Misc. Mss., M. H.S., from the Holmes-Mather papers.

GOVERNOR JOSEPH DUDLEY

Anna Regina —

At a Great and General Court or Assembly for Her Majesty's Province of the
Massachusetts Bay in New England begun and held at Boston upon Wednesday the
Twenty eighth of May 1707. And continued by several Prorogations unto Wednesday
the 29th of October following, being their Third Sessions —

Thursday
Decemr 4th 1707 —

In the Council

The Governour, Council & House having Accepted and Approved the Choice made by the Fellows of Harvard College
in Council of Mr John Leverett to be President in the room of the President of the P. College to fill up that Vacancy

Ordered That the House of Representatives Consider of and Grant a suitable Salary to be paid to the President
annually out of the Publick Treasury for his Encouragement and support during his Continuance in that Office
residing at Cambridge, and Discharging the proper Dutys to a President belonging and Orderly Devote himself
to that service —

And forasmuch as the Constitution and Establishment of that House and the Government thereof hath its
Original from an Act of the General Court made and pass'd in the year One Thousand Six Hundred & fifty —
which has not been Repealed or Nulled

The President and Fellows of the P. College are Directed from time to time to regulate themselves according to the
Rules of the Constitution by the Act aforesaid And to Exercise the Power and Authority thereby
granted for the Government of that House And to support thereof —

Saturday
Decemr 20th 1707 —

In the House of Representatives Ordered that the Vote passed in Council the 4th Curt referring to the College with
the Amendment annexed thereto And that further addition hereon Viz. That the Sum for Salary be One
Hundred and Sixty pounds, to which the Council Voted an Agreement —

By His Excellency the Governour —

Consented to — Dudley

G P Addington Secry

prerogative; and snatches of Leverett's own letter suggest that that charge was true. One gathers, too, that his many years of teaching had made Leverett somewhat austere; that as Speaker he had not been 'one of the boys' in the General Court. And he had been rendered ridiculous when returning with the defeated troops from Port Royal, having shared their chamber-pot salutes from the upper windows in the North End of Boston.[1]

The Council, after the humble addresses of the Fellows and the ministers had been read, voted (November 11, 1707) that the election of Mr. Leverett be accepted. But the House, where rural piety was strongest, non-concurred, and talked of another president *pro tempore.* It looked like a deadlock. 'The House of Deputies is out of Humour,' remarked Governor Dudley.[2]

His Excellency, whose education, begun on the parental farm and continued at Harvard, had been perfected in the House of Commons, thought up an ingenious horse-trade. If the lower House would concur in the election of Leverett and vote him a suitable salary, Governor and Council would agree to discard the 'Temporary Settlement,' forget about the Charter of 1700, and declare the Charter of 1650 in force again! Such a concession on the part of Her Majesty's Governor, a tacit recognition of the old Bay Colony principle that the General Court had a right to charter a college without permission from the Crown, carried the House off its feet. All personal objections to Leverett vanished when that constitutional point was yielded by Dudley. And the trade had the further merit (which the Representatives did not have the wit to see until too late) that if the Charter of 1650 were restored, the Corporation must be reduced from seventeen members to seven, thus (if nothing were said to the contrary) giving the Governor the chance to select from the large *de facto* Corporation that elected Leverett the five Fellows most acceptable to him and to the President.[3]

1. 6 *Coll. M. H. S.,* iii. 335–36, 387–90.
2. *C. S. M.,* xv. pp. lix, lx; Sewall, *Diary,* ii. 203–04.
3. This was done on the day of Leverett's inauguration. Dudley reduced the Corporation to the President, the two Brattles (Thomas as Treasurer), Pemberton, Flynt, Remington, and Nehemiah Hobart (Sewall, *Diary,* ii. 209). Thus all but one or two of those who voted for Leverett were left in the Corporation. Most of the other fellows under the Temporary Settlement became Overseers *ex officio.* See the angry protest of the Mathers against this game in 1 *Coll. M. H. S.,* iii. 126–38, and Dudley's rebuke.

Restoration of the Charter of 1650

After considerable shuffling of bills and resolves between the two Houses,[1] an agreement was reached on December 6, 1707, in the shape of a concurrent resolve, the engrossed and signed copy of which is a basic constitutional document of Harvard University.[2]

The Century of Enlightenment opened somewhat belatedly in Harvard College on Wednesday the fourteenth of January, 1708, with the installation of Mr. President Leverett. His Excellency Governor Joseph Dudley, 'attended by Mr. President, the Fellows and the Overseers[3] went into the Hall; and, In presence of the Scholars and a numerous Company of Gentlemen from severall Parts, Declared Mr. John Leverett to be the Reverend President of the said College, and put the Care of that Seminary into His Hands agreable to the Choice of the Fellows of The House,' delivering to him the College Seal, keys, records, and the Charter of 1650, and 'Directing Him to Govern that House, and the Scholars there, with Duty and Allegiance to Our Soveraign Lady The Queen, And Obedience to Her Majesty's Laws.'[4]

Sons of Harvard

In the long run, a college or university is known by her fruits. She will be judged by the character of her alumni, and the services they perform to the communities in which they reside. But she is not entitled to claim full credit for their achievements; the human material that goes into the academic hopper to a considerable degree determines the quality of the product. On

---

1. Sewall, *Diary*, II. 205; *C. S. M.*, xv. p. lx. The House tried to insert in the bill a promise that Judge Leverett resign his several civil offices, but was satisfied with the clause that he 'intirely Devote himselfe' to Harvard. According to A. C. Goodell, 'Leverett acted as judge of Probate as late as July 22, 1708.' *Acts and Resolves of the Province*, viii. 799.

2. Printed in Appendix E, below.

3. This was the first meeting of the Board of Overseers since 1692. The Councillors of the Province were considered equivalent to the Assistants under the old Charter. In the list of clerical Overseers present at the inauguration, the Mathers, James Allen, and Nehemiah Walter (Increase Mather's son-in-law) are conspicuously absent.

4. Nathan Prince's copy from College Book IV, 30 (printed in *C. S. M.*, xv. 381), in Holmes-Mather Mss., M. H. S. Cf. Executive Records of the Council (Mass. Archives), iv. 519, quoted in *Acts and Resolves*, viii. 799, and Sewall, *Diary*, ii. 208.

the other hand, the influence of a university is not confined to her alumni. Whatever they do, wherever they go, they carry the reputation of their alma mater, and everyone with whom they come in contact must in some measure be affected by her imprint on their minds and characters. In the colonial period, Harvard and Yale alumni enjoyed almost a monopoly of the Congregational ministry in Massachusetts, New Hampshire, and Connecticut. Consequently the example and influence of college-trained men, which to a great extent is dissipated in a democracy, reached almost every person in these three colonies. The colleges were much more integrated with the community than today.

To follow the 'Sons of the Prophets' outside the walls of their 'wilderness seminary' is beyond the scope of this history. Mr. Sibley and his successor Dr. Shipton have done that for all the seventeenth-century graduates, and for many who did not take a degree.[1] Nevertheless, we can hardly close this volume without a few brief generalizations about the 'Sons of Harvard,' or *Harvardinates*, as President Leverett liked to call his fellow alumni in preference to the favorite Hebraic phrase of his predecessors.

For the Classes 1642–1700 inclusive, we have the names of 446 men who took the Bachelor's degree, and of 97 who did not graduate. An analysis of their careers shows that by far the most popular profession for college men in the seventeenth century was the Congregational ministry. Strange had it been otherwise, when, with the exception of medicine, the ministry was the only learned profession in New England, and the one career open to young men of scholarly tastes. Teaching school for all but a very few was a mere temporary job, insufficient to

---

1. John L. Sibley, *Biographical Sketches of Graduates of Harvard University*, vol. I, Classes 1642–1658, with an appendix on non-graduates, Cambridge, 1873; vol. II, Classes 1659–1677, Cambridge, 1881; vol. III, Classes 1678–1689, Cambridge, 1885; vol. IV, Classes 1690–1700, by Clifford K. Shipton, published for the Massachusetts Historical Society by the Harvard University Press, 1933. Vol. v, Classes 1701–1712, is in active preparation. All volumes contain complete bibliographies, with locations, of each graduate's writings. Vol. IV is illustrated, and includes non-graduates as well as graduates. Sibley himself paid slight attention to the non-graduates. We probably have a complete list of these for the Classes 1651–1663, when they were relatively more numerous than at any other period, in Chesholme's accounts (*C. S. M.*, xxxi), where such information and references as can be gleaned about the non-graduates will be found in footnotes. For the Classes 1664–1689 we have the names of only a handful of the alumni who did not take degrees. Most of these will be found in *Proc. A. A. S.*, n. s. XLII. 424–27.

support a family. Law, a low business in New England, did not
become a profession until men such as John Read (1697) and
Jeremiah Gridley (1725) made it respectable. Medicine was in
good repute, but there were not a dozen communities in New
England where a physician could earn a living.[1] Career posts in
colonial governments were few, and the salaries were slender,
excepting that of the Royal Governor of Massachusetts, for
which Harvard men had to compete with members of the English governing class. But the Congregational ministry increased
in numbers with the population. It afforded a living, and
ranked as the first of those public services toward which the
community, the College authorities, and a natural ambition,
impelled the choice young men of Harvard. The Church offered
ample opportunity for the exercise of courage and leadership.
Consider, for instance, in the older communities, the careers of
the Harvard-trained Danforths, Mathers, Shepards, and Bulke-
leys; or, among the pioneers, Edward Taylor (1671) of West-
field, who organized his frontier village against the Indians, and
stood his ground in Philip's War; Joseph Green (1695), who in
his early twenties exorcised devils in a witch-ridden parish,
introduced the first public school in Salem Village, and found
time to hunt game and Indians. The Reverend Andrew Gardner (1696) was killed while on guard against an Indian attack;
Anthony Stoddard (1697) got two Indians in the next war,
when the Reverend John Williams (1683) underwent a famous
captivity. And many a son of a plain 'goodman' like Wigglesworth (1651), or of a servant like Wise (1673), rose to the ruling
class through College and Church, and thereby pegged his family to social privilege.

Harvard clerics were not all Congregationalists, nor were
their ministrations confined to New England. John Hubbard
(1695) and Jedidiah Andrews (1695) were Presbyterian ministers on Long Island and in Philadelphia. Samuel Megapolensis
(1656) ended his career as a pastor in the Netherlands. Toward
the close of the century we find sundry parsons following
New England congregations to New Jersey and the Carolinas.
Very few Harvard men went over to the Church of England
in the seventeenth century, exceptions being Samuel Myles
(1684), Rector of King's Chapel, Boston, and William Vesey

1. Even in the seventeenth century, however, we find in the Alcocks, Cookes, and
Olivers a beginning of those medical families for which Boston is famous.

(1693), the pugnacious first Rector of Trinity Church, New York. Of the twenty or more who had taken English pulpits during the Cromwellian period, a few turned Anglican at the Restoration, but most were ejected; and some of these suffered hardships and died in miserable circumstances. But ministers as a whole were longer lived than their fellow alumni. Of the Classes 1642–1689, 46 per cent became clergymen; but of the members of those Classes who were living in 1700, 64 per cent were clergymen.

Not many Harvard alumni followed government as a career, and the civil lists of Massachusetts and Connecticut show that college men enjoyed no inside track to the magistracy. Not quite half the Councillors in the late seventeenth and early eighteenth centuries were Harvard alumni. But almost every son of Harvard performed some sort of public service. Without exception, the laymen who lived in New England served in unpaid or ill-paid offices such as town constable and selectman, and, in Boston, on the visiting committees that went from house to house to check disorder and see that the children were properly brought up. John Winthrop (1700) is the only graduate I have found who considered himself too good for these humble offices. Typical of what New England then expected of her college men was the case of Charlestown against Samuel Phipps (1671), who declined to serve as town constable on the ground that he was a Master of Arts, and kept a private school. The inhabitants, highly indignant, begged the Governor and Council to force Phipps to take the office. For, said they, 'If Masters of Arts will take up secular employments,' they 'ought to help bear the same burdens with other men of the same employments.' Charlestown being a seaport, 'exposed to riots and routs by rude strangers frequenting the same, . . . our head constable should be a man of more than ordinary parts, for the discreet management of himself upon such occasions.' And Mr. Phipps became the constable.[1]

One of the common burdens that Harvard men were not expected to share was military service. Warfare was supposed to be too rough a profession for college men; students, as we have seen, were forbidden to 'train,' and Masters of Arts were especially exempted from militia service by a Massachusetts Act of

1. Sibley, II. 342–43.

1692; but many of them waived exemption and took an active part in militia training. The only Harvard men who participated in King Philip's War were chaplains and 'chirurgeons.' Some were wounded, but the first Harvard man on record to lose his life in the King's service was Daniel Denison (1690), who died on the expedition against Quebec that year. Ephraim Savage (1662), Wainwright (1686), Moody (1689), and Tyng (1691) were professional soldiers for a good part of their lives, and Berry (1685), master mariner, was killed fighting a French privateer. In the eighteenth century, we find a considerable number of graduates and a few undergraduates taking part in the French and Indian wars and the struggle for independence; but it was not until the war against Germany that the American public expected all college men to serve in the army or navy, or that college men as a whole responded.[1]

In education, almost all the public grammar schools of New England were taught by young Harvard graduates, as a stopgap before entering the ministry or some other profession; and Yale was founded, organized, and for many years taught and governed by Harvard graduates.[2] Jeremiah Dummer (1699) obtained for Yale her excellent library, and with Cotton Mather's assistance procured the gift that gave our first child and oldest rival her name.

The number of Harvard graduates in business and agriculture was greater than the statistics indicate, since most of those in public service obtained their support from farming and mercantile ventures. Generally speaking, New England boys were not sent to college in the seventeenth century unless their parents aimed at something higher than trade or agriculture. Yet some of the leading mercantile families of New England, such as Pynchon, Talcott, Sherman, Higginson, were founded or continued by Harvard graduates. Among them were the only travellers in the academic family. England or the West Indies were generally the limits of these voyages; but both Bezaleel Sherman (1661) and Nathaniel Higginson (1670) were India merchants, and the latter was President of the Council or Gov-

---

1. S. E. Morison, in *Harvard Graduates' Mag.*, xxvi. 554–74.

2. Going through Sibley, I find that at least 11 Harvard graduates before the Class of 1689, and 10 of the Classes 1690–1700, were founders, benefactors, trustees, rectors, or tutors of early Yale; and the services of Governor Belcher (1699) to the College of New Jersey are generously acknowledged by the historian of Princeton University, Mr. V. Lansing Collins.

ernor of Madras, the first on record 'who retired from the Presidency without a stain upon his name.' [1]

The only professional writer who attended Harvard in the seventeenth century was John Crowne, the Restoration dramatist; but almost all the printed sermons, tracts, histories, pamphlets, and verse composed by native New Englanders before 1700 were by Harvard-trained parsons. It would be more pious than discriminating to call any one of them a creative artist or original scholar; yet George Stirk (1646) and Thomas Brattle (1676) may be counted among the minor experimental scientists of this 'century of genius.' Some of the Harvard-trained magistrates and colonial governors, such as Joseph Dudley, Jonathan Belcher, Gurdon Saltonstall, Edmund Quincy, and Jonathan Law, showed high ability; but Increase Mather is the only alumnus fairly entitled to the rank of statesman. It would be unreasonable to expect anything more in the social, economic, and political conditions under which all provincial college graduates lived. Achievement enough to have maintained unbroken the tradition of integrity and public service that the puritans had brought to New England. When new opportunities opened with the American Revolution, Harvard men were not found wanting.

The first table that follows shows the principal occupations of all Harvard alumni, graduates or otherwise, of whom the facts are known, of the Classes 1642–1700.[2]

The second table (p. 563) shows the occupations of living alumni in 1700; a sort of Harvard alumni directory compiled at the turn of the century, just after Commencement 1700, to indicate how many Harvard men are living, and where, and what doing.

On the basis of these statistics, and the biographies in Sibley, it will not be difficult to imagine the 'typical Harvard man' [3] of

1. J. Talboys Wheeler, *Madras in the Olden Time*, I. 335. Elihu Yale, sometime of New Haven, was his immediate predecessor.

2. The old triennial catalogues from 1782 italicized names to indicate clergymen, but did not do so unless they were formally settled and ordained. In these tables all are considered clergymen who made the Christian ministry or preaching their principal occupation, whether ordained or not. In cases where a man followed two or more occupations, simultaneously or successively, the ministry takes precedence, medicine comes second, public service third, then trading or planting. Thus, a merchant of Boston who was also a Councillor is counted as a public servant; a parson who also practised physic is counted as a clergyman; and the several doctor-politicians of the period go down as physicians. All the College presidents except Leverett are counted as clergymen.

3. In the *Harvard Alumni Bulletin*, XXXVI. 898–905, Mr. David W. Bailey, editor of the Harvard Alumni Directory, has described the average Harvard man of 1934, when

the 291 alive in 1700. He is a member of the Class of 1689 or 1690, about thirty years old, pastor of the Church of Christ in a farming community between twenty and thirty miles from Boston. He had taught school, returned to college for his M.A., become a candidate for this pulpit, and after a satisfactory try-out had been duly settled and ordained. Shortly after, he married the eighteen-year-old daughter of a well-to-do neighbor. By 1700

OCCUPATIONS OF HARVARD ALUMNI OF THE CLASSES 1642–1700

Classes	1642–1658	1659–1677	1678–1689	1690–1700	Total
Clergymen	76	62	42	86	266
Physicians	12	11	4	8	35
Public Servants *	13	17	12	25	67
Teachers †	1	8	4	4	17
Merchants	3	6	1	10	20
Planters, Gentlemen	4	5	2	7	18
Soldiers, Mariners	0	1	4	5	10
Miscellaneous ‡	2	3	0	1	6
Died Young §	11	5	11	4	31
Occupation unknown °	27	35	6	5	73
Total	149	153	86	155	543

* Governors, Councillors, Judges, Deputies (if so continued for a term of years), and permanent officials; local offices not counted.
† Schoolmasters and college tutors who made teaching a career, or who died young before doing anything else.
‡ One dramatist, one drunkard, one printer, one Indian teacher, one idiot, and one lawyer.
§ Those who died in college or within five years after graduating, without, so far as our records show, getting a job.
° Most of these are the non-graduates before 1663, whose careers have never been investigated. Some of them are not even identified.

she has borne him three children, and expects to produce another every eighteen months or two years. On weekdays our parson dresses in homespun made up by his wife; on Lord's Days and at funerals he sports a black broadcloth suit made for his ordination by a Boston tailor, and expected to last a lifetime. He still wears the full-bottomed William of Orange wig that cost him a pretty penny at Commencement. His annual

there were 66,248 living alumni. He was a member of the Class of 1916, just turning forty. He lived somewhere between Scarsdale and Tarrytown, New York, and had an office below 42nd Street on Manhattan. His occupation was a mixture of law and finance; he was married and had two children, and played squash. His interest in education was largely confined to subscribing to the Harvard Fund and visiting the annual Harvard-Yale game.

salary is £80, paid (seldom on time) half in Massachusetts currency and half in country pay, together with sufficient wood to heat two or three rooms of the parsonage, which was built for him by the parish as part of his 'settlement.' An apple orchard supplies his table with cider every other year; and the parish glebe is sufficient to grow most of his food and pasture a few head of cattle. This estate he farms himself, with the aid of a

HARVARD ALUMNI LIVING IN 1700

Occupation*				Residence			Total
Classes	1642–89	1690–00	Total		1642–89	1690–00	
Clergymen	93	57	150	Massachusetts ...	95	87	182
Physicians	10	8	18	Connecticut †	28	29	57
Public Servants ..	21	4	25	Long Island, N. Y.	4	5	9
Schoolmasters	6	16	22	New York City ..	0	1	1
Merchants	7	12	19	Rhode Island ‡ ...	3	3	6
Planters, etc.	5	6	11	Maine and N. H. ..	3	6	9
College Tutors ...	0	3	3	New Jersey	2	3	5
Soldiers and				Pennsylvania	0	1	1
Mariners	3	3	6	South Carolina ...	0	3	3
Lawyers	1	2	3	West Indies	0	4	4
Students §	0	28	28	England	10	3	13
Unknown	0	6	6	Netherlands	1	0	1
Total	146	145	291	Total	146	145	291

* Many of these occupations in 1700 were temporary, hence the discrepancy between this table and the former.
† Including Enfield and Woodstock, then in Massachusetts.
‡ Including Bristol, then in Massachusetts.
§ The class just graduated in 1700 are listed as students, and their residences as Massachusetts, except for Hooker.

negro slave (presented by his father-in-law) and volunteer help at harvest, which he reciprocates when the neighbors need a hand. By dint of hard work and intelligence he has made the glebe one of the best farms in town, keeps the fences 'hog tight, horse high, and ox strong,' and experiments with strange plants such as potatoes. He keeps one horse, with a saddle for himself and pillion for his wife; but no carriage. The housework is done by the wife and an unmarried sister who lives with them. They are as well off as any in the parish; the financial pinch will come after 1715, when prices rise, money goes down, and there are more children to feed.

Twice every Lord's Day the parson preaches; and although he

has given up the public Thursday lecture for want of interest, he presides weekly at private religious societies that meet in different parts of town; and spends considerable time calling on the people and catechizing the children. He knows by name every man, woman, and child, and most of the dogs, in his parish of several hundred souls; and is on friendly terms with all except certain frontier individualists, who wish they had an evangelical exhorter, and some of the stricter puritans, who disapprove his baptismal tolerance of five-months' babies. The village schoolmaster is his friend, and every few years sends him an ambitious lad to be fitted for Harvard. Everyone is in awe of his learning, and all except the village elders respect his opinion on a variety of subjects. During the late French and Indian war the parson did watch and ward with the other able-bodied young men. As there is no physician within twenty miles, he personally attends to most of his parishioners' ailments, and keeps on hand a supply of the more common drugs in order to prescribe as directed in Culpeper's 'English Physician.' And until the town is large enough to have a Justice of the Peace, he will draft the legal papers, write wills, and do his best to prevent the parishioners from going to law.

The parson's library, about two hundred volumes, largely in the three Learned Tongues, consists mostly of college textbooks, theology, and devotional works, acquired before he took his second degree. The classics, especially Horace and Ovid, he has worn almost threadbare with repeated readings, for he can save little from his salary to purchase new books; but occasionally books may be borrowed from brother ministers. As yet there is no newspaper in New England for him to read; he is dependent on travellers and chance gossip for news of the great world. A former pupil of John Leverett, he is friendly toward the Church of England, and inclined to overlook or explain away some of the rigors of Calvinist theology. For that reason he has dropped preaching on fine points of theology, and prefers practical discourses on the divine attributes and human conduct. Strange plants, minerals, two-headed calves, meteors, and the like, attract his curiosity, and provide anecdotes to exchange with other provincial virtuosi at Commencement. This annual journey on horseback to Cambridge is his unique vacation and only relaxation, except reading, smoking, and an occasional glass of wine.

To what can such a man look forward? Spiritual serenity and the love of his neighbors; not fame, nor even security. Custom forbids a richer parish to call him from rural duties, and there are no high offices in the Congregational church. With good luck and a scholarship, one or two of his sons will enter Harvard and become ministers themselves; the others may fulfil their parents' hopes in any respectable occupation.

The loyalties of our typical Harvard man in 1700 are, first, to God, who is as real to him as his own father, but more orderly, scientific, and merciful than his fathers' God; second, to King William, the saviour of England and the Protestant religion; and, third, to New England, his native land and nation. Such notice from her as an invitation to deliver the annual election sermon in Boston would satisfy his highest personal ambition. The rights of the Bay Province and the privileges of the Congregational churches he would maintain with equal jealousy; and while ready to admit that all respectable Protestant sects such as the Baptists and Quakers should be tolerated, he hopes to keep such persons out of his parish. The state of morality and the French menace give him considerable concern; privately and publicly he prays that New England, chastened for her sins by these terrible wars, may redeem God's covenant with her founders, and become a pattern for the rest of the world. In the century that is dawning, may the reformed churches reunite on a modified New England platform which, through its obvious superiority and marks of divine favor, will even convert the French King, and unite all Christendom in bonds of brotherhood!

APPENDICES

APPENDIX A

DOCUMENTS ON THE DIFFICULTIES OF 1653–1655

IN THIS Appendix will be found a selection of available documents on the financial and other difficulties of the College at the end of Dunster's administration and the beginning of Chauncy's, which are treated in Chapters II, XV, and XVI. One of the most important documents in the group, President Dunster's Memorandum of December, 1653, is printed in my *Founding of Harvard College* (1935), pp. 448–51; and another, Dunster's letter of resignation, will be found in the present volume, pp. 309–10.

1. ORDER OF GENERAL COURT, SEPTEMBER 10, 1653 [1]

This Court, being informed that the present condicion of the colledge at Cambridge calls for supply, doe order, that Cambridge rate for this yeare, now to be collected, be pajd into the steward of the colledge, for the discharge of any debt due from the countrje to the sajd colledge; and if there be any ouerplus, to be and remajne as the colledge stocke; and for further clearing and setling all matters in the colledge in reference to the yearely maintenance of the præsident, Fellowes, and necessary officers thereof, and repayring the howses, that so yearely complaints may be prevented, and a certajn way setled for the due encouragement of all persons concerned in that worke, doe hereby appointe Mr Increase Nowell, Captain Daniell Gookin, Captain Jno Leueret, Captain Edward Johnson, and Mr Edward Jackson, or any three of them, to be a committee to examine the state of the colledge in all respects, as hereafter is expressed, Mr Nowell to giue notice of the time and place of meeting.

1. First, to take accompt of all the incomes of the colledge proffitts arising due to the officers thereof, either by guifts, revenewes, studdjes, rents, tuitions, commencements, or any other proffitts arising due from tjme to tjme, as neere as may be, since the præsident vndertooke the worke.

2. To examine what hath binn pajd and disbursed, either for buildings, repayrings, or otherwise, pajd and received annually for the maintenance of the præsident, Fellowes, and other officers thereof.

3. To consider what hath binn yearely received by the præsident out of any of the incomes and proffitts, for his oune vse and majntenance, (as neere as convenjently may be,) euer since he came to the place of præsident; also what allowances yearely haue binn made to the Fellowes and other officers.

4. To weigh and consider what maybe fitt for an honnorable and comfortable allowance annually, for the præsident, heretofore and for the future, and how it may be pajd heereafter.

---

1. *Mass. Bay Recs.*, IV. pt. i. 178–80.

5. To consider what noumber of fellowes may be necessary for carying on the worke in the sajd colledge, and what yearely allowance they shall haue, and how to be pajd.

6. To direct some way how the necessary officers, as steward, butler, and cooke, maybe provided for, that so the schollers commons may not be so short as they now are occasioned thereby.

7. To take cognizance of all and euery matter or thing concerning the sajd colledge, in reference to the welfare thereof in outward things, and to present a way how to regulate and rectify any thing that is out of order.

8. To examine what sommes haue binn, and of late are, promised by seuer-all tounes and persons for the vse of the colledge, and to giue order for the collectjon thereof, and propose a way how such monjes may be improoved for the best bennefitt of that society for the future; and this committee are heereby authorized with full power to act in all the premises, and to make retourne of what they doe to the next Court of Election, to be confirmed, if they shall judge meete.

2. COMMITTEE'S REPORT TO THE GENERAL COURT, MAY 3, 1654[1]

The Report of the Commitee about Harvard [2]
Coledge presented to the Generall
Court held the 3: of (3) month
1654

The matters comitted vnto vs are comprehended vnder viii heads as doth appere in the order hervnto anexed: which methood wee follow in this returne.

1 is Concerning an acco[un]t of all the incomes and proffitts of the coledge either by gifts reuenues, study Rents Tuitiones Commensements etc. that hath beene paid or rece[iue]d; euer since mr Dunster the president vndertooke the place

Vnto this wee haue (as neere as wee can) presented herewith an abridg-ment of the acco[un]ts in Reference to the things mentioned; which wee hope, may tend to satisfation [3]

2 was to examine what hath been disbursted either for building repaireing or otherwise paid to the officers etc

This is resolued in the abridgement of the accounts aboue mentioned

3 To Consider what the president mr Dunster hath rece[ive]d Annualy since hee came to the place, for his owne maintenance etc

This alsoe is not only Reported in the abridgement of the acco[un]ts hervnto anexed but resolued further vnder the next head.

4 Comm[i]tee was to Consider what is fitt for an honerable and Comfort-abl[e] mainteynance for the presedent both hertofore and hereafter and how the same is to be raysed

---

1. Dunster Mss., H. U. Archives.

2. 'Haruerd' crossed out.

3. This 'abridgment,' together with the Committee's findings as to Dunster's accounts, is preserved in the H. U. Archives, 1.5.20.

To which wee answer that for the tyme past wee conceue hee should bee allowed [*blank*] per anum: of which hee hath reced only 55*li* 13*s*: 10*d* per anum, by all ways and means out of this Jurisdiction; as appers in the account the Rest is due vnto him; to be paid by the country which is the sume of [*blank*] and for the future, wee conceiue the presidents place should bee allowed 80*li* per anum: to be paid as follow vizt.

By the Ferry at Charles towne, — 40*li* per anum.

40*li* per anum either by 400*l* stocke in his hand for improvement Vntill a purchase may be bought with it to raise it anualy,[1] [or]

By so much anually out of the Contributions. 40 per anum

besides The presidents house and lands adiacent Rent Free: kept in Repaire at the Coledge Chardge. as also the benifitt of all comecemttjal[2] which wee conceue may make his menit[en]anc as good as 100 *li* per anum.

5 what number of Felowes may bee nesscesary and how to bee maintend

Answer   hauing Considerd and aduised with others Insighted[3] therin wee concaue their should bee no less then 3[4] fellowes and exceptiones[4] if so many fitt ones may be procured. whose maintaina[n]ce shalbe as folowes

each fello[5] to receue all the tuitions of the scolers vnder his chardge after the rates folow[ing] 10*s* per quarter for all fellow commonrs 8*s* per quarter for all pensionrs and 6*s* 8*d* per quarter for all sizers.

2ly each Fellow or tutor to haue his Chamber and studdy rent Free.

3: to be allowed moreouer anually to each fel[low] to be paid out of the yearly reuenue of

Charlestowne Contrib..	10*l* per anum	for the	
Ipswich Contribution		eldest fellow —	12*li* per anum
for 7 yrs	8: per anum	2:	12 per anum
Concord for 7 yeares ..	5 per anum	3—9*l* 16*s* 8*d* —	09 per anum
Boston 3 persons	10 per anum		
rents 16*s* 8*d*	16*s* 8*d*		33: 16: 8
	———		
	33 16*s* 8*d*		
	contributiones[6]		

and in case 3[7] fellowes cannot bee procured then so many as vnder god and the burden of the worke whether 2 or 3 shall equaly diuide the allowance of such Fellowes whose places are vacant, vntill they be suplied

R 6 how the nesscesary officers as steward, Butler, Cooke and vtinsels may be maintend and that the sccolers Commons, may not be so Strait as they now are

---

1. This paragraph up to this point is written on the margin.
2. Commencement fees, or entrance fees of *commensales*, fellow-commoners?
3. informed; cf. *N. E. D.*
4. '4' crossed out; 'and exceptiones' inserted above line.
5. 'tutor' crossed out.
6. The writer originally put down £13 for Boston, and assigned the second fellow £10, the third £8, and a fourth £6. He then scaled down the Boston contribution to £10, added the rents, struck out the fourth fellow, and increased the two stipends above. Thus are university budgets made!
7. '4' struck out.

An: To which wee Answer that, the best way to Remidy this by the best thoughts and councel wee can get is as Foloweth viz

To Ranke the scolers into 3 degrees as in englands vniversities

1. sizers: whose Commons are as before at   vi*d* per mess
2. pentioners, Commons to bee at   ix*d* per mess
3. Fellow Commoners to be at   xii*d* per mess

and the ⅓ part of each mess is to bee sett apart to prouide The allowances of Steward Buttler Cooke vtensells, wood etc which will conuenientle effect the same and the scolers commons Sufficient if their Frends will bee at their chardges and wee neither see nor can find any other just way how to prouide for the officers and vtinsells afforsaid (which would amount to a considerable some,) but at the chardge of the scolers for whose speciall seruice, in providing and making ready prouisions the afforsad officers and vtinsells are imployed.

7: To take cognizance of all matters and things in Refference to the owtward welfare of the colledge and to propose a way how to Regulate and Rectify any thing out of order;

An[swer] this is a lardge [theame],[1] and might admitt of many Considerations; but for the present, wee shall only me[ntion] those 3 things as wee concev nescesary to bee rectified, with our corrections in order thervnto

1 many Scollers are in arreares for their Commons etc whereby many straits and wants in provition are occationed.

Remedy. That their bee a st[r]ict and martiall order made and duly executed that all Scollers whose arrears are not duly paid quarterly; or in conuenient tyme affter, bee sent to their Frends or turnd out of Commons. and this to be without offense to anny

2 some of the Fellowes which haue done seruice; latly unrewarded [illegible] are dep[ar]ted and two remaine; are all of them in debt in the stewards booke about 56*li*; wherby the Felows are discouraged and the Steward ingaged.

Remidy That this 56*li* bee paid out of the Contributions the first that is reced; that so the said Felows and their Frends bee disingaged and incoredged and the Steward satisfied his iust debts [2]

3 The present ediffice of the Coledge, is very m[uc]h out of Repaire; both in the foundation and in the ceiling [?] which of necessity calls for present emendation also some enlardgment is wanting for to accomodate scolers

Remidy Wee Conceue that about 120*li* be paid out of the contributions for the effecting of this worke; and to this end the Comitte hath giuen order for the Colection of the Contributions hereafter mentioned to bee d[elivere]d to the corporacion to effect the said repaires speedily. vizt

Watertownes Contribution which is 36: 14: 03
Sudubery Contribution 18: 02: 06
out of Cambridge 70: 00: 00
                                                              ─────────────
                                                               124: 16: 9

of which some the president Felowes and Corporation are to giue account how is expended

---

1. Crossed out.
2. Last three words crossed out.

Rem 2 for enlardgment of more roome to entertayne scolers, their is at present no stocke to effect any brick building vnles the purchase of mr Collins house not far of which is to be sold might answer the end which posibly may be purchased [1] as an [illegible]

8 is to examine what sommes are Contributed or promised for the vse of the Coledge either from persons or townes and to giue order for the colection therof and to propose a way how the same may bee improued. for the best Beneffitt of the society. for the future

For Report vppon this wee find

1: The Contributions of the seuerll towns that haue hetherto sent their returnes; promised but not payable vntill next haruest most of it: but there is more expected beeing not yet returnd but that at present in view is more-ouer the particulers are in a lyst anexed   the totall is 572*li* 03*s*: 11*d*

From Charlstowne, thir is promised .... 10*li* per anum

From Concord for 7 yeares 5   per anum

From Ipswich for 7 yeares 8   per anum

From three persons in Boston for euer [2] 10   per anum

The rent of some lands at Cambridge and Shawshinn   xvi*s* 8*d* 16   8*d* per anum

33*li*: 16*s*. 8*d* per anum

2: for the Colection thereof wee propose that the Treasurer of the Coledge; bee impouerd to make recipt of it as it becomes due; and to that end to giue warants to all constables to colect the same, in the townes and from their hands to receue it.

3: for disposing of it wee iudge that the treasurer of the Corporation shall pay it anualy according as is aboue directed; and what is ouer plus to be disbursed; by such as the Corporation shal improue for purchase of some lands that may yeald anuall Rent vnto the vses of the Coledge; and to take good assurances in the name of the Corporation for the same

[*Endorsed*:] The Report of the Committee

3. ACCOUNT OF TOWN SUBSCRIPTIONS, 1653–1655 [3]

An [Account] of what the seuerall Townes
in this Jurisdict[ion] haue subscribed
towardes the Colledge and theire Answer
in reference thereunto.

---

1. Two or three words after this are torn. Edward Collins's property comprised the southern half of the block between Holyoke Street, Linden Street, and Mount Auburn Street; it is No. 9 on Dr. Norris's Map of Cambridge (*F. H. C.*, pp. 192–93).

2. The Cogan, Newgate, and Sedgwick-Phillips annuities.

3. Mass. Archives, lviii. 23. Obviously this is the account referred to in the previous document.

		£	s	d
	1 Salem will giue Answ: to the Committee in 2 months			
	Charlestowne promises per Annum 10*li* [1] ..	00	00	0
present [2]	Dorchester haue subscribed	70	00	0
	2 Boston subscription in there Townes men ·hands			
	Roxbury haue subscribed the sume off . . .	48	05	08
present	Watertowne subscribed the sume of	36	14	03
54	Lin will giue Answ: in two months to be paid next yeare	06	00	00 [3]
53–54 N	Cambridge subscribed the sume of	150	00	00
	3 Ipswitch will giue Answ. in two months [4] ..			
	Newbery haue promised the sume of	15	00	00
	Waymouth subscribed the sume of	10	16	6
	4 Hingham will giue Answ: in two months			
	Concord fiue pounds a yeare for 7 yeares			
	Dedham haue subscribed the sume of	70	10	00
	5 Salsbury will returne in two month.			
	Hampton haue subscribed the sum of	17	19	00
	Rowley haue subscribed the sume of.	38	00	00
present	Sudbury haue subscribed the sume of present [5]	18	02	06
	6 Branntry will returne in two months.			
	7 Gloc[ester] will giue Answ in two months			
28*li* 14*s* 6*d* 2*q* at a y[ea]r	8 Woburne will [giue] Answ in 2 months . . .	28	14 [06½]	
	Wenham subscribed the sum of	06	10	00
	9 Haverill will giue answ: in Two months in 54 [6]	04	07	
16–13 54–55	10 Reading will giue Answ: in 2 months.	16	13:	
	11 Malden will giue Answ: in 2 months			
2 mo 55	Meadfeild subscribed the some of 2 mo 55 [7]	25	01	00

12 Springfeild [8]	Andover　　about 2*l*
Dover	Hull
Strawberry banke	Nashaway
Excetter	Manchester
Kitchere	Meadford
Yorke　10*l*	Topsfeild
Welles	Marble head

---

1. '10*li*' interlined in a different but contemporary hand.
2. These marginal notes also written in a different hand. 'Present' is probably an abbreviation for 'presented,' or paid.
3. The sum, and the five previous words, added later than the rest of the line.
4. Ipswich promised £8 per annum for seven years — see previous document.
5. 'present' interlined, by the same hand that wrote 'present' in margin.
6. 'in 54' added in a different hand.
7. I.e., April, 1655. This date added by a later hand.
8. This and the following entries are in a different hand from the above.

4. Order of the General Court, May 3, 1654 [1]

The Court, on pervsall of the retourne of the committee appointed to consider of colledge buisenes, doe judge that the tenn pounds brought in vppon accompt by the president of the colledge, for his care and pajnes for these twelve yeeres last past, in looking after the affaires of the colledge, in respect of building, repayring, or otherwise, be respitted till this Court take further order therein; and that the contributions and subscriptions lately given in, or which shall heereafter be given in by seuerall tounes and persons, together with all other stocke appertayning to the colledge, shallbe committed to the care and trust of the ouerseers of the sajd colledge, who haue heereby power to give order to the treasurer of the colledge to collect the seuerall subscriptions and contributions which are or shallbe heereafter due from tjme to tjme; and in case of non-pajment thereof, that it be secured by the seuerall tounes and persons, so long as it shall remajne vnpajd, and the produce of it to be pajd to the sajd Treasurer, and to be for the maintenance of the president and Fellowes, and other necessary charges of the colledge, and the seuerall yeerely allowance of the sajd president and fellowes to be proportioned as the sajd ouerseers shall determine concerning the same.

5. Dunster's Petition to the General Court, November 16, 1654 [2]

Consider[ati]ons against present Removals, presented to the honrd generall Court. 16. November 54

I. The time of the year is unseasonable being now very near the shortest day and depth of winter

II. The place unto which, [1] unknown to mee and my family what it wilbee for habit[ati]on and Health,

2 what for a way and means of subsistance [suitable] to my talents parts or kind of imployment.

3 what for containing or conserving those goods wherewith God hath blessed mee.

4 And for disposing of my catle accustomed to the place of my residence, and the bestowing of my stoer there none of which things do or can befall the Reverend president elect.

III. The Place from which, 1. there all provitions are layd in for man and beast for the winter

2 Thither what ever rents etc. from any place to bee received are to bee brought and payd in, whether for fuel or other provisions.

---

1. *Mass. Bay Recs.*, IV. part i. 186–87.
2. Mass. Archives, lviii. 30. Dunster's main headings have been put in Roman numerals for greater clarity.

3 Thence to remove somthings now is to destroy them utterly, to leave them is will undertake (?) for them.

4 And to remove others is to hazzard them very greatly as books and houshould goods

5 So that very easily more damage may to mee thence accrew than reason can require you to Recompence.

6 Its the place which upon very damageful cond[ici]ons to myself, out of loue to the Coll: I haue builded viz by taking contry pay in lieu of bils payd in England or the sayd house had not been built yea a very considerable part of it was given mee at my request out of respect to myself albeit for the Coll: [1]

IV. The Persons. All besydes myself are only women and children on whom litle help when theer mindes ly under the actual stroak of afflictions and griefes

My wife, and sp[ecial]ly the yongest childe is extreamly sick: and so hath beene for some months, that wee durst not carry him out of doors, yet much worse now than before. If a place bee found that may bee comfortable for them and reasonably answer the obstacles abouenamed, myself will willingly bow my neck to any yoak of personal denyal for I know for what and for whom by grace I suffer.

V. The state of the Colledg. [1] Requireth my Residence untill all accounts bee made up ballanced and allowed. That the Honrd overseers and Corporation may know in what estate I leaue the Colledg de facto. That afterward there may bee no uncomfortable complaints or offence on either syde unless the Honrd Overseers and corporation Accept my Accounts given in allready to the end of the year 1652, and so acquiess.

2ly My Residence is Required in Reference to the Reverend President Elected that I may shew him what our way hath been sp[ecial]ly seeing Mr Okes and all long Resident fellowes are gone away, and others in the country haue long discontinued and know not the present state of the Coll:

3 In reference to the Servants of the house to regulate all their account and declare their work to the president elect.

VI. What Place neer the Coll: can be found is more convenient by far for the Reverend President Elect who is in a moveable posture than for mee on that account.

2ly Bec[ause] myself for sundry years was compeld to what inconvenience can befall him tho but for a few months, before your desires bee accomplished.

VII. The whole transaction of this buisiness is such which in process of time when all things come to mature consideration may very probably create griefe on all sydes yours subsequent as myne antecedent. I am not the man you take mee to bee: neither if you knew what hould and why can I perswade myselfe that you would act as I am at least tempted to think you do. But our times are in Gods hands with whom all sydes hope by grace in Christ to finde favour, which shalbee the prayer for you as myself who am Honrd Gentlemen

Yours to serve

HEN. DUNSTER

---

1. The President's Lodge is meant. For comment see *F. H. C.*, p. 296 n.

6. 'Briefe Information' of May 9, 1655[1]

A briefe Information of the present necessityes of the Colledge which the Corporation do desire may by the concurrence of the Ouerseers be presented to the Consideration of the Generall Court with earnest desires of their speedy and effectuall help for supply.

May. 9. 1655

First wee are indebted to Mr Dunster (as appears upon Accompt) near 40*li* notwithstanding that he hath had all that wee haue beene able to pay or assigne him. Justice and Equity requires that this be paid him, being due Debt, and apparent upon diligent examining of Accompts. Also besides what is due upon a strict Accompt, the former motion sometimes made by the Committee of a Hundred Pounds to be allowed Mr Dunster in consideration of his Extraordinary paines, in Raising up and carrying on the Colledge for so many yeares past, we desire it may bee seriously considered, and hope it may make much for the Countryes honrble discharge in the hearts of all, and perpetuall incouragement of their Servants in such publique works, if it be attended.

2ly. The Colledge building although it be new-groundsilled by the help of some free Contributions the last year, yet those ceasing and the worke of Reparation therewith intermitted, it remains in other respects, in a very ruinous condition. It is of absolute necessity, that it bee speedily new-cou[er]ed, being not fitt for Scholars long to abide in, as it is. And without such Reparation some time this Summer both the whole Building will decay, and So the former charge about it be lost, and the Scholars will be forced to depart. So that either help must be had herein, or else(we fear) no lesse then a Dissolution of the Colledge will follow. And it is conceived, that it will need a Hundred pounds to set it in Comfortable Repair.

All the Estate that the Colledge hath (as appears by the Inventory thereof) is only its present Buildings, Library, A few Utensils, with the Presse, and some Parcells of Land (none of which can be with any reason or to any benefitt sold to help in the Premises) and in Reall Revenue about Twelue Pounds per annum (which is a small pittance to be shared among 4 Fellowes) Besides 15*li* per annum which by the Donours appointment is for Scholarships.

The Stewards Stocke is indebted for Studyes and for Diett of former Fellowes, and to the Stewards personall Estate, and otherwaies near as much as it is.

Though we haue the Ferry, yet what the produce of it will be, we haue no certainty, and whateuer it be, it had need to goe to the Fellowes, untill there be some other Provision for them.

The Revenue of the Presse (which is but small) must at present be improved for the finishing of the Print-house, its Continuance in the Presidents house being (besides other Inconveniences) dangerous and hurtfull to the edifice thereof.

The Study-Rents were untill December last discounted with Mr Dunster. Since that time they haue beene inconsiderable. And there are other smaller charges (not here mentioned) more then will be answered by the Study-Rents, though they were more then they bee.

---

1. Mass. Archives, lviii. 32–33. Printed inaccurately in Quincy, 1. 462–65.

Hence it appears that the Corporation hath nothing under their hands, which they can make use of, either for payment of Debts, or for the Repairing of the Colledge.

There are other things wee might mention, for which there is much need of help, as, viz. for Some way of maintaining Colledge Officers and Servants by Publique Stocke, that So the Scholars charges might be lesse or their Commons better; Provision of Utensels wanting in the Kitchin and Buttery; Accommodacions for the Scholars Tables; Also some fitter way of maintenance for the Fellowes. But we are not willing to trouble or presse the Generall Court or others with any thing that we can make any shift either to bearr, or for the time to wrestle thorough. Those two things aboue-mencioned (viz. payment of Debts and repairing of the Colledge) are of present absolute necessity. And it cannot be conceived or expected, that particular persons out of their own Estates much lesse that those, who are (as most of us in the Corporation) without Estates, can carry on these things of themselues.

If this work of the Colledge be thought fitt to be upheld and continued (as, we hope, the Considerations of the Glory of God, the Honour and Interest of the Country, the good of Posterity and experiences of the benefitt and blessing thereof will constrain all men to say, it is) then something must effectually be done for help in the Premises.

Wee are loath to seeme burthensome to the Country by such Motions as these, But the Considerations foregoing haue called upon us (whom the Country haue beene pleased to imploy as their Servants in this Society) to make this faithfull Representation of the condition and necessityes thereof, that if any Decay or Ruin to so good and important a worke (as this is) should ensue (which wee hope and desire may neuer be) we might not afterward fall under Blame for our Silence.

Wee confesse sundry Petitions haue beene presented to the Generall Court in the Colledge behalfe here[to]fore, and we are not so unthankfull as not to remember and acknowledge that Sundry endeavours for our help haue beene used and that a considerable matter hath beene grannted for the Presidents maintenance. But wee hope all will consider partly not so much what hath beene said or attempted, as what hath beene done and partly that the things aboue-mencioned are distinct from that particular of the Presidents future maintenance and that unlesse this of Repairing the Colledge Building be added thereto, the worke can not stand.

Also concerning the promised maintenance for the President, we desire it might be clearly settled in some such way as may be comfortable: and that it may be commended to the Generall Court to take Order thereabout.

7. ACTION OF THE GENERAL COURT ON THE 'BRIEFE INFORMATION.'[1]

The magistrates desire that our brethren the deputies consider first of this present informacion it is a matter that will require serious agitation and speedy action.

[SIGNED] JOHN ENDECOTT Gou[erno]r.

---

1. Mass. Archives, lviii. 33–34. The first paragraph is written on the previous document.

In answer to what hath bin represented to this Court by the Feofees of the Colledge in refference to what is necissary to be done there the deputies vnderstanding that there is due to the Colledge from the Country about an hundred and fifty pounds for which we pay intrest [1] doe Judge meet that the said 150*li* should be added to the next Country Rate and Collected by the Cunstables to be payd to the Country Treasurer and by him to the Colledge Treasurer or who else this Court may or shall appoynt to be Improued for the repayring of the Colledge and to satisfy mr Dunster what shalbe Iustly due to him vppon acco[unt] and for an æquall distributions of the same vppon the seuerall Townes It is ordred that for this present yeare there shalbe an addition of one fowrth part more to the Country rate payable from each Towne for the vses and ends abouemen[tioned].

The deputies haue past this and desire our honrd. magist[rate]s Consent hereto.

WILLIAM TORREY Cleric

25: 3d 1655.

The magist[rate]s Cannot Consent heereto bec[ause] the 150*li* was given per the lady Moulson and others for schollerships which this Court Cannot alter,[2] Annually to be mayntained there, and therefore desire theire bretheren the deput[ie]s to Consider of some meete way for the repayring of the Colledge which is at so great hazard.

The magistrates desire our brethren the deputies to giue answere to their returne.   EDWARD RAWSON Secretary.

21. 9 mo 55   JO: ENDECOTT Gou[verno]r

---

1. The last five words are interlined. The reference is to the Mowlson-Bridges scholarship fund — see *F. H. C.*, pp. 310–11.
2. Last five words interlined.

APPENDIX B

THESES AND QUAESTIONES
1643–1708

INTRODUCTION

IN THIS Appendix will be found the full text of all Harvard Commencement Theses and Quaestiones of which copies have survived, through the year 1708, with the exception of the Theses of 1642, which may be read in my *Founding of Harvard College*, pp. 438–40, reprinted from 'New Englands First Fruits.' [1] I have not attempted to preserve all typographical peculiarities, but simply to indicate emphasis where it occurs in the original. In the dedications, for instance, the proper names only are capitalized. A few of them have already been reproduced in facsimile, and references to these will be found in the footnotes. A key to the initials in the dedicatory formulae (D.D.D., etc.) will be found in *Publications of the Colonial Society of Massachusetts*, v. 334.

The relation of theses and quaestiones to the curriculum has already been discussed in Chapter VII of this volume.[2] Briefly, the theses are propositions on the several liberal Arts and other subjects studied in the undergraduate course, which any member of the graduating class, if challenged, was supposed to be able to defend, in Latin, by the recognized rules of syllogistic disputation. It was arranged beforehand, as a part of the Commencement Act, that designated students should defend certain theses, which (beginning with the sheets for 1653) are distinguished from the others by special type, or an index finger.[3] The quaestiones were defended or opposed by candidates for the Master's degree, at Masters' Commencement on the afternoon of Commencement Day. Examples of actual arguments spoken on these occasions may be found in this volume, pp. 144, 228–32, 277–79.

The Scottish origin of the printed Theses has been noted in my *Founding of Harvard College*, pp. 135–37, where facsimiles of Harvard and Edinburgh thesis sheets are reproduced. But the idea of printed Quaestiones came from Oxford. At that University, in the early part of the seventeenth century, it was customary to circulate a printed

---

1. The 1642 theses are also reprinted in Thomas Hutchinson, *History of Massachusetts Bay*, I, appendix no. vi, but a careful study of the text indicates that he copied them from *New Englands First Fruits*, not from an original broadside.

2. Consult also Dr. James J. Walsh, *Education of the Founding Fathers* (Fordham Univ. Press, 1935), and 'Scholasticism in the Colonial Colleges,' *N. E. Q.*, v. 483–507.

3. *Magnalia*, book iv. 131.

QVÆSTIONES IN SA-
CRA THEOLOGIA DISCV-
TIENDÆ OXONII IN VESPE-
RIIS, VNDECIMO DIE
Iuly, Ann. D. 1618.

Quæstiones Inceptoris GVLIELMI LOE.

An { Sancti sint invocandi ? *Neg.*
{ Papa sit ille homo peccati ? *Aff.*
{ Sit Purgatorium post hanc vitam pro expiatione peccati ? *Neg.*

Quæstiones Inceptoris SIMONIS IVCKS.

An { Corporis Christi præsentia in cœlo simul & sacramento sit possibilis? *Neg.*
{ Voluntas in prima conversione habeat se tantùm passivè ? *Aff.*
{ Sanctorum resurgentium futura sit par gloria? *Neg.*

Quæstiones Inceptoris FRANCISCI GIBBONS.

An { Episcopus distinguatur à Presbytero jure divino? *Aff.*
{ Episcopi Anglicani differant ab Episcopis primitiuæ Ecclesiæ ? *Neg.*
{ Concilium Tridentinum sit Oecumenicum ? *Neg.*

Quæstiones Inceptoris EDMVNDI IACKSON.

An { Sola Scriptura sit norma in controversijs fidei dirimendis ? *Aff.*
{ Omnia ad salutem necessaria contineantur in Scriptura? *Aff.*
{ Scriptura sit transferenda in illam linguam quam populus intelligit ? *Aff.*

Quæstiones Inceptoris RICHARDI ETKINS.

An { Opera infidelium sint peccata ? *Aff.*
{ Reconciliatio per mortem Christi sit singulis hominibus impetrata ? *Neg.*
{ Aliquis possit finaliter excidere à gratiâ ? *Neg.*

Quæstiones Inceptoris THOMAE OTES.

An { Romani Pontificis judicium sit infallibile ? *Neg.*
{ Verus Samuel apparuerit Sauli ? *Neg.*
{ Votum paupertatis pugnet cum Euangelio? *Aff.*

OXFORD QUÆSTIONES, 1618

Ordinaria Dæmonum eiectio
hodie nulla est, ut nec posse sito.

Coelesti Satanas deiectus sede rebellis
   Humano generi maximus hostis erat,
Gentibus & fundens dubiis oracula verbis,
   Has studuit variis illaqueare dolis.
Nostra suæ peccata cruci fed Christus Iesus
   Figens, de Satana clara trophæa tulit.
Contudit & vires, sic ut nihil amplius ille
   Possit in humanum iuris habere genus.
De Satana obsessis igitur quæcunque feruntur,
   Nil, nisi quæ nullo pondere verba cadunt,
Dæmonis aut astus, aut famæ sedula cura movet,
   Vt stolido ostentent miracula talia vulgo
Mente sed hoc capeos devius error agit.

ERGO

Dæmonis est hodie non ulla eiectio, sicut
   Oblessum nemo dæmone pectus habet.

Vasa in contumeliam facta non
possunt fieri vasa salutis.

Improbus ille Latro, reprobus tamen esse negatur
   Sic voluit Dominus, sit tibi velle satis.
Nondum natus Esau misere damnatus habetur
   Noluit hunc salvum, sit tibi nolle satis.
Vocula PECCAVI placuit satis vna Davidis
   Et MISERERE satis, cum miseretur, erit.
Pectora percussit Iudas, sed robora fiunt
   Pectora, seu rigido marmore dura magis.
Quos vult obdurat, quos diligit eligit illos
   Sic pro velle suo temperat omne suum.

ERGO

Fictus es ad vitam? nec Esau deperditus vnquam.
   Factus ad interitum? nec potes esse Iacob.

list of quaestiones to be discussed by candidates for the M.A. and higher degrees, at 'Vespers,' the important full-dress disputations two days before Commencement. Part of one of the few surviving Oxford quaestiones, for 1618, is here reproduced.[1] Beginning in 1665, when there was an unusually clever group of candidates at Harvard, these young inceptors introduced verses on their quaestio sheets similar to the 'Tripos Verses' of the University of Cambridge. There, at the Bachelors' and the Great Commencement, witty Latin verses on one or two of the theses or quaestiones to be discussed were composed by the 'tripos' or 'praevaricator' and printed on a broadside for circulation in the audience.[2] One of these, undated but belonging to the period when our founders were at Cambridge, is also reproduced In that university the practice lasted well into the nineteenth century; at Harvard, for but a few years in Chauncy's administration.

Although these Harvard sheets are sometimes loosely referred to as Commencement programmes, the term is misleading. The Bachelors' broadsides are correctly termed thesis sheets, or simply *Theses*; the Masters' broadsides, quaestio sheets, or simply *Quaestiones*. The latter were printed for the last time in 1791, and in the same year we find the first Commencement programmes, called *Order of Exercises*. Theses continued to be printed as broadsides through 1810, and for ten years more in quarto format. In 1821, when the printing of Theses ceased, the customary Latin formula of dedication was adopted for the cover of the Commencement Programme. Names of candidates for other degrees than the A.B. are for the first time printed in the Commencement Programme, instead of on a separate leaflet, in 1852; but the dedication is still signed by *iuvenes initiati in Artibus* and no others. In 1866 for the first time the Graduates, the President, and the Governor are *invited* by the candidates; and the Latin formula then adopted, very similar to the old Theses dedication, is still used on Commencement programmes.[3]

The College must have kept a file of Theses and Quaestiones, if only to obtain the names of graduates for the Triennial Catalogues. But

---

1. Bodleian, Wood Mss., 276a, 413. The portion of the sheet not reproduced includes quaestiones of candidates for B.C.L., B.M., and B.D., discussed both *in Vesperiis* and *in Comitiis* (Commencement). Cf. *Bodleian Quarterly Record*, VI. 107–12. In the Yale Library is a ms. sheet of quaestiones discussed by John Davenport when he took his B.D. at Oxford.

2. See *F. H. C.*, p. 73 n. The modern term 'tripos' at Cambridge is derived from the custom of first writing, and then printing, the names of the ranking B.A.'s on the back of these sheets. J. R. Tanner, *Historical Register of the University of Cambridge* (1917), p. 354.

3. William C. Lane, 'Early Harvard Broadsides,' printed in *Proc. A. A. S.*, n.s., XXIV. 296–97, and separately (1914), pp. 33–34, 38. Down to the American Revolution, or even later, the theses and quaestiones were drafted by the graduating class, who paid for the printing.

this file was destroyed in the fire of 1764, and after that it was impossible to reassemble a complete set. Theses are rarer than Quaestiones, as the large size of the sheet did not favor its preservation; and, paper being scarce, the temptation to use the blank side for other purposes was strong. A determined effort was made around 1912 by William Coolidge Lane, the Harvard College Librarian, to locate Theses and Quaestiones in other collections. The questionnaire he circulated resulted in the discovery of five sheets, previously unknown, in a bound volume, 'New England Tracts,' in the Hunterian Museum at the University of Glasgow, which was among the purchases of Dr. William Hunter the antiquary. Photographs of them were presented to the University by Sir William Osler; and there is now in the Harvard University Archives a complete file of originals, and photographs of all known originals, of our Theses and Quaestiones.

Mr. Lane published the results of his researches in an article in the *Proceedings of the American Antiquarian Society* for 1914 (n. s., XXIV. 264–304), which was printed separately as *Early Harvard Broadsides* (Worcester, 1914). No other sheets for our period have, to my knowledge, been discovered since.

These broadsides were printed by the College Press in Cambridge as long as it existed, thereafter in Boston.

The following list of dates of Commencement, 1642–1708, is taken from Mr. Albert Matthews' paper 'Harvard Commencement Days, 1642–1916,' *Publications Colonial Society of Massachusetts*, XVIII. 309–84. Dates in italics are conjectural. There was no Commencement in 1644, and the date in 1645 is unknown.

COMMENCEMENT DAYS, 1642–1708

1642	F	*Sept.*	*23*	1661	Tu	*Aug.*	*13*
1643	?	Oct.	?	1662	Tu	*Aug.*	*12*
1646	Tu	July	28	1663	Tu	Aug.	11
1647	Tu	July	27	1664	Tu	Aug.	9
1648	Tu	*July*	*25*	1665	Tu	Aug.	8
1649	Tu	July	31	1666	Tu	Aug.	14
1650	Tu	July	30	1667	Tu	Aug.	13
1651	Tu	Aug.	12	1668	Tu	Aug.	11
1652	Tu	*Aug.*	*10*	1669	Tu	Aug.	10
1653	Tu	Aug.	9	1670	Tu	Aug.	9
1653	W	Aug.	10	1671	Tu	Aug.	8
1654	Tu	Aug.	8	1672	Tu	Aug.	13
1655	Tu	Aug.	14	1673	Tu	*Aug.*	*12*
1656	Tu	Aug.	12	1674	Tu	Aug.	11
1657	Tu	*Aug.*	*11*	1675	Tu	Aug.	10
1658	Tu	Aug.	10	1676	Tu	Aug.	8
1659	Tu	Aug.	9	1677	Tu	Aug.	14
1660	Tu	Aug.	14	1678	Tu	Aug.	13

1679	Tu	Aug.	12	1694	W	July	4
1680	Tu	Aug.	10	1695	W	July	3
1681	Tu	Aug.	9	1696	W	July	1
1682	Tu	Aug.	8	1697	W	July	7
1683	W	Sept.	12	1698	W	July	6
1684	Tu	July	1	1699	W	July	5
1685	W	July	1	1700	W	July	3
1686	W	July	7	1701	W	July	2
1687	W	July	6	1702	W	July	1
1688	W	July	4	1703	W	July	7
1689	W	Sept.	11	1704	W	July	5
1690	W	July	2	1705	W	July	4
1691	W	July	1	1706	W	July	3
1692	W	July	6	1707	W	July	2
1693	W	July	5	1708	W	July	7

1643 THESES [1]

Illvstrissimis Pietate, et Vera Religione, Virtvte, et Prvdentia Honoratissimis Viris, D. IOHANNI WINTHROPO, caeterisque unitarum Nov-Angliæ Coloniarum Gubernatoribus, & Magistratibus Dignissimis; Vna cum pientissimis, vigilantissimisque Ecclesiarum Presbyteris: Nec non omnibus nostræ Reip. literariæ, tam in Veteri quam in Nov-Anglia, Fautoribus benignissimis: Has Theses Philologicas & Philosophicas, quas σὺν Θεῷ, Praeside HENRICO DUNSTERO palam in Collegio Harvardino pro virili propugnare conabuntur (honoris, observantiae et gratitudinis ergo) D. D. D. in artibus liberalibus initiandi Adolescentes.

Johannes Ionesius.   Samuel Danforthus.
Samuel Matherus.   Johannes Allinus.

Theses Philologic:

Grammatic:

[i]	Linguæ prius discendæ, quam artes.
[ii]	Linguæ fœlicius usu, quam arte discuntur.
iij	Linguarum Anglicana nulli secunda.
iiij	Literæ diversæ sonum habent diversum.
v	C. et T. efferre ut S. in latinis absurdum.
vi	Sheva nec vocalis est, nec consona, nec syllabam efficit.
vij	Nullæ diphthongi pronuntiandæ ut simplices vocales.
viij	Syllabarum accentus non destruit tempus.
ix	Verba valent sicut nummus.
x	Synthesis est naturalis Syntaxis.

---

1. Copies in Hunterian Museum, Glasgow, and M. H. S. Printed in *Proc. M. H. S.*, v. 444. Facsimile in S. A. Green, *Ten Fac-simile Reproductions Relating to New England* (Boston, 1902), p. 18; and *F. H. C.*, p. 137.

Rhetoric:

[i]   Rhetorica est affectionum domina.
[ii]   Eloquentia naturalis excellit artificialem.
iij   Apte loqui praestat quam ornate.
iiij   Vel gestus fidem facit.

Logic:

[i]   Dialectica est omnium artium generalissima.
[ii]   Efficiens & finis non ingrediuntur rei essentiam.
iij   Forma simul cum reipsa ingeneratur.
iv   Posita forma ponuntur essentia, differentia & actio.
v   Et motus et res motu factæ sunt effecta
vj   Oppositorum ex uno affirmato alterum negatur.
vij   Relata sunt sibi mutuo causae.
viij   Contradictio topica negat ubique.
ix   Privantia maxime dissentiunt.
x   Genus et species sunt notæ causarum et effectorum.
xi   Omnis syllogismus est necessarius ratione formæ.
xii   Omnis quæstio non est subjectum syllogismi.
xiij   Methodus procedit ab universalibus ad singularia.

Theses Philosophic:

Ethic:

[i]   Fœlicitas moralis est finis Ethices.
[ii]   Per unum actum non generatur habitus.
iij   Habitus non pereunt sola actuum cessatione.
iiij   Virtus perfecta dari potest, vitium neutiquam.
v   Vitiorum causa est liberum arbitrium.
vi   Nullus actus deliberatus in individuo est indifferens.
vij   Mores non sequuntur temperamentum corporis.
viij   Vulgi mos non regeret nos.
ix   Est abstinens qui continens.
x   Honor sequentem fugit, fugientem sequitur.
xi   Divitiae nil conferunt fœlicitati morali.
xij   Nulla est vera amicitia inter improbos.

Physic:

[i]   Nihil agit in seipsum.
[ii]   Omnis motus sit in tempore.
iij   Non datur infinitum actu.
iiij   Pura elementa, non sunt alimenta.
v   Non datur proportio arithmetica in mixtis.
vi   In uno corpore non sunt plures animæ.
vii   Anima est tota in toto, & tota in qualibet parte.
viij   Status animæ in corpore est naturalissimus.
ix   Visio fit receptione specierum.
x   Phantasia producit reales effectus.
xi   Primum cognitum est singulare materiale.

Metaphysic:

[i] Ens qua ens, est objectum metaphysices.
[ii] Ente nihil prius, simplicius, melius, verius.
iij Datur discrimen inter ens et rem.
iv Essentia entis non suscipit magis et minus.
v Veritas est conformitas intellectus cum re.

Cantabrigiae Nov. Ang. Mens. 8, 1643.

1646 THESES [1]

Spectatissimis Întegritate, Et Syncera Religione, Virtute et Sapientia Viris Plurimum Observandis, D. JOHANNI WINTHROPO; Caeterisque Confoederatarum Nov. Angliæ Coloniarum Gubernatoribus et Magistratibus Vigilantissimis: Una Cum Reverendissimis, Doctissimis, et Pietate Ornatissimis Ecclesiarum Presbyteris: Omnibus denique tàm in Veteri, quàm in Nov-Angliâ literarum & literatorum fautoribus benignissimis, Theses has Philologicas & Philosophicas, quas [aspirante Numine] Praeside HENRICO DUNSTERO, publice in Collegio Harvardino, pro virili defendere conabuntur, (quorum hic nomina subscribuntur) Adolescentes D. D. C. Q.

Johannes Alcocus. Georgius Stirkus.
Johannes Brocus. Nathanael Whitus.

Theses Philologicæ

Grammaticæ

[1] Orthographia consuetudini serviens sæpiùs mutata est.
[2] Græcæ linguæ structura est maximè harmonica.
3 Aleph pro puncti ratione omnium vocalium sonum habet.
4 Nulla hebræorum puncta præter decem primarió constituũt syllabam.
5 Hebræi sententias contrahendo, sensum dilatant.

Rhetoricæ.

[1] Oratio affectata est ridicula.
[2] Oratoris est causam non bonam facere, sed demonstrare.
3 Natura non est ad actionem cogenda.
4 Verborum pondus â re profluit.
5 Insinuatio non est insimulatio.

Logicæ

[1] Scientiæ ad res novas inveniendas parùm valent.
[2] Quó magis in notionibus â re disceditur, eo propiùs ad errorem acceditur.

---

1. Hunterian Museum, Glasgow. Printed in *New England Quarterly*, v. 508–10; facsimile in *F. H. C.*, pp. 136–37.

3 Nullum physicè diversum est logicè idem.
4 Nihil est sui-ipsius causa.
5 Instrumenti vis consistit in usu.
6 Materiæ nullum est contrarium positivum.
7 Finis dat medijs modum.
8 Oppositorum dissensio est perpetua.
9 Relativè opposita non habent medium.
10 Quæ eidem sunt æqualia, ea & inter se.
11 Abstractum est forma concreti.
12 Genus dat æqualitèr cuique speciei.
13 Definitio perfecta constituit axioma catholicum.
14 Infirmitas axiomatum parit distinctiones.
15 Præsens & præteritum immutabile est contingens.
16 Cujusdam immutabilis judicium est opinio.
17 Quæstio tutiùs exemplo quàm canone probatur.
18 Conclusio est ipsa quæstio virtualitèr.

Theses Philosophicae.

Ethicae.

[1] Vitium ipsum est peccanti supplicium.
[2] Actio virtutis non est penes homines.
3 Finis non cadit in deliberationem.
4 Fortis non est sibi mortem consciscere.
5 Forti nil præter scelus est timendum.
6 Præstat maximum pati quàm minimum malum agere.
7 Difficilius est voluptati quàm iræ resistere.
8 Omne difficile non est molestum.
9 Veritas amicitiæ semper præferenda.
10 Amicitia virtutem non dignitatem respicit.
11 Præstat amari quàm honorari.
12 Ad res adversas amicos non invites.

Physicæ.

[1] Ars Physicæ est a rebus discenda, non in mente fingenda.
[2] Experientiæ certitudo theoriæ veritatem corroborare debet.
3 Scientia & potentia humana sunt æquè lata.
4 Natura parendo vincitur.
5 Quod contemplanti est instar causæ, id operanti est instar regulæ.
6 Intrinsecus naturæ motus est homini imperceptibilis.
7 Lumen est lucis species.
8 Motus est propria causa caloris.
9 Anima nil patitur a corpore.
10 Operatio animæ pendet a corpore.
11 Vita est unio formæ cum materia.
12 Synteresis fundatur in intellectu.

Metaph:

[1]   Materia metaphysica est forma physica sublimior.
[2]   Universale non actu existit.
3   Malum rei entitatem non ingreditur.
4   Veritas est tantùm unica.
5   Perfectum est cui nil debitum deest.

Cantabrigiæ Nov: Ang: Mens: 5. Die 28. 1646.

1647 THESES [1]

Amplissimis Consultissimis Et Multifaria Virtute Ornatissimis Viris D. JOHANNI WINTHROPO, Cæterisque Summis Rerum Nov-Anglicarum Administratoribus Præfectisque Dignissimis, Perinde Ac Venerandis Quibusque Ecclesiarum Presbyteris Singulari Pietate et Eruditione Varia Clarissimis Theologis: Quinetiam omnibus in utrâque Angliâ Musarum pariter ac Musicolarum Mecænatibus Humanissimis, Theses hasce Philologicæ & Philosophicas, quibus, Annuente Deo, Præside HENRICO DUNSTERO, publice in Collegio Harvardino propugnandis suam navabunt operam (devotissimæ observantiæ et gratitudinis ergo) artium liberalium candidati Adolescentes M. D. D. D.

Jonathan Mitchellus.   Johannes Beardonus.
Nathaneel Matherus.   Abrahamus Walverus.
Confortius Starr.   Georgius Haddenus.

Theses Philologicæ.

Grammaticæ.

[1]   Rerum potior, sed verborum prior est contemplatio.
[2]   Linguarum idiomata callere est Grammaticæ peritiæ colophon.
3   Dantur solummodo quatuor orationis partes.
4   Accentus non variat tempus syllabæ sed tonum.
5   Actica [*sic*] dialectus inter Græcos principatum obtinet.
6   Puncta capta utrinque pellunt scheva.
7   Utrumvis in verbis Hebræis tempus exprimit utrumque.
8   Nomina Hebræa verbi sui casum saepè regunt.

Rhetoricæ [2]

[1]   Dialecticæ [1] præcipuè commendat oratorem.
2.   Non tam copiæ verborum quam ponderi studendum.
3.   Allegoria ex homogeneis absolvi debet.
4   Tropos ubique infarcire vitiosum est.

---

1. Hunterian Museum, Glasgow, Fragment in M. H. S.
2. These two words are written in a contemporary hand.

5   Stylus sibi constans esset, licèt pro materia varius.
6   Poësis vividos affectus tum postulat, tum parit.
7   Non tam metrum quam mimesis poëtica lauream meretur.

Logicæ.

[1]   Omnis ars est practica.
[2]   Ars Logica est in re.
3   Species intelligibiles sunt rationes Logicæ.
4   Actus ad rem provenit a singulâ causa sed non actus rei.
5   In efficiente per accidens effectum magis est a modo causæ qùam a causa ipsa.
6   Finis est aptitudo ad usum non ipse usus.
7   Res est in loco, tempus in re.
8   Duplex affectio est ex essentia relatorum.
9   Omnia adversa sunt immediata.
10   Forma & materia membrorum est forma & materia integri.
11   Integra natura generis, est in singula specie, universa in omnibus.
12   Individua differunt formis.
13   Sola res composita potest definiri.
14   Omnis veritas propriè dicta, est axiomatis.
15   Logicus conceptus, non vox grammatica axioma conglutinat.
16   Distributio in species segregative considerata est axioma disjunctum.
17   Nulla dispositio necessariò dat consequentiam, nisi syllogistica.
18   Methodus synthetica et analytica non differunt realitèr.

Theses Philosophicæ.

Ethicæ.

[1]   Fœlicitas moralis est virtutis praxis.
[2]   Res omnes dicuntur bonæ gratia bonitatis moralis.
3   Singuli affectus possunt tum virtuti tum vitio subjici.
4   Actio moralis ab agentis animo præcipuè æstimanda.
5   Qui nescit ab agendo temperare, nescit agere.
6   Actiones per se malæ nulla mediocritate fiunt bonæ.
7   Syncera voluptas est solius virtutis comes.
8   Virtus in sua ratione formali non admittit excessum.
9   Cardinales quas vocant virtutes, virtutis affectiones sunt, non species.
10   Calocagathia est virtus perfecta.
[11   illegible]
[12] Vindicta reddit inimico parem, venia potiorem.
13   Vera Philautía est virtus fœcunda.
14   Qui amicus omnibus tàm peccat, quàm qui paucis humanus.
15   Res prosperæ vitium, adversæ virtutem optimè detegunt.

Physicæ.

[1]   Qvicquid oritur è principiis naturalibus cadit sub Physicam.
[2]   Nec materia nec forma per se est quanta aut qualis.
3   Formale primum creatum fuit ex nihilo.

4   Forma est principium substantiale.
5   Forma substantialis per se non incurrit in sensus.
6   Resolubile in principia est corruptibile.
7   Motus est in mobili non in movente.
8   Motus non est ex essentia temporis.
9   Cœlum stellatum est igneüm.
10   Elementa non sunt invicem transmutabilia.
11   Elementa manent formaliter in mistis.
12   Tonitru fit per subitam rarefactionem.
13   Species externis sensibus perceptibiles sunt substantiales.
14   Dantur plures animæ in eodem animali.
15   Anima rationalis non est forma hominis.
16   Voluntas nunquam cogitur.

Metaph:

[1]   Ens creatum eo perfectius est quo proximius ad ens primum.
[2]   Omnis compositio essentiæ arguit imperfectionem aliquam.
3   Nullum ens creatum est absolutè simplex.
4   Bonum addit enti aliquid positivum, malum nihil.
5   Ubi potentia passiva, ibi materia.
6   Existendi prior est quam substandi ratio.

Cantabrigiæ Nov: Ang: 6. Calend. Sextilis. 1647.

9 AUGUST 1653 THESES [1]

Clarissimis, Dignissimis Omnigena Virtute Consilio, et Prudentia
Viris Celeberrimis, D. JOHANNI ENDICOTTO, D. JOHANNI HAINESIO,
Inclytarum Massachusetti, et Connecticutiensis, Coloniarum Guber-
natoribus Plurimum Honorandis: Cæterisque Unitarum Nov-Angliæ
Coloniarum Summis Administratoribus; Ut et Omnibus et singulis
Pietate et Doctrina Ornatissimis Ecclesiarum Presbyteris. Omnibus
denique hujus nostræ Reipublicæ literariæ Maecenatibus benignis et
benevolis. Theses hasce, quas (favente DEO) sub Praeside HENRICO
DUNSTERO palam in Collegio Harvardino, pro viribus defendendas
humillimè suscipiunt, juvenes liberalium artium studiosi, D. D. D. Q.

Samuel Willis.	Samuel Noel.	Samuel Hooker.
Johannes Angier.	Richardus Hubbard.	Johannes Stone.
Thomas Shepard.	Johannes Whitting.	Guilielmus Thompson.

Technologicæ.

[1]   Ars est regula εὐπραξίας entis a primo.
[2]   Ars et ens á primo sunt æqualis latitudinis.
☞   ARTIUM PRÆCEPTA SUNT ÆTERNÆ VERITATIS. *Anglicè.*

---

1. Hunterian Museum, Glasgow. Facsimile in *Proc. A. A. S.,* n.s., XXIV. 274 (William C. Lane, *Early Harvard Broadsides,* pp. 14–15).

4 Ut ens et bonum sic ars et verum convertuntur.
5 Artis unitas et distinctio oritur ab ejus diverso subjecto.
6 Posita re necessariò ponuntur artes.
7 In artium præceptis nulla est invicem axiomatica contradictio.
8 Solis distributionibus et definitionibus perfecta, sed consectarijs illus-
   tratur ars.

Logicæ.

[1] SOLA dialectica concrescit cum seipsà et cum omnibus alijs artibus.
[2] Ens intelligibile est latius ente vero.
3   Ratio est artium Mercurius.
4   Arguendi affectus non actus est argumento essentialis.
5   Nihil potest esse causa sui ipsius.
6   Nil est materiæ positivè contrarium.
7   Forma non est accidens.
8   Adjuncta propria, conveniunt primò generalibus generalia contrà.
9   Omnis oppositio oritur primariò à forma.
10 ☞ OMNIA ARGUMENTA NON SUNT RELATA.
11 Privatio potest esse ubi habitus actu nunquam fuit.
12 Omnes partes simul sumptæ non sunt totum.
13 Membra non sunt partes extincto integro.
14 Genus existit in individuis.
15 Sublata aliqua specie tollitur genus.
16 Individuum est species specialissima.
17 Axioma vinculo viget et animatur.
18 Idem axioma potest affirmari et negari.
19 Non consequens sed consequentia in syllogismo est semper necessaria.

Grammaticæ.

[1] Orationis puritatem non ornatum spectat Grammatica.
2   Grammatica est perfecta sinè Rhetorica non contrà.
3   Benè Grammaticari est vocum proprietates et structuram interpretari.
4   Sola vocalis non consona est sonus integer.
5   Linguæ sunt Artium gratiâ.
6   Linguarum illa perfectissima quæ maximè grammatica.
7   Comparationis duo tantum sunt gradus.

Rhetoricæ.

[1] Rhetorica est mentis Apelles.
2   Interna sermonis exornatio externæ pronuntiationi est præponenda.
3   Tropus non figura potest esse in simplici voce.
4   Prolatio est ironiæ forma.
5   Figuræ sunt sermonis nervi.
6   Poetæ et nascuntur et fiunt.

Arithmeticæ.

[1] Arithmetica est Ars a Geometria distincta.
2   Quantitas discreta est Arithmeticæ subjectum.
3   Numerus potentia est infinitus.

4   Unitas propriè dicitur numerus.

5   Factus a primo per primum non potest dividi a cómposito alio.

6   Potest primorum inter se, uterque, alter tantum, et neuter esse primus per se.

Geometricæ.

[1]   Benè metiri est cujusque magnitudinis proportionem et affectionem perspicere.

2   In singula specie figurarum unica tantum est ordinata.

3   Diameter, & centrum figuræ coincidunt.

4   Triangula æquantur ternis angulis.

5   In omni triangulo majus latus majorem angulum subtendi.

6   Figura rotunda omnes alias comprehendit.

7   Perimeter omnium circulorum est æquè rotundus.

8   Diametro in circulo respondet maximus circulus in sphærico.

Physicæ.

[1]   Physica est regula rei natæ.

2   Constantis naturæ nulla est generatio aut corruptio.

3   Materia prima erat informis.

4   Pura materia nec est una nec multiplex.

5   Formæ non materia elementorum fuerunt immediatè creata.

6   Quantitas a materia, qualitas a forma præcipuè oritur.

7   Qualitas non existit extrà subjectum proprium.

8   Qualitas genuina non dcstruit subjectum suum.

9   Anima vegetativa et sensitiva non rationalis fiunt ex elementis.

10   ☞ NULLA ANIMA EST FORMA ANIMATI.

11   Anima rationalis est divisibilis.

12   Destructa quavis anima compositum perit.

13   ☞ STELLÆ SUNT ANIMATÆ.

14   Voluntas sequitur non obsequitur dictamini intellêctus.

15   Voluntas movet sensus internos imperio tantum politico non despotico.

16   Voluntas potest pati non cogi.

Cantabrigiæ Nov-Angliæ Quint: Id: Sextilis Anno Dom: M.D.C. LIII.

9 August 1653 Quaestiones [1]

Quæstiones In Philosophia Discutiendæ Sub Henr: Dunstero Præside, Col: Harvard: Cantab: N:-Angl: In Comitiis Per Inceptores In Artib: Nono Die Sextilis M. DC. LIII.

I   An Materia & forma separatim existere possint?
                  Negat Respondens   Joshua Hubberdus.

II   An anima patitur a corpore?
                  Negat Respondens   Jeremiah Hubberdus.

III   An Astrologia judicialis est licita?
                  Negat Respondens   Samuel Philipsius.

---

1. Hunterian Museum, Glasgow. Facsimile in *F. H. C.*, p. 251.

IIII   An Elementa sunt solæ causæ essentiales mistorum?

Negat Respondens   Leonardus Hoaretius.

V   An Aliquid creatum annihilatur?

Negat Respondens   Jonathan Inceus.

10 August 1653 Theses [1]

Authoritatis Pondere, Iudicii Robore, Consiliique Gravitate Viris Vere Ornatissimis, ut et Æquitatis Almæ Peractione Celeberrimis D. Johanni Endicotto Eximiæ Massachusettensis Coloniæ Rectori Fidelissimo, Pluribus Nominibus Observando; Cæterisque totius hujusce Politiæ Nov-Angl: Procuratoribus Studiosissime Colendis, nec non etiam qua Doctrina, qua Pietate, Splendidissimis Ecclesiarum Luminibus, Reverentia (Quanta Potestesse maxima) Prosequendis: Universis porrò et singulis passim locorum ingenuarum Artium cultoribus, et patronis humanissimis, Theses hasce, quas (favente Numine) sub Henrico Dunstero Collegij Harvardini Præside, in propatulo pro virium suarum modulo defensum ire nervos intendunt suos, (officij, observantiæ, & gratitudinis ergo) tenelli Musarum alumni P. D. D. D Q

Edvardus Rawson.	Joshua Moodæus.
Samuel Bradstreet.	Joshua Ambrosius.
Joshua Long.	Nehemias Ambrosius.
Samuel Whiting.	Thomas Crosbæus.

Theses Technologicæ.

[1]   Ars est entis regula.
2   Proprium et formale recipiens artis est intellectus.
3   Ens arti adæquatur.
4   'Αφαιρεσις est et ejusdem, & diversarum artium.
5   Non ens non est entis causa.
6   Quicquid est, est positivè bonum.

Logicæ.

[1]   Dialectica est Sol microcosmi.
2   Argumenta sunt Logici radij.
3   Ens et non ens sunt subjectum dialectices.
4   Nihil arguit seipsum.
[5]   Causa et effectum sunt ὁμόχρονα.
☞   FORMA NON INFORMAT MATERIAM SED TOTUM COMPOSITUM.
7   Opposita æquè dissentanea sunt sed non æqualiter dissentiunt.
8   Privantia quàm maximè pugnant.
9   Orta sunt primorum symbola.

---

1. Hunterian Museum, Glasgow. Facsimile in *Proc. A. A. S.*, n.s., xxiv. 276 (W. C. Lane, *op. cit.*, pp. 16–17).

10   Conjugata contrariorum inter se contrariantur.
11   Sublatâ quavis parte tollitur totum.
12   Natura communis non existit nisi in singularibus.
13   Species formaliter distinguuntur.
14   Nullum testimonium humanum per se est αὐτόπιστον.
15   Scientia est necessariorum, opinio contingentium.
16   Axioma discretum non ingreditur syllogismum.
17   Logica non docet fallacias.
18   Methodus intelligentiæ parens est, magistra memoriæ.

Grammaticæ.

[1]   In Arte Grammatica nulla datur Anomalia.
2   Vocales per se sunt mobiles.
3   Nominum genera inter trinarium numerum comprehenduntur.
4   Substantiva rem abstractam, adjectiva rem concretam denotant.
5   Litera gutturalis in lingua sancta punctat et se & literam præcedentem.
6   Benoni usurpatur pro præsenti quo carent Hebræi.
7   Omnis præpositio dissyllaba apud Græcos accentuatur in ultima.

Rhetoricæ.

[1]   Rhetorica est affectuum hortus.
2   Elocutio est florum Rhetoricorum area, Pronuntiatio odorum **ex**-piratio.
3   Tropus et Figura sunt flores Rhetorici.
4   Metaphora est rhetorices Rosa.
5   .Prolatio est vividus Ironiæ color.
6   Allegoria est Troporum servia.
7   Figura Tropo naribus jucundior.
8   Styli affectatio est Herba noxia.
9   In horto Rhetorico nidulans, Emphasis est avis dulcissimè modulans.
10   Elegantia numeri est Rhetoricæ sepes.

Theses Mathematicæ.

[1]   Numerus numeratus pendet à numero numeranti.
2   Numeratio per integros & per partes idem valet.
3   Ut unitas ad multiplicantem, sic multiplicandus ad factum.
4   Ut dividendus ad divisorem, sic quotus ad unitatem.
5   Parium pares sunt Toti, Reliqui, Facti.
6   Linea fit è fluxu punctorum.
7   Omnes figuræ isoperimetræ non sunt æquales.
8   Quadratum dupli est quadruplum ad quadratum dimidij.
9   Quadratum è diagonio quadrati est duplum ejus.
10   Radius circuli est latus inscripti sexanguli.
11   Ordinata sex triangula, sexangulatria planum, octahedra novem soli-dum complent locum.

Physicæ.

[1]   Nvllum super-naturale est contra-naturale.
2   Materiæ plurimum ubi perfectionis minimum.

3   Corpora in latione sunt contigua.
4   Omnis natura est extremis finita suis & divisione.
5   Locus et corpus se mutuò terminant.
6   ☞ MUNDUS EST IN LOCO.
7   Quælibet stella de proprio lucet.
8   Non dantur duæ primæ qualitates in eodem elemento.
9   ☞ GENERATIO ET CORRUPTIO FIVNT IN INSTANTI.
10 Meteora sunt corpora perfecta, imperfectè mista.
11 Mare fontium perennium est fons.
12 Idem numero animal accidentaliter differat à seipso.
13 Anima rationalis in statu separato intelligit.
14 Nihil est in voluntate quod non fuit priùs in intellectu.
15 ☞ VOLUNTAS EST LIBERA.
16 Malum non appetitur formaliter.

Ethicæ.

[1] Ad beatitudinem via regia est virtus.
2   Nullus vir bonus potest dici miser, nec malus fœlix.
3   Vitia vincere victoria maxima.
4   Patiens est fortis.
5   Ebrietas non excusat delictum.
6   Donum non tam ex dati valore, quàm ex dantis animo pensandum
7   Tacere simpliciter non est præstantius quam loqui.
8   Comitas est societatis ciuilis vinculum.
9   Amare quàm amari melius.
10 Vera voluptas est socia virtutis.
11 Finis quò ultimo proximior eò melior.

Cantabrigiæ Nov-Angl: Decimo Sextilis Anno Dom: CIↃ IↃC LIII.

1655   Quaestiones [1]

Quæstiones in Philosophia Discutiendæ Sub Carolo Chauncæo Præside, Col: Harvard: Cantab: N-Angl: In Comitiis Per Inceptores In Artib: Decimo Quarto Die Sextilis 1655.

I.   An Quælibet natura sit patibilis?   Affirm: Thomas Shepard.
II.   An Prima materia habuerit formam?   Neg: Samuel Nowel.
III.   An Anima rationalis sit forma hominis?
                                       Affirm: Richardus Hubberd.
IIII. An Totum et partes essentialiter differant?
                                       Affirm: Johannes Whitting.
V.   An Omne ens perfectum possit perfectè definiri?
                                       Affirm: Samuel Hooker.

Quibus accedit Oratio *Demegorica,* Johannis Angeir.

---

1. Harvard University Archives; another copy in the writer's study.

1656 Quaestiones [1]

Quæstiones In Philosophia Discutiendæ, Sub Carolo Chauncæo, SS. Theol: Bac: Præside Col: Harvard: Cantab: Nov-Angl: In Comitiis, Per Inceptores in Artibus, Duodecimo Die Sextilis, M. DC. L VI.

I. An Substantia creetur?   Affirmat Respondens Samuel Bradstreet.
II. An Ens Arti adæquetur?   Affirmat Respondens Joshua Long.
III. An Detur Maximum et Minimum in Naturâ?
                                   Affirmat Respondens Samuel Whiting.
IIII. An Intelligentiæ sint materiatæ?
                                   Affirmat Respondens Joshua Moodæus.
V. An Creaturæ existentia sit Contingens?
                                   Affirmat Respondens Nehemias Ambrosius.

1658 Quaestio [2]

Quæstio In Philosophia Discutienda, Sub Carolo Chauncæo, S. S. Theol: Bac: Præside Col: Harvard: Cantab: Nov-Angl: In Comitiis, Per Inceptorem In Artibus, Decimo Die Sextilis M. DC. LVIII.
An Voluntas semper sequatur ultimum dictamen intellectus practici?
                                   Negat Gershom Bulklæus.

> Concilij quoties princeps dictamina spernit,
>   Et meliora videns deteriora facit?
> Angelici causam lapsus quis dixerit esse
>   Dictamen mentis? quippe salubre fuit.
> Vel causam lapsus mihi quis narrabit Adami?
>   Namque intellectus non fuit error ei.
> Nullus Dæmon erat qui non fuit ante δαήμων;
>   Nec sine peccato mentibus error inest.
> Impulit in vitium ergò imperiosa voluntas,
>   Quod benè mens dictat, Non, ait illa, Placet.
> Stat contrà Ratio: Stat pro ratione Voluntas,
>   Noluntas potiùs nonne vocanda tibi?

Ergò,

> Non mentis semper sequitur dictata voluntas,
>   Sed tum Medeam, non sapit illa Deum.

1659 Quaestiones [3]

Quæstiones In Philosophia Discutiendæ, Sub Carolo Chauncæo, S. S. Theol: Bac: Præside Col: Harvard: Cantabrigiæ, Nov.-Angl: In Comitiis, Per Inceptores In Artibus, Die Nono Sextilis: M. DC. LIX.

1. H. U. Archives. Printed in Sibley, 1, 358–59.
2. Hunterian Museum, Glasgow.
3. H. U. Archives. Printed in Sibley, 1. 593.

I   An Privatio sit causa rerum naturalium?
Negat Respondens Robertus Payneus.

II   Utrùm anima sit subjectum capax cognitionis infinitæ?
Affirmat Respondens Johannes Eliotus.

III   An quicquid movetur, ab alio moveatur?
Affirmat Respondens Thomas Gravesius.

IIII   Utrùm forma ducatur de potentià materiæ?
Negat Respondens Johannes Emersonus.

1660 Quaestiones [1]

Quæstiones In Philosophia Discutiendæ, Sub CAROLO CHAUNCÆO SS. Theol: Bac: Præside Col: Harvard: Cantabrigiæ, Nov-Angl: In Comitiis, Per Inceptores In Artibus, Decimo-Quarto Die Sextilis 1660.

I.   An detur Concursus Immediatus primæ causæ cum secundâ?
Affirmat Respondens Zecharias Symmes.

II.   Utrum Locus, Motus, et Tempus univocè competant spiritibus?
Negat Respondens Zecharias Brigden.

III.   An Actus Creandi sit æternus?
Affirmat Respondens Johannes Cotton.

IIII.   Utrum Intellectus et voluntas sint facultates realiter distinctæ?
Affirmat Respondens Johannes Hale.

V.   An Motus sanguinis sit Circularis?
Affirmat Respondens Elischa Cooke.

VI.   Utrum Notitia Entis primi sit homini naturalis?
Affirmat Respondens Barnabas Chauncy.

1663 Mock Theses

This document, now in the University Archives, was long in possession of the Woodbridge family of Connecticut. It was printed, with facsimile, translation, and comments, by the donor, Henry Herbert Edes, in *Publications Colonial Society of Massachusetts*, v. 322–39. By some it has been regarded as a manuscript copy of the official printed theses, no copy of which has survived; but internal evidence seems conclusive as to its burlesque character. The dedication is obviously a mockery of the customary formula: note the heaping up of adjectives and superlatives, the description of the aged and strong-tempered Governor Endecott as 'uncommon venerable' and a 'mighty satrap.' King and Crown are never referred to on Harvard thesis sheets before the Dominion period (*v.* 1687); and if a loyal and respectful allusion had been intended, the form would have been 'Domini Regis' or 'Caroli II Angliæ (etc.) Regis' and not this mock-Roman 'Imperial Majesty.' Doubtless a pun is also concealed in the

1. H. U. Archives. Printed in Sibley, i. 488.

description of the ministers as *Angeli* instead of *Presbyteri* or *Theologi*, and of the Overseers of the College as *Spectatores* instead of *Inspectores*. Moreover, those dedicating the theses are not named, and describe themselves as *iuvenes in Artibus velites* (young snipers in the Arts), a phrase never used on the genuine theses, where *iuvenes* are always humble *adolescentes*, *musarum alumni*, *in artibus initiati*, or the like. The year is given as that of the 'Great Jubilee,' perhaps a hint that all students' debts to the College should be wiped out.

Most of the theses might have found a place on a genuine thesis sheet; and some of them are so found; others, such as *Logicae* 1, 2, 4; *Rhetoricae* 2, and *Grammaticae* 6 ('Ha Ha He is a well-known sign of hilarity'), are signals to the knowing reader. Part of the fun was making the whole thing seem realistic or possible; it was near enough to the norm to fool people — a favorite form of adolescent wit, as in the old Med. Fac. catalogues, and the fake Crimsons printed by the Harvard Lampoon.

I have added a number to each thesis for convenience in reference.

Viris terque quaterque Conclamatissimis omni Laudis Gradu majoribus. Quocunque honoris Fastigio ornandis, onerandis, honorandis, probitatisque omnigenæ celebritate clarescentibus. Ipsi Cæsareæ majestatis vicario D. Iohanni Endicotto celeberrimæ Massathusettensis Coloniæ Satrapæ megalæo, non vulgariter venerabili uniuscujusque item feliciter conjunctarum N-Angliæ Coloniarum Prætoribus, plùs plurimo celebrandis. Earundemque Synarchis nullo non honoris gradu cumulandis, cumulatis. multumque Reverendis Ecclesiarum Angelis haud nequicquam observandis. Rerum Academicarum Spectatoribus spectatissimis quorum memoriam alet posteritas Intuebitur æternitas: omni etiam literarum foventi, literatorum faventi: Theses hasce (quarum Numine secundante sub Præside Carolo Chauncæo S. S. Theol: Bac: in Col: Harv: pro tenuibus virium fibris ut veritatem propugnent Labores exantlabunt) Iuvenes in Artibus velites d d d Q

Theses technologicæ.

1 Creatura speculum in quo Ars est Imago sapientiæ æternæ.
2 Datur enti & egressus ab infinito, & progressus in infinitum.
3 Encyclopædia est sphæra Activitatis Rationalis.
4 Præcepta Artis nec ortum nec occasum nôrunt.
5 Natura est Artis Nutrix, Ars Naturæ est Adjutrix.
6 Ars a Naturâ originis potitur, Natura ab Arte actionem perfectivam patitur.
7 Natura est Artis exemplar, Ars Naturæ exemplum.
8 Entia a primo sunt ab ente primo participia præteriti, præsentis & futuri temporis.

Logicæ.

1 Logica est respectu specierum Intellegendarum Nervus opticus.
2 Inventio est fodina, judicium Argumentorum Lapis Heraclius.
3 Finis causarum omnium est primum mobile.
4 Materia est formæ cathedra, Forma materiæ Episcopus.
5 Efficiens est compositi Architectus.
6 Universalia sunt in se ἀειφανεῖς in re ἀφανεῖς Asterismi.
7 Species & Individua sunt prosapia & genus generis.
8 Substantia est Accidentium πανδοχεῖον.
9 Accidens commune est per totam sphærem substantiarum planeta.
10 Subjectum est Adjunctorum Bajulus.
11 Majus & minus Extensionem, magìs & minùs Intensionem sonant.
12 Relata sunt Gemini contemporanei.
13 Contraria Antœci sunt, Disparata Periœci.
14 Contradictoria totum mundum dividunt & Imperant.
15 Qualitas est Similitudinis origo & dissimilitudinis Scaturigo.
16 Naturâ proteron Hysteron est cognitione Hysteron proteron.
17 Dichotomia est Logica Anatomia.
18 Αυτὸς ἔφη est ipsa divini testimonij forma.
19 Syllogismus est triangulum cujus basis est conclusio.
20 Lumen conclusionis Eliditur et Elicitur ex chalybe & silice præmissarum.
21 Dilemma est Amphisbæna venenosa.
22 Sophisma est Argumentorum mangonium.
23 Methodus est Ataxiæ Antagonista, & Syntagmatis axiomatum Catastasis.

Grammaticæ.

1 Grammatica est Janua Linguarum & philosophorum Proscholium.
2 Orthographia & Orthoœpia Ancillantur Grammaticæ.
3 Quatuor Elementa Gutturalia (apud Hebræos) inter se transmutantur.
4 Etymologia est verborum fractio Analytica.
5 Finis & Funis sunt dubij generis.
6 Ha Ha He vox est hilaris bene Nota.
7 Poeta est inventionis factor.
8 Licentia poetica est Hæresis Grammatica.

Theses Rhetoricæ.

1 Grammaticæ Epilogus est Rhetoricæ Prologus.
2 Rhetorica est Rationis et orationis purpurissatio.
3 Rhetoris est Sophistici verba dando verba dare.
4 Systole vel Diastole sunt Hyperboles Causa Synectica.
5 Aposiopesis est Enthymema Rhetoricum.
6 Monotonia est Rhetorica Ἄμουσος.
7 Gestus est Suadæ personatio.

Mathematicæ:

1 Mathesis est Intellectûs Diadema.
2 Arithmetica est præcipuum organum Mathematicum.

3 Ciphræ dant quod non habent.
4 Fractiones sunt unitatis Analysis Anatomica.
5 Geometres est Nebulo Angularis.
6 Linea & superficies sunt principia interna corporis mathematici.
7 Basis est Figuræ hypopodium.
8 Astronomia est Corporum Cælestium Sceletonin Intellectum.
9 Non dantur orbes distincti nisi κατ' Ανθρωποπάθειαν.
10 Planetæ sunt Stellæ fixæ, Stellæ fixæ sunt paralyticæ.
11 Sol est exercitûs cælestis Imperator.
12 Tempus est Soboles motûs cælestis.

Ethicæ.

1 Ethica est vitiorum Emplastrum corrosivum.
2 Virtus est vitiorum extremorum Progenita.
3 Virtus nescit & latitudinem & declinationem.
4 Finis, & bonum, per se sunt parallela.
5 Dives est Amphiscius.
6 Honos est Ignis fatuus fugientes sequens sequentes fugiens.
7 Saligia est vitiorum Synopsis.
8 Homo vitiosus est Centaurus.
9 Posito bono temperamento Corporis ponitur virtus, & vice versâ.
10 Rex Lex & Grex sunt partes, Rempublicam constituentes.

Physicæ.

1 Physiologus est corporum Naturalium & Naturæ dissutor.
2 Natura est omnium Actionum Naturalium directrix & Rectrix.
3 Materia prima a Quantitate fermentata est.
4 Elementa sunt corporum mixtorum terminus a quo & ad quem.
5 In Elementatis datur bellum civile.
6 Aer est globi terreni Pericardium.
7 Quævis forma cum quâvis materiâ non vult matrimonio conjungi.
8 In animantibus unio animæ cum corpore est Eorum forma.
9 Planta est animantis Embryon.
10 Quantitas est Elementorum contrariorum in mistis Anacampseros.
11 Sol est ignis, nubes sunt pluviæ Alembici.
12 Omnis sensus exterior est mercurius politicus.
13 Sensus internus est omnium specierum sensibilium Xenodochium.
14 Homo est omnium entium sporades constellatæ.
15 Spiritus animales sunt Hyphen Animæ rationalis & corporis.
16 Caput est intellectûs, Cor voluntatis Solium.

Cantabriæ Nov-Angliæ: Quinto Idûs Augusti Anno Magni Iubilæi
MDCLXIII.

1663 QUAESTIONES [1]

Quæstiones In Philosophia Discutiendæ, Sub CAROLO CHAUNCÆO SS. Theol. Bac. Præside Col. Harvard. Cantabrigiæ, Nov-Angl. In Comitiis Per Inceptores In Artibus, Undecimo Die Sextilis M. DC. LXIII.

Quas Antecedit Oratio Gratulatoria, Nathanielis Collinsii.

I.   An discrimen boni & mali à lege Naturæ cognoscatur.
Affirmat Respondens Simon Bradstreet.

II.   An Anima rationalis sit Natura immortalis.
Affirmat Respondens Samuel Eliotus.

III.   An præcepta Artis sint homini lapso cognoscibilia.
Negat Respondens Petrus Bulklæus.

1664 QUAESTIONES [2]

Quæstiones In Philosophia Discutiendæ, . . . Die Nono Sextilis M. DC. LXIV.

Quas Antecedit ORATIO GRATULATORIA, Isrælis Chauncæi.

I.   Utrum Anima Rationalis sit ex traduce.
Negat Respondens Johannes Bellinghamus.

II.   Utrum Detur Idæa omnium Entium in primò Ente.
Affirmat Resp. Nathaniel Chauncæus.

III.   Utrum Detur Concursus per Modum Principii.
Affirmat Resp. Elnathan Chauncæus.

IV.   Utrum Mundus potuerit creari ab Æterno.
Negat Resp. Josephus Whitingus.

V.   Utrum Decretum Dei tollat Liberum Arbitrium.
Negat Resp. Calebus Watsonus.

1665 QUAESTIONES [3]

Quæstiones In Philosophia Discutiendæ, . . . Die Octavo Sextilis M. DC. LXV.

I.   Utrum Deus puniat peccata necessitate naturæ.
Affirmat Respondens Solomon Stoddardus.

O tu, quæ sapis alta nimis, Sapientia prima,
Quæque Gigantæis ausibus astra petis,

---

1. H. U. Archives. Printed in Sibley, II. 53.

2. H. U. Archives. Printed in Sibley, II. 72–73. The omitted part of the heading in this and following Quaestiones is identical with that of 1663.

3. H. U. Archives. Printed in Sibley, II. 101–02. Translation of II on p. 257, above.

Aut velut Icariis assumptis, tolleris, alis
  In Cœlum, similem non metuendo casum,
Disce φρονεῖν & σωφρονεείν — NON subdere fata.
  Concipe nos ausos, nec voluisse Deum:
Justitiam at punire malos natura requirit,
  Peccatum pugnat cum bonitate Dei.

Ω Βαθός! hic clama miser, & mirare videndo
  Peccati salvos posse tot esse reos.

II.   An ulla substantia creata sit immaterialis.
                                Negat Respondens Moses Fiskæus.

Naturam Angelicam, mentesque hac lege teneri,
  Iudice quis sensu vel ratione putet?
Verum est quod carnem nec habet, neque spiritus ossa.
  Materiam quam tu Spiritibusque dabis?
Quatuor ex causis effectum existere constat,
  Actus non puros esse creata patet.
Materiata tamen sunt hæc immateriata,
  Quæ sine materia, materiata tamen.

1666 QUAESTIONES [1]

Quæstiones In Philosophia Discutiendæ, . . . Die Decimo Quarto
Sextilis M. DC. LXVI.

I.   Utrum omnes Disciplinae tendant ad εὐπραξίαν;
                                Affirmat Respondens Johannes Reyner.

A Disciplinis capiunt benefacta periti
  Artifices, tellus quos alit atque mare.
Cur benefactores rari sunt discipulorum?
  Artes munificæ quod placuêre [minus].
Cur tot Doctores mala, quæ sunt facta, tuentur,
  Discendi finis si bona praxis erat?
Ingenuas quia non didicêre fidelitèr artes,
  Nec pravum ingenium dedidicêre suum.

Ergò

Solvant artifices sua discipulis benefacta,
Εὐπράττειν illis discipulique, dabunt.

II.   Utrum Malum sit privativum.
                                Affirmat Respondens Thomas Mighell.

Quæ mala naturæ, morum, pœnæque, videto:
  Per se quæ mala sunt, sunt hominive mala.

---

1. H. U. Archives. Printed in Sibley, II. 133–34. See above, p. 124, for translation
of Reyner's verse.

Id privativum, quod mores inficit, esto:
  Pravum privatum est, exuiturque bono.
Nempe negativè mala, sunt non entia: fœlix
  Namque status noster sic foret absque malis.
Insunt (heu!) nobis, sed non sunt esse reali:
  Obsunt, quod nihil est, id nec obesse potest.

Ergò

Ne privêre bonis, aufer mala: non sapit ille,
  Qui bona nancisci quærit agendo mala.

1668 Quaestiones [1]

Quæstiones In Philosophia Discutiendæ, . . . Die Undecimo-Sextilis MDCLXVIII.

[1]   Utrum detur causa aliqua externa volitionis divinæ.

                          Negat Respondes Benjamin Eliotus.

Omnia consilio fecit Deus, idque *volendo*,
  Nolendoque etiam de libero arbitrio:
    Nec *prævisa fides*, *meritum* nec causa salutis
  Prævisum *vitium* nec reprobare facit.
    Quos vult indurat, quorum vult & miseretur,
  Externam causam, quærere, (stultè) cave
    Ultimus est finis, primus Deus efficiensque
  Causa Dei si sit, *non-Deus*, ergo Deus.

2   An detur in Deo scientia Media?

                          Negat Respondens Josephus Dudleus.

Objectum cujus *non-scibile* dicito vanum
  Scire tuum, versas pectore namque dolum.
Dividere à vero contradicentia falsum
  Dixerunt Logici: *non datur ens medium*,
    Nec norunt *medium*, contingens atque necesse
Decretum anticipans, estne quid absque *Deo*?
  Hic male dicetur MEDIO TUTISSIMUS IBIS
    Hinc etenim è MEDIO TOLLITUR *ipse Deus*.

3.   An omne bonum sit necessariò sui communicativum?

                          Affirmat Respondens Jabez Foxius.

Apparens pictumve bonum, bona quæque jucunda,
  Utilia effundunt non bona, sæpe mala,
Sed bona, quæ vere, quæ per se, maxima summum,
  Præcipue spargunt, de bonitate bona.
Qualis causa datur causatum tale bonoque
  Hinc de thesauro, quæ bona multa fluunt.

---

1. H. U. Archives. Printed in Sibley, II. 163–64.

1669 QUAESTIONES [1]

Quæstiones Duæ, *Pro Modulo*, Discutiendae ... Die Decimo Sextilis M. DC. LXIX.

An Protoplasti per lapsum amiserint Dona Naturalia?

Affirmat Respondens, Josephus Brownæus.

Integra post lapsum naturæ Dona *Papistæ*
  Contendunt, *nostri* hæc perdita jure dolent:
Hinc illi vires *Naturæ* sufficientes,
  Ut salvus fiat quilibet, esse putant:
Sed contrà certum est *Naturâ, filius iræ*
  Censetur lapsus, sic statuente Deo:
Deque novo quorsum ne expedit esse *creandos,*
  Et nasci, satis est si genitura prior?
Supra *naturam* quoque perdita dona fatemur,
  Queîs Protoplasti non caruêre prius:
Cum vitâ perdit, peccatis mortuus, illa,
  Et quæ *naturæ* dona fuêre simul.

Ergò

Cum sic naturam sanctam violavit Adamus,
  Quid Monstri Genius *posteritatis erit?*

An Homo sit Causa libera suarum Actionum?

Affirmat Respondens, Johannes Richardsonus.

Delectum quærit *ratio, natura* ligavit
  Ἐν δὲ πρὸς ἕν remanens limite fixa suo:
Libertas soli, semper, sic convenit omni,
  Re verâ compos qui rationis erit.
Sic nihil est hominum, quo carcere clausa voluntas
  Non operum dici libera Causa potest.
Sed non prima tamen, nec ad omnia libera causa est,
  Est quæ causa boni libera, quæque mali:
Nec libertati *Concursus Numinis* obstat,
  In quo *vita* datur, *motus,* & *esse* simul:
Humanos etiam quamvis determinet actus,
  Nemo tamen dicat facta coacta sibi.

Ergò,

Seu bona seu mala sint, homo libera causa vocandus.
  Fiant, non fiant; *libera causa manet:*
Arbitrium servum *sic libera causa malorum est,*
  Arbitriumque bonum *libera causa boni.*

---

1. H. U. Archives. Printed in Sibley, II. 205–06.

1670 Theses [1]

Viris Authoritate Præcipuis, Prudentia Celeberrimis Venerandis
RICHARDO BELLINGHAMO IOHANNI WINTHROPO THOMÆ PRINCÆO
Confœderatarum N. Angliæ Coloniarum Masathuset. Connecticut.
Plimouthen. Primatibus. Unà cum omnibus in Regimine Politico in
singulis Coloniis probè constitutis. Nec minùs Reverendis Reipu-
blicæ nostræ Ecclesiasticæ Rectoribus, Sacrorum Mystagogis, qui-
buscunque, etiam exiguis nostræ Academiæ cœptis benignè annuen-
tibus, Artibus Scientiisque, liberalibus πολυμάθεσι, & φιλομάθεσι
Vobis, ut Literarum Patronis, Theses hasce submissi quas (aspirante
Deo) sub tutelâ Caroli Chauncæi SS. Theol. Bac. Collegii Harvardini
Præsidis, propugnandas suscepimus Juvenes in Artibus Tyrones.

Nathaniel Higginson.   Thomas Clark.   ⎫
Ammi-Ruhama Corlett.   Georgius Burrough.   ⎬ D.D.DQ.
                                                 ⎭

Theses Technologicæ.

[1]   Ars est regula entis secundi, qua operando ad ens primum redit, à quo
       prodiit essendo.
2   Ars reflexa est phasma lucis divinæ resplendentis in nubem intellectus.
3   Ens à primo est artis fulcrum, ars entis in actione pixis.
4   Encyclopædia est circulus septem sectionibus, cujus centrum est Deus.
5   Regulæ artium in creaturis sunt radii sapientiæ divinæ.
6   Geneseωs regula retrograda est regula progressus analyseωs.
7   Artis varietas fluit ex varietate actuum rerum quos gubernat.

Logicæ.

[1]   Logica est ars dirigendæ humanæ rationis juxta regulas rationis rerum.
2   Inventio & judicium sunt intellectus gemelli.
3   Ratio & argumentum sunt parallela.
4   Causæ sunt effecti quatuor elementa.
5   Finis est causarum Primum Mobile.
6   Materia est principium subjectivum, forma effectivum actionis.
7   Contraria paribus inter se concurrunt telis.
8   Privatio est habitus apocope.
9   Similitudines non sunt Isosceles.
10   Genus summum est primum descendendo, ultimum ascendendo.
11   Genus subalternum est Janus Bifax.
12   Definitio est essentiæ perimeter.
13   Definitiones & distributiones sunt artium animæ.
14   Inartificiale argumentum est artificialis cliens.

---

1. The unique copy in the M. H. S. is torn. The dedication, which has been printed
in *Proc. A. A. S.*, n.s., xxiv. 280 (W. C. Lane, *op. cit.*, p. 19), is arranged with an elaborate series of braces in order to have the right governor correspond to the right colony.

15 Syllogismus est veritatis antipilanus.
16 Sophismata sunt paralogismi.
17 Methodus est ordinis archetypus.

Grammaticæ.

[1] Oratio est rationis clavis, ut ratio est orationis clavus.
2 Etymologia est verborum inventio, Syntaxis dispositio.
3 Orthographia est bene scribendi Lydius lapis.
4 Consona absenti vocali est ἀγκυλόγλωσσος.
5 Vocalis est vocis Harmonia.
6 Opus potius dandi casum quàm auferendi postulat.
7 Fas est indeclinabile.
8 Verba vestiendi accusandi casum admittunt.

Theses Rhetoricæ.

[1] Rhetorica est Eloquentiae uber, tropus & figura sunt papillæ.
2 Tropus est dictionis exergasia.
3 Ænigma est Rhetoricæ nodus Gordianus.
4 Aposiopesis est Enthymema Rhetoricum.
5 Synœceiosis est iræ vagina.
6 Hysterologia est figura canchrina.

Mathematicæ.

[1] Arithmetica concrescit quoad usum in cæteris Mathematicis.
2 Novem notæ figurarum sunt Mathematicum Alphabetum.
3 Numerus est corpus aggregat[um] ex unita[tib]us.
4] Substractio est avari manticularius.
5 Lineæ Parallelæ extensæ tantùm ad Græcas [se]secant calendas.
6 Trigonometria est Matheseως vertebra.
7 Horizon est Solis gena.
8 Zenith & Nadir sunt Antipodes.

Physicæ.

[1] Physica est prattomenon praxeως ar[   ].
2 Tempus est Hemerodromus.
☞ *Non Datur Transmutatio Elementorum.*
3 Concordia corporis mixti fit ex discordiâ simplicium.
4 Generatio & corruptio sunt Genesis & Analysis Physica.
5 Calor innatus & humidum radicale sunt vitæ grallæ.
6 Corpus est Animæ Gazophylacium.
7 Homo est medium participationis naturæ constantis, & inconstantis.
☞ *Anima Rationalis Creatur.*

Ethicæ.

[1] ☞ *Ethica Est Specie Distincta a Theologia.*
2 Ethica est bonorum morum pædagogus.
3 Virtutis via, respectu extremorum, jacet inter Scyllam et Charabdin.
4 Vitium est mentis declinatio ab æquatore virtutis.

5   Boni voluntas paret rationi, mali ratio voluntati.
6   Adulator est natura polypus.
7   Hypocrisis est pietatis Pa[   ]
8   Intemperantia est rationis Tor[   ]
9   Prodigalitas est divitiarum Epi[tome]
10   Avaritia est argenteus Hydrops.
11   Justitia est Mundi Atlas.

Cantabrigiæ Nov-Angliæ die nono Sextilis Anno M. DC. LXX

1674 QUAESTIONES [1]

Quæstiones Pro modulo Discutiendæ Sub LEONARDO HOAR. M. D. Col: Harvardini Cantab: in Nov-Anglia Præside Per Inceptores in Artibus in Comitiis Tertio Idus Sextiles M. DC. LXXIV.

[I.]   An Peccatum Originale sit & Peccatum & Poena?
Affirmat Respondens Samuel Sewall.
II.   An Necessitas Decreti tollat libertatem & Contingentiam Creaturæ?
Negat Respondens Petrus Thacherus.
III.   An Cœlum Stellatum sit Igneum?
Affirmat Respondens Thomas Weld.
IV.   An Detur Theologia Naturalis ad Salutem Sufficiens?
Negat Respondens Johannes Boules.

1675 QUAESTIONES [2]

Quæstiones Pro modulo Discutiendæ Sub Reverendo URIANO OAKES, Ecclesiæ Cantabrigiensis Pastore, Et Harvardini Collegii In Cantabrigia Nov-Anglorum Præside pro tempore, Per Inceptores In Artibus In Comitiis Quarto Iduum Sextilium 1675.

[I.]   An detur absolutum Decretum Reprobationis.
Affirmat Respondens Isaacus Foster.
II.   An Anima rationalis fiat ex traduce.
Negat Respondens Samuel Phips.
III.   An Species Intelligibiles sint Rationes Logicæ
Affirmat Respondens Samuel Danforth.
IV.   An Attributa Dei differant realiter ab Essentia.
Negat Respondens Guilielmus Adams.

Antecedit Oratio Gratulatoria.
Accedit Oratio Valedictoria.

1676 QUAESTIONES [3]

Quæstiones Pro modulo Discutiendæ, . . . Sexto Idus Sextiles MDCLXXVI.

1. H. U. Archives. Printed in Sibley, II. 335–36.
2. H. U. Archives. Printed with notes in Sibley, II. 413–14.
3. H. U. Archives. Printed in Sibley, II. 415. Heading same as 1675.

I.   An Voluntas semper determinetur ab ultimo Intellectus practici Judicio?   Negat Respondens Samuel Angier.

II.   An impossibile sit Mundum fuisse ab æterno?

                                    Affirmat Respondens Johannes Wise.

1678 THESES [1]

Illustrissimis Viris Tam Pietate, quam Prudentiâ atque Auctoritate spectatissimis; Ornatissimis D. JOHANNI LEVERETTO D. JOSIÆ WINSLOWÆO D. GUILIELMO LEITTO Fœderatarum Nov-Angliæ Coloniarum Massachuset Plimouth Connectitut: Gubernatoribus Honoratissimis: Cœterisque in Magistratus Onere et Honore Conjugatis, ad Reipublicæ clavum jugiter excubantibus, incolumitatis publicæ apprimé studiosis; Nec non Reverendissimis cum Academiæ, tum Ecclesiarum Curatoribus, Theologis Doctissimis et Gravissimis; Omnibus denuó et singulis bonarum Literarum candidatis, benevolis Academiæ Ενεργέταις Theses hasce, quas (ἐάνπερ ἐπιτρέπῃ ὁ Θεὸς) Sub Rev: URIANO OAKES, Ecclesiæ Cantabrigiensis Pastore, Collegii Harvardini Præside pro tempore, κᾱτᾱσκευαστικῶς κᾱί Ἀνᾱσκευαστικῶς discutiendas, proponunt juvenes φιλαλήθεις κᾱί φιλομαθεῖς

Johannes Cottonus.   Grindallus Rawsonus.

Cottonus Matherus.   Urianus Oakes.   D.D.D Q.

Theses Technologicæ:

[1]   Ars est ordinata Intelligentiæ, Scientiæ, Sapientiæ, & Prudentiæ colligatio & concursus.

2.   Ars præcipuè consistit in Theoriâ Regulæ, & Praxis secundum Regulam.

3.   Utrumque perficitur per Analysin & Genesin.

4.   Libri Scripturæ & Creaturæ sunt mineralia ex quibus haec Regula est effodienda.

5   Author entium est Author Artium.

6   Praecepta Artis id agunt, ut veteri querelæ, Ars longa, vita brevis, medeantur.

7.   Ευπραξία est objectum & finis artis.

8.   Praxis est Theoriæ finis, medium finis ultimi.

9.   Usu confunduntur, speculatione separantur prattomena.

10.   Genesis & Analysis eadem vestigia premunt.

11.   In compositione mundi Genesis fuit, in ejusdemque resolutione Analysis erit maximè conspicua.

12.   Ars ut naturam juvet, non ut impediat adhibetur.

13   Non ab artifice Ars, sed ab arte artifex creatur.

14.   Aliquis in omnibus, nullus in singulis, non est κατά παντος verum.

☞   NON DATUR METAPHYSICA AB ALIIS DISCIPLINIS DISTINCTA.

16.   In artium orbe adhuc restat multa Terra incognita.

---

1. M. H. S. and Hunterian Museum, Glasgow. Facsimile above, p. 167.

Logicæ.

[1] Dialectica est Ars rationis.
2 Logicæ munus totum est discernere & disponere.
3. Affectio est forma Argumenti.
4. Causa cognoscitur per effectum tanquam per aliquid notius nobis, effectus vero per causam, tanquam per aliquid notius naturâ.
5. Fortuna (quæ dicitur) est particula divinæ providentiæ.
6. Materia est omnium entium a primo communis.
7. Forma est principium distinctionis.
8. Posita forma, ponuntur esse, distinctio, & operatio.
9. Finis rei nihil aliud est quam rei bonitas, movens efficientem, perficiens effectum.
10. Finis in intentione est finis conceptus, finis in executione est finis natus.
11. Existentia est Essentia actualis.
12. Locus & Tempus sunt entia merè Logica.
13 Diversis & Oppositis æquè convenit dissentire, sed non convenit æquè dissentire.
14. Sola opposita realiter distinguuntur.
15. Comparatio id agit, ut comparata æque nota evadant.
16. Distributio maxime accurata est dichotomia.
17. Totum in distributione, est pars in definitione.
18. Pars in distributione est totum in definitione.
19. Genus habet naturam distinctam à speciebus, non separatam.
20. Testimonium divinum est firmissimum.
21. Omnis veritas est certa, licet non necessaria.
22. Discreta Axiomata non concludunt, sed distinguunt.
23. De axiomate immediatè, de syllogismo mediaté fit judicium.
24. Nulla datur syllogismi contingentia.
25. Tertium Argumentum est syllogismi Arbiter.
26. Explicatus primus est syllogismus refutationis.

Grammaticæ.

[1] Grammatica est Antidotus contrà confusarum linguarum maledictionem.
2. Suum Idioma servare est omni linguæ privilegium necessarium.
3. Prima sermonis gratia est purè loqui.
4. Notæ rerum aliæ possunt cudi præter verba et literas.
5. Aliquid de populorum moribus potest colligi ex ipsorum linguis.
6. Distinctio inter verba Homonyma est præcipuus Orthographiæ usus.
7. Quantitas & accentus sunt syllabarum condimenta.
8. Syntaxis est cynosura quæ lectorem dirigit in sensum sententiarum.

Rhetoricæ.

[1] Rhetoricæ munus est dictamina Rationis Phantasiæ applicare.
2 Rhetorica facit bonum apparens.
3 Copia Troporum fluxit ex inopiâ verborum.

4   Omnis tropus in axiomatibus si non aptissime adhibitus, est Cate-
       chresis.
5   Hyperbole vel supra vel infra metam semper volat.
6   Hyberbole quamvis ultra fidem, non tamen ultra modum esse debet.
7   Allegoria est metaphorarum conventus.
8   Tropus doctis, figura Idiotis est elocutionis pars mellitissima.
9   Apostrophe est orationis circumactio, ut auditores commodius, in-
       opinatè opprimat.

Mathematicæ

[1]   Ultima unitas est numeri forma.
2   Extractio radicum est arithmeticæ pars longè dignissima.
3   Lineæ Geometricæ sunt reales, quamvis non sensibus perceptibiles.
4   Linea non constat è punctis.
5   Lineæ solidæ oriuntur è corporis sectione.
6   Aequalitas est mensura inæqualitatis.
7   Recto non datur rectius.
8   Ubi Anguli sunt aquicruri Basis tantummodo constituit differentiam.
9   Pyramis est solidorum prima.
10   Æquator est præcipua temporis mensura.
11   Astronomiæ pars utilissima non adhuc ex hypothesibus colligenda
       exhibetur.
12   Astrologia, quæ dicitur judiciaria est sani judicii expers.

Physicæ.

[1]   Physica est ars bene naturandi.
2   Physicam tractandi ordo perfectissimus exhibetur in primo Geneseως
       Capite:
3:     Adæquatum Physicæ subjectum est Natura:
4:     Non in tempore, sed cum tempore mundus creabatur:
5:     Infinita non possunt esse princ[i]pia:
6:     Natura non agit nisi virtute primæ causae:
7:     Angeli sunt quanti quamvis non corporei:
8:     Omnis inconstans natura est perosa:
9:     Elementa non agunt et patiuntur nisi per qualitates:
10.   Mons[t]ra sunt ἁμαρτήματα naturæ impeditæ:
11:    Gene[r]atio et Corruptio non sunt propriè motus sed termini motus:
12:    Qualitatum recep[t]ione non fit αλλότης in subjecto sed ἀλλοιότης.
13:    Sonus non est mera elisio æris:
☞   DANTUR TRES ANIMÆ IN EODEM HOMINE.
15   Res intelligitur Intellectione rectâ Veritas Intellectione reflexâ.
☞   VOLUNTAS SEMPER DETERMINATUR AB ULTIMO INTELLECTUS PRACTICI
       JUDICIO.
☞   ETHICA NON DATUR SPECIE DISTINCTA A THEOLOGIA.

Cantabrigiæ Nov-Anglorum Idibus Sextilibus: MDCLXXVIII.

1678 QUAESTIONES [1]

Quæstiones Pro modulo Discutiendæ, . . . Idibus Sextilibus MDCLXXVIII.

I.   An Cognitio Angelica sit discursiva?
                        Affirmat Respondens Johannes Pike.
II.   An concursus Causa Prima tollat libertatem secundæ?
                        Negat Respondens Jonathan Russellus.
III.   An calor sit febri essentialis?   Negat Respondens Petrus Oliverus.
IV.   An status animæ separatæ sit naturalis?
                        Affirmat Respondens Samuel Andrew.
V.   An Eclipsis solis tempore passionis Christi fuit naturalis?
                        Negat Respondens Timotheus Woodbridge.
VI.   An hepar sanguificet?   Negat Respondens Daniel Allin.
VII.   An potentiæ animæ rationalis agant inorganicé?
                        Affirmat Respondens Johannes Emersonus.
VIII. An præcepta Philosophica sint Theologicis contradictoria?
                        Negat Respondens Nathaniel Gookinus.

His Antecedit Gratulatoria, & Accedit Valedictoria Oratio.

1679 QUAESTIONES [2]

Quæstiones Pro modulo Discutiendæ . . . Pridie Idus Sextiles MDCLXXIX.

An Detur in Deo Scientia media?   Negat Respondens Thomas Shepardus.
An notitia Dei sit homini naturalis?
                        Affirmat Respondens Thomas Brattle.

His accedit Oratio Valedictoria.

1680 QUAESTIONES [3]

Quæstiones Pro modulo Discutiendæ, Sub Reverendo URIANO OAKES, Ecclesiæ Cantabrigiensis Pastore, Et Collegii Harvardini in Cantabrigia Nov-Anglorum Præside, Per Inceptores In Artibus In Comitiis Ante Diem IV Idus Sextiles Anno Dom. M. DC. LXXX.

[I]   An detur liberum Arbitrium in non Renatis, ad bonum Spirituale?
                        Negat Respondens Thomas Cheeverus.
II   An Annihilatio sit opus Omnipotentiæ?
                        Affirmat Respondens Johannes Danforthus.

---

1. H. U. Archives. Printed in Sibley II. 447–48. Heading same as 1675.
2. H. U. Archives. Printed in Sibley, II. 481. Heading same as 1675.
3. H. U. Archives. Printed in Sibley, II. 500–01.

III   An Virtus consistat in Mediocritate?

> Negat Respondens Edvardus Paysonus.

IIII   An Conscientia errans obliget ad Peccandum?

> Negat Respondens Josephus Capen.

His accedit ORATIO valedictoria.

1681 Quaestiones [1]

Quæstiones In Philosophia Discutiendæ Sub Reverendo CRESCENTIO MATHERO, A.M. Apud Bostonienses V. D. M. In Comitiis Academicis Moderatore perquàm Honorando, Collegii Harvardini Curatore, & Socio Vigilantissimo; Cantabrigiæ Nov-Anglorum: Per Inceptores in Artibus Die quinto ante Idus Sextiles MDCLXXXI.

An Interitus Mundi visibilis futurus sit substantialis?

> Negat Respondens Johannes Cottonus.

An Puncta Hebraica sint originis divinæ?

> Affirmat Respondens Cottonus Matherus.

An Status Animæ separatæ sit naturalis?

> Affirmat Respondens Grindallus Rawsonus.

1682 Quaestiones [2]

Quæstiones In Philosophia Discutiendæ, . . . Die Sexto ante Idus Sextiles MDCLXXXII.

An Anima Rationalis sit Immortalis?

> Affirmat Respondens Jonathan Danforth.

An genus Existat extra intellectum? Affirmat Respondens Edvardus Oakes.
An Angeli habeant materiam et formam?

> Affirmat Respondens Jacobus Alling.

An Anima Rationalis agat inorganice?

> Affirmat Respondens Thomas Barnardus.

His Antecedit Salutatoria et Accedit Valedicttoria [sic] Oratio

1683 Quaestiones [3]

An Detur Concursus Causæ primæ cum omni Causâ Secundâ?

> Affirmat Resp. J. L[everett].

An Detur Summum Malum?   Negat Resp. G. B[rattle].
An Mundus sit Ens Necessarium?   Negat Resp. P. G[reen].

---

1. H. U. Archives. Printed in Sibley, III. 1. The sheet has three-eighths inch black border of mourning for President Oakes, who died on July 25, 1681.

2. H. U. Archives. Printed in Sibley, III. 170. Heading same as previous year, except that Mather's fellowship is not mentioned.

3. No printed copy extant; these are in John Leverett's ms. notebook at the M. H. S. (Sibley, III. 179). The date was September 12. *C. S. M.*, XVIII. 329.

1684 Quaestiones [1]

Quæstiones Pro Modulo Discutiendæ Sub Reverendo JOHANNE ROGERSIO Collegii Harvardini Cantabrigiæ Nov-Anglorum Præside Per Inceptores In Artibus Calend: Quintilis MDCLXXXIIII.

An Vlla Actio sit Absolute indifferens?

       Negat Respondens Samuel Mitchellus.

An Gratia sit universalis?   Negat Respondens Johannes Cottonus.

An Creatio et conservatio realiter differunt?

       Negat Respondens Johannes Hastings.

An Anima generatur?   Negat Respondens Noadiah Russellus.

An Creatio mundi sit rationibus philosophicis demonstrabilis?

       Affirmat Respondens Jacobus Pierpontus.

An notitia Dei sit homini naturalis?

       Affirmat Respondens Samuel Russellus.

An decretum Dei sit ipse Deus?

       Affirmat Respondens Gulielmus Denisonus.

An Lex humana ligat conscientiam?

       Affirmat Respondens Josephus Eliotus.

His accedit Oratio valedictoria.

1686 Quaestiones [2]

Theses Discvtiendæ, Sub Reverendo CRESCENTIO MATHERO, Comitiorum Academicorum in Collegio Harvardino Præside: Cantabrigiæ Nov-Anglorum, Per Inceptores In Artibus, Nonis Julii. M.DC.LXXXVI.

An datur Accidens realiter a substantia distinctum?

       Negat Respondens Samuel Danforthus.

An Voluntas determinatur ab ultimo Intellectus Practici judicio?

       Affirmat Respondens Johannes Williams.

An Terra movetur?   Affirmat Respondens Guilielmus Williams.

1687 Theses [3]

Præcellenti et Illustrissimo Viro D. EDMUNDO ANDROS, Equiti Aurato: Regiæ Cubiculis, Stratego & Gubernatori summo D. Regis Territorii, & Dominii apud Nov-Anglos in America: Una cum cæteris Senatoribus spectatissimis, Omnibus denique & singulis (hic & ubique) Artium Liberalium philomusis candidissimis, & Mecænatibus benig-

---

1. H. U. Archives. Printed in Sibley, III. 210–11. Ms. note in Samuel Sewall's hand after 'Praeside': 'Gradus Collati sunt per Reverendum Gulielmum Hubbard.' President Rogers was taken ill Commencement morning and Hubbard presided (above, p. 443).

2. H. U. Archives. Printed in Sibley, III. 242.

3. H. U. Archives. Facsimile in W. C. Lane, *op. cit.*, pp. 22–23.

nissimis; Theses hasce, quas sub Auspicio Reverendi D. Crescentii
Matheri Collegii Harvardini, quod est Cantabrigiæ Nov-Anglorum
Rectoris vigjliantissimi, defendendas proponunt Iuvenes in Artibus
Initiati. L. M. D. D. D. Q.

Johannes Davenport.		Josephus Dassett.
Johannes Clark.	Daniel Brewer.	Henricus Newman.
Nathanael Rogers.	Timotheus Stevens.	Josias Dwight.
Jonathan Mitchell.	Nathanael Welsh.	Sethus Shove.

Theses Technologicæ.

[1] Ars est idea εὐπραξίας regulis catholicis methodicè delineata.
2   Idea est res percepta, prout est in intellectu objectivé.
3   Idea vel á mente ut principio effectivo profluit, vel ab objecto, ut causâ
    exemplari.
4   Artis subjectum est res, vel rei modus.
5   Res, et substantia in unoquoque tertio conveniunt.
6   Eupraxia nostra ab Analysi incipit, desinit in Genesi.
7   Praxis est Entis effectum, Prattomenou causa.
8   Arti omni æque competit Praxis, ac theoria.
9   *Impossibile est idem esse, et non esse; non est primum principium.*
10 Prattomena usu conjunguntur, præceptis sejunguntur.
☞ NON DATUR METAPHYSICA AB OMNIBUS ALIIS DISCIPLINIS DISTINCTA.
☞ ETHICA A THEOLOGIA NON REALITER DIFFERT.

Logicæ.

[1] Logica est Ars recté cogitandi.
2   Partes Logicæ integrales duæ sunt, Inventio et Dispositio.
3   Inventio dirigit intellectum in clarâ et distinctâ rerum perceptione.
4   Quot sunt Idearum relationes, tot sunt Inventionis Topica.
☞ ARGUMENTA, QUA TALIA, NON PERCIPIUNTUR A BRUTIS.
6   Argumenta absoluté consentanea sunt fons scientiæ, modo quodam con-
    sentanea opinionis.
7   Causa quá talis non est prior effecto.
8   Causarum contrariarum contraria sunt effecta.
9   Instrumentum non agit, nisi dispositivé.
10 Dissentanea æquè sunt dissentanea, sed non æqué dissentiunt.
11 Contrariorum ejusdem generis unum uni tantúm, diversi autem unum
    pluribus potest opponi.
12 Tota Relatorum natura in Relatione consistit.
13 Si Privantium unum adest, alterum abest.
14 Imparia pariter differunt.
15 Similia magis ad illustrandum in Axiomate, quám ad probandum in
    syllogismo sunt accomodata.
16 In Conjugatis Logicis, concretum ab abstracto derivatur.
17 Firmior est argumentatio á nomine ad notationem, quám contrá.
18 Rationes á notationibus tum tantúm sunt efficaces, quando nomina se-
    cundum rerum naturas sunt imposita.

19   Definitio constat è solis causis internis.
20   Judicii norma est rerum inventarum Dispositio.
21   Res ipsæ sunt normæ veritatis Axiomaticæ.
22   Axioma contingens respicit et futurum et præteritum.
23   In omni contradictione Axiomaticâ includitur Topica.
24   Simplici tantûm axiomati competit esse generale aut speciale.
25   Axioma disjunctum est necessariæ veritatis ex partibus non necessariis.
26   Syllogismus methodicé arguit.
27   Ex præmissis veris conclusio tantûm vera, ex falsis non modó falsa, sed vera sequi potest.
28   In Methodo cryptica valet regulâ, sc. *Artis est celare artem.*

Grammaticæ.

[1]   Grammatica est Ars puré scribendi, ac distincté loquendi.
2   Nulla vox incipere potest á gemino scheva.
3   Consona vocalibus destituta est dissona.
4   Consona inter duas vocales pertinet ad posteriorem.
5   Genera positiva sunt tantûm duo.
6   Adjectivis non congruunt genera, sed terminationes ad genus.
7   Omnis ablativus regitur á præpositione expressâ vel intellectâ.

Rhetoricæ.

[1]   Rhetoricæ objectum specificum est oratio ornata:
2   Principia Rhetoricæ constitutiva sunt Elocutio, et Pronunciatio.
3   Tropum necessitas genuit, jucunditas celebravit.
4   Metalepsis est in unâ voce troporum multiplicitas, Allegoria in pluribus continuatio.
5   Metonymia est tropus petitus á consentaneis, Ironia á dissentaneis, Metaphora á comparatis, Synechdoche ab ortis argumentis.
6   Figura sententiæ est cognatior animo, dictionis cognatior auribus.
7   Pronunciatio est accomodanda naturæ dicentis, et rei.

Theses Mathematicæ.

[1]   Matheseωs puræ objectum est multitudo, vel magnitudo.
2   Numerus non datur maximus.
3   Ciphra nunquam occupare debet extremum sinistræ locum.
4   Numerus integrorum major est, qui pluribus notis constat, fractorum, minor, qui majorem habet denominationem.
5   Impares multitudine pari producunt parem, impari imparem.
6   Par et impar invicem multiplicantes, producunt parem.
7   Numerus á simplici notâ multiplicatus aut divisus, non nisi unicâ notâ augetur, aut minuitur.
8   Divisor quó minor est eó Quotiens est major.
9   Linea recta non recipit magis aut minus.
10   Omnis circulus est polygonus.
11   Angulus á linearum rectarum sectione fit rectilineus, perpendicularitate rectangulus.
12   Triangulum est basis Gæodeticorum organorum.
13   Triangulum in plano est rectilineum, in sphæra circulare.

14 Arcus sphærici trianguli est minor semicirculo.
15 Tres anguli rectilinei trianguli sunt æquales, sphærici sunt majores duobus rectangulis.
16 Tot sunt Meridiani, quot in Æquatore sunt puncta verticalia.
17 Horizon regionis singularis est immobilis, universalis mobilis.
18 In sphærâ rectâ oriuntur omnia sidera, in obliquâ quædam, in parallelâ nulla.

Physicæ.

[1] Physicæ subjectum est res naturalis.
2   Extensio est ipsa essentia materiæ.
3   Materiæ partes sunt vel sensiles, vel insensiles.
4   Forma est materiæ accidentaria, corpori essentialia.
5   Privatio non est principium corporis naturalis.
6   Quantum naturæ nec augmentatur, nec, diminuitur.
7   Omnis motus tendit ad rectam lineam.
8   Quicquid movetur, suo movetur motu.
☞   QUIES EST ÆQUE POSITIVA, AC MOTUS.
10 Rarefactio non est augmentatio, nec condensatio diminutio.
11 Tempus non realiter existit, sed est mensura existentiæ.
12 Tempus præsens habet partes indefinitas.
13 Locus internus nonnisi nostro concipiendi modo differt ab ipso corpore.
☞   GRAVITAS EST VIS ATTRACTRIX TERRÆ.
15 Calor in motu, frigus in quiete consistit.
16 Nulla corpora solida et tangibilia originaliter sunt calida.
17 Corpus minús densum est magis frigidum, minús rarum minús (*sic*) calidum.
18 Corpus densissimum rarissimo est siccius.
19 Corpora densa lucem reddunt, minús densa imbibunt.
20 Maculæ lunæ ab inæquali partium densitate proveniunt.
☞   RADII LUMINOSI SUNT CORPOREI.
22 Cœli & sublunarium materia est eadem.
23 Stellæ fixæ proprio lumine, erraticæ mutuatitio fulgent.
☞   SOL EST STELLA FIXA
25 Elementa sunt principia syntheseως et analyseως.
✽ 1 TERRA NON EST CENTRUM MUNDI.
27 Generatio est principium Corruptionis.
✽   PARELII NON SUNT PRODIGIA.
29 Nulla natura potest operari in distans.
☞   MAGNES NON OCCULTA VIRTUTE, SED REALIBUS EFFLUVIIS AGIT.
31 Sensus humanus non est mensura rerum.
✽   SENSUS EXTERNUS EST UNICUS
33 Visus, auditus, gustus, et olfactus sunt tactús modi.
34 Color est lux á corporibus diversis diversimodé resiliens.
35 Sonus nihil aliud est, nisi motus corporis realis.
36 Pisces respirant per attractionem & remissionem aeris.
37 Dantur montes & valles submarinæ.

---

1. A character or 'printer's flower' from the typeset border, used apparently because the supply of indexes was insufficient.

His Accedit Oratio Salutatoria.

Cantabrigiæ Nov-Anglorum. Anno à Christo nato, M DC. LXXXVII.

1687 QUAESTIONES [1]

Quæstiones Pro Modvlo Discvtiendæ, Sub Reverendo CRESCENTIO MATHERO Collegii Harvardini Cantabrigiæ Nov-Anglorum Rectore, Per Inceptores In Artibus, In Comitiis Pridie Nonarum Julii. M.DC. LXXXVII.

An Extensio eripiat cogitandi facultatem?

Negat Respondens Johannes Denisonus.

An Vmbra moveat?   Negat Respondens Johannes Rogersius.
An Puncta Hebræa sint divinæ originis?

Affirmat Respondens Gurdonus Saltonstallus.

An Curatio per pulverem sympatheticum sit licita?

Affirmat Respondens Samuel Myles.

An Detur Lapis aurificus?   Affirmat Respondens Nehemiah Walterus.
An Detur forma substantialis?   Negat Respondens Josephus Webb.
An Successio sit de essentia durationis creatæ?

Affirmat Respondens Benjamin Rolfe.

1688 QUAESTIONES [2]

Quæstiones Discutiendae Sub Reverendo D. GUILIELMO HUBBARDO Apud Gippœnses U. D. M. Et Comitiorum Academicorum in Collegio Harvardino Præside Cantabrigiæ Nov-Anglorum Per Inceptores in Artibus Quarto Nonarum Julii M.DC.LXXXVIII.

An Dominium Temporale fundetur in Gratia?

Negat Respondens Thomas Dvdley

An Primæva hominis Sanctitas fuerat qualitas Naturalis?

Affirmat Respondens Warhamus Matherus

An Detur Vacuum?   Affirmat Respondens Nathanael Matherus
An Cognitio Angelorum sit Discursiva?

Affirmat Respondens Rovlandus Cottonus

An Interitus mundi futurus sit Substantialis?

Negat Respondens Henricus Gibbs

An Vna et eadem sit Materia cœlestium et Terrestrium corporum?

Affirmat Respondens Thomas Berryus

An Quicquid est in Deo sit Ipse Deus?

Affirmat Respondens Johannes Whitingus

An Cogitatio superet Materiæ vires?   Affirmat Respondens Edvardus Mills

---

1. H. U. Archives. Printed in Sibley, III. 270–71.
2. H. U. Archives. Printed in Sibley, III. 316–18. On this, the sole surviving copy, Samuel Sewall wrote a *q* against the 1st, 2d, 7th, 8th and last quæstiones, with the explanation 'Quæstiones quiescentes,' to which he adds 'Nulli ad Primum Gradum admissi sunt.' There was no Bachelors' Commencement that year.

An Diversificatio corporum Oriatur a Motu?

Affirmat Respondens Johannes Eliotus

An Præcepta philosophica Theologicis contradicant?

Nega: Respondens Johannes White

An Pneumatica sit Scientia a Metaphysica et Theologia distincta?

Affirmat Respondens Jonathan Pierpont.

His Antecedit Oratio Salutatoria.

1689 THESES [1]

Amplissimo Ac Celeberrimo Viro D. SIMONI BRADSTREETO Coloniæ Massachusensis Moderatori Maxime Spectando. Cunctisque quibus jus et Imperium apud Nov-Anglos mandatur, nec-non Reverendis Ecclesiarum Præsbyteris; Omnibus denique ac singulis de Academia Harvardina bené meritis, Literarum literatorumque fautoribus. Theses Hasce quas sub inspectione D. GVILIELMI BRATTLE Collegii Harvardini Socii fidelissimi, discutiendas proponunt, Juvenes in Artibus initiati. D. D. D. Q.

Jacobus Allyn	Guilielmus Partrigg	Benjamin Marston
Samuel Moody	Richardus Whittingham	Johannes Eveleth
Guilielmus Payn	Johannes Emerson	Benjamin Pierpont
Addington Davenport	Johannes Sparhawk	Johannes Hancock
Johannes Haynes		Thomas Swan.

Theses Technologicæ.

[1] Ars est variorum præceptorum methodus βιωφελης.
2   Artes sunt Radii Divinæ sapientiæ.
3   Ars non existit primarió in actu exercito.
4   Non ens, quatenus non ens, non est materia artis.
5   Genesis et Analysis se invicem dissolvendis opus persolvunt.
6   Ars est generalis aut specialis, respectu usûs non objecti.

Theses Logicæ.

☞   LOGICA EST ARS COGITANDI.
I.   Tot sunt partes Logicæ quot sunt operationes menti[s.]
2   Perceptio, Judicium, et Discursus sunt partes Log[icæ.]
3   Nulli rei assensum præbemus aut denegamus quæ percep[tionis]nostræ eximussim non respondet.
4   Ablegatio dubiorum juvat ad scientiam comparandam.
5   Sensus non nisi ex accidenti res detegunt.
☞   SOLA MENTE PERCIPIMUS QUICQUID PERC[IPIMUS.]
6   Perceptionis nostræ certitudo ab Intellectu pendet.
7   Substantiæ non incurrunt in sensus.
8   Nullæ species corporeæ ad puram Intellectionem requi[runtur.]

---

1. This mutilated copy in the H. U. Archives is the only one extant.

9   Veritas aut Falsitas non est in Intellectu.
10   Vniver[salia] sunt tantum modi cogitandi.
11   Posi[ta] S[pecie] ponitur et Genus Sublata [specie et] Genus tollitur.
12   [   ] cum re quam afficiunt non faciunt compositum.
13   Causa non dat quod non habet.
☞   NON DANTUR PLURES CAUSÆ.
14   Efficiens et Causa proprié sunt Synonyma.
15   Materia est Principium (non Causa) ex quo.
16   Forma non causat sed causatur.
17   Finis est tantum modus efficientis.
18   Quale est Subjectum, talia sunt Adjuncta.
19   Quod convenit toti, convenit ejus parti.
20   Similibus similia congruunt.
21   Similia illustrant non probant.
22   Quod unius contrarii capax est, capax est alterius.
23   Sublatâ contradictione tollitur omnis disputatio.
24   A privatione ad habitum in plerisque datur regressus.
25   Quantus et qualis est testis, tantum et tale est testimonium.
26   Ad Propositionem assensus aut dissensus requiritur.
27   Propositiones Contingentes necessarió veræ sunt aut falsæ disjunctivæ.
28   Contingens propositio vera, in falsam mutari nequit.
29   In divisione Generis divisum potest in recto de singulis partibus prædicari.
30   In Divisione Integri divisum non potest de membris nisi in obliquo prædicari.
31   In Definitione requiritur Genus Proximum.
32   Ratiocinari est unum ex alio cognito cognoscere.
33   Intellectus non potest non assentiri propositioni claræ et evidenti.
34   Ex attentâ rei alicujus consideratione Analysis oritur.
35   In omni methodo à notiori ad minùs notum transeundum est.
36   Synthesis à terminis generalioribus ad magis particulares progreditur.

Theses Grammaticæ.

[1]   Grammatica est ars loquendi et scribendi.
2   Interjectiones sunt solum sonus [*sic*] inarticulati, ideoque nullam orationis partem constituunt.
3   Omnis ablativus regitur à præpositione expressâ vel suppressâ.
4   Duos accusativos nullum regit verbum, sed unus á præpositione suppressâ gubernatur.
5   Prosodia ordine naturæ Etymologiæ et syntaxi præponi debet.
6   Semicolon est nota Respirationis paulo majoris quam in commate, sed minoris quam in colo.
7   Participium est nomen, habens á verbo adsignificationem et constructionem.
8   Pronomina sunt nomina.
9   Nomen est quædam Imago, quâ quid noscitur.
10   Casus dicuntur obliqui quia cadunt â Recto.
11   Duo tantum genera novit ratio naturæ, masculinum et fœmininum.

12   Si adjectiva non essent, nulla essent apud grammaticos verba de genere.
13   Nominativus in Impersonalibus ipsis includitur.
14   Nullum nomen, verbum, aut participium proprié regit Dativum.
15   Omnes literæ hebrææ sunt in uno versu, *Isaiæ 5. 25.*
16   Quinque sunt organa pronuntiationis apud Hebræos.

Theses Rhetoricæ.

[1]   Rhetoricæ subjectum adæquatum est modus ornaté dicendi.
2   Mutua rerum affectio est cor tropi.
3   Tropica locutio propriè accepta parit absurditatem.
4   Metaphora est tropus luculentissimus.
5   Figuræ dictionis suavitati potius quam affectui inserviunt.
6   Interrogatio rhetorica differt a Vulgari.

Theses Mathematicæ.

[1]   Geometria de continuâ quantitate, Arithmetica de discretâ tractat.
[2]   Geodesia est Geometria practica.
[3   Linea] Geometrica est mensura lineæ Physicæ.
[4   Quale] unitas in numero, tale est punctum in lineâ.
[5   Linea pe]rpendicularis est mater et magistra Geometriæ.
[6   Qua linea] rectâ, itá angulo recto non datur rectior.
[7   Linea lo]ngitudines, libella altitudines, norma angulos explorat.
[8   Figura] rotundâ omnes radii æquantur.
[9   Ciphræ] non sunt numeri.
[10   Pun]cta est brevissima.
[11   Sphæra] est omnium Circulorum præstantissimus.
[12   ] solari terra, non sol, patitur.
[13   Multiplica]tio est multiplex additio, Divisio est multiplex subductio.
[14   ] non docent falsum, sed verum ex fa[lsitat]e.

Theses Physicæ.

[1]   Scopus Philosophi est scire rerum naturas.
2   Res naturales ab Artificialibus non distinguuntur.
☞   CREATIO MUNDI EST NATURALITER DEMONSTRABILIS.
☞   QUALITATES AUT MODI EX SE NUNQUAM PEREUNT.
3   Rarefactio fit per materiæ introductionem.
4   Nulla dantur Indivisibilia corpora.
5   Dantur in mundo partes Insensibiles.
6   Corporum diversitas á modificantione partium pendet.
☞   OMNE CORPUS EST POROSUM.
7   Potentia naturalis consistit in partium dispositione.
☞   CORPORA EX SE NEC GRAVITANT NEC LEVITANT.
8   Non datur Spatium sine extensione.
☞   MOTUS ET QUIES SUNT TANTUM RERUM MODI.
9   Nullus est motus in natura Violentus.
10   Corpora tantum habent principium dispositivum ad motum.
11   Non datur Quies in puncto reflectionis.
☞   FRIGORIS NATURA CONSISTIT IN QUIETE.

12   Dura sunt quorum partes quiete junguntur.
13   Fluida quorum exiguæ particulæ sunt in motu.
14   Rara et Densa, á figura et situ originem suam habent.
15   Ablatis poris nulla est inter corpora distinctio.
16   Modus varius esse potest et tamen semper unus manere.
17   Tempus non minus est quietis mensura quam motus.
18   Mundus non est Infinitus sed Indefinité extensus.
☞   MATERIA NEC GENERATUR NEC CORRUMPITUR.
19   Sol est generalis causa omnium effectuum qui in terra producuntur.
☞   FONTES ET FLUMINA ORTUM SUUM HABENT A MARI.
20   Sonitu Campanarum tonitrus desinit.
21   Animal in Rationale et Irrationale non recté dividitur.
☞   BRUTA VALENT RATIONE. Anglicè
22   Carnium esus non est homini naturalis.
23   Motus Sanguinis est Mechanicus.
24   Diversitas sensuum à diversitate nervorum pendet.
25   Sonorum variteas [sic] á diversitate motus pendet.
26   Anima semper Cogitat.
27   Anima in Infantibus nec major nec minor est quam in Adultis.
28   Anima perturbari potest in operationibus suis ex prava organorum dispositione.
☞   DANTUR VENEFICIA.
29   Veneficia sunt impii hominum cum Dæmonibus fœderis [sic] effecta.
30   Idea Dei menti humanæ est innata.
31   Ingeniorum diversitas à corporis dispositione oritur.
32   Passiones sedem suam primariam in Cerebro habent.
☞   PASSIONES ANIMÆ SUNT SUA NATURA BONÆ.

His Antecedit Oratio Salutatoria, Habita in Comitiis.

Cantabrigiæ Nov-Anglorum. Anno Domini. M.DC.LXXX.IX.

1689 QUAESTIONES [1]

Quæstiones Pro Modulo Discutiendæ Sub D. GUILIELMO BRATTLE Collegii Harvardini Cantabrigiæ Nov-Anglorum Socio Vigilantissimo, Per Inceptores In Artibus in Comitiis tertio Idus Septembris. M.DC. LXXX.IX.

An Leges humanæ obligent conscientiam?
                Affirmat Respondens Benjaminus Lynde.
An Anima sit sua natura immortalis?
                Affirmat Respondens Georgius Philips.
An Res adiaphoræ sint materia idonea legum humanarum?
                Negat Respondens Nicholaus Morton.

His accedit Oratio Valedictoria.

1. H. U. Archives. Printed in Sibley, III. 353–54.

1690 Quaestiones [1]

Quæstiones Pro Modulo Discutiendæ Sub Clar. D. Johanne Leveretto, Collegii Harvardini Cantabrigiæ Nov-Anglorum Socio Fidelissimo, Per Inceptores In Artibus in Comitiis Sexto Nonas Quintilis. M,DC,XC.

An Dubitatio sit indubitatæ Philosophiæ initium?
                    Affirmat Respondens Johannes Davenport.
An Morborum sedes sit Anima sensitiva?
                    Affirmat Respondens Johannes Clark.
An Vitiositas rationi repugnet?   Affirmat Respondens Nathaniel Rogers.
An Duella sint licita?   Negat Respondens Jonathan Mitchel.
An Stratagemata in bello sint illicita?   Negat Respondens Daniel Brewer.
An Imago Dei sit homini in statu creato naturalis?
                    Affirmat Respondens Timotheus Stevens.
An Detur Atheus in judicio?   Negat Respondens Josephus Dasset.
An Morbi sint Contagiosi?   Affirmat Respondens Henricus Newman.
An Conservatio sit continuata creatio?   Affirmat Respondens Sethus Shove.

His Accedit Oratio Valedictoria.

1691 Theses [2]

Consultissimo, Pariter Ac Perhonorifico Viro, D. Simoni Brad-streeto, Massachusettensis Coloniæ Rectori Cumprimis Honorando, Cæterisque Consulibus, Communis Omnium Salutis Apprime Studiosis: Unà cum Ducibus Ecclesiarum fidelissimis, Omnibus denique & Singulis Literatorum Mecænatibus, Literarum Antistitibus; Hasce Theses quas Sub. D. Johanne Leveretto, & D. Guilielmo Brattle Collegii Harvardini Sociis, Discutiendas proponunt Juvenes, Artium Candidati; L. M. D. C. Q.

Johannes Tyng		Christopherus Tappan
Ebenezer Pemberton	Josephus Lord	Samuel Emery
Thomas Mackarty		Thomas Atkinsonus.

Theses Technologicæ.

[1]   Technologia tradit habitudinem & sedes Artium.
2   Ars est ordinata præceptorum methodus, quâ quidvis utile docetur.
3   Ars est Artificis circinus.
4   ens primum est Artis Alpha et Omega.
5   Encylcopædia est Artium Amaltheum cornu.
6   Omnes Artes sororio vinculo inter se alligantur.
7   Ars constare debet ex præceptis scientificis.

---

1. H. U. Archives. Printed in Sibley, iii. 368-69.
2. H. U. Archives. Printed in Sibley, iv. 93.

8   Omnis Ars est interna & externa.
9   Natura est index Artium.
10   Sapientia, Prudentia, Scientia & Ars non realiter differunt.
11   Ens fictum est Entis veri Parelion.
12   Non Entis nulla sunt prædicata.
13   Subjectum tractationis in unâ disciplinâ potest esse subjectum operationis in aliâ.
14   Objecta formalia sunt objecta unicæ disciplinæ.

Theses Logicæ.

[1] Logica est Ars utendi ratione in cognitione quærendâ.
2   Logica est Ars generalissima.
3   Logica dirigit rationem & orationem hominis.
4   Logicæ objectum formale est Ratio: Materiale est Ens & Non-Ens.
☞   ENS QUATENUS ENS EST OBJECTUM LOGICÆ.
5   Argumentum est ratio rerum.
6   Mutatâ affectione mutatur argumentum.
7   Argumentum non actu arguit nisi in discursu.
8   Pura intellectio, Imagi[n]atio & Sensus sunt modi perceptionis.
9   Quicquid percipitur est vel res, vel modus rei, vel res modificata.
☞   ACCIDENS PERIPATETICUM NON PERTINET AD LOGICAM.
10   Causa fiendi est etiam causa essendi.
☞   QUICQUID PRÆDICATUR DE CAUSA PRÆDICATUR ETIAM DE EFFECTU.
11   Modi Efficientis causæ sunt tantùm adjuncta, non formæ essentiales.
12   Vis Instrumenti consistit in usu.
13   Actio convenit rei ratione formæ; passio ratione materiæ.
14   Finis est causarum primum mobile.
15   Finis & bonum controversantur.
16   Objectum est modus subjecti.
17   Materia circa quam est objectum, materia in quâ est subjectum.
18   Unum subjectum infini[t]a sustinere protest [sic] adjuncta.
19   Diversa ita dissentiunt ut uni subjecto inesse possint.
20   Diversa divisa non ingrediuntur syllogismum.
21   Disparata inter se non semper eodem gradu opponuntur.
22   Adversa se invicem expellunt.
23   Contradictoria nec admittunt medium participationis nec abnegationis.
24   Paria non admittunt majus & minus, neque magis & minus.
☞   GENUS ÆQUALITER PRÆDICATUR DE SPECIEBUS.
25   Species tantum definitionem admittunt.
26   Testimonium parit fidem.
27   Axioma necessarium parit scientiam, contingens opinionem.
28   Disjunctum axioma potest esse necessarium ubi nulla pars est necessaria.
29   Omnis syllogismus est necessarius ratione formæ.
30   Enthymema est claudus syllogismus.
31   Sorites est Dialecticæ scala.
32   Methodus est Ars memoriæ.

Theses Grammaticæ.

[1] Grammatica est Ars tradens modum purè Loquendi.
2 Grammatica est Artium referatrix.
3 Omnes linguæ ex Hebræa sunt ortæ.
4 Syllaba est pars vocis divisibilis.
5 Numeri & personæ adsignificatum, est commune dictionibus flexibilibus.
6 Genus in substantivis feré discernit sexum.
7 Genus Neutrum est tantúm genus negativum.
8 Substantivis tantúm competit genus.
9 Multis singularibus respondet unum plurale.
10 Referri ad nomen est pronominis anima.
11 Verbi anima est conjugatio.
12 Participium est medium participationis inter nomen & verbum.
13 Extra verbalia substantivum regit tantum genitivum.
14 Opus & usus tantúm genitivum regunt.

Theses Rhetoricæ.

[1] Rhetoricæ subjectum tractationis est modus ornandi orationem.
2 Rhetorica differt ab Oratoriâ, ut angustius á latiori.
3 Rhetorica est affectuum syren.
4 Omni tropo semper inesse debet verecundia.
5 Catachresis est tropus rusticus.
6 Allegoriæ sunt Logicæ parabolæ.
7 Antiphrasis est adulatoris toga.
8 Climax est figuræ ἀνάβασις.
9 Aposiopesis est dictionis Embryo.
10 Figuræ sententiæ virilem quandam dignitatem obtinent præ figuris dictionis.

Theses Mathematicæ.

[1] Arithmetica est princeps inter Mathematicas scientias.
2 Subjectum Arithmeticæ est numerus.
3 Fractiones non sunt numeri.
4 Ciphra per se nihil significat.
5 Subtractio est contraria additioni.
6 Divisio est integri corruptio.
7 Punctum est lineæ ἔσχατον.
8 Lineæ parallelæ ad Græcas calendas concurrent.
9 Angulus rectus est Matheseως magister.
10 Anguli obliqui nullâ lege æquantur.
11 Cognito angulo alterutro reliquus non ignorabitur.
12 Planetæ ab occidente in orientem moventur.
13 Datis cælis solidis nulla foret dierum & noctium successio.
14 Planetæ sunt individua vaga.
15 Sole existente in apogæo vel perigæo nulla datur prostaphæresis.
16 Quó minor est parallaxis eó remotius est Phænomenon.

Theses Physicæ.

[1] Physiologia est naturæ theatrum.
2 Physica est scientia corporis naturalis in quantum naturale est.
3 Principium corporum est unicum; sc. materia.
4 Materia omnium corporum est eadem.
5 Materia est formæ basis.
6 Forma oritur é terminatione partium materiæ.
7 Materia prima est mentis chimæra.
8 Omnes formæ sunt tantùm modi materiæ.
9 Corpora differunt tantùm diversa positione & figurâ partium materiæ.
10 Omne corpus est extensum.
11 Raritas est magna quantitas in paucâ materiâ; Densitas parva quantitas in multâ materiâ.

☞ CORPORA NATURALIA PER SE NEQUE ASCENDUNT, NEQUE DESCENDUNT.

12 Gravitas & Levitas fiunt ab externo agente.
13 Qualitates occultæ sunt ignorantiæ asyla.
14 Locus externus non est de essentiâ corporis naturalis.
15 Locus est immobilis.
16 Tempus non est Ens permanens sed successivum.
17 Cessante motu non cessat tempus.
18 Motus per se calefacit, per accidens refrigerat.
19 Non datur motus violentus.
20 Motio terræ est causa maris reciprocationis.
21 Calor in motu frigus in quiete consistit.

☞ ELEMENTA PERIPATETICA SUNT PHYSICÆ HETEROGENEA.

22 Aqua est corpus humidissimum.
23 Aer est corpus fluidissimum.
24 Ignis Elementaris est niger cygnus.
25 Magnes virtutem exercet effluvia emittendo.
26 Metalla non specificé differunt.

☞ SENSUS EXTERNUS EST UNICUS.

27 Anima est cœlum empyreum microcosmi.
28 Voluntas non semper determinatur ab ultimo intellectus practici judicio.
29 Indifferentia est de essentia liberi arbitrii.
30 Mundi creatio ratione naturali demonstratur.
31 Non datur annihilatio.

His antecedit Oratio gratulatoria habita in Comitiis.
Cantabrigiæ Nov-Anglorum Calendis Julii. M. DC. XCI.

1692 QUAESTIONES [1]

Quæstiones Pro Modulo Discutiendæ Sub Clarissimo Pariter ac Reverendissimo D. CRESCENTIO MATHERO, Collegii Harvardini quod est Cantabrigiæ, Apud Nov-Anglos Præside quam maxime literato.

1. H. U. Archives. Printed in Sibley, III. 404–05.

In Comitiis Per Inceptores In Artibus Die Sexto Quintilis M DC XC II.

His Antecedit Oratio Salutatoria.

An voluntas semper sequatur ultimum Dictamen Intellectus?
Affirmat Respondens Jacobus Allen.
An Detur in Deo Scientia media? Negat Respondens Samuel Moodæus.
An Dominium Temporale fundetur in Gratia?
Negat Respondens Johannes Emersonus.
An Bona Intentio sufficiat ad Bonitatem Actionis?
Negat Respondens Johannes Sparhawk.
An Cogitatio sit ipsa essentia Animæ?
Negat Respondens Benjamin Pierpont.
An Cognitio Angelorum sit Discursiva?
Affirmat Respondens Johannes Hancock.

His Accedit Oratio Valedictoria.

1693 Theses [1]

Amplissimo, Honoratissimo, Pariter Ac Perillustri Viro, D. Guilielmo Phipps, Equiti Aurato, Provinciæ Massachusettensis Gubernatori; ac totius Nov-Angliæ Stratego; Cæterisque Senatoribus Consultissimis, ad Clavum Reipublicæ sedentibus; unà cum Fidelissimis Ecclesiarum Presbyteris; Unicuique demum Literis Literatisque, ac nostræ Academiæ (ubicunque terrarum) Benefico ac Benevolo: Theses hasce, quas sub Reverendo admodum ac Clarissimo Viro D. Crescentio Mathero, Collegii Harvardini, quod est Cantabrigiæ Nov-Anglorum Præside Lectissimo defendendas proponunt Juvenes in Artibus initiati; D. D. D. Q.

Isaacus Chaunceus	Nathanael Hodson	Josephus Baxter
Stephanus Buckinghamus	Penn Townsend	Guilielmus Veazie
Henricus Flintæus	Nathanael Williams	Nathanael Huntting
Simon Bradstreet	Georgius Denison	Benjamin Ruggles
Johannes Wadæus	Johannes Woodward	Guilielmus Grosvenor.

His Antecedit Oratio Salutatoria.

Theses Technologicæ.

1 Ars est methodica Comprehensio Præceptorum homogeneorum.
2 Artium Dignitas consistit in Subjecto et Fine.
3 Natura est Ars inchoata; Ars natura consummata.
4 Sublatâ naturâ, tollitur Ars.
5 Præcepta Artium non formamus, sed formata invenimus.

---

1. New York Public Library. Printed in Sibley, iv. 146.

6   Ens est Primum mobile, quo Orbes Artium circumgyrantur.
7   Non-Ens non intelligitur nisi sub ratione et gratiâ Entis.
☞   *Secta Peripateticorum non est omnibus aliis præferenda.*

Theses Logicæ.

1   LOGICA est Ars dirigens Intellectum in suis Operationibus.
2   Logica est Artium omnium prima et maximè universalis.
3   Objectum Logicæ est ubique.
4   Partes Logicæ concurrunt cum Operationibus mentis.
5   Apprehensio est simplex Rerum, quæ menti sistuntur, Contemplatio.
6   Perceptio est mens Ideam sibi præsentem exhibens.
7   Omne percipitur vel Intellectu, vel Imaginatione, vel sensu.
8   Objectum Intellectus latius sese extendit, quàm Objectum Imaginationis.
☞   *Spiritus non sunt proprié Objecta Imaginationis.*
10 Substantia non cognoscitur nisi per Intellectum.
11 Quæcunque substantia est vel Intellectualis vel Materialis.
12 Genus inter Universalia Dignitate et Ordine primum Locum obtinet.
13 Genus Generi adversatur; Genus speciebus disparatur.
14 Individua et Universalia sunt Opposita.
15 Totum est quod continet Partes, estque in eas divisibile.
☞   *Partes actualitér non sunt in Toto.*
17 Definitiones Rerum multum conducunt ad Perceptionum confusionem vitandum.
18 In nominum Usu nunquam à Receptis recedendum est.
19 Complexio potest cadere in omnes partes Propositionis.
20 Veritas Disjunctivarum Propositionum dependet a Partium Oppositione.
21 Discursus est è pluribus Judiciis unius Electio.
22 In quovis Ratiocinio Præmissæ debent esse notiores Conclusione.
23 Forma Syllogismi est legitima medii Dispositio cum Partibus Quæstionis.
24 Argumentationes dicuntur Imperfectæ non ratione materiæ, sed Formæ.
25 Methodus Ideas, Judicia et Ratiocinationes ordinat.

Theses Grammaticæ.

1   GRAMMATICA est Janua Linguarum.
2   Litera est Vocis Punctum Indivisibile.
3   Diphthongus est Vocalium Consonantia.
4   Anima Consonantis est Relatio ad Vocalem.
5   Verbum et nomen sunt solum declinabilia.
6   Partes Orationis Inflexiles Flexibilibus sunt serviles.
7   Heteroclita sunt vel Variantia, vel Deficientia vel Redundantia.
8   Lingua Hebræa est omnium Linguarum Ἀρχέτυπος.

Theses Rhetoricæ.

1   RHETORICA est Ars ornatè Loquendi ac Scribendi.
2   Elocutio procedit ab Animi, Pronunciatio à Corporis Eloquentiâ.

3   Figuræ sententiæ sunt vel in Logismo, vel Dialogismo.
4   Auxesis et Meiosis sunt modi Hyperbolici.
5   Metalepsis est in verbo, Allegoria in sententiâ, Troporum Coalitio.
6   Corporis Gestus est Eloquentia muta.

Theses Mathematicæ.

1   ARITHMETICA est Mathematum Organon.
2   Numerus est æternus à parte post.
3   Positio dat esse Ciphræ.
4   Progressio est Climax Arithmetica.
5   Geometræ utuntur Lineis et Punctis, ut Astronomi Circulis Cœlestibus.
6   Hypotheses sunt Principia Astronomiæ.
7   Stellæ Fixæ nimis distant à sole, ut ab eo Lumen accipiant.
8   Luna plus illuminatur in novilunio, quàm in Plenilunio.
☞   *Corpora Caelestia sunt Corruptibilia.*

Theses Physicæ.

1   PHYSICA est Ars benè naturandi.
2   Omnis materia est uniformis.
☞   *Extensio est ipsa Corporis Forma.*
☞   ATOMI SUNT PRINCIPIA CORPORUM NATURALIUM.
☞   *Omnis Divisio fit per motum.*
☞   *Sine Poris nulla foret Divisio.*
7   Motus Circularis neque est Ascendens, neque Descendens.
☞   *Extra Corpus non datur motus aut Quies.*
9   Quicquid movetur circularitèr, à Centro recedere conatur.
10   Corpora moventur in Circulo.
☞   *Forma in Partium Configuratione consistit.*
12   Corpora nullam habent Inclinationem naturalem ad Ascensum aut Descensum.
☞   *Locus est unius Corporis ad aliud Vicinitas.*
14   Sublato Corpore, tollitur Distantia.
15   Necessaria est inter Corpora Connexio.
16   Corpus in spatio Imaginario non est hic aut illic.
17   Dura Corpora sunt, quorum Partes Quiete conjunguntur.
18   Fluida sunt, quorum Particulæ sunt in motu.
☞   *Generatio est Partium Dispositio.*
☞   *Corruptio est Partium unitarum Disjunctio.*
☞   *Non competit Terræ Gravitas intrinseca.*
☞   MAGNES AGIT REALIBUS EFFLUVIIS.
23   Aer non est humidus suâ naturâ.
24   Nulla Figura Orbi universo assignari potest.

His Succedit Oratio Salutatoria habita in Comitiis.
Cantabrigiæ Nov-Anglorum Tertio Nonarum Julii. M. DC. XCIII.

1693 Quaestiones [1]

Quæstiones Pro Modulo Discutiendæ Sub Clarissimo Pariter ac Reverendissimo D. Crescentio Mathero, Collegii Harvardini quod est Cantabrigiæ, Apud Nov-Anglos Præside quam maxime literato. In Comitiis Per Inceptores In Artibus Die Quinto Quintilis M DC XC III.

I.   An ante Ultimum Diem Judicii fuerit Beatum millennium?
       Affirmat Respondens Paulus Dudlæus.
II.   An Detur Lapis Aurificus?   Affirmat Respondens Samuel Matherus.
III.   An Curatio Vulnerum per pulverem Sympatheticum sit Licita?
       Affirmat Respondens Johannes Willard.
IV.   An Annima [sic] Rationalis sit Sua Natura Immortalis?
       Affirmat Respondens Johannes Jonesius.
V.   An Cognitio Dei sit Homini Naturalis?
       Affirmat Respondens Josephus Whiting.
VI.   An Vis Plastica mundi Possit applicari ad Peragendum opus veneficum?   Affirmat Responde[n]s Nathanael Clap.
VII.   An Creatio mundi sit Rationibus Philosophicis Demonstrabilis?
       Affirmat Respondens Josephus Belcherus.
VIII. An Motus fiat sine vacuo?   Affirmat Respondens Johannes Clark.
IX.   An Annihilatio sit opus omnipotentiæ?
       Affirmat Respondens Samuel Mansfeild.
X.   An Status animæ separatus sit naturalis?
       Affirmat Respondens Petrus Burr.
XI.   An Astrologia Quæ dicitur gudiciaria falsis Hypothesibus nitatur?
       Affirmat Respondens Johannes Newmarch.
XII.   An Gradus Accademici sint Laudabiles?
       Affirmat Respondens Thomas Greenwood.
XIII. An Atomi ob Solam Imporositatem sunt Indivisibiles?
       Affirmat Respondens Benjamin Wadsworth.
XIV. An Angeli sint Materiati?   Affirmat Respondens Thomus Ruggles.
XV.   An Hodiernæ Literæ Hebraicæ sint Primigeniæ?
       Affirmat Respondens Stephanus Mix.
XVI. An Detur Quadratura circuli?
       Affirmat Respondens Edmundus Goffe.
XVII. An Lingua Hebraica sit omnium Antiquissima?
       Affirmat Respondens Benjamin Eastabrookæus.

His Accedit Oratio Valedictoria.

1694 Quaestiones [2]

Quæstiones, Quas pro modulo Discutiendas Sub Celeberrimo Viro, D. Crescentio Mathero, Academiæ Harvardinæ, quæ est Cantabrigiæ apud Nov-Anglos, Præside Dignissimo; In Comitiis proponunt Laureæ Magistralis Candidati, Die Quarto quintilis. M. DC. XC. IV.

1. H. U. Archives.   2. H. U. Archives.

An Extensio competat Spiritibus?   Affirmat Respondens Johannes Tyng.
An Novitas Essendi sit de Essentia Creaturæ?
                              Affirmat Respondens Ebenezer Pemberton.
An Planetariorum Divinationes sint licitæ?
                              Negat Respondens Thomas Macarty.
An Arminianismus sit Neopelagianismus?
                              Affirmat Respondens Josephus Lord.
An Mundi Interitus fuerit Substantialis?
                              Negat Respondens Christopherus Tappan.
An Methodus Ampraldiana parunt a methodo Arminiana differat?
                              Affirmat Respondens Samuel Emery.
An Indifferentia sit de Essentia liberi Arbitrii?
                              Negat Respondens Timotheus Edwards.

His Accedit Oratio Valedictoria.

1695 Quaestiones [1]

Quæstiones . . . Die Tertio Quintilis. M DC XC V.

An Detur in non-Renatis Liberum Arbitrium ad bonum Spirituale?
                              Negat Respondens Benjamin Colman.
An Sola Fides, quatenus apprehendit Christi Merita, et Illis innititur, Justi-
ficet?   Affirmat Respondens Ebenezer White.
An Gentes ex Naturæ Lumine Salutem possint Consequi?
                              Negat Respondens Johannes Mors.
An Pontifex Romanus sit Ille Antichristus, Quem futurum Scriptura præ-
dixit?   Affirmat Respondens Caleb Cushing.

1696 Quaestiones [2]

Quæstiones . . . Kalendas Quintilis. M DC XC VI.

An Fides Justificans a bonis operibus sejungi possit?
                              Negat Respondens Isaacus Chauncæus.
An Aliqua Usura sit licita?   Affirmat Respondens Henricus Flintæus.
An Vere Fideles possint totaliter et finaliter deficere?
                              Negat Respondens Simon Bradstreet.
An Libri Apocryphi sint canonici?   Negat Respondens Johannes Wade.
An Justitia Vindicatrix sit Deo naturalis?
                              Affirmat Respondens Nathanael Williams.
An Credentes teneantur ad obedientiam Legis?
                              Affirmat Respondens Johannes Woodward.
An Sola Fides justificet?   Affirmat Respondens Josephus Baxter.

---

1. H. U. Archives. Printed in Sibley, IV. 119. In this and the remaining quæstiones of the Mather administration, the headings show but slight variations from that of 1694. After some attempt to find new epithets for President Mather, he becomes stabilized as *Clarissimus pariter ac Reverendissimus Dominus.*
2. H. U. Archives.

An Vitium sit rectæ Rationi contrarium?

Affirmat Respondens Nathanael Huntting.

An Ad Redemptionis nostræ Pretium, tam activa quam passiva Christi spectet Obedientia?   Affirmat Respondens Benjamin Ruggles.

An Fraudes quæ vocantur piæ, sint Illicitæ?

Affirmat Respondens Gulielmus Grosvenor.

His accedit Oratio Valedictoria.

1697 QUAESTIONES [1]

Quæstiones . . . Nonas Quintilis. M DC XC VII.

An Jesuitæ possint esse Boni Subditi?

Negat Respondens Adamus Winthrop.

An Virtutes Ethnicorum sint Veræ Virtutes?

Negat Respondens Eliphalet Adams.

An Dominium temporale fundetur in Gratia?

Negat Respondens Johannes Ballantine.

An Detur Omnibus Auxilium [S]ufficiens ad Salutem?

Negat Respondens Jabez Fitch.

His Accedit Oratio Valedictoria.

1698 QUAESTIONES [2]

Quæstiones Pro Modulo Discutiendae . . . Collegii Harvardini . . . Die Sexto Quintilis. M DC XC VIII.

An Regimen Monarchicum sit Optimum?

Affirmat Respondens Gualterus Price.

An Mendici sint tolerandi in Republica?

Negat Respondens Richardus Saltonstall.

An Sola Fides Justificet?   Affirmat Respondens Nathanael Saltonstall.

An vere Fidelis Certus esse Possit de sua Salute?

Affirmat Respondens Johannes Hubbard.

An Ecclesia Romana Hodierna sit vera Christi Ecclesia?

Negat Respondens Simon Willard.

An Detur Magnetica Vulnerum curatio?

Affirmat Respondens Abijah Savage.

An Detur Medicamentum Universale?   Affirmat Respondens Oliver Noyse.

An Christus pro Omnibus, et Singulis sit mortuus?

Negat Respondens Thomas Blowers.

An Irrenati opus vere Bonum Possint præstare?

Negat Respondens Ephraim Little.

An Curatio Morborum, Quæ Vocatur Characteristica sit licita?

Negat Respondens Johannes Perkins.

---

1. H. U. Archives.

2. H. U. Archives. Printed in Sibley, IV. 219. Note, in the heading, the return to *Collegium Harvardinum.*

An Politeia Ecclesiastica, sit quoad substantiam Immutabilis?

Affirmat Respondens Jedidiah Andrews.

An Mundus potuerit esse ab Æterno?

Negat Respondens Johannes Robinson.

An Pronitas ad malum fluat ex principiis Naturæ Integræ?

Negat Respondens Josephus Green.

An Liceat Gladio Animadvertere in Hæreticos.

Negat Respondens Josephus Mors.

1699 QUAESTIONES [1]

Quæstiones . . . Die quinto quintilis. M DC XC IX.

An Fides justificans a bonis Operibus sejungi possit?

Negat Respondens Thomas Phipps.

An Americani sint Israelitæ? Negat Respondens Georgius Vaughan.

An Motus sanguinis sit circularis?

Affirmat Respondens Roulandus Cottonus.

An Gratia sufficiens ad salutem concedatur omnibus?

Negat Respondens Petrus Thacher.

An Salus populi sit suprema lex?

Affirmat Respondens Dudlæus Woodbridge.

An Detur in Deo scientia media? Negat Respondens Jonathan Remington.

An Sola Editio Hebræa V T, et Græca N T sit authentica?

Affirmat Respondens Samuel Whitman.

An Quilibet in qualibet Religione salvari possit?

Negat Respondens Andreas Gardner.

An Religio vi et Armis sit propaganda? Negat Respondens Samuel Melyen.

1700 QUAESTIONES [2]

Quæstiones . . . Academiæ Harvardinæ . . . Die Tertio Quintilis. MDCC.

An Christus sit Mediator Angelorum?

Negat Respondens Timotheus Lindal.

An Unum et Idem Fœdus Gratiæ, quoad Substantiam, fuerit in utroque Testamento? Affirmat Respondens Ezekiel Lewis.

An Dominium Temporale fundetur in Gratia?

Negat Respondens Elisha Cooke.

An Sancta Ecclesia Catholica, quam credimus, constet ex solis Electis?

Affirmat Respondens Antonius Stoddard.

An Baptismus Laicus, ullo in Casu, sit licitus?

Negat Respondens Samuel Burr.

An jus eligendi Pastores pertineat ad totam Ecclesiam?

Affirmat Respondens Samuel Moody.

---

1. H. U. Archives.
2. H. U. Archives. **Back to** *Academia Harvardina* this year.

An Voluntas Semper sequatur ultimum Dictamen Intellectus?
                    Affirmat Respondens Johannes Swift.
An Obedientia Christi, nobis imputata, sit Causa Meritoria Justificationis
    nostræ?   Affirmat Respondens Josephus Parsonus.

1701 QUAESTIONES [1]

Quæstiones . . . Collegii Harvardini . . . Die Secundo Quintilis.
MDCCI.

An Theologia naturalis sufficiens sit ad Salutem?
                    Negat Respondens Thomas Symmes.
An Detur in non Renatis liberum arbitrium ad bonum Spirituale?
                    Negat Respondens Josias Cotton.
An Aliquis sit Philosophiæ in Theologia Usus?
                    Affirmat Respondens Samuel Mather.
An Mundus potuerit esse ab æterno?   Negat Respondens Josias Willard.
An Textus Originales puri, et incorrupti ad nos pervenerint?
                    Affirmat Respondens Dudleius Bradstreet.
An Sint Morbi qui Remediis galenicis non sanantur, sed tantum Chemicis?
                    Affirmat Respondens Petrus Cutler.
An Dentur Athei, proprie dicti?   Negat Respondens Johannes Foxius.
An Trinitatis Mysterium sit Articulus fidei fundamentalis?
                    Affirmat Respondens Nathanael Hubbard.
An Prædestinatio publice doceri, ac prædicari debeat?
                    Affirmat Respondens Samuel Wolcot.
An Fœdus gratiæ unquam universale fuerit?
                    Negat Respondens Johannes White.
An Christus gehennales Peccati pœnas in anima Sustinuerit?
                    Affirmat Respondens Josias Torrey.
An Vere et Proprie Christus, Loco nostro, justitiæ divinæ satisfecerit?
                    Affirmat Respondens Oxenbridge Thacher.
An Causa justificationis nostræ sit justitia inhærens?
                    Negat Respondens Richardus Billings.

1702 QUAESTIONES [2]

Quæstiones Pro Modulo Discutiendæ Sub Eximio, ac Reverendo
Domino D. SAMUEL WILLARD, Universitatis Cantabrigiensis Nov-
Anglorum Vice-Præside Perquam Literis Perito, Comitiis per Incep-
tores in Artibus Die Primo Quintilis, M DC C II.

An Curaturæ Existentia sit Contingens?
                    Affirmat Respondens Jonathan Belcher.
An Actus possit esse in genere moris, qui sit Indifferens?
                    Negat Respondens Johannes Bulkley.

---

1. H. U. Archives. *Collegium* again.
2. H. U. Archives. *Universitas Cantabrigiensis!*

An Existentia Angelorum possit demonstrari lumine Naturæ?

> Negat Respondens Edmundus Quinsey.

An Immutabilitas decreti tollat libertatem Creaturæ?

> Negat Respondens Franciscus Goodhue.

1703 Quaestiones [1]

Quæstiones . . . Die Septimo Quintilis MDCCIII.

An Detur Vulnerum curatio, per pulverem Sympatheticum?

> Affirmat Respondens Johannes Winthrop.

An Dentur Ideæ innatæ?   Affirmat Respondens Johannes Whiting.

An homo possit velle malum, qua malum?

> Negat Respondens Robertus Breck.

An Extensio competat Spiritibus?   Affirmat Respondens David Deming.

An Destructio mundi per Noæ Diluvium, fuerit vi causarum naturalium?

> Negat Respondens Samuel Hunt.

An Decimæ debeantur sub Evangelio Jure divino?

> Affirmat Respondens Johannes Barnard.

An Cometæ ab origine creati fuerint?

> Affirmat Respondens Johannes Prentice.

An Metalla in sese invicem possint transmutari?

> Affirmat Respondens Johannes Holman.

An Anima sit ex Traduce?   Negat Respondens Johannes Veazie.

His Succedit Oratio Valedictoria.

1704 Quaestiones [2]

Quæstiones Pro Modulo Discutiendæ Sub Reverendo et Perdocto Viro Domino D. Samuel Willard, Accademiæ Harvardinæ, Quæ est Cantabrigiæ Nov-Anglorum, Vice-Præside Peritissimo in Comitiis per Laureae Magistralis Candidatos. Tertio Nonarum Quintilis MDCCIV.

An Indigentia sit vinculum humanæ Societatis?

> Affirmat Respondens Thomas Banister.

An Leges morales sint juris Immutabilis?

> Affirmat Respondens Georgius Corwin.

An Mercatura sit utilis, et Necessaria Rei-publicæ?

> Affirmat Respondens Nathanael Oliver.

An Satisfactio Christi consistat cum misericordia Dei?

> Affirmat Respondens Samson Stoddard.

An Leges pure pœnales Obligent Conscientiam?

> Negat Respondens Johannes Legg.

An Deus sit Omnipræsens quoad Essentiam?

> Affirmat Respondens Theophilus Cottonus.

---

1. H. U. Archives. Printed in Sibley, IV. 496.
2. H. U. Archives.

An Naturalis Theologia sufficiat ad Salutem?

Negat Respondens Amesius Angier.

An Volenti possit fieri Injuria?　　　　Affirmat Respondens Thomas Weld.
An Detur in Deo Scientia Media?　　　Negat Respondens Timotheus Cutler.
An Intellectus in Seipsum reflectatur?

Affirmat Respondens Nicolaus Fessenden.

An Mores animi sequantur Temperamentum Corporis?

Affirmat Respondens Israel Loring.

An Æquivocatio Jesuitica sit licita?　　　Negat Respondens Thomas Tufts.
An Humanus intellectus sit Mensura Veritatis?

Negat Respondens Nicolaus Sever.

An Radix contingentiæ in causis Secundi sit ipsa Dei Voluntas?

Affirmat Respondens Samuel Wiswall.

An Homo sit creatione mortalis?　　Negat Respondens Samuel Woodbridge.
An Detur Actio humana involuntaria?

Negat Respondens Ephraim Woodbridge.

1705 Quaestiones [1]

Quæstiones . . . Collegij Harvardini . . . Die Quarto Julij M D C C V.

An Nummus necessario sit inventus?

Affirmat Respondens Guilielmus Hutchinson.

An Anima humana creetur?　　　Affirmat Respondens Ebenezer Mountfort.
An Affectus in homine pertineant ad appetitum Rationalem?

Affirmat Respondens Georgius Jaffrey.

An Mendacium sit ullo prætextu licitum?

Negat Respondens Guilielmus Burnham.

An Dentur communia principia?　　Affirmat Respondens Sampson Sheafe.
An Actio libera in Individuo sit indifferens?

Negat Respondens Peleg Wiswall.

An Trinitas Personarum divinarum cognosci possit Lumine naturæ?

Negat Respondens Johannes Odlin.

An Detur naturalis Theologia?　　　Affirmat Respondens Johannes Fiske.
An Finis ultimus cadat sub deliberatione?

Negat Respondens Johannes Bowles.

An Justitia Originalis fuerit homini Naturalis?

Affirmat Respondens Benjamin Gamblin.

An Decreta Dei sint Hypothetica?　　Negat Respondens Samuel Ruggles.
An Duella sint licita?　　　　　　　Negat Respondens Johannes Gore.

His Accedit Oratio Valedictoria.

1. H. U. Archives.

1707 Quaestiones [1]

Quæstiones . . . Die Secundo Quintilis, M DCC VII.

An Confusio Sermonis apud BABEL fuerit tantum diversitas Sententiarum?
Affirmat Respondens Guilielmus Dudlæus.
An Omne mendacium sit Illicitum? Affirmat Respondens Johannes Russel.
An Voluntas possit appetere Malum sub ratione Mali?
Negat Respondens Samuel Mighill.

1708 Theses [2]

Præclarissimo, Ac Literarum Literatorumque Patrono Summo, D. Josepho Dudlæo Armigero, Provinciæ Massachusettensis, et Neo-Hantoniensis Gubernatori Nobilissimo, Mariumque Vicinorum Vice-Admirallo Vigilantissimo, singulari Prudentia decorato, Omnique honoris Genere in æternum decorando; Ut et Patribus Conscriptis nunquam non honorandis, ad Clavum Reipublicæ Sedentibus; Una cum Reverendis, ac vineæ Dei Cultoribus indefessis; Singulis demum Celeberrimis Artium Liberalium Fautoribus; Hasce Theses Philosophicas quas (divina Aspirante gratia) Sub Patrocinio Reverendi D. D. Johannis Leveretti, Collegij Harvardini quod est Cantabrigiæ Nov-Anglorum Præsidis Spectatissimi, pro viribus defendendas Humillime proponunt Juvenes in Artibus initiati, *M. D. C. Q.*

David Jeffries	Johannes Quinzey	Compensantius Wadsworth
Ebenezer Thayer	Thomas Robie	Johannes Webb
Josias Oakes	Samuel Phillipsius	Aaron Porter
Samuel Fiske	Johannes Tufts.	Richardus Talley.
	Eleazar Williams	

Theses Technologicæ.

1   Technologiæ Objectum est omne Ens.
2   Technologia Excludi debent Infinita.
3   Ars est Æmula naturæ.
4   Subjectum Artis est fabrica rei.
5   Ars ejusque Objectum distinguuntur ut regula et res regulata.
6   Posterior Ars Prioris opere utitur.
7   Omni Arti Competit Εὐπραξία.
8   Non-Entis nulla est Scientia.
–   *Non datur Metaphysica.*

---

1. H. U. Archives.
2. Massachusetts Historical Society.

Theses Logicæ.

1 Logica est disciplinarum Norma.
2 Logica est ars generalissima.
3 Ut medicina Corpori, Sic Logica menti Auxiliator.
4 Sensus ad veritatis Cognitionem inepti sunt.
5 Objectum Intellectus Latius quam Imaginationis extenditur.
6 A Nosse ad Esse valet Consequentia.
7 Ratiocinatio gradatim a notis ad ignota progreditur.
8 Præcipitantia est Claræ perceptionis impedimentum.
9 Universalia non existunt extra intellectum.
10 Omne universale est prædicabile, et vice-versa.
11 Substantia est Summum genus.
12 Substantia, nisi per attributa, non percipitur.
13 Causa, qua talis, non est prior Effecto.
14 Occasio non est causa.
15 Figura et Motus a Substantia materiali modaliter discrepant.
16 Finis intentionalis est Causa procatarctica in Efficiendo.
17 Esse rei effectæ est e Causis, bene esse ex adjunctis.
18 Quicquid existit habet essentiam, non vice-versa.
19 Contradictio est oppositio maxima.
20 In contrariis negantibus duo non ponuntur.
+ *A privatione ad habitum non datur regressus.*
22 Quod non potest cognosci, non potest definiri, et vice-versa.
23 Tota vis axiomatis copulati in ipsa copulatione consistit.
24 Methodus est classica Axiomatum dispositio.
25 Methodus est ars memoriæ intellectualis.
26 Clara perceptio est memoriæ Subsidium.

Theses Grammaticæ.

1 Grammatica est Linguarum Clavis.
2 Grammatica sine Logica est vox, et præterea nihil.
3 Literæ sunt vocum materia prima.
4 Consonæ et vocales sunt verborum corpus et Anima.
5 Vox est dictionis principium.
6 Vox est index Animi significans aliquid a mente perceptum.
7 Voces sunt notionum tesseræ.
8 Etymologia et Syntaxis sunt grammaticæ membra.

Theses Rhetoricæ.

1 Rhetorica est ars Ornate dicendi.
2 Tropus et figura Orationem formandam, vox et gestus promulgandam, respiciunt.
3 Orationem adornat Catachresis.
4 Hyperbole est primæ magnitudinis Tropus.
5 Metaphora non quid, sed quale indicat.
6 Epizeuxis est echo Rhetorica.
7 Ænigma est Rhetoricæ nodus Gordianus.
8 Pronunciatio est Eloquentiæ vita.

Theses Mathematicæ.

1 Mathematica est doctrina quantitatis propria occulta recte facileque explicans.
2 Corpus, ut mensurabile, est objectum Mathematicæ.
3 Arithmetica et Geometria tantum sunt artes pure mathematicæ.
4 Arithmetica artium Mathematicarum est maxime regularis.
5 Nullum Multiplex est innumerum.
6 Numeri principium est unitas.
7 Numerus, in se, nullam fractionem habet.
8 Subtractio est duorum numerorum differentiæ inventio.
9 Multiplicatio est additionis Compendium.
10 Divisio est multiplicationis Analysis.
11 Cognitio Geometriæ ab Arithmetica pendet.
12 Astronomia est Scientia Mathematica mixta.
13 Retrogradatio et statio Planetarum non sunt reales.
14 Sydus in Æquatore Omni declinatione, in Eclyptica omni Latitudine caret.
15 Stellarum vera magnitudo ob suam distantiam inveniri non potest.

Theses Physicæ.

1 Physica est ars bene naturandi.
2 Objectum Physicæ est res naturalis.
3 Privatio non est principium.
4 A privatione ad habitum datur progressus.
5 Extensio est propria et inseperabilis [*sic*] materiæ affectio.
6 Neque per rarefactionem acquiritur, neque per Condensationem amittitur quantitas.
7 Generatio est tantum novæ formæ acquisitio.
8 Non dantur formæ Substantiales.
9 Accidens non est ens reale.
10 Qualitates non sunt Entia realia.
— *Omne corpus est in infinitum divisibile.*
12 Locus est immobilis.
13 Omnis Locus est impletus.
14 Angeli sunt in Loco.
— *Materia corporum cœlestium et terrestrium est eadem.*
16 Spatia cælestia sunt fluida.
17 Stellæ fixæ habent lucem nativam.
18 Orbes Solidi sunt Peripateticorum hæreses.
☞ SOL EST CENTRUM MUNDI.
— *Luna est habitabilis.*
21 Atmosphæra est Causa Crepusculi.
22 Omnis motus est Localis.
23 Mobile est objectum moventis, et Subjectum motus.
24 In motu propulsio et successio Corporum requiritur.
25 Quies non est quid positivum.
— *Lux est corpus.*
27 Color est diversa lucis modificatio.

+— *Visio fit per receptionem specierum.*

☞ NON DATUR COLOR IN TENEBRIS.

30 Ignis est materia violenter mota.

31 Homo est Synopsis mundi.

+— *Anima non est forma hominis.*

33 Anima rationalis agit inorganice.

☞ ANIMÆ RATIONALES SUNT ÆQUALES.

35 Anima rationalis in conceptione Creatur et infunditur.

+— *Anima Bruti creatur.*

+— *Sensus externus est unicus.*

His Antecedit Oratio Salutatoria.
Habita in Comitijs Cantabrigiæ Nov-Anglorum, Die Septimo Quintilis.
MDCCVIII.

1708 QUAESTIONES [1]

Quæstiones Pro Modulo Discutiendæ Sub Eximio, ac Reverendo D. D. JOHANNE LEVERETT, Collegii Harvardini Quod Est Cantabrigiæ Nov-Anglorum Præside Artibus Peritissimo, In Comitiis a Laureæ Magistralis Candidatis: Die Septimo Quintilis, M DCC VIII.

An Curatio per Pulverem Sympatheticum sit licita?

Affirmat Respondens Johannes Wilsonus.

An Eclipsis Solis tempore Passionis Christi fuit naturalis?

Negat Respondens Edvardus Holyoke.

An Successio sit de essentia Durationis Creatæ?

Affirmat Respondens Johannes Partrigg.

An Vis Magnetica terræ sit principium Gravitationis?

Affirmat Respondens Nathanael Clarke.

An Anima Rationalis Creetur?   Affirmat Respondens Josephus Hiller.

An Detur Liberum Arbitrium in non Renatis ad bonum spirituale?

Negat Respondens Guilielmus Williams.

An Beatitudo Cœlestis sit progressiva?

Affirmat Respondens Josephus Marsh.

An Cogitatio superet Materiæ vires? Affirmat Respondens Jonathan Marsh.

His Succedit Oratio Valedictoria.

---

1. H. U. Archives.

APPENDIX C

TWO LETTERS OF LEONARD HOAR

1. To his Freshman Nephew, Josiah Flynt [1]

[London] March 27, 1661

Cozen Josiah Flint,

Your first second and 3d are before me in answer to one of mine to you the last year: the which you esteemed somewhat sharp but I thought and still doe fear that it was scarce so much as was needfull: and I am sure yourself would be of the same mind if with me you knew the unutterable misery and irreparable mischeif that follows upon the mispense of those Halcyon dayes which you do yet enjoy. The which letter, whilst you fence withall in your first by those seven or eight thin-sculd-paper-put-byes And as many empty excuses; you did but lay more open your own blame-worthinesse and augment my greif insted of giving me satisfaction.

But your two latter epistles are better Containing some acknowledgment of those grand defects, discerned in you, and those errors committed by you: together with your promises of reparation and amendment by redoubling your diligence in your studyes for the time to come. Only remember to doe what you have promised, and I thereupon have believed; that I may see some testimonyes of it in all your succeeding letters; And also hear it testyfyed by others, that shall write to me concerning you. By all things that you can either revere or desire I adjure you that you doe not æmulate those unhappy youths that reckon it a high point of their wisdom to elude the expectations of their friends for a little while; whereby they indeed not only delude, but destroy themselves for ever.

Your account of the course of your studyes, as now ordered, under the worthy Mr. Chancey, is far short of my desire; for its only of what you were then about; Wheras it should have bin a delineation of your whole method and authors, from your matriculation till commencement. Therfore I can still touch but upon a few generalls for your direction.

The first is this that you would not content yourself with the doing that only which you are tasked to; Nor to doe that, meerly as much as needs must, and is expected of you: But dayly somthing more than your task: and that task also somthing better than ordinary. Thus when the classis study only Logick or Nature you may spend some one or two spare hours in Languages

---

1. M. H. S., 'Papers 1636–75' fol. 4. Printed inaccurately in 1 *Coll. M. H. S.*, VI. 100–08. The then (1799) editor of the Society touched up the original letter in ink, and used it for printer's copy, which makes the establishment of the original text somewhat difficult. For most of the authors recommended in this letter, consult the index to this volume.

Rhetorique History or Mathematiques or the like. And when they recite only the text of an author read you some other of the same subject or some commentator upon it at the same time. Also in your accustomed disputations doe not satisfy yourself only to theiv an argument but study the question before hand and if possible draw in a book on purpose a summary of the arguments and answers on all hands: unto which you may briefly subjoyn any thing choice and accurate which you have heard in the hall upon the debate of it in publick.

Nextly as you must read much that your head may be stored with notion so you must be free and much in all kinds of discourse of what you read: that your tongue may be apt to a good expression of what you doe understand. And further; of most things you must wr[ite] to; wherby you may render yourself exact in judging of what you hear or read and faithfull in remembering of what you once have known. Touching your writing take a few hints of many which I had thought to have given you. 1. let it not be in loose papers for it will prove for the most part lost labour. Secondly, nor in a fortuitous vagrant way But in distinct bookes designed for every severall purpose And the heads of all, wrote aforehand in every page with intermediate spaces left (as well as you can guesse) proportionable to the matter they are like to contain.

3. Let all those heads be in the method of the incomparable P. Ramus, as to every art which he hath wrot upon. Get his definitions and distributions into your mind and memory. Let thesse be the titles of your severall pages and repositoryes in the books aforesaid. He that is ready in these of P. Ramus, may refer all things to them And he may know where again to fetch any thing that he hath judiciously referred; for there is not one axiom of truth ever uttered, that doth not fall under some speciall rule of art.

The Genus on any page, you may (having paged your book before hand) by a figure set before it direct from what page it came: And the species thereof, one or more which, for method and understanding sake shall be set down under it, but not handled there: you may by figures after them direct to the severall pages that are made the repositoryes for the matters referrible to each of them And so need no childish confused Alphabetical indices.

Mr Alexander Richardson's Tables would be as an Ariadne's thred to you in this labyrinth. Which with other his Manuscripts in Logick Physick and Theology, by transcribing, have bin continued in your colledg ever since the foundation thereof among most that were reckoned students indeed. And if you have now lost them I know no way to recover them but of some that were of that society in former times. I suppose Mr Danforth Mr Mitchell and others have them.[1] Mr Hancock a quondam pupil of Mr. Chaunceyes hath his Divinity. But in the utter defect of this, you may make use of the grand Mr Ramus in Grammar Rhetorique Logick (the Mathematiques must be left to your industry and memory unlesse it should be some practicall branches of it, of which you may take short notes) and then for Theology (which you may yet let alone) you have Dr Ames Medulla: Of this Theme I shall be

---

1. Evidence that Jonathan Mitchell (A.B. 1647) had the Theses Logicae, at least, is found in his ms. theses, Mass. Archives, CCXL. 141. 5a. See references under 'synopses' in index, below.

larger: when you shall give me encouragement thereunto by attending to what I have written on the rest fore going.

4ly. As to the authors you should distill into your paper bookes in generall let them not be such as are already methodicall concise and pithy as possible: for it would be but to transcribe them: which is very tedious and uncouth. Rather keep such bookes by you for immediate perusall. But let them be such as are voluminous; intricate and more jejune: Or else those tractabuli that touch only on some smaller tendrells of any science. Especially if they be bookes that you doe only borrow, or hire to read. By this mean I have kept my library in a little compasse: (scarce yet having more bookes then my self can carry in my arms at once my paper bookes only excepted) and yet I have not quite lost any thing that did occur in my multifarious wandring readings. Were a man sure of a stable abode in a place for the whole time of his life, and had an estate also to expend; then indeed the bookes themselves in specie were the better way and only an index to be made of them all. But this was not like to be nor hath bin my condition: and it may be may not be yours. Wherefore, though it be somewhat laborious yet be not discouraged in prosecuting it. It is the surest way and most ready for use in all places and times, yielding the greatest evidences of your growth in knowledge and therefore also the greatest delight. It comprehends the other way of an index to: If for the bookes you read you keep a catalogue of their names authors scope and manner of handling and edition. And so for every severall tract you devise a certain mark, by which you may breifly quote the author from whence you had those collected notes and refer to him for more ample satisfaction in any article when as it shall be to tedious to transcribe him word for word.

5t. For bookes into which you should thus hoard your store Take at present only some quires of paper stitct together, which you may encrease or substract from, as you shall see occasion upon experience. Only let them that concern one thing be all ruld after one fashion; and let them be sewed and written so as that afterwards they may be bound into one volume, in case that you should never have time to digest them again into more handsome order. At least no further then a succinct epitome: or Synopsis.

6. One paper book more adde of the names of all philosophicall authors and divines of ordinary note: of all the severall sects in the schooles and in the Church. Of all the nations famed in the world; of all and singular the most misterious arts and sciences: And of them all write a Latine Alphabeticall Index which by figures shall direct to the severall pages in a book where you have noted or will note the characters commendations and censures which any of them doe give of other and some of the charriteristick differences by which they were known, the time of their rise their progresse subdivisions and several ends. I mean such fragments as shall occur of these things, to you by the by in your reading: and would for most part be lost, if not thus laid up. As for the full history of them wherever that is found, transcribe nothing out of it, for its to laborious and endlesse: but only refer to it. Much lesse doe you doe offer to gather any thing out of the workes of authors who have written volumes to this very purpose, such as are Possewine,[1]

---

1. Antonio Possevino, *Bibliotheca de Ratione Studiorum*; see *F. H. C.*, p. 268.

Sextus Senensis,[1] Gesner,[2] Draudius,[3] and the like. The great use of this is to preserve these fragments that yourself shall find in your studyes, and could not be otherwise referred. Likewise, that you may know and compare their thoughts of each other especially the moderns; and that accordingly you may be directed and cautioned in the perusal of any of them. Finally that you may have of your own store those characters and lineaments by which you may presently pencill any of them at pleasure: And this not as usually upon prejudice and peradventures; but the testimonyes of some or other that you may also produce. for alway be sure in this, that you note down the author whence you excepted any thing of this nature. But this you will judg so vast as never to be accomplished, and therfore vain to be attempted, you never having heard the names of $\frac{1}{10}$ of those things and persons that I have proposed so that you know not how so much as to begin this platform. I answer that for the progresse or compleating of this work you need not take care: Let it but grow as you studyes grow; you never need seek any thing on purpose to put into this book. And for the entrance I shall shew it easy. For if you take but one quire of paper and divide the first 2 sheets into 24 narrow columnes, and every page of the rest into two: which also must be paged. Then mark the narrow columnes each with one letter of the Alphabet. And it is ready for use: for tis but to write the name of seid place or person that next occurs into your index with the figure J at it: and again that name, with what is there said of it in your first page of the quire, with the author whence you had it, and its done. And the like of the second in the second. When the index shall grow full tis but write it over again leaving larger spaces where needed. And when that quire shall grow full tis but to take up another and carry on the same columnes and numbers. And when they grow to be five or 6 quires to this one index, why then, if that on any name swell to big for its column, tis but to refer it to some other column further forwards. On the contrary if any others have not nor are not like to yeild any thing much upon them, when more titles occur tis but croud those into them, referring them also, as the former, by the index and its figures. Thus I think I have made it facile and plain enough And beleiv me you will find it beyond your estimation, both pleasant and profitable.

7. One more Quire you may take and rule each leaf into 4 columnes And therin also note Alphabetically all those curious criticismes Etymologyes and derivations that you shall meet withall in the English Latin Greek and Hebrew tongues. I still mean by the by: while you are seeking other matters. Not which you may gather out of vocabularyes and Criticks that have purposely written on such subjects. for that were but actum agere.

---

1. The *Bibliotheca Sancta* (Venice, 1566; and later editions to 1626), by Sixtus of Siena (1520–1569), a converted Jew and Dominican. See article 'Sixtus von Siena' in Wetzer and Welte, *Kirchenlexikon*.

2. Conrad Gesner (1516–1565), the Swiss botanist, physician, universal savant, and pioneer Alpinist (cf. Arnold Lunn, *The Alps*, pp. 33–39). Hoar doubtless refers to his remarkable, though incompleted, *Bibliotheca Universalis* (Zürich, 1545–49, and later editions and epitomes), a catalogue in the three learned tongues of all known writers and books.

3. Georg Draud (1573–1635?), *Bibliotheca Classica* (Frankfort-am-Main, 1611 and 1625), a catalogue of books and authors that was superseded by Bayle's *Dictionnaire* in 1697.

8. Be forward and frequent in the use of all those things which you have read, and which you have collected: judiciously molding them up with others of your own fancy and memory according to the proposed occasions. Whether it be in the penning of epistles orations Theses or Antitheses, or determinations upon a question. Analyses of any part of an author, or imitations of him, *per modum genésews*. For so much only have you profited in your studyes as you are able to doe these. And all the contemplations and collection in the world, will but only fit you for thesse: tis practise and only your own practise that will be able to perfect you.

My charg of your choyce of company I need not inculcate: nor I hope that for your constant use of the Latine tongue in all your converse together: and that in the purest phrase of Terence and Erasmus etc Musick I had almost forgot I suspect you seek it both to soon, and to much. This be assured of that if you be not excellent at it Its worth nothing at all. And if you be excellent it will take up so much of your mind and time that you will be worth little else: And when all that excellence is attained your acquest will prove little or nothing of real profit to you unlesse you intend to take upon you the trade of fidling. Howbeit hearing your mother's desires were for it for your sisters for whom tis more proper and they also have more leisure to looke after it: For them I say I had provided the Instruments desired, But I cannot now attend the sending them being hurrying away from London by this unexpected providence of your unkle Daniells sicknesse: which with some other circumst: with which its acc[ompanied] dt. nt. a ltl dist. me.[1]

My deservedly honoured friend and colleague Mr Stoughton is coming over. he hath promised me to doe you any civill courtesy either for advice or loan of a book or the like. Therfore to him I wish you modestly to apply your self and hearken to: whom as I am sure you will find able, so I am perswaded that you will find both free and faithfull, to assist you as is meet.

I shall adde but one thing more for a conclusion: But that the crown and perfection of all the rest: which only can make your endeavours succesfull and your end blessed: And that is som thing of the dayly practice of piety and the study of the true and highest wisdome And for gods sake, and your own both present and æternall welfares sake, let me not only entereat, but enjoyn, and obtain of you, that you doe not neglect it: No not a day. For it must be constancy, constancy, as well as labour, that compleats any such work. And if you will take me for an admonitor doe it thus. Read every morning a chapter in the old Test: and every evning one in the new: using your self alwayes as much as you can to one edition of the bible. And as you read, note lightly with your pen in the margent the severall places of remarque, with severall marks. Those I use are: for such as have any thing in them new to me, notable and evident, this sign ´   for those that are obscure and worthy to consult an interpreter upon: this `   For those that are seemingly contradictory to some others, this +   For those that must be compared with others this >   For those golden sayings that are full of the soul and power of the Gospell; worthy of highest consideration and admiration, thus ∞. And if any 3 or 4 or 10 verses together be of like import I upon the first of them set down the proper mark and double it as ″ `` ≫.

---

1. doth not a little distress me.

2. Out of these latter most eminent sentences cull one or two for to expatiate upon in your own thoughts, half a quarter of an houre by way of meditation. There use your Rhetoricque, your utmost rationation, or rather indeed your sanctifyed affections: Love faith fear hope joy etc: For your direction and encouragement in this exercise, you may read the practique of Augustine Bernard or Gerard. Or our more modern worthyes I Ambrose, R Baxter, B[isho]p Hall or mr Watson,[1] as to the Theoreticall part.

3ly and lastly, those 2 being premised, close with Prayer. for this I præscribe not whether it should be linguall or mentall longer or breifer: Only let it as wel as its two preparatives, be most solemn and secret: and as tis said of Hannah, the speech of your heart. The barrenest ground, and with but mean tillage, being thus watered with these dews of heaven, will bring forth abundantly: and that, the most excellent fruites. Doe but seriously try these 3 last things, for some good while: and reckon me a Lyar in all the rest, if you find not their most sensible sweet effects. yea (as that Christian Seneca, B[isho]p Hall, said before me so I boldly say again) Doe you curse me from your death-bed, if you doe not reckon these amongst your best spent houres.

Touching the other items about your studyes, either mind them or mend them and follow better. So we shall be freinds and rejoyce in each other. But if you will neither: then (tho I am no prophet, yet) I will fortell you the certain issue of all: viz: that ere a very few years be over, with inconceivable indignation that you will call your self fool and caitif: And then, (then when it is to no purpose) [call] me what I now subscribe my self

Your faithfull freind, and loving unkle

LEON HOAR.

2. TO THE HONORABLE ROBERT BOYLE [2]

Cambridge, New-England, December the 13th, 1672.

Right honourable,

Your freedom and courteous treating me, when hither coming, giveth me the hardiness to present you with my acknowledgments, although it be but your interpellation; judging it better, that I were censured for troublesomness, than for ingratitude. Yea the chiefest of this colony, a poor, but yet pious and industrious people, know and acknowledge your kindness often and on considerable occasions expressed towards them, in their just defences, etc. although they know not where or how to publish their tabula votiva, or memorials of it unto your acceptation, but still do gratefully recommend you and your well-devoted labours in their prayers to God; and any publick affair them concerning, that shall unexpectedly emerge unto your prudence, love and candor, hoping, that nothing shall ever be believed or concluded against them before that they be heard.

---

1. Isaac Ambrose, nonconformist, writer of *Looking unto Jesus* (1658) and other devotional works; Richard Baxter, author of *The Saints Everlasting Rest* (1650); Bishop Joseph Hall of *Epistles* fame, author of *Christian Moderation* (1640); and, probably, Thomas Watson (d. 1686), Rector of St. Stephen's, Walbrook, whose *Three Treatises* reached a sixth edition in 1660.

2. As printed in Robert Boyle, *Works* (1744 ed.), v. 642–43.

Noble Sir, I am not unmindful of your desires to see what rarities the country might yield; and have taken course, that now be presented to you, first, a sort of berries, that grow closely conglomerated unto the stalk of a shrub, in its leaf, smell and taste, like the broadest leaved myrtle, or to a dwarf-bay; which, by plain distillation, yields an almost unctuous matter; and by decoction, not a resina, nor oil, but a kind of serum, such as I have not known ordinarily for any vegetables. I believe it excels for the wind-colick.

Though I thought myself an indifferent botanist for any thing could grow in *England*, yet here in our wild plants I am presently [at a loss] but I hope I shall in season search out their pedigrees; and would be free to gratify any person valuing them with their seeds, or bodies dried. Mr. *Alexander Balaam*,[1] my master in those studies, and a person well known to Mr. *Charles Howard* and Dr. *Morrison*,[2] are now in your land.

Also (pardon, I beseech you, the confidence) I make bold to present your honour with a model of our natives ships. With one of them twenty foot long they will carry six or eight persons, their house and furniture and provisions, by one padling her forwards in the stern, swifter than any sculler. And when they come to falls, or would go over the land, [the passengers] load themselves away with the ship and her freight too.

I doubt they are not for the wars; for if you but stamp hard, you may strike out the bottom; and if you lay your tongue on one side of your mouth, it may over-set.

Also Sir, a piece of their plate, a fish I call the sea-spider, and some stones, I doubt more ponderous than precious; but that your honour will prove.

It hath pleased even all to assign the college for my Sparta. I desire I may adorn it; and thereby encourage the country in its utmost throws for its resuscitation from its ruins. And we still hope some helpers from our native land; of which your honoured self, Mr. A[shurst] and some others have given a pledge.

A large well-sheltered garden and orchard for students addicted to planting; an ergasterium for mechanick fancies; and a laboratory chemical for those philosophers, that by their senses would culture their understandings, are in our design, for the students to spend their times of recreation in them; for readings or notions only are but husky provender.

And, Sir, if you will please of your mature judgment and great experience to deign us any other advice or device, by which we may become not only nominal, but real scholars, it shall, I hope, be as precious seed, of which both you and me and many by us shall have uberous provent at the great day of reckoning, which I know you do respect above all.

---

1. Alexander Balaam (fl. 1656–1680) was an English merchant, traveller, and amateur botanist. He collected seeds and plants in Tuscany for Gaston, duc d'Orléans, travelled as far as Persia, and sent specimens from Tangier (where he was recorder of the English Court Merchant) to Zanoni, director of the botanical garden at Bologna. E. M. G. Routh, *Tangier*; Britten and Boulger, *Biogr. Index Deceased British Botanists* (1931), p. 16; G. Zanoni, *Istoria Botanica* (1675), p. 73; Ernest Cosson, *Compendium Florae Atlanticae*, I (1881). 7; A. von Haller, *Bibliotheca Botanica* (1771), I. 496. I am indebted to Professor B. L. Robinson for this information.

2. Dr. Robert Morison. See above, p. 395.

If I durst, I would beg one of a sort of all your printed monuments, to enrich our library, and encourage our attempts this way.

I know nothing so stunting our hopes and labours in this way, as that we want one of a sort of the books of the learned, that come forth daily in *Europe*, of whose very names we are therefore ignorant.

To Mr. *Ashhurst* [1] I have written more. Let not, I beseech you, my prolixity tire or deter your acception of things hinted, or your honour's condonation of

Your devoted humble servant,

LEONARD HOAR.

---

1. See above, p. 439.

APPENDIX D

DOCUMENTS ON THE BUILDING OF OLD HARVARD HALL
1678–1682

1. RETURN OF THE COMMITTEE[1]

Cambridge April 24th 1678

To the Honoured Governor and Councill of the Mattachusetts

The Returne of the Committee appointed by the Generall Court to take accountt of the Stewards of the New-brick building at the Colledge is as foll. viz.

The Gentlemen Stewards of the Fabrick, upon our discourse with them and inquiry into their accompts and transactions in that affaire acquaint us and declare that (not looking on the accompts of their disbursments to be the businesse of our present meeting, and not having made up accompts with all persons concerned and imployed upon the work, they cannot without further time give a distinct and particular acountt of the disbursments at present and charge laid out upon the edfice but withall say they do judge and hope that what they have already received of the Contributions will neere hand if not wholly defray what they are already engaged to the workmen, And — Having farther enquired into the acompts of the Contributions and payments made towards the erecting of the said building by the Severall towns in the Colony, we find

	FOR MIDDLESEX					
	Subscriptions			Rest Due		
Charlestowne	268	7	8d	95	9	10d
Cambridge	182	6	0	80	0	0
Watertowne	44	13	0	9	5	9
Reading	35	0	0	10	13	4
Bilracah	18	4	8	11	16	5
Chelmsford	21	15	0	1	1	8
Malborough	15	0	0	5	3	0
Groton	Nothing Subscribed			Nothing paid		
Sudbury	26	8	4	4	15	6
Malden	No Subscription			Nothing paid		
Woborn	No Subscription			3	6	0 paid
Newtown	35	15	0	19	11	11
Concord	45	0	0	16	14	7

1. Mass. Archives, LVIII. 93–95. This return is later than the list of subscriptions in College Book III, printed in *C. S. M.*, xv. 222–23. That list is headed '1672,' but it cannot be earlier than June, 1677, since it includes Salem. The return of the stewards of May 29, 1677, and the circular letter of the General Court, that we have cited on p. 425, prove that Salem and Ipswich had at that date taken up no subscription.

Students[1]

	ll	s	d				
Mr Danll. Gookin	1	0	0		1	0	0
Mr Jno. Bridgham	2	0	0		2	0	0
Mr. Joseph Taylor	1	0	0		1	0	0
Mr Nath. Higginson	1	0	0		1	0	0
Mr Samll Danforth	6	0	0		6	0	0
Mr Isaac Foster	1	0	0		1	0	0
Mr Tho: Clarke	1	0	0		1	0	0
Mr Danll Russell	2	10	0		—		
Mr Edward Pelham	5	0	0		5	0	0

SUFFOLK

	Subscriptions			Rest Due			
	li	s	d	li	s	d	
Boston 1st Church	319	12	0	Order'd to be pd to Job Lane			
" 2 Church	291	3	0	84	9	4	
" 3 Church	390	0	0	79	7	5	
Roxbury	60	0	0	36	3	4	
Dorchester	100	0	0	70	15	5	
Milton	43	5	4	37	12	4	
Weymouth	53	9	0	15	19	0	
Brantry	100	0	0	86	12	0	
Medfield	12	17	6	9	17	6	
Dedham[2]	71	0	0	17	0	1	
Hingham	No Subscriptions			Mony pd 16*li* 1*s* 2*d*			

Students

Mr Elnath. Chancy[3]	1	0	0		1	0	0
Mr Jno Norton	1	0	0		1	0	0

ESSEX

Andover	14	0	0	4	10	0	
Rowly	45	0	0	4	11	7	
Beverly	13	0	0	2	0	0	
Glocester	4	19	1	11*d* over paid			
Wenham	11	10	0	9	18	6	
Marblehead	36	0	0	27	5	4	
Bradford	18	0	0	18	0	0	

1. The thirteen 'students' on this list are a problem. Mr. Albert Matthews believes that they were either teaching fellows or resident graduates studying for the M.A. in 1672, when the subscription list was first circulated; that they had almost all scattered (and some were dead) by 1678, and so were listed under the counties that they came from. Despite the discouraging showing on this list, Manning's accounts (printed below) show that £7 10*s* was collected from the surviving and available 'students' by 1682.

2. 'To write and send out' in margin.

3. It is difficult to account for this name among the students, for Elnathan took his second degree in 1664, and later practised medicine. Possibly he was simply residing in college as an unmarried graduate when the subscription list was circulated.

Topsfield	6	0	8	4	0	8
Newberry	32	3	0	32	3	0
Ipswich	80	0	0	68	5	0
Salem [1]	143	8	2	60	0	0 [2]
Lyn	No Subscriptions			12	0	Paid

Students

Mr Jo: Brown	7	0	0	7	0	0
Mr Jno Richardson	6	0	0	6	0	0

NORFOLK [3]

Hampton	26	0	0	26	0	0
Salisbury	21	11	9	21	11	9
Havrill	21	0	0	21	0	0
Exeter	20	0	0	10	12	0
Almes-berry	9	0	0	9	0	0

DOVER AND PORTSMOUTH [4]

Dover	70	0	0	35	0	0
Portsmouth	No Subscriptions.			Nothing paid.		

HAMPSHIRE

Springfield	45	0	0	26	12	8
Hatfield	25	0	0	25	0	0
Westfield	32	0	0	24	0	7
Hadley	52	11	0	18	2	11
Northampton	30	0	0	8	10	8

YORKSHIRE [5]

Kittery	30	0	0	3	13.	6
York	No subscriptions			Nothing paid.		
Wells	No subscriptions			Nothing paid.		
Saco	27	16	0	27	16	0
Falmouth	20	0	0	20	0	0
Scarborough	22	0	0	19	10	6

The Totall of the Subscriptions in the Colony to the said Edifice, as rendred by the said Stewards amounts unto 3028*li* 9*s* 2*d*. Remaining still due of the said Subscriptions unpaid — 1242*li* 13*s* 5*d* — Concerning which summe yet unpaid upon the perusall of the Returns now sent in by severall towns we understand that in this late warr many persons have lost their lives, the estates of many much impaired, and severall remooved, which will cause a failure of a part of

1. In the Essex Institute there is a ms. subscription list for Salem, totalling £158 5*s*, the largest being £40 from William Browne, Senior; the second, £25 from William Butler.

2. In margin: 'Beside Maj[or Ha]thorns ma[   ].'

3. Not the modern Norfolk, but parts of New Hampshire and Essex.

4. Piscataqua County.

5. Maine.

what is yet due but we hope also by the said Returnes transportation being allowed so much may be paid as may welle nigh carry on and finish the work, which the Gentlemen Stewards are now in prosecution of, including also what hath ben paid by some towns who have made no returne of Subscriptions which is not marked herein under the head of the towns respectively, and if not accompted in the above totall Summe of Subscriptions we further Signifie that Since [the] before written the Stewards informe us of 100*li* mony [   ] up of Capt Jno Richards, for the carrying on this work which is yet unpaid, and must be reimbursed out of the Subscriptions above Or otherwise as shall Seeme good to Authority — This being the furthest we are capable at present of proceeding in this matter Wee Subscribe our Selves

> Much Honoured
> Your most humble servants
> THO: BRATTLE
> SAMUELL APPLETON
> LAUR. HAMMOND
> NATHLL: SALTONSTALL

2. WILLIAM MANNING'S BUILDING ACCOUNTS [1]

the new Building for the Colledge debitor
to sundry disburstments as followeth

	£	s	d
to 200 tuns of lyme stones from Capt Dauis	080	00	00
to lighters to cary them to Cambridge	009	14	00
to Charlstown men for stones for the cellar and foundation	077	13	03
to seuerall persons for Digging the cellar and the well	014	02	08
to the brickmakers for making bricks and pauements	225	12	07
to carting brickes, clay, sand, lymestones from the waterside	055	16	06
to sundry persons for wood to burn the brickes and lyme	085	07	10
to the masons for building the house and labourers that wrought with them in the cellar and foundation whiles they wrought by the day	493	09	01
to boards and planks for the work	192	18	00
to bricks that came from lyn, Charlstown and from John Eames	023	17	00
to lead for the gutters, nayles, locks and hinges and seuerall other expenses	137	03	00
to Iron barrs for the lower windowes, casements and glasiers worke, a pump and Irons for the Chimneys	086	14	03
to payd mr lane besides what he had from the first church in boston	031	18	07
to labourers worke, laths, Coopers worke, laying lead haire and shreds and other things	045	16	07
to Joyners and carpenters for finishing worke	173	08	03
to Expences at Cambridge ordinary for Accommodation of seuerall Committees	012	12	00

---

1. Mass. Archives, LVIII. 119–20. Cf. *Mass. Bay Recs.*, v. 380.

	£	s	d
to payd the worpl. John Richards Esqr for Intrest of 100*li* borrowed of him	040	00	00
to more for carting, labour, workmanship, and land for diggin clay for the bricks and making ladders and other things	132	07	10

to my boating corn and other goods between boston Charlstown and
    Cambridge   24 02 08 ⎫
to warehouse roume for corn and other goods since June   ⎬ 034 02 08
    1672   10 00 00 ⎭

Sume is	1969	15	08

There is yet remaining belonging to the stocke	£	s	d
In sope, shooes, hats, and other English goods at the prizes they were payd in at, amounting to	070	05	40
In the masons hands ouer payd them in their account	006	06	04
In Benony Eatons hands to be payd in mault	015	11	00
In mony	007	10	00
In mr John vials hand for mault sold him — now payd [1]	003	00	00
	102	12	08

there is Also some nayles of seuerall sorts the quantity I know not
Also there is something payd in by Wooborn town the just quantity I cannot
know yet, it shall be giuen In in an after account their subscription was
27*li* 2*s*.

per Contra Creditor	£	s	d
from muddy riuer men subscribed with the first church in boston	004	05	00
from hadley that came to my hand besides the charges for transportation	033	15	03
from springfield	017	18	09
from northhampton	020	09	04
from west-field	012	08	01
from hatfield as is supposed, about 14*li* 2*s* 6*d*	014	02	06
from Charlstown	196	11	01
from the second church in boston besides 50*li*, of sir thomas Temples mony stopped by the honord gouernor leuerit in liew of 50*li* Doctor hoare had from mr Aline [2]	159	08	08
from the third church in Boston	343	16	01
from douer	32	15	00
from kittery	22	00	00
from salem	130	02	03
from marblehead besides 12*li* payd the worpl. Capt. Richards	08	19	06
from Ipswich	60	03	02
from newbury	21	04	00
from salisbury besides 814 feet pyne plank to the worpl. Capt Richards	13	04	00

---

1. These two words inserted by Manning later.
2. This probably represents part of the £300 appropriated out of the early contributions to President Hoar to pay for repairs to the President's Lodge. See above, p. 398, and Braintree item in this account.

	£	s	d
from Cambridge 154*li* 9*s* 3*d* from the village [1] 37*li* 2*s* 5*d* from the students [2] 7*li* 10*s* in all	199	01	08
from topsfield	06	00	00
from Excetor	10	00	00
from Chelmsford	18	07	00
from billerica	12	04	00
from the Reuerend mr Edward Bulckly for sir gorge Downing	06	05	00
from marlbrough	11	11	08
from gloster	05	00	00
from sudbury	24	00	08
from Dortchester	67	04	11
from Roxborough	37	16	08
from Concord	33	07	05
from dedham	61	12	00
from Rowly	40	08	05
from Watertown	41	16	03
from Andouer	12	10	00
from Weymouth	39	10	00
from lyn	20	00	00
from metfield	07	16	00
from milton	14	18	00
from Brantree besides 60*li* Doctor hoare had there	27	14	06
from wennam	04	11	03
from hingam	19	06	02
from hull	03	18	00
from maulden	10	00	00
from hauerill besides 500 foot of oak plank & 500 foot of pyne plank to Capt Richards	13	10	06
from Bradford besides 5*li* 12*s* in Capt laurence hamonds hand now payd	03	15	00
from scarbrough	02	09	06
from Beuerly	13	00	00
by mony borrowed of Capt Richards by order of the gouernor & magistrates	100	00	00
from Redding	30	17	06
sume is	1969	14	09

these are the seuerall sumes from the seuerall townes that hath been actually receiued without Reference to the Charges of transportation to boston & Cambridge

this is a true account errors in casting up excepted, of which I know not any as witnes my hand   WILLIAM MANNING
Cambridge this 29th of maye 1682

We under written being a Committee appointed by the Generall Court for to enquire into the accounts of mr Manning and mr Cooper (stewards of the Stock contributed for the building of the Colledge) do upon examination find and approve of their accounts as faire and honest only the value of 10*li* as we judge in nailes omitted to be valued

1. Newton.
2. See p. 648 above, n.

above And we do recommend it to the Generall Court to consider them for their pains As for the colledge debts we can say nothing about them without further Information

Octob. 18. 1682   RICHD SPRAGUE   HUM: DAVIE
                    JOHN WAYTE   SAMULL NOWELL
                    WILLIAM JOHNSON   ELISHA COOKE

The magistrates Approove of this Returne of the Comittee their brethren the deputies hereto Consenting
   18th of october 1682

                        EDWARD RAWSON Secret.

The Deputys Consent
  Oct. 20. 1682:

                    ELISHA HUTCHINSON
                        per order.

APPENDIX E

CONSTITUTIONAL DOCUMENTS, 1692–1707

CHARTER OF JUNE 27, 1692 [1]

An Act for Incorporateing of Harvard Colledge at Cambridge in New-England

Whereas there hath been for many years in the Towne of Cambridge in the county of Middlesex in New England, a Society commonly known by the Name of Harvard College where many Persons of known worth have, by the Blessing of Almighty God been the better fitted for Publick Imployments both in the Church and in the Civil State, And whereas, the due encouragement of all good Literature, Arts and Sciences will tend to the Honour of God, the Advantage of the Christian Protestant religion, and the great Benefit of their Majesties Subjects inhabiting this Province, both in the present and succeeding Generations. **And** considering that many Persons have bestowed Legacies Gifts Hereditaments and Revenues on the said Colledge. Be it therefore Enacted and Ordained by his Excellency the Governour, Council and Representatives of Their Majesties Province of the Massachusets Bay in New-England Convened in General Assembly. And by the Authority thereof, it is Enacted and Ordained, That the said Colledge in Cambridge in the County of Middlesex in their Majesties Province of the Massachusets Bay in New-England shall be a Corporation Consisting of Ten Persons, that is to say, a President Eight Fellowes and a Treasurer, And that the Reverend mr. Increase Mather shall be the first President, James Allen, Samuel Willard, Nehemiah Hobart, Nathanael Gookin, Cotton Mather, John Leverett, William Brattle, Nehemiah Walter, Masters of Art, shall be the eight Fellowes and John Richards Esq: the Treasurer, all of them Inhabitants in said Province. And the first ten Persons whereof the said Corporation shall consist, which said Increase Mather, James Allen, Samuel Willard, Nehemiah Hobart, Nathanael Gookin, Cotton Mather, John Leverett, William Brattle, Nehemiah Walter, John Richards and their successors shall forever hereafter in Name and Fact be one Body Politick and Corporate in Law, to all Intents

---

1. From the engrossed, signed and sealed Charter in the H. U. Archives, 1.15.120 pf, from which it was copied into College Book IV (*C. S. M.*, xv. 335–38). For bibliography, see *id.*, p. xl, note 4. The Charter is glossed by Increase Mather opposite the section on degrees, 'empowrd to give Degrees in Divinity.' The seal, originally in red wax, has crumbled away.

and Purposes: And shall have perpetual Succession, and shall be called by the Name of the President and Fellowes of Harvard Colledge, Which persons, or the greater Number of them, shall have Power and are hereby Authorized at any time or times to Elect a new President Fellowes and Treasurer, so often, and from time to time as any of the said Persons shall dy or be removed, **Provided** no such Election be made without notice given in writing under the hand of the President or Senior Fellow unto the Persons concerned seven dayes at least before such Election be made. **And** the said President Fellows and Treasurer and their successors Elective, as aforesaid shall and may purchase and acquire to themselves, or take and receive upon Free Gift or Donation any Lands Tenements or Hereditaments within the Province aforesaid not exceeding the value of Foure Thousand Pounds per Annum, And any Goods or summe of money whatsoever to the use and behoofe of the said President and Fellowes of Harvard Colledge, and also for the Encouragement of Learning **And** may sue and plead, or be sued and impleaded by the Name aforesaid in all Courts and Places of Judicature: **And** that the said President and Fellowes and their successors may have forever one Common Seale to be used in all causes and occasions of the said Corporation, and the same Seale may alter, change, breake and new make from time to time at their Pleasure. **And** the said President and Fellowes or the major Part of them from time to time may meet and choose Officers and Menial Servants for the Colledge, and them also to remove, and after death or Removal to choose such others. **And** to make from time to time such Statutes, Orders and Bylawes for the better Ordering the Affaires of the Colledge as they shall thinke fitt. **And** also, that the President and Fellows or Major Part of them with the Treasurer shall have Power to make Conclusive Bargaines for Lands and Tenements to be purchased by the said Corporation for valuable Consideration. **And** for the better Ordering the Government of the said College or Academy, **Be it Enacted** by the Authority aforesaid, That the President and Fellowes or any six of them, shall and may from time to time upon due notice or warning given by the president to the rest, hold a Meeting for the debating and concluding of Affaires concerning the Profits and Revenues of any Lands, and disposeing of their Goods. **Provided,** that all the said disposals be according to the Will of the Donors, And for Direction in all Emergent Occasions, and the Execution of all Statutes, Orders and Bylaws, In all which cases aforesaid the Conclusion shall be made by the President and Major Part of the Fellowes. And all the transactions aforesaid shall tend to, and for the use and behoofe of the President Fellowes Schollars and Officers of the said Colledge, And for all Accommodations of Buildings, Bookes and all other necessary Provisions and Furniture as may be for the Advancement and Education of youth in all manner of Good Literature, Arts and Sciences. **And Farther be it Enacted** by the Authority aforesaid, That all the Lands, Tenements and Hereditaments, Houses or Revenues within said Province to the aforesaid President Fellowes or Colledge appertaining shall from henceforth be freed from all Publick ordinary Rates and Taxes appertaining to the Province in General, **And** that the said President Fellowes and Schollars with the said servants and other necessary Officers to the said President or Colledge appertaining, which Servants and Officers are not to exceed Fifteen, vizt. Three to the President and Twelve to the Colledge belonging, shall be exempted from all

Personal Civil Offices, Military Exercises, watchings and wardings, And the Estates of the said President and Fellowes, under their owne Management to be free from all Rates and Taxes. Provided they reside and dwell in the Colledge. **And** whereas it is a laudable Custome in Universities whereby Learning has been Encouraged and Advanced to confer Academical Degrees or Titles on those who by their Proficiency as to Knowledge in Theology, Law, Physick, Mathematicks or Philosophy have been judged worthy thereof, **It is hereby Enacted** and Ordained, That the President and Fellowes of the said Colledge shall have power from time to time, to grant and admit to Academical Degrees, as in the Universities in England, such as in respect of Learning and Good Manners, they shall find worthy to be promoted there-unto. **And** whereas there have been at sundry times and by divers Persons Gifts, Grants, Devises of houses Landes Tenements, Goods chattles Legacies conveyances heretofore made to the said Harvard Colledge in Cambridge in New England or to the President and Fellowes thereof successively, The said Gifts, Grants Devises and Legacies are hereby for ever confirmed according to the true Intent and Meaning of the Donor or Donors, Grantor or Grantors, Devisor or Devisors.

Boston. Passed June 27th, 1692

Anno R[egni] R[egis]   WILLIAM PHIPS
Gulielmi et Mariae
Quarto.
    ISAAC ADDINGTON Secy.

CHARTER OF JUNE 4, 1697 [1]

Anno R[egni] R[egis]   An Act for Incorporating
Guliêlmi Tertii   Harvard Colledge at
nono   Cambridge in New
                   England

Whereas there hath beene for many yeares in the town of Cambridge in the County of Middlesex within his Majesties Province of the Massachusetts Bay in New England a Society commonly knowne by the Name of Harvard Colledge where many persons of knowne worth have, by the Blessing of Almighty God been Educated and the better fitted for Publick Imployments both in the Church, and in the Civil State. **And Whereas** due Encouragement of Good Literature Arts and Sciences will Tend to the Honour of God the Advantage of the Christian Protestant Religion and the Greate benefitt of his Majesties Subjects Inhabiting this Province both in the present and succeeding Generations and Considering that many Persons have bestowed Legacies Gifts Hereditaments and Revenues on the said Colledge. **Be it Enacted and Ordained** by the Lieutenant Governour, Council and Representatives in Generall Court Assembled, and by the Authority of

---

1. From the engrossed, signed and sealed Charter in the H. U. Archives, 1.15.130 pf. For bibliography, see *C. S. M.*, xv. p. xlvii, note 2.

the Same, That the said Colledge at Cambridge in the County of Middlesex aforesaid Shall henceforth be a Corporation consisting of Seventeene Persons That is to say, a President Vice-president Fourteen Fellowes and a Treasurer. And that Increase Mather shall be the first President, Charles Morton Vice-president, and James Allen Michael Wigglesworth Samuel Torrey Samuel Willard Nehemiah Hobart Peter Thacher John Danforth Cotton Mather John Leverett William Brattle Nehemiah Walter John White Paul Dudley and Benjamin Wadsworth Masters of Art, shall be the Fourteen Fellowes and Thomas Brattle Master of Art the Treasurer all of them Inhabitants within the said Province And the first Seventeen Persons whereof the said Corporation shall consist Which said Increase Mather Charles Morton James Allen Michael Wigglesworth Samuel Torrey Samuel Willard Nehemiah Hobart Peter Thacher John Danforth Cotton Mather John Leveritt William Brattle Nehemiah Walter John White Paul Dudley Benjamin Wadsworth and Thomas Brattle and their Successors shall forever hereafter be one body Politick and Corporate in Fact and Name to all Intents and Purposes in Law by the Name of the 𝔓𝔯𝔢𝔰𝔦𝔡𝔢𝔫𝔱 and 𝔉𝔢𝔩𝔩𝔬𝔴𝔰 𝔬𝔣 𝔥𝔞𝔯𝔟𝔞𝔯𝔡 𝔠𝔬𝔩𝔩𝔢𝔡𝔤𝔢 𝔦𝔫 𝔑𝔢𝔴 𝔈𝔫𝔤𝔩𝔞𝔫𝔡, and that by that name they shall have Perpetual Succession, and by the Same name they and their Successors shall and may be capable and Enabled as well to Implead as to be Impleaded and to prosecute demand and answer, and be answered unto in all and Singular Suites Causes, Quarrells and actions of what nature and kind soever, and also to have take acquire and purchase or receive upon Free Gift or donation any Lands Tenements or Hereditaments within the Province aforesaid not exceeding the Value of Three Thousand Pounds per Annum, and any Goods Chattells summe or Summes of money whatsoever To the use and behoofe of the said Corporacion 𝔄𝔫𝔡 the Same to Lease Grant Demise Imploy and dispose, and the Revenues issues and Profitts thereof for the Encouragement of Learning, and of the President Fellows Schollars and Officers of the said Colledge, as also for Accommodation of Buildings Bookes, and all other necessary Provisions and furniture as may be for the Advancement and Education of Youth in all manner of good Litterature Arts and Sciences. 𝔓𝔯𝔬𝔳𝔦𝔡𝔢𝔡 that all the said Disposalls be according to the Will of the Donours. 𝔄𝔫𝔡 the said PRESIDENT AND FELLOWS and their Successors may have forever One Common Seale to be used in all causes and occasions of the Corporation, and the Same Seale may alter, change breake and new make from time to time att their pleasure. 𝔄𝔫𝔡 𝔟𝔢 𝔦𝔱 𝔣𝔲𝔯𝔱𝔥𝔢𝔯 𝔢𝔫𝔞𝔠𝔱𝔢𝔡 𝔞𝔫𝔡 𝔡𝔢𝔠𝔩𝔞𝔯𝔢𝔡 by the Authority aforesaid That the said Corporation shall be and hereby are Authorized and Impowred to Elect a new President, Vice President Fellows and Treasurer, when and soe often from time to time as any of the said persons shall dye or be removed. The President Vice President Fellows and Treasurer or any of them being removable for Disabillity or Misdemeanour, and may be displaced by the Corporation Saveing to the Party Grieved his Appeale to the Visitors, a Vice President to be Annually Elected, although not occasioned by death or removall as aforesaid; And when any of the Members of the said Corporation shall settle himself without the bounds of this Province he shall be ipso facto dismist and no Longer Continue to be of the Corporation, and his place be Supplyed by the Election of a new member. 𝔄𝔫𝔡 the President for the time being, or in case of his death or Absence, the Vice President Shall and may from time to time appoint and order the assembling and meeting together of the said Corporation, to Consult Advise of, debate, and direct the affaires and businesses of the said Corporation, to choose Officers and Meniall Servants for the said Colledge, and them also to remove, and upon death or removeall to choose such others and to make Statutes orders and By Lawes for the better Ordering the affaires and Government of said Colledge or Accademy, soe as such Orders Statutes and by Lawes be not repugnant to the Lawes of this Province. And any nine or more of the members of said Corporation together with the President or Vice President being so Assembled Shall be taken held and reputed to be a full sufficient and Lawfull Assembly for the handling ordering and directing of the affaires businesses and Occurrences of the said Corporation. And in case of the Death removal or absence of the President and Vice President, the Senior Fellow for the time being may call and hold a Corporation meeting Untill the returne or New Election of a President or Vice President. Provided nevertheless that no meeting shall be held for the Displaceing or new Election of any member or members of the Corporation Fellowes of the House or the makeing of Statutes orders or by Laws for ordering of the affaires and Government of the said Colledge without Summoning a Generall Meeting as aforesaid for such Purpose, Each member of the Corporation to be notified either Verbally or in writeing eight days att least before hand of the time and occasion of Calling such Meeting. And in the passing of all Votes and Acts of the said Corporation in any of their meetings the Determinacion shall be made by the Major part, The President to have a Casting voice in case of an Equivote.

And It is Further Declared by the Authority aforesaid That after this Act shall be confirmed the President, as well as all the Fellows receiving Salary shall reside att the Colledge, and that not one shall enjoy a Fellowship with Salary for more than Seven Yeares except continued by a new Election. And that the Houseing and Lands in Cambridge aforesaid belonging to the said Corporation and being in the Personall Occupacion of the President and Fellows residing att the Colledge shall be Free from all Province or Country Rates and Taxes. And that the President Fellows and Schollars with the Servants and Necessary Officers to the President and Schollars Appertaining who shall reside att or be Constantly Imployed in Services for the Colledge (which Servants and Officers are not to exceed Ten vizt, Three to the President and seven to the Colledge belonging) shall be Exempted from all personall Civil Offices, Millitary Exercises Watchings and Wardings.

And Whereas It is a Laudable Custom in Universityes whereby Learning has been Encouraged and Advanced to conferr Accademicall Degrees or Titles on those who by their Good manners and Proficiency as to knowledge in Theology Law Physick Mathematicks or Phylosophy have been Judged worthy thereof.

Be it further enacted by the Authority aforesaid, That the President and Fellowes of the said Colledge shall have power from time to time to Grant and Admit to Accademical Degrees as in the Universities in England Such as in respect of Learning and Good manners they shall find worthy to be promoted thereunto.

And Whereas There have been at Sundry Times and by Divers Persons Gifts, Grants Devises of Houses Lands Tenements Goods Chattells Legacies and Conveyances heretofore made unto the said Colledge or to the President or Fellows thereof Successively, The said Gifts Grants Devises Legacies and Conveyances are hereby for ever ratified and confirmed according to the true intent of the Donor or Donors Grantor or Grantors Devisor or Devisors. 𝔄𝔫𝔡 in order to the Preventing of Irregularities and for the more assurance of the well Government of said Colledge, 𝔚𝔢𝔢 𝔭𝔯𝔞𝔶 his Majesty that it may be Enacted, and it is hereby 𝔈𝔫𝔞𝔠𝔱𝔢𝔡 𝔞𝔫𝔡 𝔇𝔢𝔠𝔩𝔞𝔯𝔢𝔡 That his Majesties Governour and Commander in Chiefe of this province and the Council for the time being shall be the Visitors of the said Colledge or Academy, and shall have use and exercise a power of Visitation as there shall be occasion for it.

Passed by the Council
and Assembly the 4th   [Seal of the   WM STOUGHTON
of June 1697   Province]

ISAAC ADDINGTON Secy.

'TEMPORARY SETTLEMENT' OF 1700

Order of July 13, 1700 [1]

Whereas this court have made their humble address unto his majesty for his royal charter for incorporating of Harvard Colledge, in Cambridge, within this province, and the good gouernment thereof,

Ordered, That the reverend Mr. Increase Mather, nominated to be president of said colledge, Mr. Samuel Willard, vice-president, Mr. James Allen, Mr. Michael Wigglesworth, Mr. Samuel Torry, Mr. Nehemiah Hubbard, Mr. Peter Thacher, Mr. Samuel Angier, Mr. John Danforth, Mr. Cotton Mather, Mr. Nehemiah Walter, Mr. Henry Gibbs, Mr. John White, Mr. Jonathan Pierpont and Mr. Benjamin Wadsworth, with the two senior tutors for the time being, nominated to be fellows of the said corporation, be and hereby are empowered to take the oversight, care and government of the said colledge and students there, and to direct and order payment of salaries or allowances to the officers thereof out of the revenues, rents and profits of the grants, donations and stock to the colledge belonging, and to sue for, collect and receive all such rents, profits and incomes, until his majestie's pleasure shall be known referring to the settlement of said colledge, or that this court take further order therein.

Order of March 14, 1700/01 [2]

Whereas [citing the Order of July 13, 1700]; and forasmuch as the constitution requires the president to reside at Cambridge, which is now altered by his removal from thence, to the intent that a present necessary oversight be taken of the colledge; it is therefore, —

Ordered, That the said Mr. Increase Mather, Mr. Samuel Willard, and the several other gentlemen mentioned in the aforerecited order, be and hereby are anew appointed and empowered to continue their oversight, care and

---

1. *Acts and Resolves of the Province of Massachusetts Bay*, VII. 265.
2. *Id.* 271–72.

government of the colledge, and students there, in manner as in the order is exprest, and to use and exercise the like powers and authority to them therein and thereby granted for and during such time as by the said order is set and limited; and in case of Mr. Mather's refusal, absence, sickness or death, that Mr. Samuel Willard, nominated to be vice-president, with the other gentlemen before named, be and hereby are invested with the like powers and authority aforesaid in all respects.

Council Order of April 28, 1702 [1]

A Question being moved upon the construction and intendment of the Order of the General Assembly for a temporary establishment of the oversight and government of the Colledge and Students there, whether it do contain a sufficient power to Mr. Samuel Willard nominated to be vice President, with the other Gentlemen therein named, to carry on the work of the approaching commencement and to confer Degrees upon the Commencers as has been accustomed.

Resolved. That they are sufficiently impowred thereto by said Order, and that they be desired to proceed in the said work accordingly. And that Elisha Cooke and Samuel Sewall Esquires be desired to acquaint Mr. Willard therewith.

CONCURRENT RESOLVE OF DECEMBER 6, 1707 [2]

Anno Regni Annae Reginae Septo

At a Great and General Court or Assembly for Her Majestys Province of the Massachusetts Bay in New England, begun and held at Boston upon Wednesday the Twenty eighth of May 1707. And Continued by several Prorogations unto Wednesday the 29th of October following, being their Third Session.

In Council

Thursday December 4th 1707.

The Governour and Council haveing Accepted and Approved the Choice made by the Fellows of Harvard Colledge in Cambridge, of Mr. John Leverett to be present President of the said Colledge, to fill up that Vacancy,

Propose, That the House of Representatives Consider of and Grant a sutable Salary to be paid to the said President annually, out of the Publick Treasury, for his Encouragement and Support, during his Continuance in the said Office, residing at Cambridge, and Dischargeing the proper Dutys to a President belonging, and Intirely Devote him selfe to that Service.

---

1. *Acts and Resolves of the Province*, VII. 703.

2. From the engrossed and signed copy in H. U. Archives, 1.15.150; reproduced opposite p. 555, above. This document is or should always be included with the Charter of 1650 at Presidential inaugurations — it was so included in 1933. The draft in Mass. Archives, LVIII. 263 is printed in *Acts and Resolves of the Province*, VIII. 257. Copies are also found in the ms. 'President Leverett's Diary,' pp. 6–7; and in College Book IV, printed in *C. S. M.*, XV. 380–81.

𝕬𝕹𝕯 Inasmuch as the first foundation and Establishment of that House, and the Government thereof, had it's Original from an Act of the General Court made and pass'd in the year One Thousand Six hundred and fifty which has not been repealed or Nulled,

The President and Fellows of the said Colledge are Directed, from time to time to regulate them selves according to the Rules of the Constitution by the said Act prescribed; And to Exercise the Powers and Authority's thereby Granted, for the Government of that House, and the Support thereof.

Saturday December 6th 1707

The Representatives, returned the Vote pass'd in Council the 4th current referring to the Colledge, with their Concurrance thereto; And this further Addition thereon, Vizt. That the Sum for Salary be One hundred and fifty pounds. To which the Council Voted an Agreement.

ISAAC ADDINGTON Secry.

By his Excellency the Governour

Consented to — J DUDLEY

APPENDIX F

THE University Archives, housed largely in the Widener Library,[1] undoubtedly form the most considerable archive of any educational institution in the United States. The older records have been described at different times by successive curators, and others.[2] During the last three years the Archives have been rearranged by Mr. Clarence E. Walton, Assistant Librarian. This brief inventory follows the more detailed one that Mr. Walton has recently compiled. It attempts to carry on in summary form all series which start before 1800, but ignores those that begin after that year. Several departments of the University, such as the Law School and the Museum of Comparative Zoölogy, have archives of their own which have not yet been adequately explored or inventoried.

Many of the early College Records were kept in bound volumes. These have been preserved intact; and in the nineteenth century, sundry loose papers were bound up with little respect for origin or order. Some of these have been broken up and rearranged functionally. Large quantities of uncalendared papers, many of them recent donations, remained. These have been preserved in their original order whenever it was known; otherwise they have been arranged in chronological order, under the appropriate department.

1. It may be well to explain the distinction between the different libraries of Harvard University. The Harry Elkins Widener Memorial Library Building, commonly called the *Widener Library*, is the structure in the College Yard that houses the Harvard College Library, and numerous special collections. It takes its name from the collection of books made by Harry E. Widener (A.B. 1907). Both the building and the Widener books were given to the University by Harry's mother, now Mrs. A. Hamilton Rice. The Harvard College Library is the collection of books belonging to the College and dating back to 1638, comprising some 2,000,000 volumes and pamphlets, which for the most part are housed in the Widener building. The head of it is the Harvard College Librarian (Mr. Alfred C. Potter, A.B. 1889). The Harvard University Library includes the Harvard College Library, sixteen Departmental Libraries (such as the Law Library with about 500,000 volumes, the Medical Library with about 230,000, etc.), and seven House Libraries. The Director is Dr. Robert P. Blake (A.M. 1909). Cf. William C. Lane, 'The Harvard College Library,' in *Development of Harvard University*, Chapter XXXVIII.

2. Justin Winsor on 'The Present Condition of the Archives of Harvard College,' in *Proc. A. A. S.*, n. s., IX (1893–94). 109–12; and printed separately as *The Archives of Harvard College* (Worcester, 1894); Andrew McF. Davis, 'Analysis of Early Records of Harvard College,' in *Bibliographical Contributions of the H. C. L.*, no. 50 (1895); William Garrott Brown, 'The University Archives,' *Harvard Graduates' Magazine*, VI (1897–98). 314–20; Albert Matthews, 'Notes on the Harvard College Records, 1636–1800,' *C. S. M.*, XIV. 312–18, and Introduction to *C. S. M.*, XV. pp. xiii–xxxii.

All historians of Harvard and of higher education in America have reason to be grateful to Mr. Walton and to Mrs. Dakin, who has worked under his direction, for their intelligent and devoted labors on the University Archives. Without their aid my task would have been prolonged indefinitely. They have rescued from forgotten boxes and bundles literally thousands of mss., the very existence of which was unknown.

A large number of papers relating to Harvard history were never deposited in the Archives, but carried away by presidents and other officials. Some of these, such as the Dunster and the Eliphalet Pearson papers, have been returned; others, such as part of the Leverett papers, have found their way into libraries; others, no doubt, are still in private hands. Many unofficial papers, such as students' notebooks, club records, and professors' correspondence, that are of no less interest to Harvard history than the official records, are also in private collections. Owners of mss. of any period relating to Harvard history are invited to present them, or copies of them, to the Archives, where they will be properly classified and made available to students.

In this inventory, bound volumes are so designated; all other mss. are in manila cases. The inclusive dates do not include those of photostats from other collections which, for convenience in reference, are placed with mss. of the same subject. The classification letters UA precede all shelf-marks.

CONTENTS

1. The College Books
2. Corporation Records
3. Overseers' Records
4. Harvard College Papers
5. Buildings Papers
6. Charter Papers
7. Commons Papers
8. Deeds, etc.
9. Disorders Papers
10. Donation Papers
11. Lands Papers
12. College Laws
13. Presidents' Papers
14. Professorship Papers
15. College Seals
16. Wills Papers
17. Chronological Miscellany
18. Treasurers' Records
19. Stewards' Records
20. Faculty Records
21. Library Records

1. THE 'COLLEGE BOOKS'

The oldest continuous records of Harvard College. The title was given and the numbering begun in President Wadsworth's time. They include all the known Corporation records for the periods covered, and many Overseers', Treasurers,' and miscellaneous records as well.

College Book I, 1639–1795   I.5.5

> Printed in *C. S. M.*, xv. 1–168. The only entries subsequent to 1687 are a catalogue of graduates that President Wadsworth began in 1734, and which others continued to 1795; and the College Laws of 1734.

[College Book II.]

> Destroyed in the fire of 1764. Wadsworth's index to it is printed in *C. S. M.*, xv. pp. xix–xxii, and a few other extracts are copied in documents of the fellowship controversy of 1720–23.

College Book III, 1636–1779   I.5.5

> Printed in *C. S. M.*, xv. 172–332. This book was begun by Treasurer Danforth about 1654, and includes copies of much of the material in Books I and II, as well as of other records that have been lost. Subsequent to 1686 it contains inventories and plans of college estates entered by Presidents Wadsworth and Holyoke; and in the back are transcripts of honorary degree diplomas.

College Book IV, 1686–50   I.5.5

> Printed in *C. S. M.*, xv. and xvi. 336–864. Corporation Records, 1692–1708, with a few for 1686–91, entered by President Leverett, and miscellaneous records.[1]

College Book V, 1693–13   I.50.15.56

> Treasurer Brattle's Journal and out-letters. Detained by John Hancock in 1777, and restored to the College ninety years later from the Governor's coach-house.

College Book VI or Hollis Book, 1726–79 and 1790   I.5.5

> Begun by President Wadsworth to preserve a record of Hollis donations and scholars. 63 pp., and at rear, catalogue of the official library of the Hollis Professor of Divinity, and Inventories of mathematical and philosophical apparatus, 1779 and 1790.

President Wadsworth's Index to College Books I–VI   I.5.10

College Books VII, 1750–78; VIII, 1778–1803; IX, 1803–10

       I.5.15

> Fair copies of Corporation Records made from drafts partly preserved in the Waste-book series (1.5.50). Indexed at beginning.

College Book X, 1810–27   I.5.15

> A series of Corporation waste-books, bound together and indexed at beginning.

The College Books are continued by:

1. There is a convenient chronological calendar of Corporation and Overseers' meetings in College Books I, III and IV, in *C. S. M.*, xv. p. clxix ff.

2. CORPORATION RECORDS (PRESIDENT AND FELLOWS)

Corporation Records, 1827 to the present, 1st set   I.5.20

These volumes are not numbered until 1914, and are known only by their dates. There are 9 volumes for the period 1827–1901; 18 vols. for 1901–34. This set, the one of original record to 1914, is kept in the College Treasurer's Office, 24 Milk Street, Boston, where the Corporation meets.

Corporation Records, 1650 to the present, 2d set   I.5.30

A fair copy of the first set, and of Corporation Records in the College Books as well. Numbered consecutively. Card index in President's Office.

Vol. I, 1643–1750	Vol. IV, 1795–1810
Vol. II, 1750–1778	Vol. V, 1810–1819
Vol. III, 1778–1795	Vol. VI, 1819–1827

Vols. VII–IX, 1827–1856, cover the same periods as corresponding volumes in I.5.20; vols. X–XXI, 1857–1914, cover in 12 volumes the same period as the 10 unnumbered volumes in I.5.20. Beginning with vol. XXII, 1914, the records are typed, the original being in this series, the first carbon in I.5.20, and a second carbon in the President's Office, University Hall (I.5.40). All three are bound uniformly.

MS. Indexes, incomplete   I.5.45 and 46

Corporation Waste-Books   I.5.50

Five thin volumes, 1771–80, 1780–84, 1784–1806, 1806–11, 1825–28.

3. OVERSEERS' RECORDS   II.5.5

The original Overseers' Records (College Book II) were burned in 1764, but a number of records of Overseers' meetings before 1707 are copied into College Books I, III, and IV. With the restoration of government under the Charter of 1650, on December 4, 1707, the Board of Overseers began a series of records of their own, which still continues.

Vol. I, 1707–1743	Vol. III, 1768–1788
Vol. II, 1744–1768	Vol. IV, 1788–1805

4. HARVARD COLLEGE PAPERS, 1636 TO THE PRESENT

The basis of this series is the correspondence and loose papers collected, mounted, and bound in chronological order in President Sparks's administration, and continued intermittently by subsequent curators of the Archives, who included mss. that earlier compilers overlooked, obtained new ones from outside, and removed others to different classifications. Consequently, there are two series, and several supplements.

First Series,

Vol. I, 1650–1763	Vol. III, 1785–1796	I.5.100
Vol. II, 1764–1785	Vol. IV, 1797–1805	

And seven more numbered volumes, covering the period 1805–25.

Calendar to First Series,

Vol. I, 1636–1809. Unbound II, 1805–1809.   I.5.102.
Useful to find present location of mss. formerly in H. C. Papers, but now removed.

First Series, Supplements

Supplement to Vol. I	Supplement to Vol. II	I.5.110
Supplement to Vols. III–IV	Supplement to Vols. V–VII	I.5.115

Second Series, Vols. I–XXX, covering 1826–1863   I.5.125

In 1933 the remaining loose papers in the Archives that seemed to be connected with the Corporation's activities were arranged chronologically. This series is called 'Corporation Papers.'

Corporation Papers, First Series   I.5.120

[I], 1636–1660. Subscription lists and letters from towns respecting the voluntary contribution of 1653–54; accounts of the investigating Committee of 1654 (see Chapters II and XV, and Appendix A, above).

[II], 1661–1714. Commission of Governor Bellingham, signed and sealed, to Richard Saltonstall et al. as trustees to collect money for the College in England, 1672. A few original mss. and photostats from other collections.

[III], 1715–1730, in 2 cases. (1) About 50 pieces from various sources, including all manner of college business, scholarships, scholars' bonds; (2) waste-book of Corporation meetings, copies from Fulham and S. P. G. Archives of documents on Timothy Cutler's efforts to enter Board of Overseers, etc.

[IV], 1731–1745. Suit of William Vassal against his tutor, 1733, and waste-book.

[V], 1746–1763. Waste-book, letter on Billerica Farm, a few Holyoke mss., proposed Queen's College.

[VI], 1764–1779. Waste-book, Fire of 1764, Dr. Williams' donation, Dummer Academy, book invoices, small-pox, request for loan of 'two Sea Horse Teeth in the Museum of Cambridge,' glazier's reports.

[VII], 1780–1785. Waste-book, correspondence, personal and official papers of President Willard (printed in *Proc. M. H. S.*, XLIII. 609–46 and *C. S. M.*, XIII. 115–16).

[VIII], 1786–1799. Waste-book, undated 'Proposals for promoting and encouraging Learning in the College,' including Deturs; queries from committee of General Court, 1786; examination regulations of 1790; correspondence of President Willard with European scholars and with recipients of honorary degrees; account of Commencement, 1794; memorial of professors and tutors demanding higher salaries, with data on increased cost of living, 1794. Most of these mss. are from the papers of Prof. Eliphalet Pearson.

The series is continued in 11 cases to 1825.

Corporation Papers, Second Series   I.5.130

These are supplementary to the Harvard College Papers, Second Series. About 40 cases, 1826–1869.

Reports of Committees and Boards, chronologically arranged

For this period, 4 mss. only:

Memorial to General Court, May 3, 1654 (I. 10. 10, printed Appendix A, doc. 2); Report on highway through Rogers Farm, 1762 (I. 10. 20); Report on Quarter-Bills, *c.* 1773 (I. 10. 30); Reports on Stewards' Accounts, 1800 (I. 10. 35).

5. PAPERS RELATING TO BUILDINGS

Peyntree and Goffe, map of foundations uncovered in 1910   I. 15. 86
Old College, material collected for *F. H. C.*, Chapter XX   I. 15. 8
'Some model for a College' and 'A Plan for the New College,' [Massachusetts, 1719], printed in *C. S. M.*, XXIV.
    94–95, 100–01   I. 15. 10 and Pf
Holden Chapel   I. 15. 10. 3
Chronological file, 1764 to the present   I. 15. 10. 5
    'Bath in Charles River,' 1799–1800.

Volume on College Buildings   I. 15. 15

Mostly on the building of Holworthy and University.

6. CHARTER PAPERS, 1650–1814

Charter of 1650, engrossed and signed   I. 15. 100 Pf
    Printed in Chapter I.
Early copies of same   I. 15. 100. 5
Charter of 1672, copy "E"   I. 15. 110

See *C. S. M.*, XXI. 388–89 for refs. to earlier copies in Archives.

Charter of 1692, engrossed and sealed   I.15.120 Pf
   Printed in Appendix E.

Charter of 1697, engrossed and sealed   I.15.130 Pf
   Printed in Appendix E.

Proposed Charter of 1700, copy in John Leverett's hand   I.15.140

Resolve of December, 1707, engrossed and signed   I.15.150
   Printed in Appendix E; cf. p. 555, above.

Acts of General Court reorganizing Board of Overseers, March 6,
   1810, and February 28, 1814, engrossed and sealed.
                        I.15.160 Pf & 170 Pf

7. COMMONS PAPERS

Vol. College Commons, 1772–1820   I.15.250
   Menus, accounts, complaints, etc.

Steward Hastings' book giving dates when each student
   checked in and out, 1772–78.   I.15.255

Unbound Commons Papers, 1775–1807   I.15.260
   Report on revising regulations, 1778; report of Steward Gannett,
   c. 1780; student walk-out of 1807.

8. DEEDS AND OTHER TRANSFERS

All are original deeds, to Harvard College (or President and Fellows) unless otherwise stated; many are handsomely engrossed and
sealed. The numbers of Yard lots refer to the Norris Map in *F. H. C.*,
pp. 192–93. For leases, see § 11, below.

Seventeenth century Series   I.15.300 Pf
   John Newgate, 1650, annuity on Rumney Marsh Farm (photograph in this volume); John Cogan, 1654/55, charter of feoff-
   ment to College Marsh (printed in this volume) with plat and
   description by John Gardner, 1715/16; John and Elizabeth Betts,
   1661, Yard lot V (photograph in this volume); Theodore Atkin-
   son, October 13, 1671, land in Boston; Thomas Sweetman to
   Michael Spencer, 1677, Yard lot VI; Samuel Ward, April 9, 1680,
   Bumpkin Island, Hingham, with plat; William and Martha Smith
   to John Richards, 1686/87, mortgage deed, Boston near Mill
   Bridge; Joshua and Lidia Scottow to Samuel Sewall, 1690, Merriconeag Neck, Maine; Seth and Dorothy Perry to John Richards,
   1693, mortgage deed, Boston near Roxbury Gate; Province of
   Massachusetts Bay to Samuel and Hannah Sewall, Nov. 8, 1693,
   Merriconeag Neck, Maine; Samuel and Hannah Sewall, 1696,

Petaquamscot in the Narragansett or King's Province; Michael and Rebecca Spencer, 1697, Yard Lot VI; Thomas Danforth to Isaac Bowen, 1698, Framingham; Thomas Danforth to John Whitney, 1699, Framingham.

Eighteenth Century Series   I.15.310 and Pf

Anthony and Mary Caverley, 1738, Rogers Farm, Waltham; Christopher Grant's Indenture, 1757, Right of Way in Watertown; Joseph Christopher, 1784, Governor Pownall's land, Pownallborough, Maine.

Nineteenth Century Series, 1810–1838   I.15.320

9. Disorders Papers

Thomas Danforth's papers on disorders of 1676   I.15.350

Vol. on Condition of the College, 1821–1824   I.15.380

Papers relating to same   I.15.380.5

10. Donation Papers

Donation Lists, 1680–1867, odd papers   I.15.400

Committee of General Court's Reports on returns of selectmen on contribution for Old Harvard Hall, 1680; Schedules of donations made by or for various presidents from Holyoke to Webber and for Prof. Pearson; Donations to the Museum, c. 1793, from Sandwich Islands, India, 'Otaheitee,' Hawaii, etc.; Catalogue of Prints, c. 1800; Donations lists, 1844–67.

Vol. on Benefactors of Harvard College   I.15.410

Probably Andrew Eliot's notes for the following; includes subscriptions after fire of 1764.

Donations Book. An Account of Grants, Donations and Bequests to Harvard College to the Year 1773   I.15.420

Vol. I, 1636–1784   Vol. II, 1776–1839

Chronological record of donations, begun 1773 by Rev. Andrew Eliot, and continued by others to 1839.

Copy of same, continued to 1900, in Treasurer's Office   I.15.425

Copy, with additional data, in Treasurer's Office   I.15.430

Vol. Wills, Gifts, and Grants, 1643–1801   I.15.480

Original indenture of Lady Mowlson's donation of 1643, copies of benefactors' wills, mss. on Williams and Boyle legacies, and on attempt to recover these and Doddridge annuity in 1785; Mrs. Sarah Winslow's donation and the Town of Tyngsborough, 1790–1801.

Gift Papers, 1672–1799, unbound   I. 15.490

> Piscataqua donation; copy in Increase Mather's hand of Robert
> Thorner's will; Nathaniel Hulton's proposal to buy for the College
> 1000 acres in the Nipmuk country, 1691; Pennoyer accounts, 1706;
> Hoar-Cotton gift for President's salary; Dudleian lectureship;
> Thomas Hollis to Edmund Quincy, 1766; will of Governor
> Pownall, sealed and witnessed by John and J. Q. Adams; letters
> from Thomas B. Hollis to President Willard (printed in *Proc.
> M. H. S.*, XLIII. 609–46); donations to Museum, 1791–96, includ-
> ing minerals from French Republic and Cherokee relics; Willard's
> thanks to Trumbull for battle engravings; Madam Saltonstall's
> donation.

Most gift papers since 1800 are in the Treasurer's Office.

Hollis Letters and Papers, 1718–1774, bound vol.   I. 15.500

Hollis Letters to Leverett, bound vol., 1718–1735   I. 15.505

> Includes letters to Prof. Edw. Wigglesworth (I), with latter's ora-
> tion on Hollis.

Statutes and Orders appointed by Thomas Hollis in respect
to Sundry Donations, January 10, 1722. Bound vol.
Copy made in 1838   I. 15.510

Letters of Thomas Hollis of Lincoln's Inn, 1760–1767   I. 15.512

> To President Holyoke. From the Pearson Mss.

Hopkins Classical School, bound vol.   I. 15.515

> Contemporary records of Corporation votes on Hopkins Scholars
> in school and college, 1726–1808; visitations of the Cambridge
> Grammar School, 1810–26; Proceedings in Pres. Quincy's hand
> on establishing the Hopkins Classical School in Cambridge,
> 1829–39; Statutes of this school, and proceedings at its disband-
> ment in 1854. The records of the School are in a separate vol.
> (I.15.526).

Receipts and Expenditures of Hopkins money, 1771–1837,
bound vol.   I. 15.520

Papers relating to Hopkins affairs in 19th century   I. 15.525

Otisfield (Maine), College share in grant, 1771–1787   I. 15.528

Ward Nicholas Boylston gift to Medical School, 1800–
1811   I. 15.529.5

Records relating to Dexter, Rumford, Boyl-   I. 15.540, 545,
ston Prizes in elocution, Martyn Paine   547, 605, 635, 660,
fund, Soldiers Field, Noble Lecture, and   670, 672, 680, 684,
Randall Charities Corporation.   686, 688.

11. Lands Papers, 1683 to present
Unbound Series

These papers are too fragile for inspection until they have been mounted.

Lands Papers, 1683–1739   I.15.750

Letter of Treasurer Danforth to William Stoughton on Pequot Farms, 1683; Leases: Bradish Lot (B) from College to Andrew Bordman, 1705; Cambridge 2d Division lots 66 and 67 in Menotomy to Abraham Hill (1705) and Gershom Swan (1706/07); Cogan Marsh to Wm. Basset, Nathaniel Ingalls, Ephraim Stacey, et al., 1708/09, 1716, 1733, 1739, and papers on same, 1734–39; Stoughton pasture, Dorchester, to John Robinson; Petaquamscot or Narragansett farm to Stephen Gardner, 1718, and Elizabeth Cole, 1731.

Lands Papers portfolio   I.15.750 Pf

List of and papers on the Eastern (Maine) Lands granted to the College, 1759–1809.

Rowley Lands, 1704–1748   I.15.760

Billerica or Shawsheen Farm, 1708–1779   I.15.765

Bumpkin Island, 1709–1746   I.15.770

Merriconeag Neck Papers, 1683–1773, in 2 cases   I.15.780

Narragansett (Petaquamscot) Farm, 1731–1775   I.15.785.5

Rogers Farm, Waltham, 1738–1779   I.15.790

Eastern Lands, 1780–1803   I.15.795 & 795.5

The result of an inquiry by the Corporation into 'the state of the College lands in the District of Maine' in 1801. From the Pearson papers.

Account of Lands belonging to Harvard College, 1806   I.15.798

Inventory by Treasurer Storer, with all sources of income other than land noted, the manner of keeping treasurer's accounts, and 'Hints for the improvement of Houses and Lands in Cambridge,' with plans.

Bound Series

Lands, 1647–1830   I.15.775

Arranged by estates, though not consistently. Calendar in each volume.

Vol. I, 1647–1800, papers on college property in following places, sometimes with plats or maps: Boston (Gridley house and ropewalk), Bumpkin Island, Cambridge, Chelsea (Cogan Marsh),

Dorchester, Framingham, Granby, Lunenburg, Merriconeag Neck (with map of Casco Bay, 1696), Newton, Pequot Country, Rutland, Townshend, Waltham, Watertown, Winchendon, Winter Harbor (Biddeford Pool, Maine).

Vol. II, on Boston (Webb), Pulham St. Mary (Pennoyer), Waltham (Rogers), and Watertown (Hayward).

Narragansett Farm, 1731–1829   I.15.785

Samuel Sewell's Petaquamscot donation in the Narragansett country (North Kingston, R. I.)

Eastern Lands, 2 vols., each calendared   I.15.795

Vol. I, 1780–1835. Bridgeton, Pownalborough, Turner, Phillipsburg, Fryeburg, Leeds, Livermore, Bucksport, Sullivan, Miscellaneous (incl. Otisfield, Bluehill, Wiscasset).

Vol. II, 1787–1835. Lottery Lands of 1787, deal with Prentiss Mellen, 1809–27; auction sale of 1835.

12. College Laws

For convenience I have made this a chronological list of all codified Laws, whether in this archival series or elsewhere, bracketing those of which no copy is in the Archives. Cf. William C. Lane's list in *C. S. M.*, xxv. 244–53, which enumerates all known copies of ms. Laws. I have noted only the best copy of each.

Manuscript Series

[1642, 'Rules and Precepts,' *New Englands First Fruits*, 1643; reprinted in *F. H. C.*, pp. 433–35.]

1642–46. Lawes, Liberties and Orders.

College Book I. English version printed in *C. S. M.*, xv. 24–27, and in *F. H. C.*, pp. 333–37, with notes; Latin version in *C. S. M.*, xv. 29–31.

March 28, 1650. Orders relating to Duties of Steward, Butler, and Cook.

College Book I. Printed in *C. S. M.*, xv. 32–35.

May 6, 1650. Additional Orders relating to Students.

College Book I. Printed in *C. S. M.*, xv. 27–29.

1655. Lawes and Orders of Harvard College   I.15.805

The 'Chauncy Code.' Printed in *C. S. M.*, xxxi. 329–39.

1667. Rules for the Library Keeper.

College Book III. Printed in *C. S. M.*, xv. 194–96, and in this volume.

1667. Orders relating to Duties of Steward, Butler, etc.
College Book III. Printed in *C. S. M.*, xv. 201–05.

1686. Regulae, Ordinationes et Statutes. The 'Dudley Code.'
College Book IV. Printed in *C. S. M.*, xvi. 848–50.

1692. Statuta, Leges, et Privilegia. The 'Mather Code.'
I.15.841.(1715)
Warham Williams's copy, 1715, is the earliest in the Archives.
Printed in *C. S. M.*, xxxi. 344–46, from copy in M. H. S.

1734. Body of Laws for Harvard College.
College Book i. Printed in *C. S. M.*, xv. 134–35. The earliest
student's copy, by Meshech Weare, is I.15.807

1734/35. College Customs I.15.841.(1735)
In the back of Richard Waldron's Copy of 1734 Laws, bound vol.
Printed in *C. S. M.*, xxxi. 383–84.

1767. Laws of Harvard College. Official Copy, with additions
to 1788, in bound vol., with index I.15.809
Printed in *C. S. M.*, xxxi. 347–83.

Printed Series

Many of these copies in the Archives have ms. notes and emenda-
tions by Presidents and Professors. The editions through 1820 have
an *admittatur* at the end, and are often found signed by the President.
They were issued in paper covers.

The Laws of Harvard College. Boston: 1790. 66 pp. I.15.811

———————————— Boston: 1798. 67 pp. I.15.813

———————————— Cambridge: 1807. 71 pp. Ms.
index I.15.815

Laws of Harvard College for the Use of the Students,
Cambridge: 1814. 67 pp. and Appendix, 15 pp.,
with curriculum I.15.817

Laws of Harvard College for the Use of the Students,
with Preliminary Notices and an Appendix. Cambridge: 1816. xii + 50 pp., including curriculum I.15.819

Laws of Harvard College. Cambridge: 1820, iv + 56
pp. I.15.821

Laws of Harvard College, for the use of the Students,
Cambridge: 1824. 26 pp. I.15.823
An attempt to select from the laws what concerned the students.

Statutes and Laws of the University in Cambridge,
Massachusetts. Cambridge: 1825, 43 pp.   I. 15.825

———————————————— Cambridge: 1826. 40 pp.   I. 15.827

Statutes and Laws of Harvard University, relative to   I. 15.829
Undergraduates. Cambridge: 1832, 40 pp., followed
by Orders and Regulations of the Faculty, 7 pp.   I. 15.829

Statutes and Laws of the University in Cambridge,
Massachusetts ['other than those relative to Undergraduates' added in Pres. Quincy's hand]. Cam-
bridge: 1834. 24 pp.   I. 15.829

Laws of Harvard University, relative to Undergrad-
uates. Cambridge: 1841. 40 pp.   I. 15.829

———————————————: 1845. 40 pp., bound up
with faculty regulations, 11 pp.   I. 15.829

Orders and Regulations of the Faculty of Harvard
University. Cambridge: 1841. 13 pp.   I. 15.829

A Revision of the Statutes and Laws of the University
at Cambridge, prepared to be submitted to the Corporation, for whose use it is privately printed.
Cambridge: 1847. 39 pp.   I. 15.831

The Statutes and Laws of the University at Cambridge. Cambridge: 1848. 60 pp., including Orders
and Regulations of the Faculty of Harvard College,
1848.   I. 15.831.5

———————————————: 51 pp., with Faculty Regu-
lations of May, 1849 at back. 8 pp.   I. 15.831.5

———————————————: 2d edition, Cambridge:
1854. 46 pp.   I. 15.831.7

———————————————: 3d edition, Cambridge:
1860. 46 pp.   I. 15.831.9
   The paper covers to these last two bear the title Statutes and
   Laws of Harvard College.

The Statutes and Laws of Harvard College, as revised and adopted by the Corporation and concurred in by the Overseers. Cambridge: 1866.
44 pp.   I. 15.833
   This is the last of the 'College Bibles.'

Students' Copies

Several score of students' copies of the Laws from 1692 to 1816 inclusive, with *admittaturs* signed by the President.
                                                            I.15.841 & 843

13. PRESIDENTS' PAPERS

Henry Dunster Papers, 1638–1892   I.15.850

A family archive, created out of mss. given by descendants of President Dunster at various times in the nineteenth century, with photostats from other collections. Only the first three cases relate to the President. Documents on the Glover property and lawsuits are in all three. Several have been printed in this volume, and elsewhere (see bibliography in *F. H. C.*, p. 241 n.).

1638–51. Day indenture; letter of Dunster's father; Widow Glover's shoe bill; Edmund Rice and Pond Farm, Sudbury; letter of R. Saltonstall, Jr.

1652–55. Letter of William Cutter; Memorandum of December, 1653 (printed, *F. H. C.*, pp. 448–51); Sudbury farm; sermon notes; *Quadriennium* Memoir (printed, *C. S. M.*, XXXI. 291–300); Irish invitation.

1656–97. Will and estate; Sarah Bucknam's and Stephen Day's testimony; printing accounts.

Increase Mather Papers, 1690–1707   I.15.860

'Queries worthy of Consideration,' and about 10 documents of 1695–1707.

John Leverett Papers, 1686–1724   I.15.866

Papers, 1651–90. Memorandum book as Tutor, 1686–91, with 'Dudley Code' of Laws, formulae for presentation and conferring degrees, etc. Partly printed in *Proc. M. H. S.*, XIV. 226–28.

Leverett's Book of Latin Orations, 1688. Copies in Leverett's hand of Commencement and other academic orations. Given to the College by the Rev. Dr. Andrews of Newburyport in 1839. Arranged in 4 folders:—

I–III contain 4 versions of Leverett's oration of 1711, 3 of them beginning 'Non semel tantum.' IV contains President Oakes's Oratio 1 of 1672, Oratio 2 of 1675 (p. 11), Oratio [4] of 1677 (p. 29, printed in *C. S. M.*, XXXI, 405–36), Oratio 5 of 1678 (p. 54); Fragment of Oration by Leverett or Brattle of 1689 (p. 77); Nathaniel Rogers' Valedictory of 1652 (p. 93, printed from another copy in *C. S. M.*, XXXI. 394–401); Leverett's greeting to Sir Edmund Andros, 1686 (p. 99); Oratio Salutatoria, 1703 (p. 104, probably Leverett's); Leverett's Oratio of 1708 (p. 114).

Leverett's ms. digest of More's *Enchiridion Ethicum*, bound.

Civil Commissions, 1702–04.

Vellum-bound Diary, 1703–23 (formerly called College Book V, in quarto). Mostly notes of Corporation meetings. Discussion of John Locke in back.

President Leverett's Discourses, 1708–24, in 5 cases. Weekly expositions of Scripture, when President.

Notes of Sermons, 1712–13. Bound vol. of notes on sermons by Brattle, Barnard, Holyoke, Flynt, Porter, Robie, and others.

Letters, 1720–21. Controversies with General Court.

Benjamin Wadsworth's Diary relating to College affairs, 1725–36   I. 15.868
    Printed in *C. S. M.*, XXXI. 444–507.

Edward Holyoke Papers, 1739–69   I. 15.870
    Accounts with the College; Letter-book, 1766–67. Given by Mr. Hamilton V. Bail.

Samuel Locke's Commonplace Book   I. 15.872
    Begun in College. All subjects from preaching to cider-making.

Samuel Langdon Papers, 1745–90   I. 15.874
    A few letters, 1745–75, and shorthand sermon notes.

The series is continued for later Presidents. With Everett's administration, it becomes a systematic file of personal and official correspondence.

14. Professorship Papers   I. 15.955, ff.

None before 1800 except Hollis Professorship of Mathematics, statutes and papers relating to the apparatus, 1767–1826 (I. 15.960), and Hersey Professorship of Physic, papers relating to the foundation, 1782–91 (I. 15.980).

15. College Seals, and papers relating thereunto

The Colonial seals are described in this vol. and in *F. H. C.*   I. 15.1110

16. Wills Papers, 1610 to present

Copies of wills of Ezekiel Rogers and Sir Matthew Holworthy   I. 15.1210

Daniel Williams' will, 1711, printed and bound   I. 15.1240

John Barnard's will, 1769   I. 15.1260

17. Chronological Miscellany

Charlestown Ferry Papers, 1707–1806, bound volume   I.20.707

2 Supplementary papers, 1743, 1763   I.20.707.5

Fellowship Controversy of 1720–23. Copies from this and other archives   I.20.718

Papers on graduates' Indian missionary work at the charge of the Boyle bequest, beginning with Oliver Peabody (A.B. 1721), 5 cases covering 1720–1812   I.20.720

Journals of John Sergeant, missionary to the Stockbridge Indians near Oneida, 1789–1809. 3 cases   I.20.720.2

Journals of Samuel Kirkland, missionary at Oneida, 1792–94, 1796–99, 1806–07   I.20.720.4

Memoranda on Acts of General Court relating to College, 1650–1723   I.20.723

Papers on College sloops *Cyrus*, 1793–98, and *Harvard*, 1801–27   I.20.793 & 801

Papers on proposal to tax College, 1799   I.20.799

18. Treasurers' Records

A few Abbreviates of College Accounts and Inventories for the seventeenth century will be found in College Books I, III, and IV; printed in *C. S. M.*, xv, xvi.

Reports to President and Fellows, 1735 to 1876   I.50.5
> Occasional from 1735 to 1777, when Annual Reports (known as Statements since 1864) begin. After 1876 kept in Treasurer's Office.

Collected Papers, 1692 to present   I.50.6
> 2 receipts for seventeenth century, 7 cases of mss., mostly receipts, for the eighteenth, and 3 for 1800–1825.

Letter-books
> Copies of Treasurer Brattle's out-letters are in College Book V.
> Letters from, 5 letter-books and one case, 1778–1842   I.50.7
> Letters to, vols. I–XIV, 1829–1868   I.50.8

Cash Books, or 'Accounts and Receipts,' 1768 to present   I.50.15.10
> Those for 1768–1807 in 21 cases.

Inventory Papers, 1715 to date   I.50.15.36
    Inventories of College property made on the resignation or death
    of Treasurer, 1715, 1752, 1753, 1807, 1830.

Journals, Ledgers, and Journals and Ledgers combined in one vol.

Accounts of John Richards, 1669–93   I.50.15.38

Partial Copy of same, made in 1893   I.50.15.41

Journal of Thomas Brattle, 1693–1713   I.50.15.56
    This is College Book V.

Journal of Edward Hutchinson, 1721–44   I.50.15.56

Ledger of Edward Hutchinson, 1721–55   I.50.15.66

Journal of Thomas Hubbard, 1755–73   I.50.15.56

Ledger of Thomas Hubbard, 1755–73   I.50.15.66

Journals of Ebenezer Storer, 4 vols., 1777–1807   I.50.15.56
        Vol. I, 1777–85   Vol. III, 1797–1807
        Vol. II. 1785–97

Ledgers of Ebenezer Storer, 4 vols., 1777–1807   I.50.15.66
        Vol. A, 1777–85   Vol. C. 1797–1807
        Vol. B, 1785–97

Storer's copy of his Accounts, 1777–85   I.50.15.48
    The Journals and Ledgers continue to the present.

Salaries Papers, 1721 to present   I.50.15.84
    The first case contains papers for 1721–28 and 1778.

Salary Receipts, 1715 to present   I.50.15.86
    1715-1721   1732–1733
    1721–1729   1751–1752
    No more until 1818, and fragmentary thereafter.

Chronological Miscellany

Thomas Hubbard's Notes Receivable, 1752–1756   I.50.27.56

John Hancock Papers   I.50.27.73
    1754–75. Cash books and correspondence.
    1776–77. Correspondence and inventory.
    1778–79. Correspondence.

1780–85. Latin speech at Willard's inauguration; building college fence; Lafayette dinner; correspondence; settlement of 1785.

1786–1926. Adjustments, 1786–92; 'John Hancock's Side of the Story' by E. N. Vose, 1894; record of Greenough bequest.

19. Stewards' Records

Stewards' Reports to President, 1713–45, 1810–28 and
1893–present   I.70.5
> Those of 1687–1713 are in the first Quarter-bill book.

Stewards' Collected Papers, 1764–1826   I.70.6
> Loose papers supplementary to the Reports. First case, 1764–1809, contains papers on college pump, commencement dinners, 'Expence of a Corporation,' etc.

Bills and Accounts Papers, 1771 to present   I.70.15.8
> Incomplete. One bill for 1771 and a few for the 1790's.

Stewards' Journals and Ledgers   I.70.15.70 & 75

> Chesholme's Accounts (Ledger only), 1650–59.
> Printed in *C. S. M.*, xxxi.

> Andrew Bordman (II) Ledger, 1703–31.

> Andrew Bordman (II) Journal, 1719–22.

> Andrew Bordmans' (II & III) Ledger, 1719–55.

> Andrew Bordmans' (II & III) Ledger, 1728–49.
> Not a duplicate of the above.

> Andrew Bordman (II) Journal, 1733–45.

> Andrew Bordmans' (II & III) Ledger, 1740–65. Not complete.

> Andrew Bordmans' (II & III) Journal, 1745–53, with balance account of 1764.

Later Journals and Ledgers, 1795–1844   I.70.15.75

Quarter-Bill Books, 1687–1827   I.70.15.100
> Vol. 1687–1720   Vol. 1757–1769   Vol. 1784–1797
> Vol. 1720–1756   Vol. 1770–1784   Vol. 1798–1812

Quarter-Bill Papers, 1774–81, 1779–81   I.70.15.102 & Pf

Stewards' Bonds, 1753–1847   I.70.15.120

Term Bills, samples and forms, 1783 to present   I.70.15.140

Chronological Miscellany
> List of Scholars inhabiting the Several Chambers, 1741–64.   I.70.27.41

Butler's Book, 1722–1750. Bound vol. stamped 'Stew-
ard Accounts'   I.90
> There are a good many Stewards' accounts in it, and accounts for
> the building of Wadsworth House.

20. Faculty Records

(Immediate Government, 1725–1825; College Faculty, 1825–1890)

Faculty Records, official copies, bound volumes   III.5.5

I. 1725–52	III. 1766–75	V. 1782–88
II. 1752–66	IV. 1775–81	VI. 1788–97

And eleven more to 1867.

Faculty Records, Original Minutes   III.5.10
> Minute of May 2, 1760, and loose papers arranged chronologically,
> 1771–1841; bound volumes after 1841.

Faculty Papers, 1 vol. for 1719–1810   III.5.26

Report of Committee on Theses, 1800 (?)   III.10.3

Admission Books, Classes of 1729–1924   III.15.5.2
> The volumes for 1729–1823 were copied from the Faculty Records
> in 1893.

Degree Diplomas   III.15.18
> Alcock's A.B. Diploma 1676 (reproduced in this Volume); sundry
> A.B., A.M. and Doctors' diplomas of 18th and 19th centuries.

Disorders Papers   III.15.21.6

> I. 1768–81   II. 1789–1803   III. 1805–65

District Reports made to Faculty on condition of College
Chambers, 1738-c. 1775.   III.15.22

Chronological Miscellany   III.27.80
> Drafts of Faculty votes, 1780–1803.

21. Library Records

Harvard College Library Papers, 1764 to present.   III.50.6
> 16 unbound papers, 1764–1803; bound vols. begin in 1826. Frag-
> mentary to 1764.

Library Bookplates, 1765 to present.   III.50.15.20

Catalogues and Shelf-lists, printed and ms., 1723 to present.
                                                           III.50.15.50

Printed Catalogue of 1723 (see Chapter XIV).

Printed Supplements to same, 1725, 1735 (photostats).

Ms. Catalogue by Wm. Mayhew, 1769 (?), with additions for 1770.

Ms. Catalogue by Amos Adams, 1770.

Ms. Catalogue of Tracts, *c.* 1770, 3 vols.

Catalogus Librorum in Bibliotheca Cantabrigiensi Selectus, Frequentiorem in Usum Harvardinatum, qui gradu Baccalaurei in Artibus nondum sunt donati. Boston: 1773.

Ms. Classed Catalogue 'under different heads,' *c.* 1780, with additions to *c.* 1789.

Vellum-bound vol. with alphabetical catalogue through B, *c.* 1781, and Tract Catalogue, 1781.

Catalogus Bibliothecae Harvardianæ Cantabrigiæ Nov-Anglorum, Bostoniæ: 1790. 2 vols.

A Classed catalogue. 3 Interleaved copies with accessions. Ms. materials for same, by T. W. Harris.

Charging Lists, 1762–1897.   III.50.15.60

Donation Books, 1638 to present.   III.50.15.80
Copies by John L. Sibley, from College Books, etc., of records of books donated, 1638–1822. The file of bound vols. begins in 1812.

Library Invoices, 1786 to present (fragmentary to 1820).
                                                   III.50.15.140

Librarians' Papers, 1714 to present (fragmentary to 1856).
                                                   III.50.15.160

Chronological Miscellany, 1764 to present.
                                III.50.27.64–III.50.27.97
Papers Relating to Books saved from Fire of 1764; Hollis Donation Papers, 1764–1770; List of Library's most important books, 1765 (sent to Jasper Mauduit in London, to avoid duplication in purchases); Papers Relating to rebuilding of Library, 1764–1773; 'A Summary of the Library of Cambridge as it stood 1783'; List of Donations of Thomas B. Hollis, 1787; Papers relating to Boylston Medical Library. *c.* 1790; Benjamin Welles' Catalogue Books in College Library, 1797, made out for the writer's private reading.

INDEX

INDEX

Pages 1–360 are in Part I.

A single year in parentheses indicates the class of a Harvard student who did not take a degree.

The names of commencers and subjects of theses and quaestiones in Appendix B, names of fellows in Appendix E, and items in Appendix F, are not indexed.